DATE DUE			

GAYLORD M-2   PRINTED IN U.S.A.

Eyewitness Accounts of the American Revolution

Letters and Diary of John Rowe

Edited by Anne Rowe Cunningham

The New York Times & Arno Press

LETTERS AND DIARY

OF

JOHN ROWE

JOHN ROWE

LETTERS AND DIARY

OF

JOHN ROWE

BOSTON MERCHANT

1759–1762   1764–1779

EDITED BY

ANNE ROWE CUNNINGHAM

WITH EXTRACTS FROM A PAPER WRITTEN FOR THE
MASSACHUSETTS HISTORICAL SOCIETY

BY

EDWARD LILLIE PIERCE

———

BOSTON
W. B. CLARKE COMPANY
1903

ERRATA.

Page 92.   Chuckly should be Checkly.

" 136.   Canes   "   " Caner.

" 248.   Oatum   "   " Occum.

" 253.   Barker   "   " Barber.

" 171, 185, 190, 226, 253, 290, 324.   Johnnot should be Johonnot.

" 267.   Boutman should be Boutineau.

PREFACE.

THESE extracts from the Letters and Diary of my
great-great-uncle, John Rowe, are printed, because it
seemed that such valuable records of life in Boston
nearly one hundred and fifty years ago, ought to be
put beyond the possibility of loss; and also, that
they might interest a larger public, than that which
listened to Mʳ Pierce's paper, and the very few who
have had the privilege of reading the original manuscript.

Exeter Place called for his early home in England,
Rowe Place and Rowe's Wharf, bring his name
down to the Boston of to-day, and there are many
living who remember Rowe Street, and the last of
Rowe's Pasture.

I wish to thank Dʳ Joseph Rowe Webster, Mʳ
C. W. Amory, Mʳˢ Charles Amory, Miss Sutermeis-
ter, and Messʳˢ Houghton, Mifflin & Co. for permission to copy photographs of family portraits and
houses, and the Massachusetts Historical Society
for allowing me to reprint from their "Proceedings" parts of Mʳ Pierce's paper, all of which add
greatly to the value of the book.

ANNE ROWE CUNNINGHAM.

Milton, Mass.,
November, 1902.

ILLUSTRATIONS.

FACING
PAGE

JOHN ROWE . . . . *Frontispiece*
 From portrait owned by Dr. Joseph Rowe Webster.

MRS. ROWE: HANNAH SPEAKMAN 4
 From portrait owned by Mrs. Charles Amory.

FIRE BUCKET, 1760 74

JOHN ROWE'S HOUSE IN POND LANE (BEDFORD STREET) . 112
 By permission of Messrs. Houghton, Mifflin & Co.

MRS. JOHN LINZEE: SUSANNA INMAN 197

RALPH INMAN 220

CAPT. JOHN LINZEE 223
 All three from portraits owned by Mr. C. W. Amory.

ROWE ESTATE AT MILTON 333
 Bought of Gov. Belcher's Heirs in 1781. (See Letters of
 James Murray, pages 252-3.) By permission of Miss Suter-
 meister.

MRS. RALPH INMAN: SUSANNAH SPEAKMAN 397
 From portrait owned by Mr. C. W. Amory.

INTRODUCTION

PARTS OF A PAPER WRITTEN BY

MR. EDWARD LILLIE PIERCE

FOR THE

MASSACHUSETTS HISTORICAL SOCIETY

THE Diary of John Rowe, a Boston merchant, includes the period from Sept. 8, 1764, to July 15, 1779, with three breaks in it,— one from Aug. 17, 1765, to April 10, 1766, another from June 1, 1775, to December 24 of the same year, and the third from Nov. 19, 1776, to Aug. 12, 1778. The missing volume which makes the second break was, according to his memorandum in the next volume, "mislaid or taken out of his store"; the other two breaks are supposed to have occurred since his death. The Diary is paged continuously, the last page being numbered 2493; and as this page completes a volume, it is likely that later volumes have disappeared.

At the time Rowe's Diary begins,— in September, 1764,— the British government was just putting in force its scheme of taxing the Colonies for the purpose as avowed of "defraying the expenses of defending, protecting, and securing the same." The Sugar Act, which imposed duties not only on sugar and molasses but on other articles hitherto exempt, had been passed the previous spring. Otis's pamphlet on "The Rights of the British Colonies asserted and proved" had been issued. In May and during the summer and autumn, protests against the new policy were being made by the Boston town-meeting and the General Court. The Stamp Act was to follow the Sugar Act in less than a twelve-month. Rowe's Diary thus opens at the initial stage of the Revolution.

The Diary comprises the period of the imposition of the new and hated taxes, the passage and repeal of the Stamp Act, the Boston massacre, the throwing overboard of the tea, the beginning of civil war at Lexington and Concord, the siege of Boston, the evacuation by the British troops, and the visit of the French fleet to the town. The battle of Bunker Hill occurred during the period included in a lost volume.

Boston was, at the period covered by the Diary, a town of sixteen thousand inhabitants,— about the present population of Northampton, or Quincy, in this State, and Concord, New Hampshire, or Burlington, Vermont.

John Rowe was born in Exeter England Nov. 27th (Nov. 16th Old Style) 1715 died in Boston Feb. 17th 1787. He was the oldest of the eleven children of Joseph & Mary (possibly Hawker) Rowe & grandson of Oliver Rowe, Clerk, who in his will dated 25th Feb'y 1706, leaves all his lands to his "eldest son John & his Heirs forever." Three of the sons of Joseph & Mary Rowe emigrated to America, John, Jacob and W[m] Syntal. "John was here as early as 1736, when he was only twenty one years old, as he purchased that year a warehouse on Long Wharf. This early purchase indicates that he brought considerable means with him; and besides he continued to own property in his native city till his death, bequeathing it to the sons of his brother Joseph who remained behind." Jacob came to America some seven years later as we learn from a letter of their sister Rebecca (Rowe) Robins dated "Exon June 1^{rst} 1784." Writing to Jacob, but referring to John, she says "What a pleasure would it be to see a Bro. after seven & forty year"! & adds "You have been wanting forty year." In a much earlier letter before her marriage dated "Exon Aug. 26th 1751 " she writes "In our early days we were indeed blest beyond measure. But then how soon was it blasted. I never, I thank God, set my mind on Riches." Wm Syntal Rowe came to Boston in 1749 or 50 but only remained on a visit to his brothers, sailing thence to Oporto where he went into business. Jacob moved later to Quebec & became asst. commissary-general. After his brother John's death he returned to Boston. His descendants, through his son John, the "Jack" of the Diary are the only members of the family known to be in this country.

John Rowe and his wife were doubtless buried (though no record of interment is preserved) in his vault under the first Trinity Church, a wooden building; and the vault is not supposed to have been disturbed by the subsequent construction of the stone edifice. The vaults were being cleared at the time of the fire of 1872; and the remains found in Rowe's are probably among the "unknown" which were then removed to the Trinity Church tomb in Mt. Auburn Cemetery.

John Rowe was married in 1743 to Hannah Speakman, who survived him eighteen years, dying July 9, 1805, at the age of eighty.[1] Her sister was the first wife of Ralph Inman, the Cambridge Loyalist, with whose family Rowe continued always to be very intimate. The sisters are said to have been twins. Rowe bought in 1764 the estate on the north side of Pond Lane, now Bedford Street, where he lived till his death, and where his widow remained till her death. The year after his purchase he pulled down the house he found standing there on the north side of the lane, and built a new one, into which he moved Oct. 16, 1766. This house with grounds about it was sold in 1817 by Rowe's heirs to Judge William Prescott;[2] and here he and his son the historian lived. It was demolished in 1845. Rowe owned a considerable tract, measuring nearly three acres, known as "Rowe's Pasture." Without attempting to define its limits accurately, it may be said in a general way that it extended from Bedford Street to Essex Street, with Washington (then Newbury) and Kingston streets as western and eastern limits, not,

[1] A portrait of Mrs. Rowe is in the possession of Mrs. Charles Amory, Jr., of Boston.

[2] Shurtleff's Topographical and Historical Description of Boston, p. 409.

MRS. ROWE

however, touching Washington Street at any point, and small lots belonging to other people perhaps jutting in here and there. On this ample tract he raised, as his Diary shows, crops of hay and vegetables, and pastured sheep and cattle. He owned houses and lots on the south side of Essex Street as well as in other parts of the town; and one of his wharves still bears his name. He owned property in other towns,— Dighton, Plymouth, Malden, Medford, Gloucester, Milton, Hardwick, Stoughton, Grafton, Shelburne, Deerfield, and also in Hartford and Woodstock, Connecticut.

Rowe became one of the foremost merchants of Boston. The "Massachusetts Centinel," in noting his death, calls him "an eminent merchant of this place." John Adams [1] names him among the very rich men with whom he had been acquainted in the way of business, placing him among those who had acquired wealth by their own industry,— unlike Hancock, Bowdoin, and Pitts, who had acquired it by descent or marriage. His ships traversed the ocean, and ran along the coast. One of them carried Josiah Quincy, Jr., to Charleston, South Carolina, in February, 1773.

His imported merchandise was miscellaneous, meeting the wants of the people of that day. We get glimpses of what it was here and there. On May 31, 1765, his "warehouse fell in with fish." He dealt largely in salt. On July 3, 1767, a quantity of silk stockings, ribbons, Spanish silk,

[1] Works, ii. 296.

and Indian and English taffetys were stolen at night from his store. The British troops, when evacuating Boston in March, 1776, took from him " linens, checks, cloths, and woolens," goods of the value of 2260 pounds sterling. Mrs. Commodore Hood visited his store, Dec. 8, 1768, and bought twenty-four yards of superfine silk.

A vessel (probably Rowe's) arrives, July 22, 1767, from Madeira with seventy pipes of wine. Governor Hutchinson's accounts[1] show a purchase, July 19, 1770, of Rowe of a quarter cask of port-wine for eight pounds. He was the owner of one of the tea-ships, though in history less is said of his cargo than of Francis Rotch's, which arriving first was the first to be dealt with. Until the conflict between the Colonies and the mother country became one of force, he was largely purveyor for the English fleet, which was rarely absent altogether from the harbor. He was one of the Proprietors of Long Wharf, — that ancient corporation in which leading merchants like Hancock, Winslow, Oliver, Wells, and Boutineau were shareholders. He was also one of the Proprietors of Point Shirley.

Rowe's sentiments in relation to the controversy with Great Britain were those of a moderate, holding in this respect the same position as that of his relatives, intimate friends, and the mass of his fellow-merchants. He was a public-spirited citizen, and wished well to his town and colony, no one more so. He was as strongly opposed as any to the new

[1] Diary and Letters, i. 77.

restrictions on trade which the parent country had put in force, and generally he was not in sympathy with its repressive policy.[1] He served on committees appointed by the town or by merchants to set forth the grievances of the Colony, sometimes willingly and sometimes not so willingly. He was a member of a committee, Sept. 18, 1765 (Otis, chairman), to express the thanks of the town to Conway and Barré for " their noble, generous, and patriotick speeches " in Parliament, and served on similar committees, April 21, 1766, Dec. 4, 1767, and March 14, 1768, — the last being appointed for a recognition of John Dickinson's " Farmer's Letters." He served on a committee, Dec. 18, 1765 (Samuel Adams, chairman), to protest against the shutting up of the courts; on committees, Nov. 20, Dec. 17 and 21, 1767, and June 15 and 17, 1768, to instruct the representatives; on a committee, Oct. 28, 1767, of which he was chairman, to prevent importations, particularly of foreign superfluities, and encourage domestic produce and manufactures; on a large committee, June 14, 1768, to wait on Governor Bernard with a petition for the redress of grievances; and on a committee, September 12 of the same year, to wait on the Governor and inquire as to the reported coming of troops to Boston, and to recommend measures required in the emergency. He signed, Sept. 14, 1768, as one of the selectmen, an address

[1] S. G. Drake, in his " History of Boston," p. 657, states Rowe's signature to a petition to the General Court as early as Dec. 17, 1760, charging the Crown officers with appropriating to their own use money derived from forfeitures.

to other towns, protesting against Bernard's dissolving the General Court and against the taxes levied by Parliament. He was chairman of a committee, in June, 1779, to fix the prices of merchandise, and to bring to punishment offenders against the Act prohibiting monopolies and forestalling.[1] As chairman of a merchants' committee, he signed, June 22, 1779, in its behalf a communication to Congress, testifying their patriotic devotion, and reprobating the attempt of " sordid and unprincipled wretches " to depreciate the paper currency by which independence had been almost secured, and " to force a currency of gold and silver on its ruins." This document also expresses " anxiety for the security of that important staple, the fishery," as the main support of the future commerce of the Northern States. Congress, on receiving the petition, passed a resolution of thanks, July 27, 1779, which was communicated to the committee by Elbridge Gerry, James Lovell, and Samuel Holten, then members from Massachusetts.

Rowe, however, while considering the conduct of the British government impolitic and harsh, was indisposed to carry opposition beyond argument, appeal, and protest; and at no time did he favor measures looking to forcible resistance and independence. His position is misconceived when he is classed with the " Patriots,"— the party who supported separation from the mother country, and had in view the use of force outside of law to pro-

1 Independent Chronicle, June 24, 1779.

mote that end.[1] He did not join the patriotic exodus from Boston when the siege began, preferring
to remain in order to protect his property.[2] This
may have counted against him with the Patriots;
for when after the British evacuation he proposed
to join in the ceremonies for the interment of Dr.
Warren, a brother Mason, he encountered rude
treatment from the populace, and found it prudent
to withdraw. His close relations with the family of
Captain John Linzee, an English navy officer, must
have made him an object of suspicion. The popu-
lar feeling was, however, soothed in time by his
amiable manners, the good offices he freely distributed among his townsmen, his active service on
a relief committee, and his general usefulness as a
citizen; so that before peace was reached he was
elected a representative to the General Court. The
looting and pillaging attending the close of the
British occupation, in which he was a sufferer, must
have sensibly cooled his attachment to the country
of his birth.

The words " who knows how tea will mingle with

[1] This error is found in Frothingham's "Siege of Boston," p. 23;
John Adams's Works, ii. 158, note; F. S. Drake's "Tea Leaves," p.
63. Gordon in his History, i. 209, says Rowe was "a merchant who
had been active on the side of liberty in matters of trade,"—a
statement which, limited to "matters of trade," is true enough.
S. G. Drake's "History of Boston," p. 700, note, citing an anony-
mous memorandum, gives currency to the absurd imputation that
Rowe led the mob in the assault on Hutchinson's house. Hutchinson himself may have thought (Diary and Letters, i. 67) that the
class of merchants to whom Rowe belonged had stirred up violence
against the Crown officers.

[2] He seems, however, to have applied, April 28, 1775, for a pass
to go out with his effects, which was for some reason refused.

salt water?" said to have been spoken by Rowe in the Old South Meeting House on the evening of Dec. 16, 1773, with a view to instigate the destruction of the tea, must, in the light of his Diary, be regarded as apochryphal.

Rowe was childless; but his house was well filled with young people,— his wife's nephews the Speakmans, her nephew George Inman (and his cousin John Inman) and her nieces Sarah and Susanna Inman. The last-named was adopted by him, and called familiarly "Sucky" in his Diary.[1]   Born March 23, 1754, she married, Sept. 1, 1772, at the age of eighteen, Captain John Linzee, then commanding the British warship "Beaver," brother of Captain, afterward Rear-Admiral, Robert Linzee, and also of Admiral Samuel Hood's wife.[2]   He had been an *habitué* for three years at Rowe's house, where she was living.   Rowe was very fond of her, and the day after her marriage gave her husband written authority to draw on him every New Year's Day for twenty pounds sterling; and his will, as well as his wife's, provided liberally for her and her children. Three days after her wedding he records: "Capt.

---

[1] Sarah died, Sept. 14, 1773, after a brief illness.   George's career is elsewhere noted.

[2] Rowe's Diary states that Robert and John were brothers.   See also "The Dictionary of National [English] Biography" under "Samuel Hood, Admiral Viscount."   It should be mentioned, however, that the traditions of Captain John Linzee's family do not agree with the statement of Rowe's Diary that he was the brother of Admiral Robert Linzee.

The late William Amory, of Boston, owned the portraits of Captain John and Mrs. Linzee, his grandfather and grandmother, and also of Mrs. Linzee's parents, Mr. and Mrs. Ralph Inman; and they remain with the Amory family.

Linzee sailed this forenoon and carried my dear Sucky with him; I wish them happy together." Absent for nearly three years, they arrived in Boston Easter Sunday, April 16, 1775, in the " Falcon," which he was then commanding, bringing with them their first-born, Samuel Hood Linzee, the future admiral, born Dec. 27, 1773. Rowe brought the three to his house the same day. Linzee was just in time to take part in the first armed conflict of the Revolution. On April 19, 1775, Rowe records: " Capt. Linzee and Capt. Collins in two small armed vessels were ordered to bring off the troops to Boston, but Lord Percy and Generall Smith thought proper to encamp on Bunker Hill this night." The fact of this order has escaped the attention of historians. Linzee had also on the 20th an engagement with the American troops below Cambridge bridge.

Mrs. Linzee and her child remained for the next nine months with Rowe, or with her father then living in town,— her husband while active on duty being with her from time to time. He was at Rowe's house at dinner and for the evening on the day before and the day after the battle of Lexington, and was there each day till his next sailing, May 1, from Boston; and now and then till after the siege his presence at Rowe's house is recorded.[1] He commanded, June 19, the " Falcon," one of the six vessels which cannonaded the American works on

[1] Linzee's name appears as being at Rowe's April 17, 18, 20, 21, 22, 23, 24, 25, 26, 27, 28, 29, 30, Dec. 27, 28, 1775 ; Jan. 2, 7, 11, 14, 1776. Rowe's Diary from May 30, 1775, to Dec. 25, 1775, is missing.

Bunker Hill. He sailed, Jan. 20, 1776, in the "Falcon" for England, taking his wife, his son, and infant daughter Hannah, born in Boston, and also his brother-in-law George Inman. Later he commanded the "Pearl"; and after the war, as commander of the "Penelope," he was in Boston Harbor, Sept. 9, 1790, and applied to Governor Hancock for permission to enter the harbor with his ship, offering to fire a salute and expecting one in return. Hancock's answer is not known, but it was certainly one of consent; for it appears that the "Penelope" sailed from Boston, September 17, leaving, however, its commander behind, "lying very dangerously ill of a fever at his house in this town." [1] He recovered, and resumed his command. His wife with her children about this time made her way to Boston, and occupied a house on Essex Street, bequeathed to her by Rowe, subject to his wife's life estate, whence, according to a letter of her husband, still preserved,[2] there was an open walk across the field to Mrs. Rowe's house on Pond Lane. Linzee resigned his commission in 1791, and joined his wife in Boston. She died a year later, at the age of thirty-nine, the mother of nine children. He removed to Milton, to a house near the bridge over the Neponset River, where, according to tradition and Samuel Breck's "Recollections," he lived an eccentric and lonely life, dying, in 1798, at the age of fifty-six. His eldest son, the admiral, has de-

---

[1] Massachusetts Centinel, Sept. 18, 1790.

[2] Some of Captain Linzee's letters are in the possession of his grandson John W. Linzee, of Boston.

scendants in England, not however bearing his
name. His other children remained in this country ;
and some of their descendants bearing his name
live in or near Boston. From Captain Linzee's
eldest daughter, born in Boston, descended a branch
of the Boston Amorys, one of whom became the
wife of William H. Prescott, grandson of Colonel
William Prescott; and thus in the historian's descendants is united the blood of combatants on
opposite sides on the memorable June 17, 1775.
Their swords crossed are a possession of this Society. (Mass^tts Hist. Society.)

After the marriage of Sucky Inman Mr. Rowe
adopted Jack, son of his brother Jacob at Quebec
& we quote some parts of a letter in which he
announces the boy's arrival at Boston.

BOSTON, Oct. 25th, 1772

DR BROTHER,— The Beginning of last week
Capt Truman arriv'd here & Brought mee your favor
of the 24th September — he also handed mee your
son Jack who is very well & a Merry Smart little
fellow. I shall take care of him & Mrs Rowe seems
well pleased with him.

He is to go to School on Tuesday to Mr Holbrooke I dont think to let him stay longer there
than this winter but that will depend on Some
Progrefs a Clergyman Mr Nicholls is making in a
New School.

Mrs Rowe is now very well but has been Rather
Dull in Parting with her niece Sucky Inman who is

married to Capt John Linzee, who commands the
Beaver Man of Warr & is gone to England.

Our United Affection & Good Wishes attend you
your Spouse & Family & you shall hear from mee
from time to time Letting you know how Jack goes
on &

I Remain yr affectionate Brother

& hum Serv

J Rowe

Jack went to Rev. Mr Nicholls school at Salem
and later (that school being broken up soon after
the battle of Lexington) removed to the school of
Rev. Phillips Payson at Chelsea.

Rowe held various trusts and offices. He was
treasurer of the Charitable Society, and spent many
evenings at its meetings. From 1750 (his connection with the order began some years earlier) till his
death he held high offices in the Masonic fraternity,
and in 1768 became Grand Master of the order in
North America. The lodge in Boston suspended
its regular meetings April 19, 1775, till it was called
together in 1787 to attend his funeral; and a few
months afterwards it resumed its sessions.

Rowe often served by the choice of town-meet-
ings on important business committees (Aug. 26,
1765; Jan. 7, May 7, 1766); was once at least
moderator (March 30, 1774); served as one of the
fire-wards, whose meetings he often mentions; was
sometimes overseer of the poor; and was selectman
for the years 1766, 1767, and 1768, declining a

re-election in March, 1769. He was a candidate
for Representative at the election in May, 1765,
when he failed, receiving 238 votes,— James Otis,
who was chosen, receiving 388, and the other successful candidates, Thacher, Cushing, and Gray, a
still larger number. At the special election in
September, 1765, for filling the vacancy caused by
the death of Oxenbridge Thacher, there was no
choice on the first ballot,— the vote being Samuel
Adams 247, Rowe 137, John Ruddock 110, and
John Hancock 40. Adams was chosen on the next
ballot, and this was the beginning of his legislative
career. The next May, Rowe, who had 309, was
defeated by Hancock, who had 437,— Otis, Cushing, and Adams receiving each between six and
seven hundred.[1] The story is, as told by Gordon
in his History,[2] that Adams promoted the election
of Hancock, saying, when Rowe's name was mentioned for the place, and pointing at the same time
to Hancock's house, " Is there not another John
that may do better ? " This piece of gossip, which
has been much copied,[3] is quite untrustworthy.
It is not unlikely, however, that Adams threw his
influence against Rowe, not thinking him earnest
enough for the work in hand, or perhaps piqued by
his rivalry at the special election. Rowe was again
unsuccessful in 1767, when he received only 134

[1] Drake's "History of Boston," p. 719, is in error in stating
Rowe's election at this time.
[2] I. 142.
[3] John Adams's Works, ii. 158, note; Wells's "Life of Samuel
Adams," i. 119.

votes; and he was not afterwards a candidate for a considerable period. He was, however, chosen a member for the years 1780–1784. As a member in 1780 (being chosen also at the election in October), he took part in the inauguration of the State Constitution. He failed of a re-election in 1781, when there were several candidates, Samuel Adams heading the list; but Adams, already chosen a Senator, elected to go to the higher chamber, and at a special election (June 12) Rowe received 300 out of 394 votes cast.[1] Why Adams, chosen a Senator a few weeks before, was placed on the Representative ticket, particularly as his subsequent choice between the two offices shows that he did not wish to go to the House, is not easily understood.

Rowe was greatly interested in Trinity Church, connecting himself with it somewhere between 1741 and 1744,— probably in 1743, at the time of his marriage, when it was only eight years old.[2] Late in that year he bought pew 82, as appears by the records. His wife's relatives the Speakmans appear to have been connected with it from the first. The subscription list, open from 1741 to 1744 for its organ, bears his name with twenty pounds annexed to it. He was chosen a vestryman in 1760, and continued to be one till his death, except for one or two years (1776–1777), when he was warden. He became a communicant in 1766. He was from the

---

[1] Adams's biographer, Wells, does not refer to this double election, only mentioning his election as Senator.

[2] The manuscript records of Trinity Church have assisted in filling out the Diary as to Rowe's connection with it.

first a generous giver, and for most of the time of his connection with the church he contributed a larger sum to its funds than any one else. He was rarely absent from both Sunday services, except when ill, or troubled in spirit, or the barber failed to come; notes always the text, which he copies at length; follows closely the sermons, which he remarks upon as "very clever," "very elegant," "most excellent," "delightful," "sensible," "serious," "very polite," "pathetic and moving," "metaphysical," or "well delivered." He has much to say of parish affairs,— Mr. Banister's ejectment suit against the church (Dec. 31, 1764; Jan. 2, Feb. 18, March 19, 1765), being appointed (Jan. 6, 1765) on the church committee in relation to it; the cracking of the church's bell (March 6, 1774), which was given a few months later (October 2) to a sister church in Norwich, Conn.; the collections for the poor at Christmas (£400 8s., old tenor, Dec. 25, 1773); the raising of the minister's salary (April 5, 1765); the new organ in 1770 (October 5 and December 9); the proposed alteration of the church (July 26, 1772), as to which he regrets to see the gentlemen so indifferent; the convention of the Episcopal clergy (June 17, 1767); the death of Rev. William Hooper, who expired instantaneously in his garden, April 14, 1767, " to the great grief and sorrow of his people and the loss of his family," whom Rowe calls his own "most valuable and worthy and never to be forgotten friend"; and the contribution of £253 for " good Mrs. Hooper," May 13, 1770.

Rowe was the intimate friend of the successive
ministers, Hooper, Walter, Parker, and of their
families as well. Their evenings, particularly Sunday evenings, were often passed at his house. He
" smoaked a pipe," June 11, 1765, with Mr. Hooper.
Mr. Parker, in recognition of his uniform kindness,
named a son for him ; and Rowe, in recognition of
the friendship, bequeathed a legacy to the father
and an estate on Pond Lane to the son, his namesake. He was a peacemaker, composing differences
between ministers, as when Mr. Walter on one
occasion took umbrage at some behavior of Mr.
Hooper (July 13, 16, 1765). The clergy would
have a sunnier life if all parishioners were as
friendly critics of their sermons as was he,— when,
for instance, he wrote, Aug. 15, 1773, " Mr. Walter
shines more and more in his preaching," and, a
week later, " he is so good a man that my pen
cannot describe his virtues."

Now and then a stranger clergyman appears. On
June 9, 1765, " The Rev. Mr. Cooper, President of
the Colledge at New York, preached." The record
for May 10, 1772, is, " Mr. Thompson of Scituate
read prayers and preached [in the morning and the
afternoon]. . . . Both these sermons were honestly
designed but very lengthy."

Nearly a year after Mr. Hooper's death, April 4,
1768, Rev. William Walter was chosen unanimously
his successor,[1] with a salary of 156 pounds sterling,

---

[1] The " Memorial History of Boston," iii. 128, implies an immediate succession. A. H. Chester's " Trinity Church," published in
1888, contains a similar error.

and a gratuity of 50 pounds sterling for the year
to Mrs. Hooper.

Rowe took especial interest in the calling of new
ministers, and a good voice seems to have been an
essential requisite in a candidate. Dec. 7, 1777,
a " young gentleman from Andover," who had been
recommended for assistant, " read prayers in the
church this morning to several of us that we might
judge of his voice, and I think he has a pleasant and
agreeable voice." Oct. 5, 1773, Rev. Samuel
Parker of Portsmouth read several chapters privately
in the church to " the gentlemen of the vestry "
to show what his voice was. He was found to
have " a good voice," and to read " with propriety " ;
" was much liked," and the wardens and vestry
" were all of them for him " as assistant (October
7, 10). He sailed for England, Nov. 6, 1773, for
ordination, and arrived home May 16, 1774.
Rowe's record for May 22 is that he then " preached
for the first time from 123^d Psalm and the 1st verse
a sensible, good discourse, and very well delivered
for his first time of preaching."

The parting of the ways was at hand. Mr. Parker
informed the wardens and vestry, July 18, 1776,
that he could not with safety perform the entire service as before, that he was interrupted the previous
Lord's Day when reading the prayers for the King,
and that he had received threats of interruption and
insult in case of a repetition, and was fearful of
damage to the church ; and he desired counsel and
advice. The wardens and vestry decided (the pro-

prietors concurring), as the only alternative for shutting up the church, in view of the temper and spirit of the people, to request the minister to omit the part of the liturgy which related to the King; and Mr. Parker acted accordingly.

Mr. Walter left for England in 1776. The proprietors, April 10, 1776, invested Mr. Parker, the assistant minister, for one year with all the powers of incumbent minister. Three years afterwards they voted, June 13, 1779, after correspondence with Mr. Parker, that "the church has not an incumbent minister, 12 yeas, 4 nays." Two of the proprietors, Colonel Hatch and Mr. Bethune, withdrew before the vote. A week later Mr. Parker was chosen incumbent minister at a salary of three pounds sterling a week; and after some reflection on the propriety of taking the place in view of his friendly relations with Mr. Walter, he accepted, July 25.[1] Some idea of the condition of the church shortly after the siege had ended may be had from Rowe's entry May 26, 1776: "Mr. Parker preached a well adapted and good discourse. I staid at the sacrament this day, about fifty communicants." The proprietors of King's Chapel proposed, April 4, 1776, in view of the financial difficulty in keeping both churches open, a united service at the Chapel for both churches, with Mr. Parker as the minister; but Trinity Church (Rowe being chairman of the committee) declined to suspend their own services.

[1] The "Memorial History of Boston," iii. 129, says that "Mr. Parker became rector soon after the war," which is not strictly correct. A. H. Chester's "Trinity Church," p. 11, has the same error.

Rowe, while a loyal Episcopalian, was observant of what was going on in other denominations, sometimes attending their special services, as the installation of Rev. Samuel Blair, in Dr. Sewall's Meeting House, Nov. 19, 1766, where Mr. Pemberton prayed and Mr. Blair preached; the ordination of Rev. Simeon Howard at the West Church, May 6, 1767, where Dr. Chauncy preached, and " before and after the ceremony there was an anthem sung"; the preaching of an Indian minister, Mr. Occum (Aug. 22, 1773), at Mr. Moorhead's, the Presbyterian church in Long Lane, afterwards Federal Street; the election sermon of Rev. Mr. Shute of Hingham (May 25, 1768),—" a very long sermon, being an hour and forty minutes." The entry July 9, 1766, is: "This morning about five of clock the Rev^d Dr. Mayhew died much lamented by great numbers of people." These seem to have been the best days of the Quakers in Boston, who had had a place of worship in the town for more than a hundred years. Rowe notes, July 21, 1769: "This afternoon Mrs. Rachel Willson, the famous Quaker preacher, preached in Faneuil Hall to at least twelve hundred people; she seems to be a woman of good understanding."

A very interesting religious event of this period in Massachusetts was the visit of the most renowned evangelist of modern times, George Whitefield. These were his last days; he was to sleep in the land he loved so well; and his sepulchre is where his voice was last heard calling sinners to repent-

ance. He came to us in the midst of great excite-
ment on public affairs; and it is pleasant to think
of him that our fathers had his sympathies, and that
in the last letter he is known to have written, just a
week before his death, he said feelingly: " Poor
New England is much to be pitied, Boston most of
all. How falsely misrepresented!" Whitefield
came from Wrentham to Boston Aug. 14, 1770.
He preached at the old North Church the 15th, at
Dr. Sewall's the 16th, at Dr. Eliot's the 17th, at
Mr. Pemberton's the 18th, at the New North
(Dr. Eliot's) the 20th, at Dr. Sewall's the 21st
and 22d, at the New North the 23d, at Dr. Sewall's
the 24th, at Cambridge the 27th, at Charlestown the
28th,[1] at the Old South the 29th, at the New North
the 30th, at Jamaica Plain the 31st, at Milton September 1st, at Roxbury the 2d, at the Old South
the 3d; and on the 4th he set out for Portsmouth.
The Diary does not give a record of services on
August 19th, 25th, and 26th.[2] Rowe heard him
twice, on August 16th and 24th, and notes the text
on both occasions, saying of the first sermon (text
Zechariah ix. 12, 1st clause), " I liked his discourse,"
and of the second (text St. Matthew xxii. 11–13),
" This was in my opinion a clever discourse." His
entry Sunday, September 30, is, " The Rev^d Mr.
Whitfield died suddenly this morning at Newberry,

[1] Tyerman's "Life of Whitefield," ii. 592, reverses the dates at
Cambridge and Charlestown.

[2] His biographer, Tyerman (ii. 592), says that he preached at
Malden the 19th and at Medford on the 26th. Neither he nor the
Boston newspapers take note specially of his preaching on the 25th.

much lamented." His death was at 6 A.M., probably
of *angina pectoris ;* and a special messenger must
have been despatched to carry the intelligence to
Boston.[1]

Among the pageants of the town, funeral ceremonies were the foremost. Those of eminent clergymen and lawyers and of civil or military officers drew
a multitude of spectators. Rev. Dr. Mayhew was
buried July 11, 1766,— a day when the thermometer stood at 90°. Besides a long procession of
men and women on foot, preceding and following
the remains, were fifty-seven carriages, of which
sixteen were coaches and chariots,— Dr. Chauncy
making the prayer and many clergymen attending.
Similar rites accompanied, April 17, 1767, "the
mournful funeral of Rowe's worthy and much
lamented friend," Rev. Mr. Hooper, with "a great
concourse and multitude of people attending the
solemnity hardly to be conceived, . . . so great at
the [Trinity] church that a great many gentlemen
and ladies could not get in. . . . Rev[d] Mr. Walter
preached a very pathetick and moving discourse."
" A great concourse of people attended the funeral "
of the Rev. Mr. Moorhead, Dec. 6, 1773. The
funerals of Captain Hay of the warship " Tamar,"
March 23, 1773, and particularly of Lieutenant-

[1] Some of the clergymen were not well affected towards Whitefield's théology and methods. This was the case with Rev. Nathaniel Robbins of Milton, who refused to admit Whitefield to his
church; and the latter preached in the open air on Milton Hill, in
front of the house which was the former home of William Foye,
provincial treasurer, under an elm which stood till the storm of
1851. Teele's "History of Milton," pp. 116, 117.

Governor Andrew Oliver, March 8, 1774, combined
civic and military pomp,— coaches, chariots, solemn
music, Hancock and his Cadets, the firing of
minute-guns, and the presence of officials of high
rank.   Henry Vassall's funeral at Cambridge,
March 22, 1769, is described as "a very handsome
funeral and a great number of people and carriages."   But the most august rites in honor of the
dead accompanied, Sept. 12, 1767, the burial of
Jeremiah Gridley, the great lawyer of the Province,
father of the bar of Boston, master and guide of
John Adams in legal studies, Grand Master of the
Masons (Rowe being then Deputy Grand Master).
Preceding the remains were the officers of his regiment and one hundred and sixty-one Masons in full
regalia and bearing the symbols of the order; and
following them were the Lieutenant-Governor, the
judges and James Otis as bearers, then relatives,
lawyers in their robes, gentlemen of the town, a
great many coaches, chariots, and chaises, with
"such a multitude of spectators as Rowe had never
before seen since he had been in New England."
After the interment the procession returned in the
same order to the Town House, whence the body
had been taken at the beginning.   Rowe remarks of
the display : "I do not much approve of such parade
and show ; but as it was his and his relations' desire,
I could not well avoid giving my consent."

Rowe was a leader in all social affairs.   Every
colonial mansion was open to him.   As merchant,
Mason, member of clubs, an officer of Trinity

Church, a citizen active in public concerns, a leader
in public and private festivities, he knew every one
in the town who was not altogether obscure. In
his Diary all the principal personages pass again
and again before us, whether official persons or
conspicuous citizens,— Bernard, Hutchinson, Otis,
Hancock, Bowdoin, Cushing, the Quincys, Adamses,
Olivers, Gridleys, Boylstons, Auchmutys, Grays, Vassalls, Pitts, Inches, Phillips, Brimmer, Apthorp,
Boutineau, Goldthwait, Swift, Hallowell, Timmins,
Amory, all the leading clergymen and physicians,
and a hundred more bearing familiar names.
When the British evacuated Boston at the end of
the siege, many of his best friends and some
of his kinsfolk left also; and their names appear
in Sabine's "Loyalists," and in Hutchinson's and
Curwen's journals, and in the records of confis-
cated estates which we could wish our fathers had
not left us as subjects of explanation and apology.

The amount of gayety and feasting in Boston in
the period preceding the Revolution appears promi-
nently in Rowe's Diary. It is safe to say that nothing like it exists to-day in any American town of less
than twenty thousand inhabitants. The hour of
dining was in the early afternoon, and that of the
supper in the evening. Rowe records a great
number of private meals, with names of guests,—
friends, relatives, officers of the army and navy, or
visitors from other Colonies or from Europe. We
get only glimpses of the menu. French novelties
had not yet come into vogue; and the dishes were

substantial, mostly English. We hear nothing of
soups; but turtle (how served it is not stated),
venison, and salmon seem to have been the choic-
est dishes which could be set before guests. The
only vegetable named is green peas, picked from
his own garden (June 16, 1767). Of the fruits
which now complete a dinner or give relish to a
breakfast or tea, nothing is said except that at Inman's one afternoon (July 6, 1768) there was at
tea "a fine desert of cherrys and strawberries,"
the last doubtless growing wild. "A good large
plumb cake" accompanied, June 5, 1769, "a fine
ball and excellent music in Faneuil Hall."

The Diary suggests the beverages of the time.
Then, as in more modern periods, Boston people
delighted in Old Madeira. Hutchinson, in his alma-
nac for 1770, notes: "July 19, paid John Rowe
for a qr. cask of Port, £8." At a dinner at
Rowe's, July 5, 1765, "Christo. Minot was very
wroth with Mr. Inman for introducing some sterlg.
Madeira on his new coat from one of the Leghorn
glasses not well managed." May 1, 1766, "After
dinner came Capt. Solo. Davis and Mr. H. Bethune
to drink Welch ale." At the dinner on the Queen's
birthday at Concert Hall (Jan. 18, 1771) there was
"very good dancing and good musick, but very bad
wine and punch." At Mrs. Cordis's tavern (March
25, 1767) her patrons "regulated the price of wine
and punch with her, twenty shillings a double bowl
punch, thirty shillings a bottle Madeira." March 7,
1767, "we went to Capt. Bennets and drank a bottle
of Madeira with Lewis Gray and Capt. Doble.

The private dinners at which Rowe was host or
guest bring before us the principal citizens of
Boston at that time. One misses altogether, in
the repeated lists of names, Paul Revere, and
finds only in a very few instances Samuel Adams
sharing in the conviviality. The last-named, with
Hancock and Cushing, dines with Rowe May 5,
1767, and again Feb. 15, 1774, in company with
Colonel James Warren of Plymouth, and other
guests, not of Boston, bearing military titles.
Rowe meets Adams at a dinner at Henderson
Inches's, Jan. 7, 1775, in company with the
clergymen Hunt and Bacon, Ezekiel Goldthwait,
Cushing, and Arnold Wells. Otherwise Samuel
Adams is not traced at dinners and clubs, except
at the Fire Club.

Rowe's relations as friend and client with John
Adams seem to have been very cordial, and the
latter was as often in Boston life as his residence
at Quincy much of the time permitted. Rowe
meets " Mr. Adams of Braintree, lawyer," at
Bracket's, the tavern, Jan. 28, 1765, in company
with gentlemen nearly all bearing military titles.
At a missing point in Rowe's Diary, John Adams
enters in his, Dec. 20, 1765 : [1] " Went to Boston ;
dined with Mr. Rowe in company with Messrs.
Gridley, Otis, Kent, and Dudley." Rowe has at
dinner, Sept. 4, 1766, " Mr. Addams of Braintree,
lawyer," in company with " Mr. Payne of Taunton," and also has Adams to dine Feb. 24, 1767.

[1] Works, ii. 158.

He notes, March 6, 1769, a dinner at Major Cunningham's with him, "his two sons, all his officers of his company, the Rev. Dr. Elliot, Mr. Henderson Inches, Mr. John Adams, lawyer," and others. June 16, 1769, Rowe's guests were James Otis, Mrs. Otis, Mr. Walton and Mr. Dennison of New York, Brigadier-General Brattle, John Adams, Mr. Dana the lawyer, Mr. Benjamin Kent the lawyer, Mr. John Timmins, Captain Solomon Davis, Thomas and William Apthorp. Adams records in his own Diary, Feb. 26, 1770, calling at Rowe's house to warm himself, and their going out together to attend a funeral. Adams, as appears by Rowe's Diary Aug. 19, 1766, June 17, Nov. 2, 3, 1772, had law business in Taunton and Ipswich in which Rowe was concerned as client or witness.

Rowe had pleasant relations with James Otis, and they met from time to time in a social and friendly way (July 6, 1768; June 16, 1769). Rowe dined, April 1, 1767, at Otis's, where were Mrs. Otis, Jeremiah Gridley, Mr. Grant of Halifax, Mr. Hughes, Andrew Belcher, Mr. Amiel, and John Dennie. He was also in friendly intercourse with John Hancock.

Some entertainments given by Rowe may be noted: Jan. 9, 1770, "Dined at home with his Honor, the Lieut.-Govern^r, his brother Foster Hutchinson, Esq., Colo. Dalrymple, Capt. Caldwell, Mr. Nicholas Boylston, Mr. Inman, Mr. John Lane, Mrs. Rowe." Aug. 6, 1770, "I dined at home with Colin Campbell, Esq., and his lady,

Colo. Dalrymple and Capt. Mason of the 14th regiment, Capt. Robertson and his son, Capt. Rob[t] Linzee,[1] Capt. Bellew, Capt. Porter, Mr. Inman, Mrs. Rowe, and Sucky." Feb. 23, 1774, the party consisted of John Hancock, Joseph Hawley, Robert Treat Paine, John Pickering, Jedediah Preble of Falmouth (Portland), Isaac Lathrop of Plymouth, William Sever of Kingston, Gorham of Charlestown, and the Inmans. Frequently before the war Rowe gave dinners to the British officers, military and naval (Oct. 19, 1770; Feb. 25, Nov. 15, 1774; Feb. 15 and April 13, 1775), and, after the British evacuated, to American officers (Sept. 4, 1776). "A genteel dance" was given for "Sucky" Inman, Feb. 21, 1770, at which military officers were most prominent,— among them Captain Preston, who was shortly to become an historical character.

There were dinners which Rowe attended,— at Governor Bernard's, Nov. 23, 1764, where were Boutineau, Pitts, Erving, Hancock, Samuel Wentworth, and Dr. Chauncy; at the Surveyor-General's (John Temple) Feb. 2, 1767, where were the Secretary (Andrew Oliver), Mrs. Robert Temple, Colonel Gorham, Dr. Bulfinch, Rev. Mr. Walter, Rev. Mr. Troutbeck, and "Miss Alice Whipple, the fair Quaker"; at Governor Hutchinson's, Dec. 30, 1772, where were the families of himself and Lieutenant-Governor Oliver, Dr. Gardner, the clergymen Caner, Byles, Walter, and Troutbeck; at Nicholas Boylston's, whose sumptuous furniture im-

---

[1] Afterwards Rear Admiral, brother of Captain John Linzee.

pressed John Adams [1] (Jan. 2, 1768; Jan. 4, Oct. 31,
1769; May 16, 1770), and at whose entertainments
the distinguished people of the town were to be found;
at Hancock's, Aug. 8, 1766, where were James Pitts,
Treasurer Gray, James Otis, Thomas Cushing, and
Benjamin Gerrish, and Dec. 12, 1772, where were
" Madam Hancock, Solo. Davis, Judge Read, Thos.
Brown, Thos. Brattle, Timo. Fitch, Tuthill Hubbard and James Perkins "; and " the fattest venison " which Rowe had ever seen was served.

Rowe recounts the guests at numerous dinners he
attended,— as at Ezekiel Goldthwait's in Roxbury,
Aug. 23, 1766; Thomas Flucker's, April 16, 1773;
Ralph Inman's in Boston, July 13, 1776; Tuthill
Hubbard's, Aug. 7, 1776; and Mrs. Coffin's, Nov.
19, 1778.

Rowe kept open house for friends from the
country, and he notes their dining with him,—
Tristram Dalton of Newberry (July 16, 1765; May
16, 18, 1766; Aug. 19, 1772; March 30, 1774;
Oct. 27, Nov. 3, 1776; Feb. 14, 19, 1779); Epps
Sergeant of Gloucester (Aug. 17, 1768; March
22, June 17, 1772); Captain Thomas Gerry
of Marblehead (Sept. 13, 1769), and his son El-
bridge, then rising to distinction (May 26, 1767;
June 29, 1770); Robert Treat Paine of Taunton
(Feb. 8, March 1, 1767); Colonel John Chandler of
Worcester and Colonel John Murray of Rutland
(March 1, June 8, 10, 1767; Dec. 3, 5, 1769); and
General Timothy Ruggles of Hardwick (March 1,

---

[1] Works, ii. 179,

1767). He had (Sunday, Jan. 10, 1768) General Winslow of Marshfield to dine with him; and after church he spent an hour at Mrs. Bracket's, the tavern, with General Winslow, General Ruggles, Colonel Bradford, Mr. Sever of Kingston, and Major Alden.

Occasionally there were guests from other Colonies,— an Izzard, Burrows, and Powell from South Carolina, or a Livingston, King, and Mercer from New York (July 15, Aug. 21, 1767 ; Aug. 6, 7, 8, Sept. 6, 7, Oct. 15, 19, 21, 23, 1776); visitors or traders from the West Indies (Aug. 27, 1772; Sept. 6, 1776); Mr. Conner of Madeira and Mr. Conner of Teneriffe (Nov. 16, 1772); occasionally Frenchmen and Spaniards (July 16, 1772); and Englishmen who came for trade or curiosity (Oct. 12, Nov. 23, 1772), now and then bearing titles, as for instance Lord and Lady William Campbell (Oct. 25, 30, 1771; July 4, 1772). The English officers, civil and military, were much in social request; and some of them had to seek Rowe's good offices to relieve them from arrest for debt or other difficulties, as in the cases of Sir Thomas Rich of the "Senegal" (Nov. 7, 1771), and Captain John Linzee (Aug. 26, 27, 28, 31, 1772). Rowe often notes the sailing or arrival of passengers, both English and American, to or from England; and there seems to have been more communication between the town and the mother country than between the town and the Colonies lying southward. It is thus easy to understand how Boston at an early day acquired a distinctively English stamp.

A romantic character appears transiently in Rowe's pages,— Lady Frankland (Agnes Surriage), born in 1726, a Marblehead girl, celebrated in Holmes's ballad, who attracted the eye of Sir Charles Henry Frankland, great-grandson of Frances Cromwell, the daughter of the Protector.[1] He had come to Boston as royal collector in 1741. Though closely identified with King's Chapel as vestryman in the years 1743–44 and 1746–54, he was a benefactor of Trinity Church, giving, as appears by its records, a subscription for its first organ which was exceeded only by the amounts contributed by Peter Faneuil and Henry Vassall. Besides his city house next to Hutchinson's, he bought, as is well known, an estate in Hopkinton, now Ashland, where he placed his mistress, whom several years afterwards he married at Lisbon, in gratitude for her having rescued him at the time of the earthquake in 1755. Sir Henry and Lady Frankland were again in Boston in 1756, and they entertained the Rowes and Inmans Jan. 26, 1757. They left the country Feb. 23, 1758.

Once or twice more Frankland came to Boston, and returning to England died near Bath, Jan. 11, 1768. He was accompanied by Henry Cromwell, said to be his natural son, born in February, 1741, before his acquaintance with the Marblehead girl whom he took with him to Boston and Hopkinton.

---

[1] Sir Charles Henry Frankland, by Elias Nason; Foote's Annals of King's Chapel, i. 515–518. Frankland did not come to his title till the death of his uncle in 1747. His memorandum book or journal is preserved in the cabinet of this Society.

A few months after her husband's death Lady Frankland and Henry Cromwell sailed for Boston.

Lady Frankland and Cromwell were of a party at Menotomy Pond Aug. 28, 1773; and they disappear at this date from Rowe's Diary. Lady Frankland probably left shortly after for her estate in Hopkinton. She and Cromwell remained there till 1775, when after some obstruction they were allowed by the Provincial Congress to go to Boston, and not long after sailed for England, never to return.[1] The curious history of Agnes Surriage is only pursued thus far in order to illustrate Rowe's Diary. It may be added that she married in 1782 John Drew, a banker of Chichester, and died, April 23, 1783, at the age of fifty-seven. The only glimpses of her sojourn in Boston after her return as a widow are now for the first time obtained from Rowe's Diary.

Henry Cromwell's origin is involved in obscurity. Sir Charles Henry Frankland is usually named as his putative father, but the history which comes nearest the time makes him the natural son of Sir Thomas Frankland, Sir Charles's uncle and immediate predecessor in the title.[2] No writer makes any suggestion as to his maternity. He entered the English navy, rose to be a captain, and was with Admiral Kempenfelt in an action off the French coast Nov. 14, 1781. He is said to have been liv-

---

[1] Memorial History of Boston, iii. 77.

[2] Noble's Memoirs of the House of Cromwell, ii. 423, 424. Noble makes two mistakes,— giving Agnes's name as "Brown," and giving "Colchester" instead of Chichester as the place where she passed the latter part of her life.

ing and to have had a family in Chichester in 1796.
Nason makes a statement which is not trustworthy,
— that, "being unwilling to fight against his native
country, he retired from the service previous to the
close of the Revolution." There is no evidence of
his American birth, and the dates indicate an English birth. It appears by Steel's " List of the Royal
Navy," page 20, that his first commission was in
1781, and that, instead of leaving the navy, he was
still in it in 1797, with the rank of captain.

Weddings were the occasion of good cheer and
gayety. Rowe mentions, Nov. 8, 1764, "Mr.
Thos. Amory married Miss Betty Coffin this evening; there was a great company at old Mr. Coffin's
on the occasion, and a great dance." [1]   He records,
Jan. 13, 1767, "a wedding frollick" at John Erving, Jr.'s, where he " had the pleasure to dance with
the bride." Feb. 2, 1768. " This morning Miss
Polly Hooper was married in Trinity Church to Mr.
John Russell Spence by the Rev[d] Mr. Walter; a
great concourse of people attended on the occasion.
Dined at Mrs. Hooper's with her, the new bridegroom and bride." A large number of guests were
present,— Hallowells, Apthorps, Murrays, Green-
leafs, and others,— remaining to tea and joining in
the evening in a dance. " We were merry, and
spent the whole day very clever and agreeable."

There were once in two weeks in the winter and
spring, beginning with the first of January, dancing-

---

[1] The bride's portrait belongs to the family of the late William
Amory of Boston.

assemblies at Concert Hall. The Governor and military and naval officers quite often attended them, and Rowe describes them many times as " very brilliant." The number of gentlemen and ladies in attendance was usually rather more than a hundred, and sometimes it rose to two hundred. Feb. 10, 1768. " Spent the evening at the assembly, which was a very brilliant one, the Governour and Lady, all the commissioners, Mr. Harrison, and too many to enumerate." March 15, 1769. " Spent the evening at the assembly with the Governour, Commodore, General, Colo. Kerr, Colo. Lesly, Major Furlong, Major Fleming, Major Fordyce, a great number of officers of the navy and army and gentlemen and ladies of the town, that it was a brilliant assembly and very good dancing."

There were several political clubs in Boston in Rowe's time, but he belonged to none of them. He was however an habitual visitor at clubs social or commercial, going almost every evening to one or another. More often than any other he sought the " Possee "; but what was its bond of fellowship is not known. It had a limited number of members, as follows: John Avery, John Box, William Coffin, Senior, Samuel Deming, Deacon Thomas Foster, Benjamin Greene, Rufus Greene, William Henshaw, Francis Johonnot, James Richardson, and John Rowe. Samuel Swift, the lawyer, usually met with them, though perhaps rather as a guest than as a member. Occasionally a member introduced a guest who lived in the country.

The Fire Club, meeting at Mrs. Cordis's or at Ingersoll's, was made up of George Bethune, Melatiah Bourne, James Boutineau, Nicholas and Thomas Boylston, John Brown, John Dennie, Solomon Davis, Benjamin Faneuil, Samuel Fitch, Thomas Flucker, Harrison Gray, Capt. Jerry Green, Joseph Green, Dr. William Lloyd, Master John Lovell, William Molineux, and William Sheaffe. Rowe's first meeting with them was Sept. 5, 1768. On the same page where he states this fact he writes, "The word, Ask more," which may have been the password. Joseph Green, who was present Sept. 4, 1769, is mentioned as "the poet."

Rowe attended, Nov. 7, 14, 1764, the Wednesday Night Club, probably having no connection with the Wednesday Evening Club of a later date. He also mentions, July 4, 1767, meeting the "No. 5 Club," made up of prominent citizens whom he names.

The chief rendezvous of the leading citizens was, however, at Mrs. Cordis's,— "the British Coffee House in the front room towards the Long wharf where the Merchants Club has met this twenty years."[1] Lawyers as well as merchants came hither, probably every evening. In 1767 the meetings were at Mrs. Cordis's; but about 1772 they were held at Colonel Joseph Ingersoll's Bunch of Grapes in King Street, and when he left Boston, at Captain Marston's, either in King Street or Merchants' Row. The names of persons whom Rowe met at these resorts — some on one evening and some on another, and all of them recurring again and again in his pages — are John Amiel, George Apthorp, Nat. and George Bethune, Joshua Blanchard, Melatiah and William Bourne, James Boutineau, John and Nicholas Boylston, Thomas Brattle, Edward, Solomon, and William Davis, John Dennie, Joseph Dowse, John Erving, Samuel Fitch, Thomas Flucker, Ezekiel Goldthwait, Thomas Gray, Treasurer Harrison Gray, John Hancock, Samuel Hughes, Nat. Hide, Henderson Inches, Joseph Jackson, William Molineux, James Otis, Edward Payne, James Perkins, Dr. William Lee Perkins, Samuel Quincy, Joseph Scott, John Timmins, James Warden, Edward Wendell, and Joshua Winslow, and the lawyers Gridley, Sewall, and Swift.

The habit of frequenting insurance offices for reading newspapers and hearing gossip belongs to a later date; but Rowe records, Aug. 22, 1768: "Spent the evening at the North Insurance office with James Otis, Solo. Davis, John Erving, Thos. Brattle, Capt. Vernon, Nat. Barber, Andrew Clark, and John White."

Club life as well as public festivities were mostly suspended after the battle of Lexington, except on special occasions like the visit of the French fleet.

The usual drives in the country were round Jamaica Pond or in Roxbury and Dorchester, sometimes "over the Neck round the little Square" (July 29, Aug. 10, 1774), and sometimes as far as Milton (April 6, 1769). Rowe often drove to Roxbury to see his old friend and relative Robert Gould, an invalid, till the latter's death early in 1772 (May 5, June 22, 1765). In the summer of 1771 he used to drive to Savin Hill, " a very agreeable rural spot," to a place which his friend Thomas Brattle had hired, where an agreeable company sometimes gathered for afternoon tea (May 16, June 3). The drive we may presume was often in a chaise; but sometimes Mrs. Rowe "took an airing in the chariot" (Sept. 2, 1766). The drives were to the south, as communication with the north was so circuitous. For instance, a party set out, Nov. 10, 1772, in Paddock's coach for Salem (Rowe's chaise accompanying it). " We went all round through Cambridge and dined at Martin's ; we got to Salem about four of clock."

The suburbs of Boston were attractive in those as in later days. At Milton lived Thomas Hutchinson, in a house standing till 1872, which looked out on river and ocean in front and the Blue Hills in the rear,— a house then filled with sons and daughters. He loved that home on Unquity Hill, parted from it with deep regret, and sighed in exile to return to it. Rowe drove to Hutchinson's mansion to make calls, and sometimes on official business (June 16, Sept. 11, 1766 ; July 13, 1773). He had friendly relations with Daniel Vose, the merchant of the place, at whose house " at the Milton Bridge," still standing near the railway station, the Suffolk Resolves were passed ; and dined there, May 6, 1769, in company with Dr. Catherwood, Joshua Winslow, Jr., and others. But the house in Milton which

he sought the most was that of James Smith on
Brush Hill, still standing, and for a long period the
home of the late James M. Robbins. Smith, who
died in 1769 at the age of eighty, was a wealthy
sugar-refiner, and owned an estate of one hundred
and seventy-one acres running to the Neponset
River.[1] He had also a farm at Watertown, where he
gave a distinguished dinner-party July 15, 1767.
His second wife, Mrs. Elizabeth Campbell, born
Murray, was of a Scotch family; and her maiden
name is found in the middle names of her descendants, the late Mr. Robbins, and others who are still
living in Milton. She became by a third marriage Rowe's kinswoman.[2] He records in a quaint
way the courtship of herself and his brother-in-
law Inman: July 22, 1771. "After dinner [at
Rowe's] Mr. Inman introduced his design to Mrs.
Smith." August 16. "Afternoon Mr. Inman and
Mrs. Rowe paid a visit to Mrs. Smith over to Goldthwait's. Mr. Inman came home well pleased and
agreed on his plan of matrimony." Rowe notes
the publication of banns at King's Chapel, September 1, and the marriage "at the seat of Mr. Ezekiel
Goldthwait," September 26, followed by a dinner at
Inman's, where Rowe passed the evening and the
night. Rowe was often at this Brush Hill house,
once at least taking a sleigh-ride there (Jan. 30,
1765); and once Mrs. Rowe was badly bruised (Aug.

[1] Pictures of the Hutchinson, Vose, and Smith houses are in
Teele's "History of Milton."

[2] She and her second husband, James Smith, are buried at
King's Chapel.

18, 1767) by her carriage being upset as she was driving there. It was Rowe's stopping-place as he was returning from fishing or business excursions (July 20, 1765; July 22, 1766). Under this roof often gathered gay dinner-companies, where were James Murray and wife; his daughters Anna, Betsey, and Dorothy [1] (the last afterwards the wife of Rev. John Forbes); old Madam Belcher, the Governor's widow, and Mrs. Belcher, widow of Andrew Belcher, who was both Madam's daughter and daughter-in-law; the Hoopers, Inmans, Vassalls, Amiels, Auchmutys, Goulds, Temples, Hallowells, Goldthwaits, Miss Blowers, Rev. Edward Winslow; and Milton neighbors, the Pratts and Clarks (March 28, July 19, 20, 1765; July 24, Oct. 23, 1766; Aug. 18, 1767; Feb. 7, 25, 1769). Rowe writes of the dinner, March 16, 1773, "We were very merry." These happy days at Brush Hill were then coming to a close, the greater number of the festive company sharing the fate of Loyalists and exiles. The Murray ladies succeeded in saving the estate itself from confiscation by remaining upon it and keeping very quiet during the war.[2]

There were then attractive houses at Cambridge. Rowe records festivities at several of them, — at Colonel Thomas Oliver's (Dec. 9, 1766; Feb. 22, 1768; Aug. 17, 1769), where were the Brattles, Temples, Vassalls, Byards, Phippses, Van Hornes Edward Winslow, and Richard Lechmere; and at

---

[1] She is buried at King's Chapel. Her portrait is in the possession of her grandson, John M. Forbes, of Milton.

[2] Teele's "History of Milton," pp. 173, 174, 421, 422.

John and Henry Vassall's, where were similar companies (Feb. 16, 1765; Dec. 12, 1766; Feb. 17, 1768). His record for Feb. 20, 1768, was of a dinner at Ten Hills (Mr. Robert Temple's), where were "Mrs. Temple, Mrs. Elizth Hubbard, Miss Henrietta Temple and 4 daughters of Mr. Temple's, also Colo. James Otis, his son James Otis, Mr. Wm Bayard, Major Robt. Byard, Mr. Lavicount, Mr. Dewar, Capt. Sheaffe of Charlestown, Colo. Saltonstall of Haverhill." A dinner at Colonel David Phipps's (July 7, 1768) has been noted elsewhere.

In no house in or about Boston were there more lavish entertainments than at Ralph Inman's in Cambridge, a house the site of which is just behind the present City Hall. No buildings then intervening to obstruct the view, it looked out on the Charles River and Boston beyond. Noble trees stood in the spacious grounds about it.[1] Rowe as a kinsman was often here for family and friendly gatherings, some of which have been elsewhere noted (Oct. 18, 1764; June 21, Aug. 2, Oct. 23, 1771; Aug. 25, 1773).

The entertainments at Inman's and at College rooms on Commencement Day surpass anything since known in that renowned home of culture and hospitality, except perhaps "the class spreads" given in recent years at the Hemenway Gymnasium and Beck Hall. Rowe makes these records: July 17, 1765. "Commencement Day. Went to Cam-

---

[1] Drake's "Historic Fields and Mansions of Middlesex," p. 187, gives a description and picture of the house.

bridge, Mrs. Rowe, Polly Hooper, and Sucky; dined
at Edward Winslow's room, a very large company;
went to Mr. Hooper's room, also to Col. Taylor's."
Young Winslow was to die an exile in New Brunswick. The next day there was a dinner at Mr.
Hooper's (probably Robert Hooper of the Class of
1765), "with a very large company"; and in the
evening a dance at the Town House given by young
Nathaniel Sparhawk, another of the Class of 1765,
at whose request Rowe "officiated as master of the
ceremony." Sparhawk and probably Hooper became Loyalists. A similar festivity is recorded July
16, 1766. Again, July 20, 1768: "I went to Cambridge, stopped at Mr. Inman's, dined with a very
large company at Jos. Henshaw's, paid a visit to
Tutor Hancock's, met the Rev^d Mr. Barnard of
Marblehead, afterwards paid a visit to Mrs. Green's
where were a very large company, too many to enumerate." July 21. "A very hot day. I came to
town this morning and returned to Cambridge;
dined with Mr. David Greene, with a very large
company, spent the evening there. We had a dance.
I was master of the ceremonies; slept at Mr.
Inman's." Greene of the Class of 1768 became a
Loyalist. July 17, 1771: "I went to Cambridge
and dined with Mr. Inman, Polly Jones, and Sally
Inman; after dinner I went to Colo. Murray's room
in the New Colledge,[1] where there was a large company, the Governour, Councill and too many to enumerate. I staid till six." Colonel John Murray

1 Hollis Hall.

and his son Daniel of the graduating class, also his son Samuel of the class of the following year, became Loyalists.

The fullest record of festivities at Cambridge is in July, 1772. On the 15th Rowe dined at Samuel Murray's room, where were Colonel Murray the father, Colonel Saltonstall, Judge Sewall, Colonel Oliver, Samuel Quincy, Major Vassall, and many other guests whose names are given. Rowe adds: " After dinner we were visited by the Governour and Council, Admirall Montague and many other gentlemen too many to enumeràte. I paid a visit to Mr. Jonathan William's son and also Dr. Whitworth's son, both which took their degree." The record of the next day is as follows: " I went early to Mr. Inman's, who made the genteelest entertainment I ever saw on account of his son George taking his degree yesterday. He had three hundred forty-seven gentlemen and ladies dined, two hundred and ten at one table, amongst the company the Governour and family, the Lieut-Governour and family, the Admirall and family, and all the remainder gentlemen and ladies of character and reputation; the whole was conducted with much ease and pleasure, and all joyned in making each other happy; such an entertainment has not been made in New England before on any occasion." A ball at the Town House in Cambridge followed, where " all were very happy and cheerful" and Rowe slept at Inman's. George Inman, whose college life closed so merrily, left his home three years later to join the British army, and died at Grenada in the West Indies in 1789.

These annual festivities were approaching a suspension; and Rowe records, July 20, 1774, that " the distressed situation of the town and Province prevents Commencement Day being kept publick as usual." Inman's house became General Putnam's headquarters during the siege of Boston,— an event which is commemorated by an inscription on a stone slab placed on its site by the city of Cambridge. The building itself, removed twenty and more years ago, is now a double tenement house, recently bereft of its piazza, numbered 64 and 66 on Brookline Street in that city, and making the southeast corner of Brookline and Auburn streets.

Ralph Inman's estate escaped confiscation, and he returned to live and die upon it, and to bequeath it by a will proved in July, 1788. He has posterity other than the Linzees living in Boston, New York, and Philadelphia, descending from the daughters of his son George, who came with their mother from Grenada to Massachusetts soon after their father's death, and who were liberally provided for in the wills of their grandfather and of Hannah Rowe.

Another well-known suburban house was that of Isaac Royall at " Mystick," or Medford. There, May 3, 1766, besides Rowe, were " Miss Polly and Miss Betsy Royal, General Brattle, Treasurer Gray, James Otis, Esq., Thos. Cushion [Cushing], Esq., and Mr. Nathl. Sparhawk." There also, July 22, 1768, were " the Governour and Council, Danforth,

Gray, Flucker, Bowdoin, Isaac Royal, Mr. Pepperell." This company were to be scattered a few
years later, the hosts and the larger number of
guests becoming Loyalists. Royall is gratefully
remembered by jurists for the professorship
founded by him at Cambridge.

Rowe attended, Aug. 23, 1773, a large dinner-
party at " Mallden " given by Captain Haskins,
where were several whose names have already appeared in other connections in these pages.

All the notable houses in the Province were open
to Rowe, — those of the Speakmans, his relatives
in Marlborough; Colonel John Murray at Rutland
(May 21, 23, 1766); General Timothy Ruggles at
Hardwick (May 21, 22, 1766); Colonel John
Chandler at Worcester (May 12, 1767); Robert
Treat Paine and Captain Cobb at Taunton (May 8,
July 3, 1766; July 30, 1767); Edward Winslow
at Plymouth (May 2, 1765; April 28, 1768;
April 27, 1769; April 30, May 21, 1770; April
24, 25, 1771); Nathaniel Ray Thomas (May 1,
1765; April 28, 1769) and General Winslow
(April 29, 30, 1767; April 25, 26, 1769; May 1,
2, 1770; April 23, 1771), both at Marshfield;
Major Goldthwait's country home at " Westown "
(May 13, 1767); those of several friends in Salem,
among them Colonel Pickman and Joseph Dowse
(Oct. 1, 1767); Captain Thomas Gerry at Marblehead (July 31, 1765; July 28, 1776), where were
his sons Thomas, John, and Elbridge; and of
Tristram Dalton at " Newberry Old Town," where

Rowe dined, July 26, 1776, when returning from
Portsmouth. Of Dalton's place he writes : " This
seat of Mr. Dalton's is most delightfully situated,
and has the most extensive prospect I ever saw,
particularly of the River Merrimack and the sea
beyond, Newberryport and Hampton Beach."
One gets the impression from this Diary that in
the days before the Revolution there was a country
life in New England in large houses remote from
Boston (not summer cottages only) more interesting and having greater social vitality than anything
like it in those or similar localities in our time.

The public feasting in Boston at this time was
beyond anything now seen in places of the same
population. There were merchants' dinners, St.
Patrick dinners, charitable society dinners, Masonic
dinners, artillery election dinners, dinners on board
vessels of war and commerce,[1] dinners at Faneuil
Hall to celebrate the close of the school year, with
clergymen and official or eminent persons as guests,
dinners of the Proprietors of Long Wharf, dinners
on Spectacle, Rainsford, and Noddle's islands, and
at the Light House. There were dinners, often
with dancing, to celebrate the King's accession to
the throne, and the King's and Queen's birthdays,
and to express the public joy at the repeal of the
Stamp Act. Rowe was present at all these, often
serving as chairman or toastmaster ; and he describes with much zest the entertainments as " gen-

---

[1] April 21, 1774, on board Rowe's own ship, the " Montagu."

teel." He seemed to enjoy more than any the Masonic dinners which came twice a year, in June and December, and he always gives the names of the brethren present. Dec. 27, 1764, he wrote: "I don't remember St. John, as long as I have belonged to the fraternity, has been celebrated with more decorum and more pleasure." The merchants' dinner at the Coffee House, Dec. 2, 1766, Rowe presiding, to Capt. John Gideon, commander of the warship "Jamaica," just before sailing, was a notable festivity. Here were all the principal merchants and citizens, including Hancock, Otis, Edmund Quincy, Cushing, the Boylstons, Amorys, and Hallowells. Rowe says: "And a very genteel entertainment it was." A committee, of which Rowe was a member, had been appointed the day before by the town to express its thanks to Captain Gideon for his conduct while stationed at Boston.

Sometimes our ancestors feasted on a roasted ox, or "barbikue,"—"the ox being carried through the streets in triumph" the day before,— at the Turk's Head, on the Common, at Faneuil Hall, and Dennis Island (Sept. 28, 1764; Aug. 13, 1765; Aug. 1, 1766; Aug. 16, 1768; May 29, 30, 1770). These were not occasions for the masses only; but the leading people, ladies as well as gentlemen,— Hutchinsons, Olivers, Grays, Belchers, Sheaffes, Auchmutys, Swifts, and Goldthwaits,— took part.

The places for feasting when the company was very large were Faneuil Hall and Concert Hall,—

the latter resort situated on the south corner of
Court and Hanover streets, and standing till a
modern period,[1] — but considerable parties were
entertained at Mrs. Cordis's Coffee House; Colonel
Joseph Ingersoll's Bunch of Grapes in King Street
(Captain Marston was his successor there, 1775–
1779); Bracket's, Gardner's, and King's Arms on
the Neck; the Peacock, Greaton's (the Greyhound),
Richards's, and Blany's in Roxbury; Kent's and
John Champney's (the Turk's Head) in Dorchester;
Coolidge's "at Watertown Bridge"; Weatherby's
at Menotomy Pond, and places of refreshment at
Fresh Pond and Spot Pond. These festivities included a pleasant suburban drive of ladies and
gentlemen round Jamaica Pond (in winter in
sleighs), a dinner and tea and a dance in the evening, joined in not by the young only, but also by
middle-aged people of foremost rank in the town.
Sometimes each paid his own score, but at other
times one of the party was host and the rest guests.
The French consul was the host at Marston's Feb.
27, 1779; and Colonel Dalrymple, Francis Waldo,
and John Lane on other occasions at the Peacock
(July 10, Aug. 20, Oct. 30, 1771).

Eighty gentlemen, "a high campaign," went,
Aug. 11, 1767, to witness a launch at Weymouth.
An excursion to a remoter point may be chronicled
in this connection, Aug. 6, 1772: "This morning
Mr. Hancock, Dr. Cooper, Mr. Brattle, Mr. Tuthill
Hubbard, Mr. Saml. Calef, Mr. Winthrop of Cam-

[1] It was finally demolished in 1869.

bridge, Mr. Nicho. Bowes and Capt. Hood went from Boston in the Providence packet to visit the eastern parts of this province and also on a party of pleasure. My servant Henry Smith and Davis the barber's man went with them as attendants." The party returned August 22.

There were a succession of enjoyable inns on the highways leading from Boston southward to Plymouth and Taunton, and also to the east and west. Most sought by Rowe was Doty's,[1] in Stoughton, now Canton, just beyond the Blue Hills, standing till it was burned in December, 1888, its site now a race-course. Here met in 1774 the " County Congress," with Warren at the head of the Boston delegation, by which at an adjourned meeting held at the house of Daniel Vose in Milton were passed the famous Suffolk Resolves. Here during the siege lived Ezekiel Price, who drove often to Milton to learn the news and observe from the hill the movements of the British ships in the harbor. Rowe had occasion on fishing-excursions or journeys to Dighton on business (the affairs of Ebenezer Stetson, an insolvent debtor), to stop often at this tavern, and he managed whenever he could to pass the night there. Once when returning from Dighton, May 9, 1766, he wrote : " We supped and slept there, and I set it down as an extraordinary house of entertainment, and very good beds." Other country taverns which he frequented were

---

[1] An account of this tavern, with a picture, is given in Huntoon's "History of Canton," pp. 335-341.

Brackett's in Braintree, Deacon Cushing's in Hingham, Elisha Ford's in Marshfield, Spears's and Hall's
in Pembroke, Howland's in Plymouth, Newcomb's
in Sandwich, Stone's in Stoughton, Widow Noyes's
in Sharon (then Stoughtonham, where one of the
Edmund Quincys seemed to be an *habitué*), Howard's and Kingman's in Easton, McWhorter's in
Taunton, Tapley's, Johnson's, and Norwood's in
Lynn, Goodhue's in Salem, " a good tavern and
good lodging " (Oct. 1, 1767), Treadwell's in Ipswich, Widow Ames's and Woodward's (both being
the same) [1] and Gay's in Dedham, Mackintosh's in
Needham, Pratt's at Needham Bridge, and Fisher's
on Charles River in the upper part of that town,
Bullard's in Natick (where Rowe dined July 3,
1765, " on fish which Mrs. Bullard dressed very
well "), Mann's in Wrentham, and Bryant's in Sudbury. These wayside inns, sometimes the resort of
parties of gentlemen and ladies driving from Boston,
appear attractive in Rowe's pages ; but John Adams
does not give so favorable an account of them. [2]

Fresh-water fishing was a great sport in those
days, and Rowe was one of the jolliest and most
expert fishermen. We read in John Adams's Diary
(II. 238) a note, June 2, 1770, from Goldthwait to
Adams, who was to start the next day for Ports-

---

[1] These taverns were in Dedham village. Mrs. Ames was the
mother of Fisher Ames, and married Woodward for her second
husband. At Woodward's the " County Congress," which afterwards passed the Suffolk Resolves at Milton, met.

[2] Works, ii. 123, and elsewhere.

mouth on a professional errand: "Do you call to-morrow and dine with us at Flax Pond near Salem. Rowe, Davis, Brattle, and half a dozen as clever fellows as ever were born, are to dine there under the shady trees by the pond upon fish and bacon and pease, &c. ; and as to Madeira, nothing can come up to it. Do you call. We'll give you a genteel dinner and fix you off on your journey." Rowe took care to provide himself with all a fisher-man's needs, as imported rods (June 11, 1765); sometimes "lost several fine hooks and snoods" (Sept. 10, 1768), once lost "the top of his rod line and hooks by a very large pickerell" (Sept. 17, 1764), and once left behind his "fishing rod and leather dram bottle" (Oct. 2, 1767). His com-panions on these excursions were often Samuel Calef or Henry Ayres, and sometimes his clerical friends. In the early part of the Diary he was fishing mostly in Flax Pond in Lynn, and in the latter part mostly in Charles River at Dedham and Needham, keeping a boat at Dedham, which he sent up the river, June 12, 1776, and stopping sometimes at Kendrick's or other taverns in the town or vicinity, but oftener at Richards's (prob-ably Timothy Richards), who, though not a tavern-keeper, received him in a friendly way. Other fishing-resorts frequented by him were Menotomy Pond, with Wyndship's tavern near by; Fresh Pond; Spot Pond; Jamaica Pond; Ponkapoag Pond (Doty's tavern near by), and perhaps Hough-ton's in the vicinity (Aug. 2, 1766); Mossepong (or

Massapoag) Pond (July 30, 1767) in Sharon; ponds
or streams in Natick and Wrentham; "the Great
Worster Pond"[1] in Shrewsbury, where he was
entertained at "Mr. Furnaces" and fished at
"Worster Bridge" (May 12, 13, July 6, 1767);
and a pond "at the upper end of Mallden" (July 2,
1767). To the south were sheets of water inviting
the fisherman,— in Hingham, Taunton, Duxbury,
Pembroke, and Plymouth; and with all these Rowe
was familiar.

Sometimes the luck was poor, but generally it
was very good. Four or five dozen was an ordinary catch; but often the fishing-party brought
back ten or even twenty dozen,— sometimes pickerel two feet long and weighing nearly four pounds
(one caught June 29, 1770, weighing four and a
quarter pounds); perch fifteen, sixteen, and eighteen inches long, and weighing three and a half
pounds; and trout eighteen inches long.

Ladies were sometimes of the party, and passed
the night at the tavern near by; but they do not
appear to have joined in the sport. At Kendrick's
on Charles River, July 27, 1765, Pitts, Bowdoin,
Boutineau, Bourne, and Flucker were accompanied
by their wives for the day, and Nicholas Boylston
was of the party. At Doty's tavern in Stoughton
the fishing-party was joined, Aug. 21, 1776, by
"the two Mrs. Belchers, Miss Clark, Miss Dolly
Murray, Mrs. Jones, Miss Blowers, Miss Amiel,
Mr. Hutchinson, and Mr. Waller." At Flax

---

[1] Long Pond, or Lake Quinsigamond.

Pond, June 29, 1770, the ladies of the Wendell, Goldthwait, Wells, Gerry, and Winslow families joined the party. June 8, 1773. Admiral Montagu's wife and other ladies were at Mann's tavern in Wrentham for the night, when Rowe and the Admiral were fishing there. Aug. 28, 1773. At Menotomy Pond were Montagu and his wife and daughter, Lady Frankland and Henry Cromwell, the ladies Lechmere, Simpson, Inman, Flucker, several military and naval officers, Commissioner Hulton, and Collector Harrison. "We were very jolly. The Admirall, Capt. Williams, and I had very poor luck, the fish very small."

Rowe, when visiting Plymouth for business or pleasure, did not fail to take advantage of ponds and brooks in that town and vicinity,— at Duxbury Mills, April 28, 1767, where five dozen trout were caught; at Pembroke, May 20, 1769, April 30, 1770, and May 5, 1773, each time catching fifty, fifty-eight, and sixty trout; at South Pond, Plymouth, Aug. 12, 1766, where he "caught a very large perch, measured 18 inches and weighed three pounds and half"; and May 31, 1771, when he had very good sport, afterwards dining at Mr. Richman's. "We were very merry; some young ladies came there a fishing and to pay a visit, particularly Miss Polly Brimhall of Plymouth and two daughters of Mr. Richman."

The hooking of turtles is sometimes recorded,— one at Fresh Pond, June 25, 1765, weighing thirty

pounds. Except " trying for some smelts " once or
twice (Oct. 5, 18, 1764), Rowe says nothing of salt-
water fishing, although the harbor of Boston
within the memory of living people has been good
fishing-ground. He records, June 19, 1765, a
strange apparition in our waters : " This morning
our fishermen caught a large fish in the shape of
a shark twenty foot long ; his teeth were different
from a shark's teeth." The next day's record is :
" They cut up the fish, and filled two large hogsheads with his liver."

We have sports which were unknown to our
fathers ; but they had fishing-resorts within
one or two hours' drive from Boston which we can
only have by long journeys to the Rangeley Lakes
and the Adirondacks.

In the period immediately preceding the Revolution, the port of Boston was a lively scene. War-
vessels were leaving for or coming in from Halifax
or the South or England, or going out on short
cruises. The sailing and arrival of merchant vessels, several in a day, were town topics of keen interest. April 19, 1765. " Above thirty sail of vessells arrived from the Vineyard this afternoon."
Rowe mentions the clearing of ships for Nova Scotia and New Brunswick, the West Indies, Lisbon,
Oporto, Cadiz, Gibraltar, Alicante, Madeira, Suri-
nam, Glasgow, Newcastle, Bristol, Plymouth, Whitby, London, or their arrival from those ports, Liverpool not having then attained the prominence
it has since held. Passages between English ports

and Boston ranged from five to eight weeks;
but Captain Bruce made the run from London
(arriving Oct. 20, 1764) to Boston in twenty-
six days, which Rowe mentions as "the shortest
passage ever known."[1] Later he records a still
shorter passage, April 20, 1769: "This afternoon
Capt. Post arrived from Glasgow in a short passage
of twenty-two days." Another short passage is
noted May 8, 1767: "This day arrived Capt. Delano from London in 27 days passage."

Rowe notes the arrival, May 11, 1774, of a vessel from Scotland, with upwards of a hundred passengers,— the only instance of a body of immi-
grants mentioned in the Diary.

The town was not without commercial panics;
and a serious one occurred in January, 1765. On
the 16th Nathaniel Wheelwright "stopt payment
and kept in his room. A great number of people
will suffer by him. . . . The trade has been much
alarmed." That evening at Mrs. Cordis's the conversation was on his affairs; and Mr. Inman went to
the Assembly probably to start legislative action.
"A general consternation in town occasioned by
these repeated bankruptcies. That the General
Court which are now sitting determine to make an
act for the relief of insolvent debtors,— which will
be very seasonable." The General Court, in consequence of the application, passed the Act of March
9, 1765, which was approved by the Privy Council,

[1] Province Acts and Resolves, iv. 777-781, 793-795.

though such an act had been disallowed eight years
before. Scollay's and Wheelwright's estates were
distributed under the new Act.[1]

Arbitration was usually resorted to by merchants
for adjusting disputes which arose in the way of
trade. Rowe and merchants of his standing often
sat on such boards, which met usually at the Coffee
House or Colonel Ingersoll's tavern. His records
of such sessions are so frequent that it is not worth
while to give the dates.

Rowe's Diary discloses a great number of fires in
Boston at this period. They started in many instances from foul chimneys and bakehouses. " 'Twas
a terrible foul chimney," is a record he sometimes
makes (Feb. 2, 1765). The citizens, it must be said
to their credit, worked with energy and organiza-
tion, and generally got the better of the fire before
it spread beyond the building where it started (Oct.
12, 1767). There were as early as 1768 as many
as six fire-engines, and John Hancock gave another
in 1772.[2] Rowe commends "the dexterity and
clever behaviour of the South End Engine men"
(Jan. 24, 1765). On April 2, 1768, when there
were several alarms, "one poor man lost his life by
falling off a ladder." The fire-wards were substantial citizens like Samuel Adams, Hancock, Captain
Adino Paddock, Captain Thomas Dawes, John Scol-

---

[1] There were shorter passages going eastward: Richard Clarke
made one in twenty-one days (S. Curwen's Journal and Letters, p.
43); General Burgoyne made one "in less than twenty-four days"
(Hutchinson's Diary and Letters, i. 587).

[2] Memorial History of Boston, iii. 151.

lay, and Rowe, who got excused from further service March 9, 1772. There was a Fire Club, already mentioned, which was composed of the most substantial citizens. Rowe went to the fires and fought them vigorously, coming home afterwards "much wet and tired," and going to bed (Jan. 18, 1765; June 15, 1766). His leathern bucket, marked, in large letters, "John Rowe, 1760," is still in the possession of his great-grand-niece.

The most disastrous fire of the period was on Feb. 4, 1767, breaking out in "a baker's warehouse and spreading round about the neighborhood, that it consumed more than twenty houses, among which were Mr. Jonathan Williams's dwelling-house, several houses of Mr. John Hancock, several belonging to Capt. Ball; it began at ten of clock and continued until three in the morning." Public and private charity was invoked in behalf of the sufferers, forty of whom were reduced to extreme poverty. The selectmen promptly sent a petition to the General Court asking for a grant of relief for the sufferers, and that body voted £400 to be paid to the selectmen for the purpose. The selectmen (Rowe being one) received a statement of losses, and distributed the fund March 6, 10, 12, 27. They addressed a letter to the churches, asking for contributions April 5. In Trinity Church, May 17, there was a collection for the sufferers by the late fire. "Mr. Walter behaved extremely clever on this occasion, and urged his congregation to their usual benevolence." The selectmen also distributed the fund which came from the churches (June 5, 12). A collection was taken, Aug. 7, 1768, in Trinity Church for sufferers by fire at Montreal. It is pleasant to note how the well-to-do people of Boston at that day were sympathetic, as they have been ever since, with others, near or remote, who were afflicted with misfortune.

Curiously enough, Rowe, who was keen in noting fires, makes no reference to that in Fish Street, Aug. 10, 1774, attended with loss of life, which is mentioned in Thomas Newell's Diary; but he notes, October 6 of the same year: " A large fire happened at Salem last night; Dr. Witaker's meeting house and eighteen houses were destroyed."

The lighting of the streets of London, the significance of which inspired a well-known passage of the third chapter of Macaulay's History, took place in the last year of Charles the Second's reign. Somewhat less than a century later this reform was introduced into Boston; and Rowe was one of its leaders, quite likely its originator. Thomas Newell's Diary mentions only the first lighting, and also his beginning (Jan. 8, 1774) to make the tops of the glass lamps; but Rowe gives in detail the progress of the enterprise, which occupied his attention for a year.[1]

Pope's Day, November 5, with its rival North End and South End processions, and their contest or " battle," sometimes at Mill Bridge on Han-

[1] Rowe does not mention the loss of the first lamps sent from England by the wreck of a tea-ship off Cape Cod in December, 1773,— a fact stated in John Andrews's letters.

over Street, is described by Rowe. In 1764 the sheriff, justices, and militia undertook to destroy the figures, but the populace was too much for them. Several thousand people were in attendance, and there was a fatal injury. This "foolish custom," as Rowe calls it, became in later years, as in 1769, 1773, and 1774, less of an affair, and then died out altogether.

The lottery still existed in this Puritan community, legalized for public objects. Rowe bought, March 19, 1767, seven tickets of John Ruddock, and sold one, kept two for himself, and gave the rest to Mrs. Rowe and the Inmans.

The fashion of duelling still lingered, Feb. 23, 1765 : " Colo. Bourn of M'head and Jerahmiel Bowers challenged each other with sword and pistoll yesterday about the excise."

Rowe gives incidents of crimes and punishments.

Boston does not seem to have been the orderly and well-governed town which our fathers sometimes proclaimed it to be. There was no constabulary force which amounted to anything when such a force was required. The mobs of Pope's Day, as already seen, had their own way, defying even the militia. The populace arrested at pleasure the infliction of public punishments judicially ordered, and sometimes superadded discretionary pelting of their own (Sept. 11, Oct. 4, 1764 ; Jan. 11, 1770 ; March 28, 1771). When the political troubles came, they sacked and destroyed the

houses of unpopular citizens and magistrates.
They stripped the offender naked, covered him
with tar, decked him with feathers, and transported
him in this plight, without hindrance, through the
main thoroughfares as a spectacle for a jeering
multitude (Oct. 28, 1769 ; May 18, 1770 ; March
9, 1775).   One cannot help asking where at such
times were the selectmen, the twelve constables,
the militia, Hancock and his Cadets, and the principal citizens who were so effective when fires were
to be extinguished or patriotic enterprises to be
executed.   On the whole, Boston is now a safer
place to live in for one who asserts the right to
differ with his neighbors than it was in those
good old days.

1764—1779

DIARY OF JOHN ROWE

BOSTON MERCHANT

1764

Journal begins Sept. 8, 1764.

Sept. 10. Rose very early this morning & settled with Capt. Jarvis. Wind So. West. Capt Jarvis put off the Long Wharf about twelve of Clock — in him went passengers Mr Apthorp of Cambridge Mr Binning of Halifax Mother Douglass & neice, Young Sam Wentworth & Mr Kimball. Dined at home with Mr Bannister & Mr Inman. Was much diverted in the Common, being Training Day.

Sept. 11. Very damp morning. Wind North East. Capt Jarvis in Nantasket Roads. The regiment appeared in the Common this afternoon. One of the soldiers behaved saucily to his Captain upon which they called a Court Martial and ordered him to Ride the Wooden Horse, but the mob got foul of the wooden horse & broke it so that the Fellow escaped. Spent the eve'ng at the Coffee House with Mr Treasurer Gray, Mr Gridley the Lawyer,

Mr John Boylston & Capt Davies. Also Mr Ezek^l Golthwait. Found by Mr Golthwait & the Treasurer that Fletcher's bond d'ld & was sworn too yesterday & that he had given Rec^{ts} for £6300 — d paid the Treasurer £1300 — this information pleased me very much.

Sept. 12. Went after dinner to Faneuiell & heard Clement Jackson, Wm Tyng, Lewis Gray young Jarvis, young Welsh & Mr Archibald Neale tryed for assaulting Fletcher.

Sept. 13. Went to Court. the Jury bro^t in their Verdict against Clement Jackson, Wm Tyng & young Jarvis. the Rest they acquitted. Went to Court this afternoon. heard the Trial between John Bannister & Mr Henderson the Judges summed up in favour of Mr Bannister.

Sept. 14. The storm abated, the Sun Shining & a fair morning. Capt Jarvis sailed this morning from Nantasket Roads. The Jury bro^t in their Verdict in favour of Mr Bannister.

Sept. 15. A beautiful morning. went a fishing at Jamaica Pond. had poor luck.

Sept. 17. Rose very early before six, went with Mrs Rowe to Flax pond in comp^y with Mr Inman & S. Mr Jon^a Simpson & the Revd Mr Walter. were Joyned by John Lane & Henry Ayres & Capt Tracy of Newberry. had very Good Sport. in the afternoon I lost the Top of my Rod Line & Hooks by a very large Pickerell.

Sept. 18. Dined this day at John Champney's on Mr Inman's Pigg which proved Tuff & the Company as follows. Surveyor General Mr Boutineau, Mr Hale, Mr Wentworth, Mr Paxton, Solo. Davis Na^l Bethune, Benjn Hallowell junr Mr Butler, Mr Inman Mr Lane, Mr Henry Ayres, J. Rowe.

Sept. 19. Capt Tilghman arr^d. In the afternoon met the Committee about Mr Hancock's donation to the Town. Spent the eve'ng on board Capt Jacobson.

Sept. 21. Went to Flax pond at twelve of Clock arr^d there at four in the afternoon. Rained very fast. had tolerable good luck. went from there to Johnson's on Lynn Plain. when I came there found young Mr Lewis & Sheriff had taken up two people that had stole Goods from Colo. Lee. Spent the eve^{ng} at Johnson's with Sam Calef & slept there.

Sept. 22. Rose early this morning, went to Flax pond, fished with Mr Saml Calef had great sport. caught two Pickerell one was two foot long & weighed three pounds & three quarters & about four dozen large Pond Perch, one measured fourteen inches. Capt Lessly arrived this day from a Cruise & Got no Prizes.

Sept. 23. Did not go to Church this forenoon occasioned by the Barber not coming to shave me. Capt Antrobus arr^d in Nantasket in the Maidstone, Man of War. Just after dinner Capt Bishop & Capt Gidyion came to our house & got a piece of a Round of Beef. Was well pleased they stayed all the afternoon & drank tea.

Sept. 24. Rose very early this morning &

settled a mistake with Capt Brown.   Capt Brown
sailed this day.   Old Mr Gould sent for me &
told me he had some thoughts of making his
will, upon which desire I called Mr Golthwait,
who took from him minutes on that affair which
I thought were very Just.   The first was that
after his debts etc were paid Mrs Troutbeck was to
have her fortune & the Rest to be divided between Mrs Troutbeck & Wm Gould & John Gould's
Children, all the Furniture to Mrs Troutbeck excepting the plate which is to be divided between
Wm Gould & her.   Mr Gould has given four
Legacies his two sisters a hundred pounds sterling
each, his Brother fifty pounds ster'g & Mrs Shaw
twenty pounds & his third part of the House.
Spent the eve^{ng} at the Coffee House with the
Merch^{ts} Committee.

Sept. 25.   Mr Lane set out for New York with
Mr Thos Palmer.   Capt Pring sailed this day for Cape
Fear.   Mr Harrison, Collector of New Haven came
to town.   Went in the afternoon to see old M^r
Gould who still continues ill of the Gout.

Sept. 28.   Dined at the Turk's Head on a Bar-
becue with James Smith & wife, Mr John Jones and
wife, Mr Arnold Wells & wife, Mr Waldo & wife,
Ezekiel Golthwait & wife, Mr Inman, Mr Ayers,
Madam Belcher & Daughter, Miss Oliver, Miss
Blowers, myself & Mrs Rowe.

Sept. 29.   The *Black Act* takes place this
day.   Mr Cockle suspended from his office yesterday at Salem, which the people at that place

Rejoiced at, by Firing Guns, making Bonfires,
Entertainments, &c & the Surveyor General
much applauded by the merchants in the Town
of Boston for his Good & Spirited Behaviour.
Enterd at the Custom House Capt Ashburn &
Capt Barthlet. Took a Ride this afternoon with
Mrs Rowe.

October 2. Went to the Collectors and Surveyor
General's about the Molasses Act who agreed the
Advocate General should determine the method of
gauging molasses, whether should be Winchester
measure or Wine Measure. Spent the eve^{ng} at
the Posee. Settled the arbitration between Elisha
Doane & Mr Whitney.

Oct. 3. Spent the evening at Wednesday night
Club.

Oct. 4. Went after dinner upon Boston Neck
& saw John & Ann Richardson set on the Gallows
for Cruelly & Willfully endeavouring to starve
their Child. the man behaved in the most
audacious manner so that the mob pelted him
which was what he deserved. Spent the eve^{ng} at
the Charitable Society with Jos. Dowse Esq, Capt
John Hammock, Mr Wm Coffin Sen^t Mr Danl Hubbard & Mr Robert Jenkins — gave away Charity
about twenty dollars — Capt Brownot took away
his Bag to sail for Bristol this afternoon.

Oct. 6. The post brought me letters from Messrs
Lane & Booth per packet dated 11th August.

Oct. 9. Intended to have met Mr Henry Ayres
at Flax pond but my Business would not permit
me.

Oct. 10.   Capt Coffin arr^d yesterday from London. Capt Dashwood arr^d from London, also Capt Calef arr^d from London, & Capt Mallard in the ma'rt ship from Lisbon. went in the afternoon to Mr Rob's Funeral & was one of the Bearers.

Oct. 12.   Spent the evening at Colo. Jugendts' on the Arbitration of Clement Jackson & the Underwriters.

Oct. 13.   Went with Henry Ayres to Monomy pond, had very bad sport, came to Mr Inman's & dined (with a numerous company)

Oct. 17.   Spent the evening at the Merchnts Meeting Capt Gardner arr^d from Bristol & Capt Hugh Montgomerie from Glasgow.

Oct. 18.   Went a fishing for Smelts with Mr Fenton but got none.

Oct. 19.   Cleared out Capt Barthlet, entered in Capt Robert Montgomerie.   The General Court met this day.

Oct. 20.   Capt Jacobson & Davis sailed this morning for London.   Capt Bruce arr^d this eve^{ng} in Seventy Six days from London, the shortest passage ever known & bro^t News of Hunter's arrival.

Oct. 21.   Capt Bennet brought me word the Gov^t had stopped Barthlet which made me very Angry.

Oct. 23   Mr Stetsn's Brigg arr^d from Lisbon & Capt Barnes from Cadiz.   Spent the evening at Colo. Ingersoll's with Mr Doane & Henderson Inches on the Arbitration between Clement Jackson & the Underwriters.

Oct. 25.   The King's Accession to the Throne.

The Troop & Cadets mustered in King's St. Capt
James Montgomerie sails this day. Capt Marshall
arr^d from London.

Oct. 26. Went after dinner to see a Show at the
White Horse wh was a very faint Representation of
the City of Jerusalem, in short 'tis a great Imposition on the Publick. I dont Remember to have
seen so much Rainfall in so short a time.

Oct. 28. Stopt at Church with the Church
Warden & Vestry on Mr Bannister's affair they
chose a Committee, namely Mr Doane Mr Rufus
Greene, Mr Boutineau & Mr Simpson.

Oct. 31. Dull & heavy weather. A snow arrived
yesterday with Dr. Gardner's settlers for Kennebeck. This day half after twelve Capt Dashwood's
Brigg caught on fire occasioned by the Tar boiling
over the Caboose.

November 2. Went to the Coffee House in the
afternoon on an Arbitration between Mr Jno Chipman & Mr Wm Davis, & Joseph Greene Esq, Solo.
Davis & myself sat & finished it. Spent the eve'ng
at the Masters' Lodge.

Nov. 4. Took a walk after church with Mr Erving & found Capt Sherrard arr^d from Newcastle &
Capt Cockran from Newfoundland.

Nov. 5. A sorrowful accident happened this
forenoon at the North End. the wheel of the carriage that the Pope was fixed on run over a Boy's
head & he died instantly. The Sheriff, Justices,
Officers of the Militia were ordered to destroy both
S^o & North End Popes. In the afternoon they got

the North End Pope pulled to pieces. they went to
the S° End but could not Conquer upon which the
South End people brought out their pope &
went in Triumph to the Northward and at the Mill
Bridge a Battle begun between the people of Both
Parts of the Town. The North End people having
repaired their pope, but the South End people
got the Battle (many were hurt & bruised on
both sides) & Brought away the North End pope
& burnt Both of them at the Gallows on the Neck.
Several thousand people following them, hallow-
ing &c.

Nov. 6. Capt Robt Caldwell arr^d from St Jubes
with a cargo of salt which I bought at eight shillings sterling p hhd. Mr Richd Smith told me he
had secured about one hundred half Barrels of Gunpowder belonging to Gilbert Berkley of Phila.
Spent the eve'ng at the Coffee House.

Nov. 7. Entered Capt Robert Caldwell, took
out a register for Capt Mitchell, gave bond for him
& also for Capt Ashburn's Mediterranean pass.
Spent the eve'ng at the Wednesday night Club.

Nov. 8. Bought the salt out of Mr Gould's
ship this day. Spent part of the evening at the
Coffee House. Mr Thos. Amory married Miss Betty
Coffin this evening there was a great company at
old Mr Coffins on the occasion & a great Dance

Nov. 12. Capt Ashburne sailed this forenoon
for Alicante with a fair wind. Spent the eve'ng at
the Coffee House with Treasurer Gray, Solo. Davis,
James Perkins John Boylston & Nicholas Boylston
& James Warden.

Nov. 17 Agreed for Mr Thompsons Estate this day at £415. Law money.

Nov. 19. A great number of vessels from Phila. Maryland, North Carolina, Providence & two from Surrinam arr^d this day — also six from Nantucket.

Nov. 20. Capt Scot arrived in Nantasket from London having the small pox on board. Spent the eve'ng at the Posee Club.

Nov. 22. Dined at the Govern^{rs} with Mr Boutineau Mr Pitts, Mr Erving, Mr Jno Hancock, Mr Sam. Wentworth, the Govern^r & Lady & Dr Chauncy. In the eve'ng was at an Arbitration between Mr Arnold Wells & young Mr Austin of Charlestown. The Arbitrators were Mr Nicho^s Boylston Mr Tho. Gray & myself.

Nov. 23. Spent part of the evening at the Coffee House on an Arbitration between James Russell & John Avery Esq^{rs} against Mr Aaron Porter of Halifax. The arbitrators were Mr Thos. Gray, Mitabiah Bourne Esq & myself.

Nov. 24. About half past six old Mr Palfrey's Chimney got on fire — made a most Terrible Blaze — the Town was much alarmed & there was some Danger.

Nov. 29. Thanksgiving Day. Went to the warehouse this forenoon & was very glad to be alone to examine my Books. Capt Mitchell sailed this morning ab^o Eight of Clock & also Capt Logie. Both bound for London   Went after dinner to Robt Goulds & Old Mr Goulds found him much indis-

posed. Mr Inman & George slept at our house tonight

December 3. Spent the eve'ng with the Committee of Merch^{ts} & others about the Loaf Sugar.
present Jos. Winslow Esqr Mr Thos Gray, M^r
Treasurer Gray, Mr Edwd Paine, Mr Richard Clark,
Ezek Golthwait, Mr James Warden, Mr Thos. Ivers,
Capt Solo. Davis, Mr John Dennie, Mr Mitabiah
Bourne. Voted that Mr Ivers Bring an Action at
this Court against the Collector for asking the duty
of five Shilling sterling pr hundred on Loaf Sugar
cleared out at his office

Dec. 7. Major Rogers was Committed to Goal
yesterday

Dec. 9. Sunday. The Vestry met after church
& made Choice of Stephen Greenleaf & James
Boutineau Esqr to be a Committee to defend the
Law Suit Mr Banister has Commenced against the
church.

Dec. 10. Capt Diamond sailed this day for London. Capt Valentine sailed this day for Surrinam.
Wrote a letter to John Bannister on the affairs of
the Church.

Dec. 13. Went with Nat Wheelwright, Dr
Gardiner to Old Mr Goulds & came to an agreement ab^o Capt Phillips Cargo.

Dec. 16. Mr Wentworth was sent for by the
Governour & Interrogated by him concerning a
dispute between him & the Surveyor Generall.
Have had a sore throat three or four Days.

Dec. 17. Got my Letters by the packet from

Mefs^{rs} Booth & Lane. Cleard out Capt James
Oliver & dispatched him this day for Madeira.

Dec. 18. Was much out of order with a Cough
& sore throat in the night, begins to snow & held
tell nine of Clock. The Fortune Sloop Capt Bishop
arrivd this day from Hallifax

Dec. 19. Continued very cold all the whole Day
— dind at home could not go to Cambridge for the
severity of the Weather. Spent the evening at
the Free Mason's Lodge with thirty Brethren.

Dec. 21. My acquaintance Mr J^{no} Morley died
this morning.

Dec. 22. Very cold, have been very Unwell in
the Night the snow falls very fast, went with M^{rs}
Rowe a Slaying. Capt Scot in Mr John Hancock's Briggatine sailed for London.

Dec. 24. Went to Town Meeting this afternoon.
Mr Sampson Salter was Chose a Collector of
Taxes in the Room of Mr Harris who could not
attend through Infirmity of Body. The Surveyor
General & the Collector had a warm dispute this
day.

Dec. 25. Christmas Day. Went to Church.
Mr Walter read prayers & Mr Hooper preached
from 1st Chap. of the Gospel of St John & 17th
Verse. I was much pleased with the Discourse.
A great number of people at Church. Mr Hooper
sent the Box to me to collect for the poor. Dined
at home with Capt Bishop, Mr Inman, Capt Bruce,
Capt Montgomery, Capt Blake, Mr Jonas Clark.
Mrs Rowe & Sucky Stayed at home all the after-
noon with the above company.

Dec. 27. Dined with the Brethren of St John's Lodge being the anniversary of the feast of St John's Lodge at which were present the following Brethren Jerry Gridley Esq, Wm Pourvier, Jn° Jay, Hugh McDaniel, Ph. Dumaresque, J. Wheelwright, Seth Blodget, Edm^d Quincy, J. Box Jr, John Bryant, Lewis Gray, Sam Quincy, George Gardner, James Jackson, Sam Fitch, Christo' Clark, Wm Jackson, Shubael Hussey, Jn° Amiel, Wm Perkins, Thos. Dawes, Elias Dupee, John Perkins, And. Lapier, Jn° Blake, Henry Price, J. Rowe, Robt Jenkins, Richd Gridley, Archi^d McNeal, Abram Savage, J. Cutter, Jn° Box Senr, Jn° Gardner, Edm^d Quincy Jr, Wm Tyng, And. Johnnot, Jos. Golthwait, James Charity. With the aforesaid company we spent the day very agreeably & very joyfully. I dont remember St John as long as I have belonged to the Fraternity has been celebrated with more decorum & more pleasure.

Dec. 30. Mr Charles Apthorp came to Town last night & Brough an acc^t of Mr Rice's our late Organist arr'd at N. Y. in Capt Lacy.

Dec. 31. Had a great deal of Talk with Mr Bannister about his Lawsuit with Trinity Church & find him very Obstinate however he made the following proposal which I Record for Fear he should forget it, that if the Church would give him a pew & pay one hundred & fifty Ounces of Silver, besides the Charges on that amo^t, he would on these Conditions give them any discharge & sign any Deed that they shall get drawn. this is as near what he said as can be.

1 7 6 5

Jan. 1. New Years day. Dined at home with Capt. George Phillips, Mr Inman, Christo Minot Mrs Rowe & Sucky. Went in the afternoon to young Thos. Brinley's Funerall. Bruce endeavored to go this day but was stopped by the Ice.

Jan. 2. Went the forenoon to Mr Robt Auchmootys, with Mr Rufus Greene, Mr Boutineau & Mr Stephen Greenleaf to consult him on Bannister's action against the church.

Jan. 8. Capt Skillings arrivd this day from London after a passage of nine weeks.

Jan. 9. Capt John Skimmer came passenger in Skillings & bro^t me a letter from Jarvis. Settled the affair between Mr John Denim & Mr John Spooner this forenoon. The General Court met today & made a house.

Jan. 11. Went after dinner to the Court & heard the Tryal between Mr Ivers & Mr Hale relative to the Duties on Loaf Sugar. Very warm Debates on both sides but the Jury found for the plaintiff Mr Ivers, which was generally thought a good verdict.

Jan. 12. Was called by Mr Henderson Inches & Capt Jno Blake. Went to the warehouse & settled with them. Capt Blake sailed from Hancock's Wharf about twelve of Clock with a fair wind. Capt Dunn in Robt Gould's Snow sailed just before Blake for So Carolina. Messrs Ben^j & Edwd Davis' Brigg sailed for Bristol.

Jan. 14.   Still very cold.   The Harbour almost froze over.

Jan. 15.   The Trade has been much alarmed this day.   Mr Wheelwright stopt payment & kept in his room.   A great number of people will suffer by him.   Spent the eve'ng at Mrs Cordis'.   the Conversation of the eve'ng was on Nat Wheelwrights affaire.   Mr Inman went to the Afsembly.

Jan. 18.   Spent the eve'ng at Mr Collector Hale's at his lodgings with Mr Robt Temple, Mr Saml Wentworth, Mr Inman, Mr Steward Collector of New London, Mr Roberston Collector of Newport, Mr Thomas of Marshfield & the Comptroller of Halifax — also Capt Bishop Comm^r of the Fortune Sloop of War.   About half an hour after nine of Clock the Town was alarmed by the Cry of Fire which happened in an Out-house of M^r McNeal the Baker, did some damage but was Reduced in about an hour & half.   got myself much wet.

Jan. 19.   Very bad acc^{ts} Mr John Scollay shut up.   Mr John Dennie shut up & Peter Bourne at the North End.   Am like to be a large sufferer by Scollay.   Extream bad & slippery walking.

Jan. 20.   Was much out of order today occasioned by the Distress the Town is in, occasioned principally by the failure of Mr Wheelwright.   Was sent for this forenoon on My Friend Jos. Scot's affairs.   he seemed greatly distressed.   Was sent for by Sheriff Greenleaf on John Scollay's affairs.   Did not go to Church, my mind too much disturbed.

FIRE BUCKET 1760

Jan. 21. Mr Cudworth the Sheriff came here
on Business & Mr Cary on the Affairs of Wm Has-
king & Co who shut up this morning as did my
Friend Joseph Scot. A General Consternation in
Town, occasioned by these Repeated Bankruptcies.
That the General Court which are now sitting determine to make an Act for the Relief of Insolvent
Debtors, which will be very seasonable at this
time. Spent the eve'ng at the Royal Exchange
with the Grand Committee of Charity.

Jan. 24. Sent Mr Mallet to the H   after Jno
Scollay schooner. Spent the eve'ng with the Doc-
tors & the Proprietors of Point Shirley, namely
Dr Gardiner, Dr Gardiner Junr, Dr Sprague, Dr
Bullfinch, Ezk^l Golthwait Esqr, Mr Inman, Mr Nat
Holmes, Mr John Hancock & Mr Pitts. as M^r In-
man & I came home a fire happened at the So End
in a Dutch Bake House which Burnt it down but by
the Dexterity & Clever Behaviour of the South End
Engine men it did not spread.

Jan. 25. Madame Hutchinson buried this afternoon.

Jan. 26. Mr Arthur Savage fell down in an
Apoplectick fit & soon expired. this happened
yesterday in the afternoon at Mr Kent the Lawyer's
office. Spent the afternoon at Mr Henderson
Inches on the affairs of Clement Jackson & the
Underwriters.

Jan. 30. These last four days have been the
coldest of any for 12 years past together. the
Harbour froze in.

Febry 2. Heard of M[r] Henry Bromfield's Snow being cast away at Cape Ann the night before last. About eight this eve'ng was alarmed by Fire which proved to be the Chimney of the Great House at the Head of Long Lane. The two South End Engines were there. twas a Terrible Foul Chimney.

Febry 7. Cap[t] M[c]Kinstosh & others tryed before M[r] Justice Dana & Justice Storey for the 5th of Nov. affair.

Febry 12. Spent the eve'ng at M[rs] Cordis' with the Committee from the General Court on the Excise Act, namely James Otis Esq[r] M[r] Tho[s] Cushing, Thos. Gray M[r] Saunders of Cape Ann, M[r] Lee of Cambridge M[r] Crocker of Barnstaple, Sam[l] Wells Esq[r], M[r] Bourne of Marblehead, Rob[t] Hooper of ditto, W[m] Story, W[m] Mollineaux, Nich[l] Boylston, Sam[l] Sturgis, W[m] Coffin Sen[r], Jos. Henshaw, W[m] Richardson, Solo. Davis, John Erving Jun[r], Joshua Winslow Esq[r] & several others, proceeded to the Choice of Managers when M[r] Wells, M[r] Hooper & M[r] Justice Story were Chose.

Febry 13. This Forenoon I appeared with the Petitioners on acc[t] of the Excise on the floor of the House & was heard on that subject. Spent the eve'ng at Solo. Davis' with the Firewards.

Febry 18. Met M[r] Banister, M[r] Boutineau M' Jn[o] Simpson & M[r] Greenleaf on the affairs of Trinity Church & agreed the plan of settlement. M[r] Reed the Lawyer is ordered to prepare the writings.

Febry 21. The General Court are still on the Excise.

Febry 23. Colo. Bourne of M'head & Jeramiel Bowers challenged each other with sword & pistol yesterday ab^t the Excise.

Febry 26. Went after dinner before the Council & was heard on the floor, relative to the Excise Bill.

Mar. 4. Dined this day with Capt James Cunningham at his house with Gen. Winslow, Mr Byles the minister, Saml Wells Joshua Henshaw Francis Wells & the officers belonging to Capt Cunningham's Comp^y also Deacon Elliot.

Mar. 11. Made a Great Struggle about the Warden Act but could not prevail.

Mar. 13. B^t Capt Potts cargo of Salt this day. went in the evening over to Gardners to see the Orphan acted which was miserably performed. ab^t 210 persons there.

Mar. 15. Mr Inman & Mr Bannister went to Brush Hill & dind with Jemmy Smith.

Mar. 19. Went to the Superior Court this forenoon & heard the learned Debate before the Judges in the Case of John Bannister & others. came home to dinner & went after dinner on Capt Jno Phillips Arbitration, adjourned till tomorrow ten of Clock. Set on Clement Jackson's affairs with Mr Douse &. Mr Henderson Inches and came to a Resolution to give in our Award. went in the eve'ng & heard more argument on John Bannister's Affair. both Mr Auchmooty & Mr Otis behaved very well & I was pleased with Mr Dana in this argument.

Mar. 20. Mr Inman had fine Lamb today for dinner, the whole weighed 28 lbs. this is the first Lamb I have tasted this season.

Mar. 23. Went to Fanewill Hall in the afternoon there met the Committee on Mr Hancock's Donation, Mr Otis, Mr Nat. Bethune, Mr Thos Flucker, Mr John Ruddock, Mr Saml Sewall, Mr John Barnat, Mr Esek^l Goldthwait & myself. Voted that The Town accept of the Donation & that a proper piece of Ground be laid out in the Common for that use.

Mar. 24. A very heavy storm all night & this morning snow & rain very fast. The weather so very bad that Mrs Row & I stayed at home from Church this forenoon — high water about half after one — the Highest Tide I have known since I have been in New England accompanied with the Greatest Storm, so the Damage it has done is almost incredible, almost every Wharf in Town has suffered, mine in particular. A number of vessels drove from their Anchors & many lost their masts. One sunk at my wharf. Went down to my wharf & several others & was amazed to see the destruction, my damage will not be Repaired for two thousand pounds, old tenor, but as it's the Providence of God, I am content about it. Visited all the Stores I hire & have not found so much Salt &c. washed away as I expected.

Mar. 25. Lady Day. Town meeting. Went to my wharf & found a great deal of damage done. Went to town meeting & got the Vote accepted for Mr Hancock's donation. Dined at Mr Robt Auch-

mooty's with the Surveyor General Mr Hale, M'
Paxton, Mr Hallowell, the Comptroller Mr Geo. Apthorp & Chris. Minot.   Snow'd all night & the face
of the Ground appears as much winter as in the
midst of it.

Mar. 28.   Last eve'ng the Creditors of Mr Wheelwright met & heard the Report of their Committee
who advised them to take up with Mr Charles Apthorp's proposal.   Dined at Brush Hill with James
Smith & wife, M^r   Hooper & wife, Miss Dolly
Murray, Miss Polly Hooper, Mrs Rowe Sucky &
Mr Inman.

Apr. 2.   Capt Edward Forbes arrivd in Town
this day from Liverpool by way of Plymouth in
Colo Warren's Schooner.

Apr. 5.   Good Friday.   After church the vestry
met on Mr Walters affairs & unanimously agreed
to add fifty pounds Ster^g P Annum to his Salary.

Apr. 7.   Found myself a little Lame occasiond
by wearing a pair of Shoes that pinched my Right
foot & obliged me to stay at home.

Apr. 9.   Easter Monday.   Went to church in the
forenoon & chose the Wardens, Stephen Greenleaf
& Rufus Greene.   Also Vestrymen, myself, James
Boutineaux, Jona. Simpson, Wm Coffin Senr, John
Erving Junr, John Gooch, Thos. Greene, Joseph
Douse, Benj^m Greene, James Perkins, Saml Hughes,
Gillam Phillips.   Voted the Revd Mr Walter fifty
pounds Sterling to be added to his Salary & taxed
the Pews $\frac{1}{5}$ pt on the floor, the Gallery Pews
8^d pt.

Apr. 10.   The Charitable Society met this day at Mrs Cordis' & dined, as usual, had a Genteel dinner & twenty three dined there, made choice of officers for the Year ensuing — as follows — J. Rowe Treasurer, Dr. Silvester Gardiner Deputy Treas^r, Mr Wm Price, Mr Wm Coffin, Mr Robt Jenkins, Capt John Hammock, Mr Danl Hubbard & Mr Thos Greene Trustees.

Wind N E. it has Continued in this quarter 21 days, all but one halfday.

Apr. 20.   Agreed with Mr Eben Lewis to build me a Schooner forty four foot Keel, seventeen foot Beam & seven foot $\frac{1}{2}$ in the Hold a £19.10 p ton to have a long Quarter deck.   Went after dinner round by Jamaica Pond came back to Greatons & spent an hour with James Otis, Nath Bethune, Solo. Davis, Colo Richd Gridley, Saml Hughes & Thos Gray.

Apr. 22.   This morning Mr Longly & Parker began to pull down my House in Pond Lane. Went to Fanewill Hall & met the Committee about the Town Affairs.   Mr Tho' Cushion, Mr Tho' Flucker, Mr James Boutineaux, Mr Tho' Gray, M^r Ed. Payne, Mr Wm Phillips & myself.

Apr. 23.   Sold the Schooners Cargo this forenoon at Publick Vendue & I think very well.

Apr. 30.   Mr Pickering sent me a dozen fine large Trout.   Set out after dinner from Boston for Plymouth in company with the Revd Mr Walter, Mr Sam Calef, Major Vassall, Joshua Loring jun^r & Edwd Winslow Jr.   Stopt at Bracketts, Braintree. reached Cushing's & spent the eve'ng & slept there.

May 1. Set out early this morning, reached
Pembroke went fishing had bad luck, began to
Rain which was much wanted. got to Duxbury Mills, went a fishing, had tolerable luck.
dined at Mr Nath. Ray Thomas on a mess of Trout.
spent the eve'ng & slept there.

May 2. Set out early this morning for Plymouth. called at Silas Mortons. Reached Plymouth at ten in the forenoon. I went about my
Business. dined at Mr Edwd Winslow's with him,
Mrs Winslow, Miss Penny & Miss Sally Winslow,
Major Vafsall, Jos. Loring, Edwd Winslow Jr. M^r
Walter, Mr Calef & Mr Pelham Winslow. Spent
the eve'ng at the same place with the same company & Miss Joanna White. Slept at Capt White's
— engaged fish from several people this afternoon.

May 3. Breakfasted at Capt Whites. Went a
fishing with Mr Wm Watson, had very good sport.
I caught one very large Trout & several other
very fine ones. Dined at Colo. Geo. Watson's with
Mr Walter, Mr Calef, Mr Watson & daughter. Set
out after dinner for home. Stopt at Pembroke at
Spears & got in the eve'ng to Cushings. there met
Mr Gill of Boston. spent the eve'ng & slept there.
heard of Whitmarsh sailing.

May 4. Hingham. Breakfasted at Cushings
stopt at Bracketts, there settled the reckoning.
Reached home between 10 & 11 in the forenoon.

May 6. Two Gentlemen came fr Newberry to
sell a Cargo of Coals which I Bought.

May 10. Went in the evening to Concert Hall

at an entertainment of the Officers of the Army &
Navy. A Great Number of Gentlemen & Ladies
there & a Genteel pretty entertainment.

May 11. Went fishing at Manotomy Pond with
Sam[1] Calef had very good Sport, dined at Winship's,
the tavern there & fished there in the afternoon had
also very Good Sport, we caught at least ten doz^n
of Pond Perch & several Pickerel, came home &
spent the evening at the " Possee."

May 14. This day the Town of Boston chose
Representatives namely

James Otis	Esqre	388	Votes
Oxna Thatcher	"	427	"
Thos' Cushing	"	538	"
Thos' Gray	"	570	"

I myself had 238 votes. The number of votes was
641.

May 16. Capt Edwards arriv'd from the Isle of
Wight in fiue weeks. He came out in Comp^{ny} with
Jarvis. A Brigg from Salter —— also arr'd.

May 19. Capt Hunter sailed early this morning
from below, this forenoon arr'd two vessels from
Bristol, Capt Southcot in a Snow & Capt Canidge in
a Brigg both consigned to Mr James Griffin. Col.
Henry Vassall sailed this afternoon in Capt Phillips
for Antigua. Capt Logie came ashore after church
with Capt Marshall from London. Capt Davis is
also arr'd fr London.

May 24. Went to Lynn after dinner with M^r
John Lane & spent the eve'ng at Tapley's with

Mr Hale, Mr Lane & Mr Geo. Apthorp.   Stayed at
Tapley's all night.

May 25.   Rose very early, went to Flax Pond &
breakfasted there with Miss Becky, went a fishing,
had great sport, dined with Miss Becky, Mr Hale,
Mr Geo Apthorp, Mr J. Lane & Mr Inman — came
home with Mr Hale & spent the evening with the
Revd Mr Walter found Old Mrs Graves dead.

May 29.   Colo. Chandler chose Councillor in
the Room of Mr Hancock.   Went to Fresh Pond
& dined with Mr Benjn Fanewill Senr & wife, M^r
Geo. Bethune & wife, Major J^{no} Vaſsall & wife
Mr Wm Sheaff & wife, Mr J^{no} Coffin & wife Mr Frol-
let, Mrs Cutter & Solo. Davis.

May 30.   Went to Doctor Sewall's meeting &
heard Dr Chauncy preach.   Went in the eve'ng at
Blodgets with a Number of the General Court
where they were Shoeing Colts — that is, the New
Members that are Chosen treat the Council & House
of Representatives.

May 31.   This day my Warehouse fell in with
fish.   Went to Town Meeting this afternoon, adjourned till this day Week.

June 3.   Artillery Election — Went to the Brick
Meeting & heard Mr Gad. Hitchcock of Pembrooke
preach from the 21th Chapter of St. James & 1st
Verse.   Went in the afternoon to old Mr Letchmere's funeral.

June 4.   King's Birthday.   Went early in the
morning with Wm Sheaff.& Saml Calef to Manotomy
pond.   had very Good Sport fishing — were joyned

by Solo. Davis & Geo. Bethune—we all dined
together at Wyndships—M[r] Sheaff & I went fishing at Fresh Pond in the afternoon.

June 5. Dined at home on a trout that measured 18 inches with Ezek[l] Golthwait, Cap[t] Rob[t]
Jarvis & M[rs] Rowe It has rained all day which
was much wanted & came by the providence
of God in Good Time. Spent the eve'ng at the
Charitable Society.

June 10. M[r] Miller began to mow the Land
next the Barn.

June 19. This morning our fishermen caught a
large fish in the shape of a Shark Twenty foot long,
his Teeth were different from a Shark's teeth—
Went after dinner to Jamaica pond with Cap[t]
Jacobson, had pretty good Sport.

June 20. This day they cut up the Fish &
filled two large hogsheads with his Liver. Went
in the afternoon to Fresh Pond with Sam[l] Calef.

June 23. Dined at home with M[r] J Lane, M[rs]
Rowe Sucky W[m] Speakman & Cap[t] Buddicome that
arr[d] from London last night, in whom came passenger
M[r] Arthur Savage who is appointed Comptroller of
Falmouth, Casco Bay.

June 25. Went after dinner to Fresh Pond with
Sam. Calef & Geo. Apthorp, found M[r] James Perkins & Lady there—had pretty sport. I hooked
a Turtle to the best of my Judgement must weigh
30 pounds.

June 27. This afternoon M[r] David Wheeler
tryd his New Engine & it play'd very well.

June 28. I went to Marblehead about Ten of
Clock & dined at Major Reed's with Capt Southcote
& two Frenchmen. Paid a visit to several of my
Friends & came away about six got to Flax Pond
alias Gravesend & there met Mr Saml Calef. wee
fished & supped & stayed there all night — very
agreeably entertained.

July 2. Paid a Visit to Wm Gould & found
his Affairs under a Cloud.

July 3. Rose very early this morning & went
with Mr Saml Calef to Natick Pond. was obliged to
stop three hours at Pratt's at Needham it rained so
hard, however wee had very good sport. Dined
at Bullard's on Fish which Mrs Bullard dressed
very well. In the afternoon came Colo. Brattell,
Colo. Danforth, Col Watts on affairs of the Government.

July 5. Dined at home with Mr James Welsh,
Mr Edward Walker, Capt Jacobson, Christo Minot,
Mr Inman, Sam Calef, Mrs Rowe & Sucky. Christo
Minot was very wroth with Mr Inman for Introduc-
ing some ster^g Madeira on his New Coat from one
of the Leghorn Glasses not well managed.

July 9. Mr Inman had an unlucky Fall in getting on his horse wh Bruised him. this eve'ng M^r
Scolley's Creditors met at the Coffee House & made
Choice of Wm Phillips, John Erving & myself to
act as Trustees in his affairs.

July 13. Rose very early this morning, went to
Monotomy Pond with the Revd Mr Auchmooty &
Mr Sam Calef had great sport, we caught above

sixteen doz^n of pond & sea perch — made a Rough Day of it & came home in the evening & spent it at home with the Revd Mr Walter who had taken umbrage at Mr Hooper's behaviour which I endeavoured to Reconcile & hope shall be able to effect it.

July 16.   The Revd Mr Walter & John Erving Junr came to breakfast.   A misunderstanding having happened between Mr Hooper & Mr Walter was very happily made up this forenoon.

July 17.   Commencement Day, went to Cambridge.   Mrs Rowe Polly Hooper & Suky — dined at Edwd Winslows Room, a very Large Company.

July 18.   Went to Town early this morning, staid till noon.   went to Cambridge & dined at Mr Hooper's with a very Large Company after dinner visited Col. Fowler, Colo. Stoddard Mr Ed^{wd} Winslow.   In the evening went to the Town House to a Dance with a very Large Company.   Colo. Sparhawk's Son made it, he desired me to officiate as Master of the Ceremony which I did to Oblige him.

July 19.   Set out with the Revd Mr Auchmooty & Saml Calef for Mrs Prat's at Milton.   (Welles house, Beals & afterwards Brook's house, now moved to E. Milton,   Mrs P.   Mr Auchmooty's daughter & her daughter Bella married Saml Wells.)

July 20.   Rose very early this morning.   Mr Calef, the Revd Mr Auchmooty & myself went to a pond beyond the Blue Hills & put up at Mr Joseph Gooch — went fishing — had very fine Diversion — the weather very hot — came from thence to M^r

James Smiths' & dined with him & wife, the Rev^d
Mr Winslow the Revd Mr Auchmooty & his Daugh-
ter Bella, Mr Robt Auchmooty & wife — Mr Robt
Temple & wife — Mr Inman, Mrs Rowe — Mrs Prat
Polly Overing & Miss Bella Prat & Mr Saml Calef.

July 24.   This afternoon spent on Benj^m & Edwd
Davis' arbitration — Mr Gerry came to Town &
brought an acc^t of the Niger, Man of War, taking
three Schooners out of the Harbour of St. Peters,
one belonging to his Father & two to Epps Sargent.

July 27.   Rose very early this morning.   went
with M Saml Calef to Capt Kendrick's on Charles
River a fishing — had very good sport — dined
there with James Pitts & wife, James Boudoin, Esq.
& wife, James Boutineau & wife, Melabiah Bourn
& wife, Mr John Erving Junr, Mr Geo. Erving, Thos
Flucker & wife, Mr Nicho. Boylston, Mr Saml Calef,
Miss Hannah Flucker — Went to Mr Inman's after
dinner — there I met Mrs Rowe, Mr Saml Hughes
& wife — drank tea there, came home & spent the
evening at home.

Aug. 5.   Was much alarmed in hearing Capt
Forbes in bad circumstances.   went to the Coffee
House on Arbitration between Capt Geo. St Barb &
Capt Robt Robins with Nat. Bethune & Melabiah
Bourne.

Aug. 6.   Capt Forbes shut up his shop this day
— am much grieved for him, as he is An Old Acquaintance & Friend.   Spent the eve'ng at M^{rs}
Cordis' with Jerry Gridley, Bro. Daniel, Bro. Jenkins, Bro. Cutter, Bro. Box Senr, Bro. Joseph Gard-

ner, Bro. Fitch, Bro. Savage, Bro. Quincy — they came to the choice of a Treasurer in Room of Capt Forbes — they unanimously chose myself.

Aug. 11. Capt Harlow arrived from Bristol & brought the Good News that Mr Pitt was again in the Ministry.

Aug. 12. Dined this day on board the Jamaica, Man of War with Capt Gidoin, Capt Bishop, The Surveyor General, Mr Temple, Mr Paxton, Mr Hale, Mr Hallowell Senr, Mr B. Hallowel Junr, Mr Jordan, a gentleman from Barbadoes, Major Vafsall, Colo. Phipps, Mr Inman, Mr Thos Palmer, Thos Apthorp, Geo. Apthorp, Mr Peet Lieut of the Jamaica, Christo Minot & Mr Sam Wentworth — came ashore about six of Clock & spent the Evening at the Coffee House with Treasurer Gray, Nicho. Boylston, John Boylston, James Otis, Melabiah Bourn, Mr Wm Mollineaux & Solo. Davis.

Aug. 13. Dined at the Turk's Head on a Barbikue with the following persons — James Otis Esqr & wife, The Treas. Gray & wife, The Honble Foster, Hutchinson Esq & wife, Mr Sam. Hughes & wife, Mr James Perkins & wife, Capt Solomon Davis & wife, Mr Wm Sheaff & wife, Mr John Armiel & wife, Mr Ralph Inman & Mrs Rowe — Capt Freeman, Mr Wentworth's vessell & Job Prince's Brigg all three sailed for London this day.

Aug. 14. A Great Number of people assembled at Deacon Elliots Corner this morning to see the Stamp Officer hung in Effigy with a Libel on the Breast, on Deacon Elliot's tree & along side him a

Boot stuffed with representation, which represented
the Devil coming out of Burk — this stamp officer
hung up all Day — at night they cut him down,
layd him out & carried in Triumph amidst the ac-
clamations of many thousands who were gathered
together on that occasion. They proceeded from
the S° End down the Main Street, through the Town
House & Round by Oliver's Dock — they pull'd
down a New Building which some people thought
was building for a Stamp Office & did some Mischief
to Mr Andrew Oliver's house (which I think they
were much to blame).

Aug. 16. Heard that Mr Andrew Oliver had resigned his Commission in Form on which there was
great Rejoicing the last evening in Boston.

Vol II of the Diary from Aug 16th 1765 to April
11th 1766 (pages 186 to 323 inclusive) is missing.

1766

1766, April 11. A fine soft morning — dind at
home with Mr Inman Mrs Rowe & Suckey. M^r
John Scolleys Creditors met at Mrs Cordis this
afternoon I was obliged to attend some other
Business so could not be there — in the Evening I
went to Dr Sewalls Lecture & heard Mr Blair preach
a very serious Discourse.

April 12. Wet & rainy — In the afternoon finished with Capt Rowland and went over to Gardner's
with Capt Davis where we found Mr John Boylston,

M[r] James Perkins, M[r] Sam[l] Calef and M[r] Tho[s] Gray — who wee stayd with an hour.

13 April. Sunday. Capt George Rolland sailed for Antigua in Cap[t] Bruce's Ship. I went to Church in the forenoon. M[r] Walter read prayers and M[r] Hooper Preached — this I think was a very Judicious discourse. When I came home I heard of an Express being Brought to town giving an acc[t] of the Repeal of the Stamp Act, which I examined into & found the greatest probability of its being true & passed by the House of Commons on Feb'y the 8th last by a great majority, which appear[d] by a letter of that date from Mess[rs] Day & Son to M[r] Maxwell their Correspondent in Petaxion River, Maryland. in the afternoon I went to Church. M[r] Hooper Read prayers & M[r] Walter preached — this was a very elegant Discourse — and much admired.

April 14. The Selectmen met this forenoon to consider & fix on a Day for Rejoicing.

Apr. 15. Cap[t] Dobson arr'd last even'g from Newcastle consigned to me, belonging to M[r] Jonas Brown of Whitley. Cap[t] Calef arrived from London this afternoon — he left the Downs the 20 febry. He Brought good news ab[o] our American Affairs, but no certainty of the Repeal of the Stamp Act. I spent the afternoon with the Select Men — Colo. Jackson, John Ruddock, John Hancock, W[m] Phillips & Timothy Newall. We let Deer Island to the Pratts at forty pound p annum for seven years & Boston Neck to Gideon Gardiner at sixty pounds p annum.

Apr. 16. Capt Cahoon arr'd from Glasgow &
brought acc^{ts} that correspond with Capt. Calef's.

Apr. 17. The Select Men met this morning &
appointed Monday next to be a Town Meeting.

Apr. 18. Capt McClean arrived from Ireland &
confirms the acc^t of the Stamp Act being repealed.
in the afternoon I took a walk over the neck with
Mr John Timmins & Mr Thos Gray.

April 19. Capt Jacobson arrived in Nantasket
from London.

Apr. 21. A Town Meeting this Forenoon to
agree on a method of Rejoicing & Illuminations.

April 22. I went this morning with Mr Coor to
Mr Foxcraft's at Cambridge about some Business &
Returned to dinner. In the afternoon I went as a
Relation to the funeral of Mr Edward Churchs
wife.

Apr. 23. Mr William Marlet came this morning
to take his leave of me & go for New York this
forenoon. Capt Bryant sailed from Nantasket Road
this morning in the Sloop Chagford for Antigua.
Spent the eve'ng at Capt Cunningham's with the
Firewards. The Select Men met this afternoon at
Fanueil Hall.

April 24. Thursday — went to Cambridge this
Forenoon & Rode my Colt for the first Time —
went to Church & heard Mr Agar Read prayers &
preach. dined at Mr Inman's with the Surveyor
Generall Mr Robt Temple, Mr Henry Loyd & M^r
George Apthorp who set out after dinner for New
York. came home & went to see Mr Wm Vafsall

ab° his Brother Henry' Affairs.   This day was Appointed by the Govr & Council for a fast Day — which is generally appointed once a year.

Apr. 25.   Spent the eve'ng at Mr Blodgetts with the Grand Lodge — this eve'ng a Committee from St. Andrews Lodge presented a Memorial to the Grand Lodge upon which they appointed a Committee to meet them on Monday eve'ng & adjourned to next Friday eve'ng.

27 April.   went to Church in the afternoon. Mr Hooper Read prayers and Mr Walter preached this discourse of Mr Walters I Esteem'd much and think it is a very Beneficial & excellent sermon and was admired by all his Hearers.   After Church I went and p^d a visit to see Robt Gould who has got the Gout pretty Smartly.

28 April.   Spent the afternoon at the Selectmens Chambers being, the last Monday, with Colo Jackson, John Hancock, Samuel Sewall, Deacon Newall & Wm Phillips.

29 April.   I went this morning with Wm Vafsall Esqr to Cambridge & stopt at Francis Foxcrafts Esqr where wee finished the signing of Mr Dinely' Papers — din'd at Major Vafsall's.

Apr. 30.   The Select Men met this forenoon & gave orders for a Town Meeting next Tuesday.   In the afternoon I went to Mr Chukly's meeting to the ordination of Mr Bowen.   A Country minister prayed — Dr. Chauncy preached, The Revd Mr Chukly Senr gave the Charge & the Revd Mr Cooper the Right Hand of Fellowship.

May 1. Dind at Mr Robt Goulds with him &
Mrs Gould Betty & Sally Gould. The Rev^d M^r
Hooper, Mr Inman & Mr Kennedy — after Dinner
came Capt Solo Davis & Mr N. Bethune to drink
Welch Ale. Capt Davis saild for London the fore-
noon by whom I sent Mr Foxcrofts papers.

May 3. Dined at the Hon$^{'ble}$ Isaac Royal Esq at
Medford with him & Lady. Miss Polly & Miss
Betty Royal, Gen. Brattle, Treas^r Gray, James Otis
Esqr, Thos Cushing Esqr & Mr Nath. Sparhawk.
Spent part of the eve'ng at the Possee & the re-
mainder at home.

May 6. Town Meeting this forenoon for the
Choice of Representatives for the Year ensuing.
The number of Voters were 746 — the Town made
Choice of

James Otis	573
Mr Saml Adams	691
Thos Cushing	622
Jno Hancock	427

I had 309 votes.

May 8. About half-past eleven I set out from
our house with Mr Benjamin Davis for Taunton — at
two of Clock we reached Stones at Stoughton, we
dined there & went forward through Easton Woods
& stopped at Howards & reached Taunton at seven
of Clock. Spent the eve'ng at Mr Robt Treat
Paine's, the Lawyer & Slept at McQuarter's.

May 9. Went with Mr Ben^{jn} Davis to see M^r
Stetson at Dighton, found him in great Confusion,
after I had discoursed with him on his affairs I came
back with Mr B. Davis & dined at M^r McQuarters

at Taunton where I met a number of my acquaintances, namely Colo. White, Col. Richmond & his two Sons, Colo. Leonard & many others ab° half after two we set out from McQuarters for Boston & stopt at Mr Heingman's at Easton who lives on Colo. Brattles Farm — we set out from thence ab° five of Clock & stopt at Colo. Doty's at Stoughton. We supped & slept there & I set it down as an extraordinary house of Entertainment & very Good Beds.

May 10. We breakfasted at Colo. Doty's & I met Mr Abel Puffer who lives hard by, who tells me that he understood the Cure of a Bite by a Rattle Snake. About nine of Clock we set out from thence & called at Colo. Oliver's at Dorchester & reached home about twelve of Clock. In the afternoon I went over to Roxbury Plain where I spent two hours with Mr Troutbeck & wife & Capt Jacobson. Mr Auchmooty came there, I had some conversation with him ab° the nature of attachments on the Bankrupt Act.

May 13. Rose very early this morning & set out for Hopkinton on my old mare — got to Woodburns at nine of Clock & reached Colo. Jones at Hopkinton at twelve — I went to the Brook with Charles & caught a fine Red Trout — measured 14 Inches & several other Fish. Dined at Colo. Jones with him & wife, Mr John Nazro & Colo. Jones daughter. after dinner came Deacon Russell, Thomas Millens & wife & James Millens — after many debates we adjusted their acc^{ts} & settled them. Slept there.

May 14. Roes early. I went & tryed to get some trout but could not. Came away from Colo Jones after breakfast & stopt at Capt Drury's at Framingham as it rained hard — got to Mr Inman's (at Cambridge) at two in the afternoon.

May 16. Capt Shubael Coffin arr'd from London ab^o 11 of Clock & bro^t the Glorious News of the total Repeal of the Stamp Act which was signed by his Majesty King George the 3^d of Ever Glorious Memory, which God long preserve & his Illustrious House.

May 18. This being Whit Sunday Mr Walter read prayers & Mr Hooper preached. Capt Blake & Capt Strand both arr'd from London this forenoon. Went to church in the afternoon, Mr Hooper read prayers & Mr Walter preached. Both Mr Hooper's & Mr Walter's discources were much admired — after church the Vestry met ab^o cleaning the Organ & voted it to be cleaned.

May 19. This day is the Joyfull Day indeed for all America & all the people are to Rejoice this day for the Joyful News Bro^t their vessels from London that the Stamp Act is Repealed. Dined at Colo Ingersoll's with Twenty Eight Gentlemen — we drank fifteen Toasts & very Loyal they were & suited to the Occasion. In the evening there was very Grand Illuminations all over the Town. In the Common there was an Obelisk very beautifully Decorated & very grand fire works were displayed. Mr Hancock behaved very well on this occasion & treated every Person with Cheerfulness. I contrib-

uted as much to the General Joy as Any Person.
The whole was much admired & the day Crowned
with Glory & honour.

May 20.   Set out early this morning for Hardwick with Mr Saml Calef.   Reached Mr Woodburn's
before nine, then joyned Major Golthwait, from
thence we got to Sudbury at Bryant's & from thence
to Sister Speakman's at Marlborough.   There wee
dined with Mr Henry Barnes, Mrs Speakman, Mrs Instant & Miss Betsy Leddell.   After dinner wee set
out for Shrewsbury & Reached Furnefs' at six.   M^r
Calef & I went to the Great Worcester pond &
caught Two doz^n of fine Perch which wee Brought to
Furnefs' & supp^d on   Slept there & got up early &

May 21 passed through Holden.   Reached Dr. Par-
kers at Rutland at eight of Clock   called on Colo.
Murray.   Passed through Oakum & a part of New
Braintree & crossed Ware River got in Hardwick
at Capt Paul Mendall's at One.   Dined at Brigadier
Ruggles with a very large Company, after dinner
went to Vendue where Mr Thomas' things were sold.
Spent the eve'ng at Brigadier Ruggles' with him,
Colo. Murray, Mr Abram Savage, Mr Joseph Blake
Mr Saml Calef & Major Golthwait.

May 22.   Breakfasted with the Brigadier & went
to Hardwick Fair where there were a large company
of People.   Dined at Brig^r Ruggles with a very
large Company among them Mr Joseph Spooner &
Lady which I much admired also Miss Betty Ruggles.   In the afternoon I attended the Vendue —
had some conversation with Mr Asa Hatch & M^{rs}

Hatch who I concluded should remain on the Farm.

May 23.   After doing my Business Major Golthwait Mr Calef & I set out for Rutland from Hardwick   We reached Colo. Murray's & dined there with him & lady — Mrs Bliss, Miss Betty Murray & Miss Chrissy Green — after dinner we went & caught a mess of Trout.   In the evening they had Great Rejoicings at Rutland — they behaved very well, had a large Bonfire & many sky Rockets which I put them in a way to fire — there was a Genteel entertainment at ye Tavern.   afterwards wee returned to Colo. Murray's where there was a Grand Supper & entertainment prepared & Many Loyal Healths drank.   We then retired to bed.

May 24.   Wee rose early this morning & breakfasted with Colo. Murray & set out for home ab° nine in the morning.   Wee stopt at Shrewsbury at Furnefs' & Reached Marlborough at two.   We dined at Sister Speakman's.   Ab° 4 of Clock wee set out & Reached Sudbury at six & proceeded to Woodburn's, Reached it at eight — set out at nine & reached home at eleven.

May 28.   Election Day.   Mr Otis was chosen speaker of the House, but negatived by the Governour   Mr Saml Adams who had a great zeal for Liberty was chosen Clark of the House by one vote I went to meeting & heard Mr Barnard of Haverhill preach the Election Sermon from the 5th Chap. Nehemiah & the 19th Verse   I think this a sensible discourse & very Politic.   I dined with the Gover-

nour, Council &c at Fanewill Hall. The following
Gentlemen were Chose of his Majesty's Councill —
Sam[l] Danforth, Isaac Royal, John Erving Sen[r], W[m]
Brattle, James Boudoin, Tho[s] Hubbard, Israel
Williams, Harrison Gray, James Russell, Tho[s]
Flucker, Nath. Ropes, Timothy Paine, Royal Tyler,
Andrew Belcher, John Chandler, Joseph Gerrish,
James Pitts, Tho[s] Saunders — Gam. Bradford, James
Otis Sen[r], Sam[l] White, Jerahmiel Bowers, John
Hill, Nat. Sparhawk, John Bradbury, Jery Powell,
Benj[n] Lincoln & Sam[l] Dexter Esq[rs].

May 29.   M[r] Tho[s] Cushing was chosen Speaker
in the room of M[r] Otis who the Governour approved
of.   This day the Governour negatived six Councillors viz   Colo. Otis — Colo. Sparhawk, Colo. Gerrish of Newberry, Colo. Bowers of Swanzey, M[r]
Dexter of Dedham & M[r] Saunders of Gloster — this
occasions great murmurings in some & rejoicings in
others.   Spent part of the afternoon with the House
of Representatives in Shoeing Colts.

June 2.   Artillery Election — Went to Meeting
this forenoon the Rev[d] M[r] Brown of Cohasset
preached from the 5th Chap. to the Ephesians &
13[h] Verse.   Dined by invitation with the Gov[r] &
Council at Fanewill Hall & spent part of the afternoon at M[r] Jn[o] Hancock's.

June 4.   The King's Birthday & a great Holli-
day.

June 5.   Was summoned to Court on a Dispute
between Arnold Wells & Cap[t] Christo. Prince —
Heard the tryal between Colo. Brattle & Colo. Mur-

ray — the Jury found thirty pounds damages for
Colo. Brattle.   In the afternoon was obliged to Attend Court again — heard the tryal between Charles
Ward Apthorp & Co. & Mr Richd Pattershall
which went in fav^r of Mr Richd Pattershall.   Spent
the eve'ng at Colo. Ingersolls with the Charitable
Society.

June 6.   In the afternoon I went to Court &
heard the tryal between the Commissioners of the
Land Bank & the Heirs of Rentham which was a
perplexed Cause & was in favour of the Land Bank
Commissioners.   Spent the eve'ng at the Possee.

June 7.   I went this forenoon to Needham a fishing with Mr Saml Calef, Mr Thos Knights, Mr John
Stevenson & Mr Archib^d McNeal — we had middling
luck — there is a Trout Brook empties itself into
Charles River ab° a mile & half beyond Dedham
Island Crossway — dined under a large apple tree &
fished again.

June 8.   heard of the Death of Mr Nat Wheelwright at Guadaloupe.

June 10.   Gen. Ruggles & Mr Otis had some disputes & hard language this day on the Floor of the
Town House   We had this eve'ng the bad news of
Colo. Malbone's fine house on Rhode Island being
burnt down on Saturday last.

June 12.   Rose early this morning & landed
some casks out of an Eastern sloop.   Colo. Bowers
& I went to his honour the Lieut. Governour & got
a statute taken out against Eben^r Stetson.

June 15.   About half after six a fire broke out at

the North End & consumed Dr Clarks barn &
several other houses took fire but by the Dexterity
of the people wee soon extinguished it. I was
much wet & tired & came home & went to bed.

June 16. Rose very early & went to the Lieut.
Governor's at Milton & got him to appoint Trustees
for Eb. Stedson's affairs — namely Colo. Bowers,
Colo. Job. Winslow & myself.

17 June. This morning Capt Hunter arr^d from
London in a short passage. The wind SouthEast
& a splendid Rain, which was very seasonable, at
this time being very Dry din'd this day on a Tor-
tois, at Mr Wm Sheaffe — Capt Duncan Ingram arrived from Surrinam last evening.

18 June. A plentiful Rain & the weather Cold.
I spent the afternoon with the Selectmen & the
evening at the Coffee house. Capt Geneste arrived
from Liverpool.

20 June. Capt Brayley arrived from Biddeford
this morning. I paid the Normans a visit & heard
of the lofs of Capt Gwynn's ship on the Isle of
Sables.

21 June. Went with Mr Saml Calef to Monotomy Pond, din'd there & went fishing, had very
Good Sport, caught seven doz^n of Perch.

23 June. Capt Birney sailed for London this
morning. After dinner I went to Monotomy Pond
with Archib'^{d} Mr Neal & Mr Knight had pretty
Good Sport.

June 24. St. John's Day. Dined at Mr John
Greatons at Roxbury with Jer'y Gridley Esqr &

thirty nine other Brethren of the Fraternity. there
was an elegant entertainment. Spent the eve'ng at
the Merch^{ts} Meeting & adjourned until that day
month.

June 25. The Select Men, Overseers of the Poor
& a Number of the Ministers of the Town &
Country with a Number of other Gentlemen went
& visited the schools of this Town & we found them
in Good Order. the Number of Scholars in the
North writing School are 251. In the South
writing School 263. in Mr Lovells Latin School
130. in the North Latin School — We all dined
together in Fanewill Hall where there was a Genteel Entertainment and everything went on with
Pleasure &c — among the company I invited M^r
Luis, a young gentleman from London.

June 26. Capt Jacobson & I Rose very early &
went to Bullards at Natick where I sent for M^r
Louis ab° some Inch & Quarter Oak Boards &
agreed with him for as many as he & his neighbours
Could Bring. We went fishing at Natick Pond &
had very good sport. Dined at Bullard's with
Capt Jacobson went down to Charles River & fished
there. wee had very Good Sport.

June 28. We got in all our hay. I spent two
hours with Capt Jacobson on Jamaica Pond, wee
had poor Luck.

July 2. Rose very early this morning & set out
for Taunton. Stopt at Colo. Doty's at Stoughton.
was joined there by Tim° Folger, & Mr Swaine &
Kennedy. went on to Kingman's at Easton & from

thence passed by Winnisconnet & Seadding Ponds & Reached Taunton at two.   Dined at McQuarters with Capt Folger, Mr Swain, Mr Robt Jenkins & Mr Isaacs of Swanzy.   I went to Eben. Stedsons at Dighton   spent the eve'ng with him & slept there.

July 3.   Colo. Bowers & Colo. Winslow Trustees of Stedson came & wee went to Colo. Richmond the Sheriff & showed his son the Judges warrant & Got him to read my Bill of Sale for the Briggatine Abigail, before the said Bowers & Winslow.   this was the young gentleman the Sheriff, for the Colo. was gone out, for in my way from Taunton I met the old Colo. & agreed to meet him at Taunton on Monday week following.   din'd at Capt Cobbs with him & wife & in the afternoon reached Colo. Doty's at Stoughton & slept there.

July 4.   Rose very early & set off.   It rained so hard that I was obliged to stop at Milton & at Kent's at Dorchester & Greaton's, when I came there found a Large Company was going to dine on Turtle.   I stayed there to accompany them.

5 July.   After Dinner I went to old Mr Gould's with Mrs Rowe to see Mr Wentworth who I found very weak & Low.   Spent ab^o an hour a fishing with Capt Jacobson, had Little Sport.

6 July.   Capt Gwynn arriv'd from the Isl^d of Sables in a schooner belonging to Capt Soamer.

July 7.   A schooner, Capt Forbes from S^o Carolina put in here in distress & valued himself on me.

July 8.   Rose very early & went with Mr Armiel to Fresh Pond.   Had very poor Sport, caught but a dozen of Perch. Dined at Prentice's with a very large company.

July 9. This morning at five of Clock the Rev^d Dr. Mayhew died much lamented by Great Numbers of people.

July 10. Gave Mr Lander £8415 Connecticut money to exchange — the interest thereon 21–5–9.

July 11. A very hot day — the thermometer up to ninety. In the afternoon I went to the funeral of Dr. Mayhew which was a very large one. The Corps was proceeded by the Gentlemen of his Parish being fifty-seven Couple of Gentlemen then followed the Corps. The Bearers were Mr Appleton, Mr Gay of Hingham, Dr. Chauncey Mr Pemberton, Mr Elliot & Mr Cooper. Then the mourners, then the Ladies & women of his Parish, then the Clergy & Gentlemen of the Town & fifty-seven carriages among them sixteen Coaches & Chariots. Dr. Chauncey prayed in the Meetinghouse before the corps was carried out.

July 14. Rose very early & sent Kennedy to Taunton. Capt Giddins arriv'd from Halifax last night also Capt Cathcart & Capt Sherrard from S Carolina Mr Nathan Jones arriv'd from Goldsberough this morning & Capt Atwood from Halifax.

July 16. Commencement Day. I went to Cambridge with Mrs R. & dined at the Hall with the Governour & Council, President, Tutors &c. After dinner I went & visited Mr Sparhawk, Colo. Pitman Mr Douse, Mr Epps Sergeant, Colo. Jarvis Capt Cobb. Spent the evening at Mr Inmans and slept there.

July 17. Came to Town & got Capt Jno Skinner clear at the Custom House. I went to Cambridge & visited the same gentleman as yesterday, was very merry. in the eve'ng Colo. Sparhawk had a Genteel Ball at the Townhouse. Mr Pepperell desired me to officiate as Master of the Ceremony. The whole was conducted very clever. Slept at Mr Inman's.

July 19. After dinner I went over to the Governour's to get Capt Dobson's Lumber Certificate signed. Capt Bennet arr'd from Madeira.

July 20. Sunday. I went down my wharf & sent away the Capt Skinner for Oporto, & Capt Dobson for Whitby. Capt Calef also sailed for London.

July 21. Set out early this morning, reached Colo. Doty's at Eight of Clock. Got to the Wid^o Noyes at Stoughtonham at half past nine. Stopt at Kingman's & reached Taunton at one. Dined at McQuarters. After dinner Mr Sheriff Richmond & I spent two hours at Colo. White's about Eben Stedson's affairs. From thence I went to Mr Stedson's & arrived there with Colo.[1] Job Winslow till eight. Called at young Col^n Richmond's & spent an hour with him Mr Crook of Newport. Then I returned to Taunton & slept at McQuarters.

22 July. Rose very early & set out for Boston with Kennedy — got to the Widow Noye's at nine o'clk   began to be extreme hot weather — got to Mr James Smiths & dined there with him & wife & Miss Dorothy Murray.

July 23.   Capt Robert Montgomerie Cleared this forenoon.

July 24.   Thanksgiving Day.   I went with Mrs R. to Brush Hill & dined there with James Smith & wife, Mr Murray.

July 25.   Capt Montgomery sailed this day.   I spent the afternoon with the Creditors of Eben^r Stedson at Cordis' the Creditors made choice of Joshua Winslow Esq., Colo. White of Taunton & Myself.   I was called as an Evidence on the Tryal between Scollay & Dunn.   I was very sorry the Jury dismissed Capt Dunn's action & think he has been vilely used.

26 July.   I settled with Capt Thomas Forbes who sailed for London.   Capt Robertson arriv'd from Gibraltar in a Ship belonging to Mr Lane, Capt Farr.   After dinner I went to see Mr Wentworth who thinks he is on the mending hand.

27 July.   Capt Ashburn arriv'd from the Straights.   The Fortune Man of War, Capt Bishop sailed this forenoon, with a fair Wind in Whom went passengers Charles Paxton & Mr Thos Palmer.

July 28.   I went with Capt Jacobson to M'head. Dined at Martin's & reached Marblehead at dark. Spent the eve^{ng} at Capt Gerry's.

July 29.   Capt Jacobson & I went to Flax Pond, had very Good Sport.   Caught twelve dozen Perch in two hours.   Dined at Flax Pond & stopt at Mr Joseph Gould's at Lynn — from thence came home.

30 July.   Attended the Tryal of Keen for stealing the Barrell of Molasses — he was found Guilty.

1 Aug.   A hot Day din'd at Jn° Champney on a Barbekue.

2 Aug.   I went this morning with Capt Jones to the Lieu^t Governour ab° Stedsons affairs.   Afterwards to a pond ab° a mile from Colo Dotys with Mr John Lovell jun^r & Saml Calef.   wee had Good Sport & caught a great many fish tho they were small.   Mrs Rowe has been unwell but is growing much Better.

3 Aug.   Mrs Rowe continues very unwell.

4 Aug.   A very hot morning.   Mrs Rowe took a Ride.

Aug. 5.   Mrs Rowe very unwell.   The Tryal about Ridgeway's Plate was heard this day & the Jury found in favour of the Creditors.

Aug. 6.   Mrs Rowe still unwell.   There was an Eclipse of the Sun yesterday.   Met the Selectmen in the afternoon — they were all present.   48 people apply^d for License, 4 new ones approbated & five that had been Retailers before.

Aug. 11.   Mrs Rowe a little better.   Set out this morning for Plym° in comp^y with Capt Ashburn. Stopt at Mr Bracketts in Braintree & at Deacon Cushings at Hingham at Dr Hall's at Pembrooke — there wee dined.   Set out & Reached Littles at Kingston & from thence to Plymouth — we put up at Howlands.   Spent the eve'ng at Capt Gideon White's with him & wife & Miss Joanna — & slept there.

Aug. 12.   Went with Cornelius White, Ed^{wd} Winslow, & Young Bradford also Capt Ashburn to

South Pond a fishing — had very good sport. I
caught a very large Perch — measured 18 inches
& weighed three pounds & a half.   Dined at Ed^{wd}
Winslows with him & wife & Two Daughters.
After dinner we set out for home.   Reached Hall's
at Pembrooke where wee Stopt & from thence to
Cushing's & Bracket's where we lodged that night.
Colo. Ephraim Leonard, Mr Justice Williams, & M^r
Justice Elisha Toby who was this day moved into
his office, also Mr Justice Fales who is Clerk of the
Court — had some conversation with Colo. White &
Mr Adams on the affairs of Ebenezer Stedson with
B & Ed^w Davis & gave Mr Adams a Guinea as a
fee.

13 Aug.   Rose early this morning & set out &
got home to Boston & found Mrs Rowe much Better, found Capt Dashwood come in from St Kitts
having sprung his masts.   In the afternoon I went
to Mrs Forbes Funeral & was one of the Bearers.

Aug. 15.   I went to dinner on Spectacle Island.

18 Aug.   Mrs Rowe still unwell.   After Dinner
Mr Saml Calef, Mr J. Amiel, Wm Speakman & my-
self set out for Taunton.   We stopt at Colo. Doty's
Pond & caught Eight Dozen of Perch.

Aug. 20.   After I had done my Business M^r
Laughton & I set out for to come home.   We over-
took Mr Calef, Mr Armiel, & Wm Speakman at
Winnesconnet Pond — they had caught a great
many Fish which wee dined on at Howard's at
Easton.   Set out from thence & reached Col.
Doty's & slept there.

21 Aug.   Wee Rose early this morning and went a fishing   had Good Sport.   We were joyn'd by Mr James Smith & wife, Two Mrs Belchers, Miss Clark Miss Dolly Murray Mrs Jones Miss Blowers Miss Amiel Mr Hutchinson & Mr Waller.   We all Din'd at Colo Doty's.   in the evening I came home & found Mrs Rowe very unwell.

22 Aug.   Mrs Rowe still unwell, had a very Restless night   My Lord Hope arrived here from Halifax last on a snow.

23 Aug.   Mrs Rowe no sleep tonight.   din'd at Mr Ezek^l Golthwaits at Roxbury with him & wife & three Daughters, Mr James Smith & wife   Both Mrs Belchers, Mrs Jones & Mr Waller.   went in the afternoon to Jamaica Pond & fished there with Capt Jacobson   had pretty Good Sport   Mr Wentworth lies dangerously Ill at Roxbury   Mr Copeland took his Face this afternoon.

26 Aug.   Mrs Rowe growing Better.   very hot weather.

27 Aug.   The weather still very hot.   Mr Amiel & I went to Mystick & din'd there at Jones.   afterwards we went to Spot Pond & caught a Good many small Perch & Returned in the evening.   The weather changed, the wind Easterly & very Cold.

29 Aug.   Mrs Rowe not as well as yesterday.

Aug. 30.   Mr. Core came early this morning & we went to Capt Kendricks a fishing.   wee were joyned by Major Golthwait, Mr Armiel & Mr Calef. wee all dined there & a very elegant Dinner   Partridges for the first time this season.   The Garland

mann of War sailed this day on a Cruise. Capt St
John.

Aug. 31st.   Mrs Rowe (thank God) much Better.

2 Sept.   Mrs Rowe took an airing in the Chariot
this forenoon for the first time since her Illness.

4 Sept.   Rose very early this morning & settled
with Capt Dashwood who sailed ab^o Ten of Clock
Came home & took a Ride Out with Mrs Rowe.
din'd at home with M^r payne of Taunton Lawyer
& Mr Addams of Braintree Lawyer and Miss Sucky.
Spent part of the afternoon with the Creditors of
Capt James Forbes.

Sept. 6.   Thos Oliver sent for my Sorrell Mare
this morning for which he is to give me a hundred
dollars or return me the Mare again in the Spring
safe & sound. if any accident happens to her it's
at his Risque by agreement. I went this forenoon
with Capt Jacobson to Govr Barnard's to get his
despatches but they were not Reddy. Capt Marshall has arr'd in Nantasket from London having
the small-pox on board.

Sept. 7.   I met the Selectmen this morning about
Capt Marshall's affairs and sent him some provisions
etc. I went to the Charitable Lecture at Fanewill
Hall & heard the Revd Mr Elliot preach a sensible
Discourse Capt Freeman arriv'd from London this
afternoon.

Sept. 9.   Set out with John Nazzro for Dighton.
Stopt at Col. Doty's & at the Wid^o Noyes at
Stoughtonham & dined at the Wid^o Godfrey's at
Norton. Reached Taunton at three of Clock. met

Colo. White & went with him to Dighton. old Colo. Richmond was not at home. wee went to Eben Stedsons & stayed there all night.

Sept. 10. Old Colo. Richmond met us & delivered all Stedson's effects as pr inventory in presence of John Nazzro & Eben Stedson to Colo. White & me. After dinner I set out with Colo. White & drank tea at his house with Mrs White & her two daughters which appear very neat &c.

Sept. 11. Set out of Taunton for home. stopt at Howard's & at the Wid° Noyes where I met Edwd Quincy Junr & breakfasted there. wee set out for Colo Doty's Reached his home at Eleven of Clock. Mr Quincy & I went a fishing. after dinner set out for home & stopt at his honour the Lieut Governour's & I d'ld his Daughter the Sheriff Richmond's Return on Stedson's affairs with the Inventory annext.

Sept. 12. Sold my Ship — Capt Hatch — to Capt Taylor & Mr Rider — in the afternoon I went to the Funeral of my old Friend Saml Wentworth. Spent the eve'ng in part at home & the remainder at the Coffee House.

Sept. 14. Sunday. The Revd Mr Walter was Published to Miss Lidia Lynds this forenoon. Capt Oman arrived from London this morning.

17 Sept. Met the Selectmen in the afternoon — at six of Clock met the Creditors of Eben Stetson at the Coffee House.

18 Sept. Capt Marshalls snow came up from Nantasket yesterday in the afternoon. I went to

Mr Smith's Farm at Watertown Mr Fessendens Brother & dined there with Mr James Smith & wife Mr Murray & wife, Two Mrs Belchers Mr Inman, Mr Walter Colo Henry Vafsall & wife Mr Trollet, Mrs Cutler Mr J. Amiel & wife & Miss Chrifsy, Capt Buntin & Two French Gentlemen from Guadalope.

20 Sept. Capt Freeman arr'd from Bristol in him came Mr John Powell. Capt Ashburn also arriv'd from Liverpool.

21 Sept. Sunday — Both Mr Hoopers & his (Mr Walter's) were good & sensible Discourses but a little Metaphisical.

23 Sept. Capt Daverson Senr arriv'd from London. I went to Fresh Pond & din'd there on Turtle with Henry Vafsall & wife & (a large company)

Sept. 24. The Custom house attempted to seize some wine out of Malcom's cellar but were hindered from it by about two hundred people making their appearance in the street. The Governour & Council met on the affair of the Seizure but they could make nothing of it.

Sept. 25. The Governour & Council met again on this affair, & examined many Evidences, but could make nothing of it.

Sept. 26. Mr White moved into my house on Monday, the 22^n Sept at £8 p annum — this house adjournes to Mr Amiel's.

Sept. 29. Spent the afternoon at the Selectmens Room.

30 Sept. Rose very early this morning & went

a fishing with James Perkins & Sam¹ Calef wee din'd together under a tree on the Causeway beyond Dedham Island. Wee had very great sport.

2 Oct. Capᵗ Sheppard in Briggs Hallowell's Briggantine sailed for London.

3 Oct. The Selectmen met & ordered a Town Meeting on Wednesday next.

Oct. 5ʰ. Capᵗ Coppinger arr'd at Cape Ann & came to Town, from Martinico & gives an accᵗ of Ninety Sail of Vessels being lost there in a Hurricane in August.

Oct. 7. Pᵈ Green 7 Dollars for horsehire etc going to Bridgewater.

Oct. 8. Town Meeting this forenoon. The Town Voted that the Sufferers here have Compensation made them provided they apply in a parliamentary way. Yesterday in the afternoon Mʳ Samuel Holbrook was buried.

Oct. 10. Met the Selectmen at Fanewill Hall this morning. This afternoon I met the Committee on Capᵗ Dan¹ Malcom's affair — James Otis, Sam Adams, myself Edwᵈ Quincy — John Hancock, Joshua Henshaw & Edwᵈ Payne. Spent the eve'ng at the Possee.

Oct. 13. Mʳˢ R. much hurried in removing from one house to the other Met the committee on Capᵗ Malcolm's affair.

Oct. 16. Slept this night for the first time in our new house which is a Very Good, Handsome & Convenient house. Went to Little Cambridge on business The Revᵈ Mʳ Hooper went into the House I came out off this day.

JOHN ROWE'S HOUSE IN POND LANE (Bedford Street)

Oct. 19. Sunday. Stayed at home with Andrew Brimmer on business — I went to church in the afternoon Mr Hooper read prayers & Mr Walter preached from 3rd Chap. Proverbs & 6^h Verse — this was a clever sensible discourse.

Oct. 20. Dined at home with Capt Harris Hatch — set out with him for Dighton at two of Clock — wee stopt at Colo. Doty's & from thence reached Mrs Noyes' Wee spent the evening there with Edm^d Quincy Junr & a Dartmouth Man & slept there.

Oct. 21. Wee put on to Howards at Easton, there breakfasted & from thence to Taunton — wee stopt at McQuarters & thence to Dighton. There wee dined at Eben Stedson's — after dinner wee began to sell Mr Stedsons things Capt Hatch b^o the Brigg^n Abigail appurtenances & cargo for me at six hundred & ten pounds lawful money — John Nazro sold part of the Household Furniture.

Oct. 22. Wee rose very early this morning & examined the Brigg — sent for the Joyner & several other Tradesmen. Mr Stedson had agreed with the Joyner for 34 Dollars for his work & Stedson to find the stuff. After dinner wee begun the Vendue & continued until dark — from Mr Stedson's, Capt Hatch & I went to Colo. White's.

Oct. 23. Set out for Boston. We breakfasted at McQuarter's & from thence to Howards & from Howard's to the Wid^o Noyes' & from thence to James Smith's at Brush Hill. there we dined with him & Lady. Old Madam Belcher & Mrs Belcher

her Daughter, Mrs Jones, Mr Inman, Mr Cutler Mifs Blowers, Miss Anna Clark, Miss Dolly Murray & Miss Betty Murray.

Oct 24. Spent the afternoon at the Coffee House on an Arbitration between Joseph Rhodes & Geo. Stacy & Capt Brown of Marblehead. the Referees Jos. Winslow Esqr, Mr John Pidgeon & myself. Met the Arbitrators on Rhodes & Stacy affairs.

Oct. 25. Spent an hour at Normandy.

26 Oct. This morning Capt Jarvis arriv'd from London having a Long Passage of Eight Weeks & three Days. I paid a visit to Old Mr Gould who I found very Ill in the Gout.

27 Oct. Capt Hunter sailed from Nantasket Road. in the afternoon I went to the Select mens Room and attended there.

30 Oct. Capt Young arriv'd from London. After dinner I went & p^d a visit to Mr Harrison Our new Collector & spent the evening at the Coffee House.

1 Nov. Spent my time this forenoon with Mr John Pidgeon on Stacy & Rhodes affairs.

Nov. 4. The House of Assembly tried for a Compensation for the Sufferers this afternoon but did not obtain — there were 51 against it & 43 for it.

Nov. 5. This is a Day of Confusion in Boston occasioned by a foolish Custom of Carrying about the pope & the Devill &c on a large carriage thro' the streets of this Town. indeed three very large ones made their appearance this day. Finished the affair between Rhodes, Stacy & Brown.

Nov. 12. Dined at M' Francis Johannot's with him & wife & three daughters, M' Craddock, Andrew Belcher & Byfield Lyde. The Select men met this afternoon. Wee did a Good Deal of Business Capt Coffin arriv'd from London in M' Hancock's Brigg^a.

Nov. 13. This day the General Court was adjourned for three weeks. Spent the afternoon with John Scolly's Creditors.

Nov. 19. I went to Dr. Sewall's Meeting house to see the Rev^d M' Blair Installed. A great many People were there. M' Pemberton prayed & M' Blair preached from 11^h Chap. to the Romans 13 verse.

Nov. 20. Went on business to M' Otis & gave him a Guinea for a fee on M' Robt Cook's business in the Admiralty.

Nov. 22. Last night I sent my negro Cato to Bridewell for a very bad fault.

Nov. 25. Spent the afternoon with the Committee of the General Court, M' Speaker, M' Otis, M' Stephen Hall, M' Adams, M' Hancock, M' Dexter. A number of Merchants were there. Am in hopes wee shall get Redress in our Trade.

Nov. 26. Rose very early & went & paid a visit to M' Jos. Harrison & Gov' Barnard. Got Capt Robertson's affairs thro'. Met the Selectmen at their room in the afternoon. A Transport Ship arr'd bound from Halifax to Quebec but could not get up the River. She has seventy people belonging to the Royal Train of Artillery on board, forty-three women & nineteen children. The master Capt Smith values on me.

27 Nov. Thanksgiving Day. This day is my Birthday being now entering into my fifty second year.

28 Nov. Met the Committee of the General Court this afternoon.

29 Nov. Capt Smith in Mr Sam Hughes Brigg arriv'd from London this day. Received two letters from Mr Peter Hubbert dated at Manticoke River Maryland November 4^h, 1766. The Gent^m Belonging to the Train agreed with Jno Bryant for Beef & Archibald McNeal for Bread.

Dec. 2. The Merchants made a Dinner for Capt Gideon at the Coffee house & a very Genteel Entertainment it was. The Company did me the Honour to Preside & the Company consisted of the following Gentlemen. myself Capt Gideon Mr Peele Doct^r Pettigrew. Joshua Winslow Esq James Pitts Thos Flucker Jam^s Botineau Robt Hooper Esq of M'blehead. Mr Inman Mr John Erving Junr. Mr Joseph Green. Mr James Otis Mr Nich. Boylston. Mr John Boylston Mr Arnold Wells Mr Ed^w Paine Mr Edwd Davis. Mr Stephen Greenleaf Mr J^{no} Amory Mr Jonathan Amory Mr Ezek. Golthwait Mr Sam Hughes Mr Ezek^l Price Mr Benjn Hallowell Senr Mr Briggs Hallowell. Mr Robt Hallowell. Mr Thos Cushing Mr John Hancock. Mr Henderson Inches Mr John Timmins Mr James Perkins Mr Thos Brattle Mr John Powell Mr George Irving Mr Murray Mr Wm Mollineaux Mr Henry Loyd. Mr Geo. Bethune Richd Clark Jona. Simpson Edm^d Quincy Robt Gordon.

After Dinner the following Toasts were Drank
1. The King   2. The Queen & Royal Family   3
The Parliament of Great Britain   4 His Majesty's
Ministry   5 The Earl of Chatham   6 Lord Chan-
cellor   7 Gen¹ Conway   8 Earl Sherburne   9
Duke of Grafton   10 Duke of Newcastle   11 The
Earl of Chesterfield   12 Duke of Richmond   13
The Chancellor of the Exchequer   14 The Right
Hon'ble Sir Arthur Onslow   15 Gen¹ Howard   16
Colo¹ Barre   17 The Patrons of the British Colo-
nies   18 The Lords of Trade   19 The Lords of
the Admiralty   20 The Army & Navy   21 The
Extension of Trade & Commerce.   22 The United
& Inseparable Interest of Great Britain & Her
Colonies   23 May the True Interest of Great
Britain & Her Colonies be Never Hidden of their
Eyes   24 Sir Edwᵈ Hawk   25 My Lord Colvil
26 Prosperity of Nᵒ America.   27 A Good Voy-
age to the Jamaica.   Capt Wᵐ Robertson in Capᵗ
Fair's ship sailed this forenoon for London

Dec. 5.   This Day the Court voted Compensation
to the Sufferers   The Treasurer's wife, Mʳˢ Gray
was buried this afternoon   Dined on board the
Thames with him Rev Mʳ Walter, Mʳ John Hancock
(& others)

Dec. 7.   A fire broke out abᵒ four of Clock this
morning in our Lane & burnt Mʳ Snow's potash
house down with the Buildings Adjoyning.   Went
to Church this forenoon   Mʳ Walter preached a
sensible Discourse & historical

8 Dec.   Town meeting this forenoon.   Settled

with Capt Geneste & he sail'd for Lond° ab° five of Clock

9 Dec.   Capt Jarvis set out for Providence.   I p^d him £200.2/ lawfull money to pay Mr Brown this day a Brigg^a arriv'd from Bristol

11 Dec.   Capt Morrison sailed this day for the Straights   Met the Creditors of John Scollay Esq this afternoon

12 Dec.   Din'd at Major John Vafsall's at Cambridge with him & wife (& ten others)   After Dinner Miss Penny & Edwd Winslow set out from thence for Plymouth   came home with Major Byard, of New York, in his Phaeton.

17 Dec.   Settled with Decon Foster & wife about the Iron works.   Spent the afternoon with the Selectmen Colo Jackson Mr Saml Sewall Mr Ruddock, Deacon Newall, Deacon Phillips & John Hancock Esq & the eve'ng at Mrs Cordis'.

18 Dec.   One Joseph Andrews, a Portugese was taken at Marblehead & brought here & put into Goal for Piracy.

20 Dec.   It has snowed all night & is very deep after Dinner put the Horses in the Sleigh but could not get over the Neck   the snow very very much drifted.

Dec. 21.   No post in.

23 Dec.   Spent the afternoon & evening with the Committee of Merchants namely Mr Edwd Payne Mr John Erving, Mr Thos Gray & Mr Sam Hughes at Colo. Ingersolls (Bunch of Grapes Tavern)

24 Dec. Mrs Speakman went out of Town this morning Capt Scott arriv'd from London Capt Bryce is also arriv'd from London.

Dec. 26. I sent Andrew Brimmer to Salem this morning on Buffams affairs Spent the eve'ng with the Free Masons Committee of Charity.

Dec. 30. Spent the eve'ng at Colo. Ingersolls with Jerry Gridley & about 40 Brethren. Another snowstorm blows very hard.

Dec. 31. A very cold Day the Ink freezes as I write.

1767

Jan. 7. Went to Town Meeting in the afternoon & spent the evening at Mr Cordis' at a very Genteel Entertainment & Dance where I presided. This eve'ng Capt Williams of the 39th Regiment was arrested by Sheriff Greenleaf on the suit of Mr John Spooner, which occasioned much noise &c in Town.

Jan. 8. The Govr Sent for me this morning. I was bound for Capt Williams. Met the Proprietors of Point Shirley at the Coffee House. Ezek^l Golthwait, Mr Pitts, Mr John Hancock & Mr Nath. Holmes & spent the eve'ng at Mrs Clappam's. Dined at Capt Solo Davis on Venison.

Jan. 13. Spent the evening at Mr John Erving Junr at a wedding Frollick — this was an agreeable Frollick & I had the pleasure to dance with the Bride Mrs Stewart.

Jan. 17. Dined at Mrs Cordis' at the invitation

of Capt Willson.   Capt Henry Smith in the Transport Sailed this day.   Capt Jarvis was ready but Sprung a Leak.

Jan. 20.   Colo. Gorham & Lady arrived in Capt Soames from Halifax.   Dined at Mrs Clappam's by Invitation from Capt Williams with him & Govr Barnard, Major Byard, Major Butler, Capt Williams, Mr Gregory Townsend & Lieu^t Carghill.

22 Jan.   Begins to snow.   Spent the evening at Capt Matchet's at the North End with him (several other gentlemen) & Capt Clark a Stranger who diverted us much in playing the slight of hand.

23 Jan.   This morning the Cause between Charles Ward Apthorpe & Mr Deblois came on & lasted the whole day   Spent an hour with the Grand Lodge & the evening at the Coffee House.

24 Jan.   After dinner I took a Ride with Major Byard over the Neck   very good Sleighing.   Spent the evening at the Pofse.

Jan. 26.   Met the Selectmen at the Representatives Rooms.   Joshua Winslow Esqr one of the Court of Sessions met us, but no other of the Justices.   Spent the afternoon at Mrs Cordis' on a Reference between Dr. Gardiner & Mr James Flagg, Mr Paine, Henderson Inches & Sam Hughes were the Referees — it was a Publick Hearing & a Great Company.

Jan. 29.   Was alarmed early this morning by the Cry of Fire — two Times two Thieves set the Goal on fire & got away — it did not do much damage. The General Court met yesterday — I met the

Creditors of Capt James Forbes.   we agreed to allow him 10 p cent on the Sum he collected.   Spent the evening at the Coffee house at a Dance.   Capt Jarvis sail'd for London.

Febry 2^d.   Mrs R. & I paid a visit to the Surveyor General & Lady where we found the Governour's Lady, the Secretary, lady & three Daughters, Sheriff Greenleaf, lady & Miss Nabby, Mrs Robt Temple & two Daughters, Colo Gorham & lady, Madam Apthorp, Dr. Bulfinch & wife, Mr Pitts & Lady, & Miss Betty, Mr Armiel & wife, Mr Inman, the Revd Mr Walter & wife, the Revd Mr Troutbeck Mrs Sheaffe & Miss Sally, Capt Phillips & wife, Mrs Boudoin, Miss Howard, Miss Alice Whipple the fair Quaker & Miss Wm Phillips.   Spent part of the afternoon with the Selectmen & a Committee of the Sessions, Sam Wells Esq, Richd Dana Esq, Joshua Winslow Esq & Foster Hutchinson.

Feb. 3rd.   Set out for Salem with Mr Sam. Calef — dined at Norwood's at Lynn — called on Mr Gould. Reached Salem at three of Clock.   I went to see Friend Buffam, had a great deal of Conversation on his Affairs — visited Mr Jos. Douse, Mr Fisher also Mr Pyncheon the Lawyer.   Spent the eve'ng at Col. Pickman's — Slept at the Tavern.

Febry 4^h.   After Breakfast set out for home & upon the Road heard of a great fire in Boston which broke out in Bray the Baker's Warehouse & spread round about the Neighborhood, that it Consumed more than Twenty houses among which was Mr Jonathan Williams Dwelling House several houses of Mr John Hancock's, several Belonging to Capt Ball — it Begun at ten of Clock & continued until Three in the morning when it was stopt. Spent the afternoon at the Selectmens Room.

Febry 6.   Spent the afternoon & evening at the Selectmen's rooms with the Committee of the Sessions & the Committee of the Town about the Sale of the Townhouse.   Sam. Wells Esq, Jos. Winslow Esq, Jerry Gridley Esq, Foster Hutchinson Esq & Richd Dana Esq — Joseph Jackson Esq, Mr Saml Sewall, Deacon Wm Phillips, Deacon Newall & myself.   We also drew a petition to the General Court in Behalf of the Sufferers by Fire.   Gave Mr Kent Capt Barker's bond to Sue.

Feb'ry 7.   A very cold night. My pump in the front yard froze.   After dinner I went Sleighing in Bracketts sleigh with Mr Paine of Taunton, John Amory, Johnathan Amory, Henry Hill, Edm^d Quincy Tertius, Saml Quincy, Dr. Jos. Gardner, Dr. Oliver Wendall & James Lovell.   We went round Jamaica Pond & Stopt at Gideon Gardners on the Neck where we were Joyned by Wm Taylor, Nat. Taylor, Gregory Townsend & Frank White & Bart^o Kneeland.

Feb'ry 9.   The two Committees of Town & County met the Committee of the General Court ab^o the Townhouse — for the General Court Capt Edwd Sheaffe, Mr Stephen Hall — for the County Saml Wells, Jos. Winslow, Jerry Gridley, Foster Hutchinson & Richd Dana Esq^{rs} — for the Town Colo. Jackson, Mr Saml Sewall, Wm Phillips, Deacon

Newall & myself. The Justices of the Town of
Boston, the Overseers of the Poor & the Select Men
met this afternoon to fix a time for a general Visitation.

Feb'ry 10. Attended the Tryal between Dr. Gardiner & Mr Flagg.

14. Feb. It has snowed all night — in the afternoon Major Byard called on me & wee took a Ride
in his Sleigh & stopt at Gardners where wee found
a Good Company.

Feb'ry 19. In the afternoon met the Creditors of
Mr John Wennid at Colo. Ingersolls & afterwards
met the Creditors of Mr Jno Nichols at the Coffee
House. Spent the evening at home with the Fire-
wards. Dined at home with Colo White of Taunton, Major Leonard of Norton, his son-in-law, Colo
Payne of Worcester, Mr Stephen Hussey of Nantucket.

Feb'ry 20. This day let Mr Pipon half the Brick
House in this Lane at ten pound lawfull money p
anum. Capt Hatch sailed this morning for London.

Feb'ry 24. This morning the Lawyers finished
their Debates on Dr Gardiner & Flagg's affairs &
the Court adjourned until the 2^d of March to give
their Opinion.

Feb'ry 26. The House of Representatives have
been all day on the Land Bank scheme. I met the
Creditors of Mr Hope.

Feb'ry 27. I sign'd the Deeds for Capt Forbes'
Houses — at four met the creditors of Sam. Buffam
at the Coffee House.

Mar. 6. Spent the afternoon at the Selectmens room. The Sufferers by Fire Brought in their acc^{ts} of what they had lost at the Fire the 3rd feb'ry — wee went through the whole acc^{ts}.

7 March. After Dinner Capt Davis Mr Inman & I paid a visit to Robert Gould who wee found laid up with the Gout — then wee went to Capt Bennets & drank a Bottle of Madeira with Lewis Gray & Capt Doble.

Mar. 9. Town Meeting today on which I attended all day.

Mar. 10. Spent the afternoon with the Selectmen, the same as last year, on the distribution of the money given by the province to the sufferers.

Mar. 11. The Superior Court set yesterday. Mr Benj^m Austin Mr J^{no} Timmins & I sat on an Arbitration between Levi Stedson & Wm Hayden & finished our Report & carried it in this forenoon. Afternoon met the Selectmen at their Room.

Mar. 12. Spent the afternoon at the Selectmen's room in Distributing money to the sufferers by Fire. Mr John Pidgeon & I met the Committee of the General Court at Mr Blodgets on Jos. Rhodes & Geo Stacey's affairs.

Mar. 13. The General Court chose Commissioners to treat with the Government of New York about the Line between them & us — The Lieut. Governor, Colo. Brattle & Mr Sheaffe of Charlestown.

Mar. 14. Still exceeding cold & sharp. It froze almost as far as the Castle tonight. Went to Court

this forenoon on an Action depending between
Colo. Gridley & Andrew Hall.

Mar. 17. St Patrick's Day. Dined at Cap[t]
Moses Bennet's with the Sons of St Patrick — M[r]
Forrest, Cap[t] Malcom, old M[r] Malcom, two Bry-
ants, Cap[t] W[m] Nichols, Cap[t] McDonald, Cap[t]
Mackay, Arch[d] McNeal, Tho[s] Bennet, James
Thompson, W[m] Thompson, Cap[t] Tho[s] Mitchell, Cap[t]
Moses Bennet, Cap[t] Matchet, M[r] W[m] Bowers, James
Otis Esq, M[r] Lewis Gray, Cap[t] Hopkins, M[r] Nath[l]
Spear, Dr Cast & a great many others I did not
know. In the afternoon I went to Court — they
voted M[r] Debert two hundred pounds st'lg for a
year's salary.

Mar. 18. This is Anniversary Day when the
parliament of Great Britain repealed the Stamp Act.
I dined at Col. Ingersoll's with the following Gen-
tlemen. Colo. Jarvis, Sam[l] Quincy, Jos. Scot, Jos.
Winslow jun[r], Gregory Townsend, M[r] Forrest,
Tho[s] Amory, Jos. Blanchard, Dan[l] Hubbard, Peter
Johannot, Tho[s] Brinley, Tim[y] Folgee, Edm[d] Quincy
Tertius, M[r] Trumball of Lebanon, Tho[s] Apthrop
Rob[t] Hallowell, John Timmins, M[r] Smith from Lon-
don, Tuthill Hubbard, W[m] Coffin jun[r], Dr W[m] Lee
Perkins, Edw[d] Davis, Sam. Calef, M[r] Josiah Quincy,
M[r] Sam[l] Treat Paine of Taunton, M[r] W[m] Davis &
M[r] Tho[s] Brattle. We had a very Genteel Dinner.
After dinner they desired me to be Toast Master on
the occasion. The following Toasts were Drank.
The King — The Queen & Royal Family — The
Parliament of Great Britain — His Majesty's Minis-

try— The Earl of Chatham — The Lord Chancellor
— General Conway — Duke of Grafton — Marquis
of Rockingham — The Chancellor of the Exchequer, Gen. Howard — Colo. Barry — Sir Wm Mer-
dith — The Five Dissenting Lords — The Patrons of
the British Colonies — The Lords of Trade — The
Lords of the Admiralty — The Army & Navy —
The Extension of Traded Commerce — The United
& Inseparable Interest of Gr. Britain & Her Colonies
May the True Interest of Great Britain & her Colonies be never off their Eyes. Prosperity to the
Province. May the 18^h Day of March 1766, the day
the Stamp Act was repealed be ever had in memory
by all True Britains & Americans — Prosperity
to the Sons of Liberty — Prosperity to the Town of
Boston. At four of Clock in the afternoon I was
obliged to attend at Fanueil Hall, where there met
a great Concourse of People to Drink the King's
Health &c prvote of the Town & the same Toasts
were drank as above. The Hall was illuminated also
Liberty Tree & sundry other Gentleman's Houses.
I never saw more Joy than on this occasion.

Mar. 19. I attended the Selectmens room this
forenoon. After met the Committee of the Affairs
of Mr Ebenezer Perry. Bought of John Ruddock
Esq 7 Lottery Tickets.

N° 1038 Gave M^{rs} R.

" 1039   "   Suky Inman

" 1040   "   Sally Inman

" 1041   "   George Inman

" 1042 Kept myself

N° 1043 Kept myself

" 1044 Sold James Kennedy.

Mar. 20. I was called on by Cap⁺ Daws to view
the Land by the Fortification. Spent an hour at
Brackets on business with Judge Danforth, General
Ruggles, Colo Bradford, Thoˢ Cobb.

Mar. 25. There was a General Council this forenoon. The Govʳ appointed Mʳ Trowbridge, a Judge
of the Superior Court, our Friend Jerry Gridly,
King's Attorney General, Mʳ Sewall, special Attorney
to act in the absence of Mʳ Gridley. Several other
promotions. Spent the evening at Mʳˢ Cordis'. This
night wee Regulated the price of wine & punch with
Mʳ Cordis. Twenty Shillings a double Bowl Punch.
Thirty Shillings a Bottle Madeira.

Mar. 27. Spent the afternoon & evening with
the Select men at Fanewill Hall where we made a
Division of the Remainder of the money to the Sufferers by Fire.

Mar. 28. Dined at Jⁿᵒ Champney's at the Turks-
head on a wager of a Rump & Dozⁿ — lost by
Thoˢ Brattle.

Mar. 31. Town meeting this forenoon. I was
on an arbitration between Cap⁺ Glover of Mhead &
the Underwriters at Mʳ Pidgeons office. The arbitrators were five — namely Foster Hutchinson Esq,
Nat. Bethune, Isaac Smith, Sam G Hughes & myself.

3 April. The Governor & his Son came to see
our New House this afternoon.

April 5. After church there was a Vestry to

consider of the Selectmen's Letter ab° a Contribution for the Sufferers by Fire.

7 April.   Met the Creditors of Mr John Cotton
and adjourned untill Fryday.

Apr. 8.   Spent the afternoon with the Justices
& Selectmen ab° laying out a New Street in Paddy's
Alley.

10 April.   Attended the Tryal between Charles
W Apthorpe & Mr Deblois.

Apr. 14.   Between 10 & 11 of Clock my most
valuable & worthy & never to be forgotten Friend
the Revd Mr Hooper fell down in his Garden & expired instantaneously to the Great Grief & Sorrow
of his People & the Loss of his Family.   Met the
Church Wardens & Vestry at three of Clock to consult on Mr Hooper's Funeral.   My Sloop Chagford
went a whaling this day.

April 15.   Met the proprietors of Long Wharf
at Mrs Cordis this afternoon, also attended the Selectmen, also the Funeral of Mrs Jeffries.   Also met
the Church Wardens & Vestry of Trinity Church.

16 April.   Met the Justices and Selectmen at the
Hall & finished the affair of the street.

Apr. 17.   I attended the mournfull funeral of
my worthy & much Lamented Friend the Rev^d M^r
Hooper.   The Great Concourse & Multitude of
People that attended this Solemnity is hardly to be
conceived   His bearers were the Rev^d Dr Chauncey,
Dr Byles, Mr Thompson of Scituate, Mr Winslow of
Braintree Mr Troutbeck & Mr Walter.   the Throng
was so great at the Church that a great many Gen-

tlemen & Ladies could not get in to the church.
Mr Troutbeck read the Burial Service on this occasion & Mr Walter preached a very Pathetick & moving Discourse from 14th Chap Revelations & 13^n^ verse.
After church returned to the House of mourning
& I endeavoured to give Comfort to the distressed
family. I intend to be their friend.

Apr. 20. I went to Trinity Church this fore-
noon for the Choice of officers the ensuing year.
Mr Greenleaf & Mr Wm Coffin sen^r^ were chosen
Church Wardens & 12 vestrymen.

Yesterday Mr Murray, Mr Donn· & mee went to
the Judge of Probate to prove Mr Hoopers will.

Apr 23. Dined at Ezek^l^ Goldthwait's with him
& wife, Capt Michael Dalton & wife, Mrs Hooper of
Marblehead, Mrs Lewis, Mrs Cumming, Miss Patty
Goldthwait, Mr Inman & Miss Goldthwait. M^rs^
Hooper went to Copley to have her Picture drawn
as did Capt Dalton & wife.

Apr. 26. Sunday. After church there was a
gathering for to make the expense of the Funeral of
Mr Hooper. They collected seventy two pounds.

Apr. 27. Set out for Plymouth in Company with
Mr Sam Calef & Mr Thos Knights. Stopt at
Bracketts, Braintree dined at Cushings at Hingham,
Reached Dr Hall's at Pembroke in the afternoon &
stayed there all Night

Apr 28. Set out early from Halls & got to Dux-
bury Mills. Stopt there & fished, had very Good
Sport. caught five Dozen Trout. Dined at Dr
Harlows. Reached Plymouth. I see all my Friends.
Slept at Capt White's

Apr. 29. Went to my Forge with Cornelius White, Pelham Winslow, Edwd Winslow jun^r. did what business I had to do. After dinner set out for Marshfield stopt at Kingston at Mr Little's, had some conversation with Miss Lydia Little. Wee set out from thence & Reached Duxbury Mills, fished there & caught ab° a Dozen Trout. In the evening wee went to Gen. Winslow's, Marshfield & slept there.

Apr 30. We went to Duxbury Brook, had very good sport. Returned to the General's & dined there. ' Set out from the General's, Reached Hall's & then for Cushing's.

May 1. Set out for home. Stopt at Brackets, got home ab° ten of Clock

May 4. Met the Selectmen & finished the Warrant for Town Meeting.

May 6. I went to the West Church to the Ordination of Mr Simeon Howard. The Revd Mr Perkins of Bridgewater Began with Prayer, The Rev^d Dr Chauncey preached from, 7^h Chap. Acts & 2^d & 3rd verses. The Revd Mr Gay of Hingham pray'd & gave the Charge. The Revd Mr Sam Mather pray'd also & the Revd Mr Appleton of Cambridge gave the Right of Fellowship. Before & after the ceremony there was an anthem sung.

May 8. Town Meeting today for the Choice of Representatives the four old ones were chose.

James Otis Esqr 574 votes.

John Hancock 618   "

Thos Cushing 557   "

Saml Adams 574 votes, myself 134.

The whole number of votes was ab^o 648.

This day arr'd Capt Delano from London, in 27 days passage.

May 11. I set out for Worcester with John Greene, John Nazro & Kennedy. Stopt at Woodburn's & Reached Hows at Marlborough stayed & slept there.

May 12. Rode thro' Marlborough, called at Mrs Speakman's. Reached Martin's at Northborough, breakfasted there, Reached Furnace's, stopt at the bridge & got half a Doz^n Trout. got to Worcester & dined at Colo. Chandler's. Met Gen. Ruggles there, examined the Commissioner's Return on Isaac Thomas' Estate. did my Business. Drank tea with Mrs Chandler & Miss Dolly Chandler, spent the even'g & slept there.

May 13. Finished what I had to do, set out with Mr John Greene for home. called at Worcester Bridge, caught one Trout & half a Dozen perch. went forward and stopt at a Brook two miles this side of Shrewsbury. caught ten Trout. Reached Mrs Speakman's at Marlborough dined there. P^d Mrs Barnes a visit, drank Tea there. Set out from thence & got to Westown. Spent the eve'ng at Major Goldthwaits & slept there.

15 May. Mr Higgins carried off Polly yesterday from the Coffee House.

May 17. Sunday. After church there was a Collection for the Sufferers by the late fire. Mr Walter behaved extremely clever on this Occasion

& urged his Congregation to their usual Benevolence.

18 May. This day Mr Inman set out with James
Smith & wife & other company for Sherburne &
Marlborough.

May 23. About Ten of Clock I went with M^r
Timothy Fitch to Medford & paid a visit to the
Revd Mr Turrell & agreed with him for his piece of
Land by my old house for four hundred dollars.
Afterwards dined at Mr Benjn Hall's at Medford.
Wee set out after dinner for Spot Pond & fished
there. We had but poor Sport. Wee caught ab^o
4 dozen of small perch, a few pickerel & three
Eylls.

May 25. I went with the Selectmen to view the
pavement by the fortification. Spent the afternoon
at the Selectmen's room, being Draught Day.

May 26. Went with Deacon Sewall & Dea. Phillips about paving the Road by the Fortification.

May 27. Election Day. I waited on the Governor & Council to the Town House, afterwards I
went with Mr Thos Brattle to Capt Kendricks &
dined there. When I came home I found the following Gentlemen were Chosen Councillors — first 18

Saml Danforth Esqrs	Thos Flucker
Isaac Royal	James Rufsell
John Irving Senr	Nath. Ropes
Wm Brattle	Tim^o Paine
James Boudoin	Royal Tyler
Thos. Hubbard	And. Belcher
Harrison Gray	Jno Chandler

James Pitts   Thos Saunders
Jos Gerrish   Jn° Worthington
   For the Late Colony of Plymouth
Gamaliel Bradford   Saml White
James Otis Senr   Jerahmiel Bowers
   For the Late Province of the Main
John Hill, Nath. Sparhawk & John Bradbury Esqs.
   For Sagadohock — Jeremiah Powell Esq.
            At Large.
    Benjamin Lincoln, Sam Dexter Esqrs.

May 28.   The Govern^r negatived five Councillors
this morning The Honble James Otis, Joseph Gerrish, Thos. Saunders Jeramiel Bowers & Saml Dexter Esqrs.

29 May.   Capt Hunter arriv'd from London in
37 Days Passage

May 30.   Dined at the Club at Mr Williams by
Pierpoint's Mills with Peter Johannot, Major Jn°
Vassall Mr John Timmins, Mr Forrest, George Brinley, Thos Brattle, Dr Wm Lee Perkins, Thos Apthorp Mr Spencer & Mr Dalrymple an officer Spent
an hour fishing with Dr Calef & Mr Brattle on
Jamaica Pond

June 1.   Artillery Election.   Dined at Fanewill
Hall by invitation with the Company of Artillery,
Governour & Council &c & heard the Revd Mr Shute
of Hingham preach a sermon to them from the 9th
Chap. Ecclesiastes & 18th verse, this was a sensible Discourse.   After dinner Mr Amiel & I set
out & Reached in the eve'ng Mr Makintosh's Tavern at Needham.   Wee were soon joyned by Capt

Jacobson, Mr Sam Calef & Mr Thos Apthorp. wee spent the evening very cheerfully together & slept there.

June 2. I rose very early this morning & Routed up my companions & set out for Bullard's pond at Natick, where went a fishing, had extraordinary Sport. We did not weigh the fish, I guess wee caught about Eighty weight. I caught 25¾ lbs weighed at Kendrick's. We came back & dined at Kendricks with Old Mad^m Apthorp Major Byard & Lady Mr Amiel & Wife Mr Inman & Mrs Rowe Mr Spence & Miss Sally Sheaffe Capt Jacobson Sam Calef, Mr Thos Apthorp, Mr Robt Apthorp, Geo Inman & Jack Wheelwright. Wee were very merry

3 June. Capt Oman sailed for London this afternoon. Spent two hours at Mr Sam Hughes on an Arbitration between Capt Glover of Marblehead and the Underwriters at the North Office. The Arbitrators were Foster Hutchinson Nat Bethune Isaac Smith, Sam Hughes & myself afterwards I went to the Funeral of Capt Ruddocks Wife.

June 4. High Training Day. Dined at Fanewill Hall by invitation from Ye Commissioned Officers with the Govr Council etc. Spent the evening at the Hall in part & the remainder at home.

June 5. Very hot. The House examined into Bottle Brown's affair ab^o drinking in the Common with Mean Company etc. Spent the afternoon & evening at the Selectmens Chamber in Distributing money to the Suffers

6 June. Still very hot. I went to Monotomy

with Sam¹ Calef & din'd at Newalls there, with him
& Andrew Hall, after dinner wee went a fishing &
Caught ab° 4 dozen of middling Perch. This evening it Lightened & thundered & Rained extream
hard. I hardly ever saw a severer storm.

8 June. About twelve of Clock I went with
Capt Duncan Ingram to Cambridge & din'd with
him at Eben' Braddocks after dinner I went to
Judge Danforths on Business & found him gone
to Boston. Called on Henry Vafsall & M' Trollet,
spent an hour with them & then Capt Ingram & I
went to Freshpond a fishing, had good Sport —
came to Town & spent the eve'ng at the Pofse

June 9. this forenoon met M' Nath¹ Bethune,
M' Foster Hutchinson M' Isaac Smith & M' Sam¹
Hughes on the arbi. between Capt Glover of Marble-
head & the Insurers of the North Office. Lent
Major Jos Goldthwait Twelve pounds and sent it
pr his servant Aaron Richards.

11 June. Last evening Gov' Wentworth arriv'd
here from the Southward. I din'd at M' Greatons
on Turtle with (twenty-eight other gentlemen)

June 13. Rose very early this morning for Natick Pond. On my way there the Horse took
fright & run against a Rock which overset the
Chaise — thank God I got no harm only broke my
fishing Cane.

June 15. Capt Brow in Capt Dashwood's Brigg
sailed yesterday for St Christopher

June 16. Dined at home with Capt Hunter,
Major Jos. Goldthwaite, M'ˢ Rowe & Suckey on

Greenpeas out of our own Garden — in the afternoon Wm Speakman & I went to Jamaica Pond a fishing, had poor Sport.

June 17.   Convention Day with the Episcopal Clergy.   I went to church this morning, Mr Troutbeck read prayers & Mr Gilchrist of Salem preached. There were present the following Clergymen — Dr Canes, Mr Troutbeck, Mr Greaton & Mr Walter of Boston — Mr Thompson of Scituate, Mr Winslow of Braintree, Mr Lyon of Taunton, Mr Usher of Bristol Mr Graves of Providence, Mr Graves of New London, Mr Fairweather of Narragansett, Mr Weeks of Marblehead, Mr Bayley of Kennebeck, Mr Wiswall of Casco & Mr Gilchrist of Salem who preached 'twas a Sensible Sermon.

18 June.   Rose very early & bought a Quantity of Timber for my Wharff of Mr Howard

June 24.   Dined at Mr Greatons with forty three Brethren   I presided.   The Right Worshipful Bro. Gridley being sick.

28th June.   Very Dry Weather, the Countrymen complain for want of Rain.   It has blown very hard all Day at the So East but no Rain.

30 June.   A little Rain in the night but Continues very Dry — in the afternoon it began to Rain & it pleas'd God to give it us in good time.   Capt Lyde arriv'd from London.

July 1.   This day we visited the Charity Schools & dined at Fanewil Hall, the Selectmen, the Overseers of the Poor, Mr Secretary Oliver, Mr Treasurer Gray &c others, it was a Genteel Dinner — ab^o Six

of Clock Mrs Rowe & I went to Cambridge & spent
the Evening at Mr Inman's.

July 3. When I came to the store I found it
broke open I lost 4 ps English Taffatyes — 2 doz^n
Silk Stockings ½ ps India Taffaty 1 ps Spanish
Silk, some Ribbons & other things not known yet.
Have been Busy all Day in searching for my Goods
but to no purpose.

6 July. Set out for Worcester. Stopt at Major
Goldthwait's he went with me, wee din'd at M^{rs}
Speakman's at Marlborough. Set out after Dinner,
Mr Wm J. Thompson Joyn'd us at Colo Williams.
Wee Reached Mr Furnaces at Shrewsbury. Wee
caught a Good mefs of Perch supped & slept there

7 July. Caught another mefs of Fish, got to
Worcester at ten of Clock, held the Vendue at
Twelve at Mr Sterns — din'd there with General
Ruggles, Mr Blake Major Thompson, Major Gold-
thwaite & Mr John Nazro the afternoon wee ad-
justed several acc^{ts}

8 July. Set out for home with Major Goldthwait. Wee stopt at Shrewsbury Pond, caught
a Mefs of Perch & din'd at Mr Barnes at Marlborough. Set out for Sudbury fish'd there, had
good sport, came to Major Goldthwaitt at Weston
& slept there.

9 July. Rose very early & got home to Breakfast, found All Well.

15 July. Commencement Day. I went to Cambridge, stopt at Mr Inman's & din'd at Mr Smith's
Farm at Watertown (with a company of thirty

five which included) "Two Madame Belchers M^r
Jas Murray & wife & Miss Dolly Murray, Mr Inman
& Mrs Rowe"

July 21.   A most Delightful Rainy morning.
God is very gracious to his People in this Dry time
& all the People ought to praise His Holy Name.

July 22. The Rain yesterday fell 5 1-2 Inches as
measured in our cistern. Mr Powells vessel arr'd
from Madeira with 70 pipes Wine.

July 23.   Attended Court on Davis & Stetson's
affairs. The Court would not receive Stetson's
affadavit & Davis got his cause.

24 July.   Went with Mr Tim^o Fitch to Flax pond,
had very Great Sport, caught upwards of Twenty
doz^n din'd there with Mr John Erving Capt Solomon
Davis, Capt Duncan Ingraham, Mr Jno Brown, M^r
Timothy Fitch, Capt Jacobson & Mr Saml Calef, wee
spent the afternoon very merry & Mr Calef & I$^.$
went to Marblehead where I met Jerry Lee & Capt
Copmer on Businefs, when done wee spent the
evening at Mr Reeds & slept there

26 July.   After church I went & paid a visit to
Old Mr Gould who is very Ill of the Gout in his
Stomach. Capt Cummings in my Brigg^a Nancy
arr'd from Liverpool this day.

July 28.   This afternoon the Creditors of Eben^r
Stetson met & voted Mr John Boylston & me to go
to Dighton.

Aug 1.   We went to Punkapong Pond & fished
there   caught 26 Dozen of Pond Perch before
ten of Clock. (2 gentlemen, Mr John Boylston &

himself) John Boylston is a Good Companion but very Fretful & Uneasy in his make. I should be very Glad to accompany him at any Time on a party of fishing, especially when the fish Bite fast.

5 Aug. Mrs Rowe's Birth Day & forty two years old this day.

12 Aug. While wee were sitting a Great Rogue who calls himself Michael Hendly was brought before the Justices, for Breaking open a shop & was admitted to Goal.

Aug 12. Yesterday there was a high Company at a launching at Weymouth of Clem^t Jackson's. near eighty gentlemen went from Boston. Spent the afternoon with the Justices of the Sessions & Select Men on the affair of the Family of the Tyler's Petition. the Select Men also set upon Licenses

Aug. 14. This day the Colours were displayed on the Tree of Liberty & ab° Sixty People Sons of Liberty met at One of Clock & drank the King's Health.

Aug. 17. After dinner wee went in quest of thieves & took up one Davidson a Peddler & Morris Morrous. found one p^r Silk Stockings & one small Bit of English Taffaty. Mr Wells committed them to Bridewell

Aug 18. Dined at Brush Hill with James Smith & wife, Mr Murray & wife, Mr Amiel & Miss Crissy, Mr Inman & Miss Polly Hooper, Mr Powell & Jacky Day — Mrs Rowe & Dolly Murray, Mr Burgoin & lady was to have been there but they overset their Carriage & bruised themselves much which hindered them.

Aug 19.   Took up three thieves this forenoon, Lawrence & Mary M⁶Guire & Patrick Marra & sent them to Goal.

Aug 22.   Spent the afternoon at the Warehouse & at Clark's Wharf.   Mʳ Hancock's Union Flag was hoisted for the first time.

23 Aug.   The Revᵈ Mʳ Sargeants son died this day.   Mʳ Wᵐ Gould sailed.

Aug. 27.   This afternoon the Grand Lodge met on the affair of the Concert Room.   Capᵗ Geneste sailed for Bellisle.   Capᵗ Brass arriv'd from Bristol.

Aug. 29.   I went with Wᵐ Speakman to Kendrick's.   after dinner wee went fishing.   coming home wee saw a Kite attack a full grown Duck.   he struck his Tallons into her side which would have killed her, but did not carry her off being Pursued by the people.   Capᵗ Robson sailed for London this day, in whom Mʳ Sears & Colo. Jarvis went paſsengers.

Sept. 1.   This afternoon James Smith was try'd & found Guilty of Stealing my Goods.

Sept. 2.   A Negro Fellow belonging to the Town of Newton was try'd for killing a man.   The Jury Brought in their Verdict not Guilty.

Sept. 4.   Dined at home on Turtogue with Mʳ Edw. Winslow of Plymouth, Mʳ Zephaniah Leaned of Rainham, Mʳ Ebenʳ Stedson of Dighton, Mʳ Trollet, Capᵗ Solo. Davis, Mʳˢ Rowe & Sucky Spent the eve'ng at the Grand Lodge with the

Master Wardens of the three Regular Lodges.   I
attended the Funeral of M͏ʳ Peleg Wiswall.

Sept. 11.   Last night at eleven of Clock departed
this Life Jerry Gridley Esq͏ʳ Grand Master of
Masons & King's Attorney.   The Brethren met together this afternoon to consult about the Funeral
procession of our Brother Gridley tomorrow.   Several votes were past which will be Recorded in the
Grand Lodge Book.

Sept. 12.   In the afternoon I attended the Funeral of our Right Worshipful Jerry Gridley Esq,
Grand Master, as Deputy Grand Master.   The officers of his Regiment marched in order first.   then
the Brethren of St. Andrew's Lodge.   then the
Stewards of the Grand Lodge.   then the Brethren
promiscuously two by two.   then the Wardens of
the Second Lodges.   then the Wardens of the first
Lodges.   then the Wardens of the Master's Lodge.
then the three Masters of the three several Lodges.
then the past Grand Officers & the Treasurer.   then
the Grand Wardens.   then myself as Deputy Grand
Master.   then the Tyler with the Grand Master's
Jewels on a Black Velvet Cushion.   The Corps
the Bearers were the Lieut. Governour, Judge Trowbridge, Justice Hubbard, John Erving Sen͏ʳ, James
Otis and M͏ʳ Sam͏ˡ Fitch.   then followed the Relations.   after them the Lawyers in their Robes.
then the Gentlemen of the Town & then a great
many Coaches, Chariots & Chaises.   Such a multitude of Spectators I never saw at anything before
since I have been in New England.   After his Body

was interred wee Returned in Form to the Town
house (from whence his Corps was taken at the Beginning of the Procession) in the same order as wee
first walked. I do not much approve of such
parade & show but as it was his Relatives desire, I
could not well avoid giving my Consent. I think
the Number of the Brethren that attended was 161.
upon the whole it was as well Conducted & in as
Good Order as the Nature of it would admit.

Sept. 15. Spent the evening at Blodget's in seeing Hinds the Balance Master perform — he is but a
clumsey Hand. Mr Inman Mrs Rowe & Sucky was
there.

18 Sept. Mr Amiel & Gardner set out in quest
of Powell this morning

Sept 24. The Sun passed the Equinox about
twelve of Clock last night. We had a very severe
Storm, it blew as hard as I ever heard it, accompanied with Thunder Lighting & very heavy Rain.
Mr Walter & wife had like to have been drowned
at Peck's Wharf   Capt Skinner arr'd from Bristol.
Mr Inman set out for Connecticut

Sept 27. Afternoon I went to Church. Mr Wal-
ter Read prayers & preached from 103rd Psalm &
19th Verse. This was a very Pathetick & Good
Discourse & very Appropriate to Mr Walter's late
Misfortune — in which wee all Rejoyce for God's
Remarkable Deliverance of him & wife.

Oct 1. Set out with Capt Ashborne for Salem.
Stopt at Flax Pond. I caught two dozen of fine
large Perch & three Pickerell. Dined at Salem at

Mr Goodhews   after dinner I paid a visit to several
of my old Acquaintances & Friends.   Mr Sam Barton, Mr Douse, Mrs Epps & Spent the evening at
Colo. Pickman's.   Slept at Goodhews.   a good Tavern & good Lodging.

Oct. 2.   Went to Mr West's Fish Fence.   Bought
his Fish, did some other Business — in my way home
stopt at Flax Pond & fished there.   Left my Fishing Rod & Leather Dram Bottle there.

Oct 5.   I waited on the Select men this forenoon
about calling a Town-meeting.   Wee agreed on
Fryday

Oct 7.   Dined at home with Stephen Hufsey,
Abijah Folger jr Richard Coffin, Isaac Paddock.
all four from Nantucket.   Capt Robert Jarvis, Capt
Saml Dashwood & Mrs Rowe Spent part of the even-
ing at the Coffee House with Treas. Gray, Thos
Gray & John Boylston & the remainder at Turner's
Ball in seeing the young Ladies Dance.

Oct 12.   About eight of Clock we were alarmed
by the cry of Fire which proved to be Edes Bake-
house at the North End.   the wind was very high
but by the Providence of God we soon got the better of it.   Capt Hohne arriv'd from London.

13 Oct.   Rose very early   Mr Walter called on
mee to go to Kendricks — but on Consultation wee
thought the weather too Cold & therefore adjourn'd
until Thursday.   Capt Copmer sail'd this day ab^o
one of Clock for Biddeford.

15 Oct.   Capt Davis & Capt Davison both from
London arriv'd this afternoon.

16 Oct. Capt Wood in a Large Ship from St
Christophers arriv'd consign'd to mee. Capt Hall
arrivd from London in 45 Days.

17 Oct. Capt Calef arrivd from London.

18 Oct. Capt Scot arriv'd this day from London.

23 Oct. Breakfasted with Capt Wood at home.
Wee set out for Richards wee fished at Dedham
Caufsway had good Sport come back to Richards
& din'd with the Revd Mr Townsend of Medway, Capt Woods & Wm Speakman. Capt Ashburn saild to Day.

27 Oct. Arriv'd the Captains Freeman & Smith
from London. Spent the afternoon at the Coffee
House with the Proprietors of Point Shirley—James
Pitts Ezek^l Goldthwait, John Hancock & Nathaniel
Holmes

28 Oct. It has blown a very heavy Storm all
Night & continued. Town Meeting this forenoon
which I attended. in the afternoon Town Meeting,
again I attended.

Oct. 29. In the afternoon attended the Town's
Committee at Fanewill Hall. Present, myself, M^r
Thos Cushing, Melabiah Bourn, Saml Austin, Hen-
derson Inches, Jonathan Williams, Edwd Payne,
John Ruddock, Joshua Henshaw & Solo. Davis.
We could not agree & therefore adjourned until to-
morrow, three of Clock.

Oct: 30. Met the Selectmen this Forenoon. In
the afternoon the Committee met by Adjournment.
Present, myself, Thos. Cushing, Melabiah Bourn,
Saml Austin, Henderson Inches, Jonathan Williams,

Edwd Payne, John Ruddock, Joshua Henshaw, Solo. Davis, Wm Greenleaf & Edm^d Quincy tertius. We agreed to divide ourselves into six Classes & to get what subscriptions we can. Mr Bourn and mee for the 9th & 10th Wards.

Oct. 31. After dinner I went over to the Governor's to get Jarvis's pass signed.

Nov. 2. Bad news from the back of the Cape. Several vessels on Shore. Green & Boylston's Brigg^a Mr Nat. Holmes' Brigg^a Mr Tuthill Hubbard's Brigg, Capt Prince's Sloop, a Connecticut Sloop & a great many others. Dind at Bullards on Turtle with (nineteen other gentlemen).

3rd Nov. Mr Robt Apthorp sailed for Jamaica this day as did Capt Scot for London.

4th Nov. Spent the afternoon with the Selectmen. Capt Watts arriv'd from London in whom several Gentlemen Pafsengers, Robt Temple, Charles Paxton, Mr Hollen & Twenty more names unknown to me, except Mr Birch, Mr Williams, Mr Porter.

5 Nov. A wet Rainy Day. Pope weather! Spent the afternoon at the Select men's Room & the evening at Colo. Ingersolls with Mr Robt Jenkins & Mr Daniel Hubbard, Gent^n of the Charitable Society.

6 Nov. Capt Jarvis saild for London & Capt Scot & Mr Nat Rogers. Spent the afternoon at the Selectmens Room.

7 Nov. This afternoon Capt Marshall arri'd at the pest house from London having the Small Pox on board. The Select men met & gave Hartly his Instructions.

9 Nov.   Met the Select men this Forenoon with Capt Marshall.

11 Nov.   The Superior Court set yesterday & too Day.   Spent the forenoon & afternoon with the Select men.   All Present & the Town Clerk.

12 Nov.   Mr Blake from Hardwick paid me a visit.   Din'd at Colo. Ingersolls on Venison with (thirteen other gentlemen) got myself pretty mellow & came home & went to Bed.

Nov. 15.   Mr Walter's child was Christened & named Lynde the Sponsors Stephen Greenleaf, Jona Simpson & wife.

Nov. 16.   This is my Birthday Old Style & am now 52 years old the 27th Current.   Attended the Superior Court all day on Eben^r Stedsons affairs & spent the eve'ng at the Coffee House with the Proprietors of Point Shirley — James Pitts John Hancock, Ezek^l Golthwait & Nat Holmes.

Nov. 20.   Attended the Trial of Thieves & the Town Meeting which was conducted with Great Propriety & Moderation.   Capt Blake arrived this afternoon which saved the Freighters above three hundred pounds Lawful money — this being the Time fixed to pay the Duties on Glass, Painter's Colour's &c.   An Imposition on America in my Opinion as Dangerous as the Stamp Act.

Dec. 3.   Thanksgiving Day.   I went to Church this morning.   Mr Walter read prayers & preached from the 97th Psalm & the 1st Verse.   This was a Clever Discourse & much approved.   Spent part of the evening at Colo. Ingersoll's with the Charitable Society & the remainder at Capt Solomon Davis'.

Dec. 4. Spent the afternoon with the Committee for giving Instructions to the Representatives, Richd Dana Esq Mr Edwd Payne, Dr Church, Henderson Inches & Ezek^l Price.

Dec. 6. I went to Church both Forenoon & Afternoon. Mr Walter read prayers & preached both Sermons from the 119th Psalm & 160th verse. Both these Sermons were Metaphysical but well pickt & adapted to the present Season.

Dec. 11. The Halifax Packet arr'd & Brought News of the Duke of York's Death.

13 Dec. The York Papers Brought acc^{ts} of Colo Scots Death, Sir John Sinclairs & Dr Grants Ladys.

14 Dec. Begins to snow & a great Storm. Din'd on board the Thames Capt Watts with (fourteen gentlemen).

15 Dec. This afternoon I attended the Funeral of Old Madame Otis.

17 Dec. Spent the afternoon with the Committee of Instructions   present Richd Dana, myself, Mr Payne, Mr Henderson Inches, Mr Ezek^l Price.

19 Dec. Snows fast again. After Dinner I went in the Sleigh over to Gardners & spent an hour with John Erving Joseph Scot, Mr Amiel, Solo Davis & Tho Brattle   Brought them home.

Dec. 21. Extreme cold. The Harbour froze in as far as the Castle. This Day the shortest in the year.

Dec. 22. Snows very fast. Town meeting this forenoon — adjourned till three in the afternoon. Town meeting this afternoon. The town received Our Report.

Dec. 25.   Christmas Day — very cold.   I went to church this forenoon.   Mr Walter read prayers & preached a very clever sermon from 2^d Chap. St Luke & 32^d verse.   I applaud Mr Walter's Behaviour very much.

Dec. 30.   Mr Barnes of Marlborough Breakfasted at our House with Mrs Speakman.   Dined at Colonel Ingersolls with the Free Mason's at the Celebration of St John.   Present (49 Brethren)   The General Court begins their Sessions this Day.

Dec. 31.   Spent the eve'ng at Mrs Cordis's where the Club had their Annual Supper.   Present — Treas. Gray, Thos. Gray, Wm Mollineux, John Erving, Solomon Davis, Nich^o Boylston, Ezekiel Golthwait, John Dennie, James Warden, Melabiah Bourn James Perkins & James Otis.

1768

Jan. 1   New Years Day.   Still very cold.

Jan. 5.   The Inferior Court set to Day.   Spent part of the eve'ng at the Coffee House & the remainder at Joseph Harrison's Esq with him, Mrs Harrison, Miss Betty, Mr Richard Harrison, Mr Inman & Mr Mills of Newhaven who entertained us most agreeably on his Violin.   I think he plays the best of any Performer I ever heard.

Jan. 13.   Town Meeting this forenoon to receive the Report of the Manufactory Committee.   In the afternoon I went to the Funeral of Mrs Rufus Greene & was one of the Bearers with Stephen

Greenleaf, James Hill, Colo. John Chandler, Mr Jonathan Simpson & Mr Wm Coffin Senr. Mrs. Rowe went to Assembly tonight.

Jan. 20.   Capt Blake sailed for Jamaica this forenoon in whom I sent my Negro Boy Cato.

Jan. 21.   About eight of Clock wee were alarm'd by the Cry of Fire which prov'd to be Mr Valleys Shop.   Wee soon got the better of it.

Jan. 26.   A famous Tryal before the Court of Sessions this day against Mrs Kneeland for stealing a Silver Spoon from Dr. Baker; it continued all Day.   The Jury brought in their Verdict, not Guilty.

Jan. 27.   Spent the evening at the Assembly. There were 27 Couple that drew.

Feb'ry 2.   This morning Miss Polly Hooper was married in Trinity Church to Mr John Russell Spence by the Revd Mr Walter.   A great concourse of People attended on the Occasion.   Dined at Mrs Hooper's with her, the new Bridegroom & Bride, Mr Thos Apthorp, Mr Robt Hallowell, Miss Nancy Boutineau, Miss Dolly Murray, Bridemen & Bridemaids, Mr Murray, Mrs Murray, Mr Stephen Greenleaf, Mrs Greenleaf, the Revd Mr Walter, Major Byard, Mrs Bayard, Mrs Rowe, Mr Thos Hooper, Mr John Hooper, Mrs Eustis Nat^h Apthorp.   In the afternoon wee were joyned by Mr Inman, Miss Suky, John Apthorp Esq & lady, Dr Bulfinch & lady, Mr Amiel, Mr John Erving & lady.   Wee all Drank Tea, spent the evening there, had a Dance, wee were merry & spent the whole day very clever & agreeable.

Feb'ry 9. Spent the forenoon at the Court House hearing the Debates before the Govr & Council & House of Representatives on the Land Bank Scheme.

Feb'ry 10. Spent the eve'ng at the Assembly which was a very Brilliant One. The Governour & lady, all the Commissioners, Mr Harrison & too many to enumerate were there. I rec^d letters pr post giving an acc^t of Geneste's arrival at Newport Rhode Island.

Feb'ry 11. Spent the evening at the Coffee House & a Disagreeable evening it was. The Topick of the Discourse was about the Seizure made by Capt Folger & the reseizure of it afterwards by Capt Hallowell. Mr Mollineux in his representation & talk used the Surveyor General Mr Temple most Cruelly and Barbarously; he abused the Character of said Gentleman most shamefully & said that if Mr Folger made any seizures or held this, that it would not be of any benefit to him, upon which one of the Company asked Mr Mollineux, who then would receive the benefit of Mr Folger's part as Informer & he replied " Why, are you at a Loss — Why, Mr Temple, the Surveyor General, & further said that there was an agreement between the Surveyor General & Folger. Intimating that the Surveyor General gave Folger his Place with a view to get money by it & swore he believed it. Mr Mollineux was asked by Mr John Erving " Surely you cannot believe the Surveyor General guilty of so Base a Design & you have behaved very Ill in

making the company think so " — his Reply was
severall Times " I do Believe it." Upon which M^r
Erving & Mollineux had some smart speeches with
each other. Some of the company were very uneasy
at these Doings, & mentioned the Commission that
Folger had Received from the Surveyor General to
be Doubtfull & not Authentic enough to make
seizures. Upon which Mr Otis said the Commission
he thought, was very Good, but that there was one
Expression in it that some People Hesitated about
& Repeated the Sentence in the Commission which
Runs thus — and in my Behalf to seize for his
Majesty's Use — Upon repeating of this Sentence
Mr Mollineux " Now Gentlemen, you see that I am
Right in what I said," & seemed to lay great Stress
upon these words — in my Behalf — signifying that
whatever seizures were made by Folger, he, the said
Folger, was not to have the profit arising from such
seizures but the Surveyor General & that the Sur-
veyor General gave him his Commission on these
terms. I mentioned in the Course of this talk, that
I had many times been in Mr Mollineux' company
but never heard him guilty of so great an. Indiscre-
tion before — Present — Solo. Davis, John Erving,
Geo. Bethune, James Otis, Wm Mollineux, Thos
Gray, James Warden & myself.

Feb'ry. 12. Spent the eve'ng at Mrs Cordis'.
Mr Mollineux was there & renew'd his Discourse as
on the last evening but soon went away.

15 Feb. The late Surveyor General Mr Fenton
P^d Mr Wm Mollineaux a Visit ab° Two of Clock.

17 Feb.   I forgot to mention the meeting of the Justices, Select men & Overseers of the Poor yesterday at Fanewill Hall to fix on a Day for a General Visitation of the Town & they fixd on Fryday. Dind at Major John Vafsalls at Cambridge.   I paid a visit to Colo. Henry Vafsall & Family where I found Dr Russell who was married to Miss Betty on Monday Last.

19 Feb.   Spent part of the Afternoon at the Funerall of Mr John Scolly's son who was most unfortunately Drown'd.

23 Feb.   Mr Inman came home this morning (from Connecticut) Capt Lewis Geneste arriv'd from Liverpool & Capt Blythe from Bristol.   Spent the evening at Normandy.

26 Feb.   Attended the Select men this Forenoon ab° a Brigg^a from Bristol Capt Sargeant having had Small Pox.

Feb'ry. 29.   Attended the Court of Admiralty this forenoon.   Mr Folger's cause was put off until Friday.

Mar. 1.   Spent the eve'ng at the Merchant's Meeting.   Wm Phillips Esq was chose Moderator. There were 98 merchts present.   they voted, that it is the Opinion of this Company that every Legal Measure for freeing the Country from the present Embarrassments should be adopted & among, the stopping the Importation of Goods from Great Britain under Certain Limitations — then Chose a Committee of nine to fix and Report to this Company on adjournment, the best measures for carrying in

execution the foregoing vote.   The following Gen-
tlemen were Chose — myself, Wm Phillips Esq. John
Hancock Esq, Arnold Wells Esq, Mr Edwd Payne,
Mr Thos Boylston John Erving jun^r, Melabiah
Bourn, Henderson Inches, it was also voted that
John Hancock Esq be desired to procure a Copy
of the Commissions of the Commissioners of the
Customs & produce the same at the next meeting —
then the meeting was adjourned until Fryday eve-
ning.

Mar. 2.   I went with the Selectmen to view the
new Engine No 6. built by Dav^d Wheeler & approved of it, it being a good one.

Mar. 3.   Spent the Forenoon with the Committee
of Merchants.   Spent the afternoon & part of the
eve'ng with the Committee of Merchants, & part
with the Charitable Society at Colo. Ingersoll's.

Mar. 4.   This day the Govr Prorogued the Assembly to the 13 April   Spent the day with the
same Committee of Merchants & in the evening wee
reported to them as follows :

The Committee of Merchants appointed at their
meeting March 1^rst 1768, having duly considered
what they had in charge, do Report the following
Resolutions viz

In consideration of the Great Scarcity of money
which for several years has been so Sensibly felt
among us & now must be Rendered much Greater
not only by the immense Sums absorbed in the Collection of the Duties lately Imposed but by the
great checks given thereby to Branches of Trades

which yeilded us the most of our money & means
of Remittance,— In consideration also of the great
Debt now standing against us, which if we go on
Increasing by the excessive Import we have been
accustomed to while our Scources of Remittance are
daily drying up, must terminate not only in Our
Own & Our Country's Ruin but that of many of
our Creditors on the other side of the Water —

In consideration farther of the Danger from some
Late Measures of our losing many Inestimable
Blessings & advantages of the British Constitution
which Constitution we have ever Rever'd as the
Basis & Security of all we enjoy in this Life, there-
fore Voted

1^{rst} That we will not for one Year send for any
European Commodities excepting Salt, Coals, Fish-
ing Lines, Fish Hooks, Hemp, Duck, Bar Lead, Shot,
Wool Cards & Card Wire &c & that the trading
towns in the province & other provinces in New
England together with those in New York, New
Jersey & Pennsylvania be Invited to accede
hereto —

2nd That we will encourage the Produce & manufactures of these colonies by the use of them in
Preference to all other manufactures —

3rd That in the Purchase of Such Articles as we
shall stand in need of, we will give a Constant Preference to such Persons as shall subscribe to these
Resolutions —

4th That we will in our Separate Capacitys inform
our several Correspondents of the Reasons & point

out to them the necessity of witholding our usual
Orders for their Manufactures — the said Impedi-
ment may be removed & Trade & Commerce may
again flourish —

5th That these Votes or Resolutions be Obliga-
tory or binding on us from & after the time that
these or other Singular or tending to the same Salu-
tary Purpose be adopted by most of the Trading
Towns in this & the neighboring Colonies —

6th That a Committee be appointed to Correspond with merchants in the before mentioned
Towns & Provinces & forward to them the foregoing Votes, & that s[d] Committee be Impowered to
call a meeting of the merchants when they think
necessary —

Mar. 9. Spent the afternoon at the Selectmen's
Room & the evening at the Merchants Meeting at
the Coffee House. The same Committee was chosen
again & the Company voted some further Resolutions —

Mar. 10. Spent the afternoon with the Selectmen. We paid a visit to one Mary Phillips who
was born Deaf & Dumb & has remained so ever
since & is now upwards of 80 years of age. M[r]
Fessenden Brought my Colt yesterday from Rutland.

Mar. 11. Spent the whole day with the Merch[ts]
Committee myself, John Hancock, Arnold Wells,
Tho[s] Boylston, Henderson Inches, Edw[d] Payne, W[m]
Phillips & Melabiah Bourn. This Day Cap[t] Bin-
ney arr'd & Brought an acc[t] of the Death of M[rs]
Scot at Dominico.

13 March.   After Church I paid a visit to M^r
James Smith who I found very weak & low, also to
Old Mr Gould who is also very Ill and full of Pain
with the Gout.

Mar. 14.   Spent this Day at the Annual Town
Meeting for the Choice of Officers — the Select men
the same as last year.

Mar. 15.   In the afternoon met the Selectmen at
Fanewill Hall to swear in ye Officers.

Mar. 18.   The Anniversary of the Repeal of the
Stamp Act.   Dined at Colo. Ingersoll's with Treas.
Gray, Harrison Gray jun^r, Henry Green, John
Timmins, Solo. Davis, Ralph Inman, Joseph Scot,
Thos Brattle, Thos Apthorp, Joshua Blanchard,
John Spence, Geo Erving, Gregory Townsend, James
Forrest & Robt Hallowel — wee had a Genteel Din-
ner & Entertainment.   After dinner the following
Toasts were drank.   1. The King — 2. The Queen
& Royal Family — 3 The Earl of Chatham — 4.
Lord Chancellor — 5 Genl Conway — 6. Marquis
of Rockingham — 7 Duke of Grafton — 8 Genl
Howard — 9 Con^l Barry — 10 Sir Wm Meredith —
11 The Extension of Trades & Commerce — 12
The United & Inseparable Interest of G^t Britain &
her Colonies — 13 Prosperity to the Province — 14
May the 18th Day of March 1766, the Day the
Stamp Act was repealed be ever had in Memory of
all True Briton & Americans — 15 Prosperity to
All Sons of Liberty — 16 Prosperity to the Town of
Boston — After these the Company were very cheer-
ful & Gay & broke up about Eight of Clock — A

considerable Mob of young fellows & negroes got
together this Evening & made great Noise & Hallooing, ab° Eight hundred appeared in King St &
at Liberty Tree & went to the North End to John
Williams the Inspector General, but did him no
Damage — which the greatest part of the Gentlemen in Town were very glad of. There were two
Effigies on Liberty Tree this morning marked C. P
& J. W. but were taken down again by Wm Speakman, Thos Crafts & John Avery Junr.

Mar 20. Very stormy, I dont remember to have
heard it blow harder than this morning — snows
very fast — very high tides, much damage done
among the Shipping & Wharfs —

Mar 21. I spent the forenoon at the Court House
to hear the Tryal between Capt Folger & Capt Hallowell about the Seizure of Tea & after the whole
morning debates it was adjourned until next Saturday morning Spent part of the afternoon with the
Towns Committee to draw a Letter of Thanks to
the Farmer for his Ingenious Letters —

Mar 22. Attended the Town Meeting all the
Day, in which many Debates about Mr Adams whose
Friends were so warm in his favor that the Gentlemen could not get a Reconsideration of the vote
passed on Monday last —

Mar. 23. As soon as I got abroad I heard very
bad news about Mr Spence — whose affairs have
been imprudently Treated by Mr Spooner — In the
afternoon attended the Funeral of the Rev^d M^r
Sam^1 Cheekly jun^r, afterwards with the Select men.

24 March.   Mr Davidson Returned this eve'ng from Scituate after having got Abiel Turner to attach Mr Spence's Sloop for my acc^t

25th.   Have been this forenoon with Mr Spooner on Mr Spence affairs.   this afternoon I attended Mr Spooner again on Mr Spences affairs — am in hopes to get them accommodated.

26 Mar.   Spent the afternoon on Mr Spooner's affairs.   This day the Lawyers plead Mr Folgers Case before the Judge of Admiralty.

27 Mar.   This forenoon I paid Mr Spence a visit. Capt Bromage arriv'd from St Kitts in 24 Days. this vessell was blown off in December last coming from Leith bound here.

30 Mar.   Spent the afternoon at the Selectmens Room & afterwards I met the proprietors of Long Wharf at the Coffee House

Mar 31.   Attended the proprietors of the Long Wharf at the Coffee House — Preasent — Joshua Winslow Esq — chosen Treasurer — Mr Secretary Oliver, Mr John Hancock, Mr James Boutineau, Mr Gillam Phillips Mr Arnold Wells, Capt Benjn Waldo Mr John Powell, Capt Job Prince, Mr Abijah Savage Mr John Savage, Mr John Stevens, Mr Jos. Henderson Mr Saml Hews, The Honble John Eving Esqr We voted that the Stock in the hands of the Wharfinger be laid out in Repairing the wharf & be put into the Hands & under the Direction of a Committee now chose viz. Capt Waldo, Mr Wells, Mr Powell, Capt Dalton & Jno Savage

April 1.   Good Friday.   I went to church this

forenoon. Mr Walter read prayers & preached a
very Pathetick & moving sermon suited to the
Solemnity of this day which was greatly admired
from the 2nd Chap. St Paul's first Epistle to the
Corinthians & 2nd Verse.

April 2. The Town several Times alarmed this
morning by the Cry of Fire. One poor man lost
his Life by falling off a Ladder.

Apr 4. This Forenoon the Wardens, Vestry &
proprietors of the Pews in Trinity Church met
according to their annual Custom to choose Officers
&c for the year ensuing but this day to choose a
a Minister in the room of my Good Friend the
Revd Mr Hooper there were 57 voters & the whole
were in favour of the Revd Mr Wm Walter. They
afterwards voted him a Salary of one hundred
fifty six pounds Ster'g p annum & forty pounds
Ster'g more for his extra services the year past —
they also voted the Widow Hooper fifty pounds
Ster'g this present year.

Apr. 7. The proprietors of Long Wharf met at
the British Coffee House & voted to build a pier
head & added Mr Secretary Oliver & Mr Boutineau
to the former Committee. This day Antony Letchmere signd his Indentures.

Apr. 8. Capt Scot arr'd from London in M^r
Hancock's Brigg^a; out eight weeks. The Select
men visited Mr Proctor's school.

Apr. 10. I went to church both forenoon &
afternoon. Mr Walter read prayers & preached
too very good Discourses on Prayer from the 2nd

Epis. Thessalonians 3rd Chap & 1^{rst} Verse " Pray for us " which sermons were well adapted to him being the first Sunday since he was unanimously chosen our minister & Incumbent.

14 April.   Fast.   I went to Cambridge Church this Forenoon.   Mr Sergeant Read prayed & preached.   Din'd at Mr Inmans with him & George, Sucky & Sally, Mrs Rowe, Mrs Eustis & Mrs Billy Gould.

15 April.   Met Mr Thos. Gray, Mr John Erving & Mr John Low'l at Colo Ingersoll's on the said John Lowell's affairs.

16 April.   After Dinner I took a Ride Round Dorchester.   Colon^l Dalrymple came to Town from New York & several officers.

22 April.   Met the Committee of Merch^{ts} at the Coffee House.   John Hancock, Melabiah Bourne, Arnold Wells, Henderson Inches, Edward Payne, Wm Phillips & adjourned untill Monday.

26 April.   Settled with Capt Lewis Geneste. After Dinner I Set out with Mr Saml Calef for Plymouth, at Gardiner wee met Mr Thos Knights who Joyn'd us.   We stopt at Brackets at Braintree & from there Reachd Cushings at Hingham.   Wee spent the evening & slept there.

27 April.   Reached Dr. Halls Pembrooke, wee Breakfasted there, from thence to Duxbury; fished there & caught upwards five Dozen of fine Trout. wee din'd at Dr Harlows.   Set out & called at Major Bradfords & from thence Reached Plymouth. I spent the evening and slept at Capt White's.

28 Aprill. Did what Business I had to do din'd
at Edwd Winslow Esq with him Mrs Winslow, M^r
Edwd Winslow jun^r Miss Dyer Miss Penny Winslow Mr Calef Mr Knights   Mr Hooker one of the
Inspectors arrivd at Plymouth with Attendance.
About three of Clock wee Returned to Duxbury,
had good Sport, I Caught about a Dozen fine
Trout. Wee went to General Winslows spent the
evening & slept there.

29 Aprill. Mr Pelham Winslow joynd us wee
went a fishing had but poor Luck. Returned to
Generalls & dind there with him Mrs Winslow Miss
Massy Little Miss Polly Little Wm Sever Esq &
Daughter Mr Pelham Winslow Mr Nat Ray Thomas
Mr Knights Mr Calef. After Dinner we set out
from thence, stopt at Fords & at Dr Halls & from
thence to Cushings & slept.

30 Aprill. Wee went to Cushings Brook. M^r
Knights caught the finest Trout I ever saw. After
Dinner set out for home stopt at Brackets paid our
Reckoning £7. 2. 6 Old Ten^r pr man for the
Journey. Stopt at Crampeys & came home and
found all well.

May 2. Met the Merchants at the Town House
in the Representatives Room — agreed to the Resolutions of the City of New York — not to write for
any Goods after the first of June, nor Import any
after the first Day of October, until the Act Impos-
ing Duties on Glass, Paper &c be repealed —

May 4. Town meeting for the choice of Representatives — the following Gentlemen were chosen

by a great majority, the whole number of voters 441.

James Otis	Esq	410
Tho[s] Cushing	"	433
John Hancock	"	432
Sam Adams	"	414

Din'd at M[r] James Otis with him, M[rs] Otis, Sam[l] Adams (and others)

9 May. Spent the afternoon with the Select men, Present Colo Jackson M[r] Ruddock M[r] Sewall M[r] Hancock M[r] Newell M[r] Phillips & myself & the Committee on M[r] W[m] Coopers acc[t] James Pitts Esq[r] Royal Tyler Tho[s] Hubbard Rich[d] Dana & Tho[s] Flucker. M[r] Sewall M[r] Phillips M[r] Newall & myself Resignd.

11 May. I went to Cambridge with M[r] Boutineau & dind at M[r] Inmans with him M[r] Gregory Townsend & M[rs] Townsend M[rs] Hooper M[rs] Rowe & Sally Inman. I went to the Dudleyan Lecture & heard M[r] Barnard of Salem preach a most sensible Discourse. Came home & found Cap[t] Jarvis arr'd from London

12 May. Spent the afternoon at the Select mens Room & the evening at the Merch[ts] Meeting in the Representatives Room.

14 May. Went with Gregory Townsend M[r] Sam[l] Calef & W[m] Speakman to Dedham Cofsway fishing had Good Sport.

18 May. The Romny Man of War Cap[t] Conell arrivd yesterday in Nantasket & this day in Kingroad. M[r] Sam[l] Hughes departed this Life Yesterday

May 23. Attended Town meeting this afternoon,
three of the Select men Resigned. Mr Sewall, M^r
Phillips Mr Newall — three were chose in their
place Jos Henshaw, Henderson Inches & Mr Saml
Pemberton.

May 24. Arr'd from London yesterday Capt
Rotch — arr'd from Liverpool this forenoon, Capt
Perkins. Arr'd from Cadiz this forenoon, Mr Bethune's Brigg. I b^o her Cargo. Arr'd from London
& Halifax, Capt Brown, & arr'd from Bristol Mr Corbet's Snow — all long Passages — Spent the afternoon with the Committee of Merchants.

25 May. Election Day. I went to Meeting &
heard Mr Shute of Hingham preach. This was a
very long sermon, being one hour & forty minutes.
In the afternoon they chose Councillors. Mr Hancock & Colo Ward new ones. I had fifty two votes.

26 May. The Governor negatived the following
Gentlemen Colo Otis Colo Bowers Colo Gerrish Colo
Ward John Hancock & Thomas Saunders Esq.

27 May. Capt Skinner arrivd from Oporto &
Ford from Hallifax

28 May. Went a fishing with Mr Thos Knights
& Mr Saml Calef at Mr Days at Strawberry Hill in
Springfield   had but poor Sport, dind there with M^r
Day & wife   came home & spent the evening with
Mrs Rowe & Sucky

31 May. I went with the Select men to visit M^r
Ruddock & take a view of Winnissimmet Ferry
way.

First June. Went to Flax pond with Mr Saml

Calef, Capt Handfield Mr Thos Jackson Senr.   Wee had good Sport, wee were joynd by M^r McKneal from Surrinam & Archibald McKneal   Wee dind at Mr Graves   wee went to Salem, wee spent the evening at Mr Goodhues & slept there.

2nd June.   Wee breakfasted at Colo Higginsons Returnd to Flax Pond.   had but Ordinary Sport — After Dinner we Returned to Boston   Spent part of the evening at the Charitable Society & the remainder at the Coffee House.

June 4.   King's Birthday.   Guns Firing, Drinking Healths etc

June 6.   Dined at the Coffee House with the Governour & Council, the Officers of the Artillery & many other Gentlemen — Mr Clark of Lexington preached a Sensible Discourse on the Occasion.

June 7.   My New Store Raised this Day.

June 8^h.   Wednesday.   A fine morning WNW. Capt Freeman arrived from Bristol in whom came Passengers Lady Frankland & Henry Cromwell. Dined at Mr Inman's with him, the Revd Mr Brown of Portsmouth the Revd Doct^r Cooper President at New York, The Revd Mr Troutbeck & wife, Mr Robt Temple & wife, The Revd Mr Sargent of Cambridge, Mrs Rowe & Sucky   came home & spent the evening with Mrs Rowe & Sucky.

9 June.   Thursday   A fine morning Wind Westerly   dined at home with Mr Henry Cromwell Lady Frankland Mr Inman Capt Solo Davis Mrs Rowe & Sucky.   after Dinner Mr Harrison & Mrs Harrison paid us a visit spent the evening at home with the same company.

June 10.   Yesterday the Select Men viewed the Ground for a Gun house & the North Battery.   A considerable mob tonight occasioned by a seizure belonging to M[r] John Hancock.   Some Damage to M[r] Harrison the Collector & his Boat Burnt.

June 13.   The Select Men waited on the Gov[r] & Council about Cap[t] Corner's pressing a man out of a Coaster — & the Affairs of the Town.

June 14.   The People Assembled under Liberty Tree from thence removed to Fanewill Hall — there it was proposed to have a Regular Town Meeting called which was accordingly done — Afternoon the Town met at Fanewill Hall, the people were so many that M[r] Otis Ye Moderator proposed adjourning to Dr Sewall's Meeting — which was accordingly voted — & they met there — A Committee of Twenty One Gentlemen were Chose to wait upon Gov[r] Barnard with a Humble Petition — which Petition to him is on File & I think a very smart Petition.   The whole Twenty One met at M[r] J[no] Hancock's & proceeded in form to Roxbury to wait on Gov[r] Barnard, M[r] Otis being Chairman introduced the Petition with a Genteel Speech.   The Gov[r] rec[d] us very cordially — spoke very sensibly to some parts of the Speech & Petition & promised an answer in the morning — The Committee returned to M[r] Hancock's in order as follows, M[r] Otis, M[r] Hancock first —

M[r] Royal Tyler —	M[r] Henderson Inches
Myself —	" Edw[d] Payne
M[r] Joshua Henshaw	" Rich[d] Dana
John Ruddock Esq	" Sam[l] Quincy

Mr Thos Cushing   Mr Melabiah Bourn
Mr Saml Adams   " Benjn Kent
Colo. Joseph Jackson   " Josiah Quincy Jr
Mr Saml Pemberton   Dr Warren

Dr Church, Dr Young & Capt Daniel Malcolm.
all in carriages —

The Man of War the Romney unmoored this
forenoon.

June 15. The Town met again at Dr Sewall's
Meeting —

June 16. Spent the afternoon with the Towns
Committee to draw Instructions to the Represen-
tatives on the Present Difficulties, that attend the
Trade of this Town, myself, Dr. Warren, Dr.
Church, Mr John Adams, Mr Dana & Mr Henderson
Inches. The Select men were ordered to attend
the Govr & Council to hear the Report of their
Committee & their Consultations with Capt John
Corner of his Majesty's Ship, the Roundy.

June 17. Spent the forenoon with the Same
Committee as yesterday. Town Meeting in the
afternoon.

June 18. Went to Mr Ballard's at Natick
Pond, there I met Capt Jacobson & Mr Sam.
Calef, wee fished there, had Great Sport — we
caught several Perch Fifteen Inches Long & one
Sixteen Inches. Capt Bellew in his Majesty's Sloop
Beaver arrivd yesterday evening from Hallifax &
Capt Marshman arriv'd from Lisbon & Jamaica con-
signed to me.

20 June. Dind at home with Mr Wm Sheaff Mr

Inman Capt Marshman Mrs Rowe Mrs Speakman &
Sucky   After Dinner wee went in Capt Marsh-
man's Boat to the Castle. Capt Brett saild for
London with Capt Hallowell Pafsenger.

22 June. Spent the afternoon with the Selectmen   Dismissed James Kennedy this Day.

23 June. Begun to mow our Pasture. Dind at
Old Mr Goulds at Roxbury on Turtle (with eighteen
others)

24 June. St Johns Day. Dind at Mr Greatons
at Roxbury with (fifty seven Brethren. names all
given) Wee spent the afternoon very agreeably

June 27. After dinner wee set out for Sherburne. wee stopt at Natick & reached Sherburne.
Wee supped & slept at Mr Richd Sanger's jun^r. I
bought a hundred tons of Oak Timber a 22/8 p ton
of Mr Sanger, for Capt Marshman who was present
also Capt Jacobson.

June 30. This day the General Court behaved
very steadily & according to the Approbation of
most Good People who have any Regard for their
Country & Posterity — that they would not Re-
scind their former Resolutions which the Earl of
Hillsborough took offense at, vide Newspapers —
number of voters in the House 109 — 17 Yeas. 92
Nays. for my own satisfaction I record the seventeen yeas, that were so mean spirited to vote away
their Blessings as Englishmen, namely their Rights,
Liberty & Properties —

1 Peter Fry Salem   2 Dr. John Calef Ipswitch
3 Jacob Fowle Marblehead   4 Richd Saltonstall

Haverill   5 Mr J^{no} Bliss Springfield   6 Israel
Williams Hatfield   7 Jn° Ashley jr Deerfield   8
Capt Jos Root Sunderland   9 John Ashley Esq
Sheffield & Great Barrington   10 Tim° Ruggles
Hardwick   11 Josiah Edson Bridgewater   12 Jn°
Sayward York   13 Mathew Mayhew Chilmark   14
Wm Brown Salem   15 Chillingsworth Foster Har-
witch   16 Mr Wm Farrigan or Journigan   17 M^r
John Chadwick Tirringham in the Co. of Berkshire

July 1.   Yesterday the Govr prorogued the General Court to the 3^d Aug.

July 4.   This Day Govr Barnard disolved the
General Court.

5 July.   Tuesday   A fine morning W at West
Dined at Greatons at Roxbury on Turtle with

James Otis & wife	John Timmins
Solomon Davis & Wife	The Wid° Greene
Joseph Scot & wife	John Erving jun^r
James Perkins & wife	Miss Bouchee
William Sheaffe & wife	Thos Brattle
Henry Cromwell & Lady Frankland	Miss Katy Wendall
Sam F Allen Otis & wife	George Bethune & wife
Joshua Winslow jun^r & wife	Benjn Fanewill jun^r & wife Mr Inman & myself

Afterwards we were Joynd by Two Mifs Perkins
Miss Joanna & Miss Betty.   We spent the Evening
& had a Dance there very agreeable.

July 6.   This Day the Select Men Visited the
School & dined at Fanewill Hall with seventy Gentlemen.

John Erving Esq^{rs} ⎫
James Bowdoin "   ⎬ *Counsellors*
Thos Hubbard "   ⎭

Harrison Gray "   ⎱ *The Representa-*
Thos Flucker "   ⎰ *tives of the Town*

Revd Mr Mather
"   Dr Byles
"   Dr Cooper
"   Mr Blain
"   Mr Bowen
"   Mr Howard

The Seven Select Men, The 12 Overseers. Colo. Marshal, Major Cunningham, Capt Dawes, Capt Wm Holmes, The Town Treasurer, The Town Clerk, Mr Sewall, Mr Astor, Mr Phillips, Mr Newall, Mr Scollay, Mr Joseph Greene, all the schoolmasters & ushers & the Boys in the Head form of Master Lovells school.

After Dinner Mr James Otis & myself went to Mr Inmans where we found Col. Phipps & wife, Mr John Apthorp & wife Capt. Solo Davis & wife, Mr Cromwell & Lady Frankland, Miss Betty Debuke, Miss Katy Wendall, Mr Inman, Mrs Rowe, Sucky & Sally Inman. We Drank Tea and had a fine Desert of Cherrys & Strawberries. I came home & spent the Evening with the members of the Charitable Society at Colo John Ingersolls. Mr Jenkins Mr Dan Hubbard & Mr John Box Senr.

7 July. Thursday A Rainy Morning W at S^o Dined at Colo David Phipps at Cambridge with him & wife Mr John Apthorp & wife Mr William Davis & wife Mr Henry Cromwell Mr Inman Lady Frankland Mrs Rowe Miss Betty Debuke Miss Katy Wendall. came home & spent the Evening at the Coffee house with Treasurer Gray Joshua Winslow Edwd Payne Wm Mollineaux John Boylston Thos Gray & James Otis.

July 9.   Saturday   A fine morning.   W S° West
Dined at Ten Hills with Mr Robt Temple & wife
Mr Cromwell Lady Frankland Mr Stewart Mr Fenton
Mrs Fenton Mr Inman Mrs Rowe Miss Bessy Tem-
ple & Mr Temple's 4 Daughters   in the afternoon
we were Joynd by Mr John Temple the Surveyor &
Lady.   Came home and spent the Evening with
Mrs Rowe.   Miss Sucky gone to Marlborough.

July 15.   Went to Flax Pond. we fished there
and had pretty good sport.   We spent the evening
at Mrs Graves' & slept at her daughter Becky's.

July 16.   Rose early & went fishing. dined at
Mrs Graves.   Came home & Mrs Rowe told me of
the Sons of Liberty visiting at Mr Williams the
evening before & that he engaged to meet them
on the Change this day which he did & great numbers, she says were present. he asked them what
Questions they had to ask him that he might answer
them but no Person made him any Reply.

July 20.   Commencement Day.   I went to Cambridge.   dined with a very large company at Jos.
Henshaws.   paid a visit to Tutor Hancock's, met
the Revd Mr Barnard of Marblehead, afterwards p'd
a visit to Mrs Greene where were a very large company, too many to enumerate.

July 21.   Dined with Mr David Greene with a
very large Company.   Spent the eve'ng there.   we
had a Dance.   I was Master of the Ceremonies.
Slept at Mr Inman's.

26 July.   Tuesday   A fine morning Wind at
West   Dined at home with Mrs Rowe Sucky & In-

man Capt Christo Prince arrived from London
Spent the afternoon with Lady Frankland M^rs
McNeal Mrs Wm Gould Mrs Rowe & Sucky & the
Evening at Mr James Richardsons with the Fire-
wards. Present Joseph Tyler Capt Waldo Mr John
Miso Wendall Mr Wm Cooper Colonel Marshall,
James Richardson John Scolley Capt Holings Capt
Gay & Capt Paddock.

28 July. Thursday A fine morning WS° West.
Dined at home, with Capt Joseph Williams M^r
Henry Cromwell Mr Tristram Dalton Mr Inman M^rs
Rowe Sucky & George Inman. In the afternoon
the Merchants met & adjourned untill Monday.
Spent the Evening at the Pofsee. Rufus Greene
Benjn Greene Francis Johnnot Wm Coffin James
Richardson John Avery Wm Henshaw Thos Foster
& Sam Swift.

July 29. This forenoon the Governour & Council met on affairs of consequence it is supposed
Relative to the Introduction of Troops which has
greatly alarmed the Inhabitants.

Aug. 1. Spent the afternoon at the General
Merchants Meeting at Fanewill Hall at which place
there were present sixty two — sixty of which signed
an agreement I have on File not to Import any
Goods. Spent the evening at Mr Barber's Insurance Office & the Silver Bowl was this evening for
the first time introduced, N° 45. Weighs 45 ounces
& holds 45 gills. Present

John Hancock   Mr Wm Bowen
Saml Adams   " John Marston

Capt Malcom	Mr John Welsh
Mr John White	Thos Cushing
Capt Cobb	Myself
Mr Daniel Parker	Capt Vernon
James Otis	John Ruddock
Major Doane	Mr Crane of the Vineyard &
Capt Mackay	Mr Nat. Barber

Aug. 2.   The Committee of Merchants met & got further subscriptions.

Aug. 7.   I went to church & Mr Walter read prayers & preached from 14 Chap. St Luke & 14th Verse.   this was a most sensible, charitable Discourse being a Collection of Charity for the Sufferers by Fire at Montreal in the province of Quebeck.

Aug. 8.   The Merch^{ts} met at Fanewill Hall   present ab^o 100.

Aug. 10.   I went with the following company to view Rainsford Island on the Province Acc^t.   Thos Cushing, James Otis, Saml Adams Joshua Henshaw Colo. Jackson John Ruddock John Hancock Saml Pemberton Henderson Inches Benjn Austin Thos Gray David Jeffries Wm Cooper Dr Chauncey Dr Elliot Saml Mathew Colo. Brattle & myself.   Wee dined there, were very merry.

Aug. 15.   Dined at Greatons with a Number of Gentlemen about one Hundred — who were very jovial & pleasant & in the forenoon a great Number of People were at Liberty Hall where there was a variety of Good Musick exhibited & Great Joy appeared in every countenance, being the Anniversary Day of the Sons of Liberty —

Aug. 16. I went to Dennis Island & dind there on a Barbicue with (23 others).

Aug. 17. After Dinner I set out with Capt Jacobson & Saml Calef for Colo. Doty's — wee fished on Punkapaud Pond — spent the eve'ng & slept at Colo. Doty's.

Aug. 18. Wee went again to fish — had great sport, caught upwards of twenty dozen & some Large Fish — set out for home, were caught in the Rain, and stopt at Mr Clarks at Milton.

24 August. Wednesday a Cold morning W at W. Dined at home with Colo Bourn of Mhead Mrs Rowe & Sucky Spent the Evening at Lady Franklands with Her and his sister, Mr Cromwell Madam Apthorp Dr Bulfinch Mrs Bulfinch Mr Inman Mrs Rowe & Sucky

25 Aug. Our Wedding Day having been married twenty three years. Mr Davidson arrivd from the Island of St Johns this day. Capt Folger saild for London. Mr John Boylston went home pafsenger in him.

29 Aug. Poor Wm Speakman was taken in a fit & had doubtful Struggles for Life.

30 August. Tuesday A fine Cold Morning W N West Superiour Court setts this Day — dined at home say at Mr Lavicount's at Cambridge with him & Mrs Lavicount Mr Cromwell & Lady Frankland Mr Wm Sheaffe & Mrs Sheaffe Colo Phipps & Mrs Phipps Mr John Apthorp his lady and Miss Bettsy Greenleaf, Capt Solomon Davis Mrs Davis Mr Inman Miss Sally Sheaffe & Mrs Rowe came home & spent the evening with Mrs Rowe.

4 Sept. In the Begginning of the evening I went to the Quarterly Lecture at Fanewill Hall. M[r] Adams of Roxbury preached a Good Sermon on the occasion

5 Sept. Wee met on an Arbitration between M[rs] Eustice & M[r] W[m] Bowes present M[r] Ezek Golthwait M[r] Ezek[l] Price M[r] Murray myself. Spent the evening at the Fire Club for the first Time The Word " Ask More "

9 Sept. The Governour told mee in Conversation Yesterday morning that he had Stav'd off the Introducing Troops as long as he could but could do it no longer.

10 Sept. I went out to Richards with Sam[l] Calef a fishing on the Cofsway — was very Lucky — caught many Perch & fine ones — Lost severall fine Hooks & Snoods.

11 Sept. After Church the Selectmen met about a Cask that was fix'd on the Saddle of the Beacon.

16 Sept. Fryday A fine Morning W N° West dined at home with Capt Jacobson M[r] Thos Brattle M[rs] Rowe & Sucky. Spent the Evening at John M[c]Neal Esq at a Rout being his Birth Day with him his Lady son & Daughter M[r] Fenton M[r] Archibald M[c]Neal & Two Daughters M[r] Robert Gould his wife Miss Bettsy & Miss Sally M[r] Phillip Dumaresque & wife M[r] Gordon Doctor Gardiners Lady & Two Daughters M[r] Lavicount & wife & M[rs] Jn° Vafsall M[r] Edw[d] Davis & wife M[r] Parsons M[r] Inman M[rs] Rowe & Miss Sucky M[r] George Brinley

his wife & Mrs Atkinson Mr Griffin from Maryland
Mr Hartley Mr Forrest Mr Robt Hallowell Dr Pettigrew Mrs Hardrigg Mrs Wm Gould & Mr Cromwell.

Sept. 20.   Afternoon I attended the Select Men
& waited on the Council to consult about Barracks
for the Troops that are expected.

Sept. 23.   King's Coronation Day.   The Convention met at Fanewill Hall this day.

Sept. 28.   This forenoon came to anchor in Nantasket Roads six sail of Men of War supposed to
have the 14th Regm^t & 29th Regm^t on board.

Sept. 29.   Arr'd three more of his Majesty's
Ships of War from Halifax so that are now in our
harbour —

The Launceston   Capt Gill
   "   Romney   "   Corner
   "   Glasgow   "   Allen
   "   Mermaid   "   Smith
   "   Bonelten   "   Wallace
   "   Martin   "   Haywood
   "   Senegall   "   Cookson
   "   Beaver   "   Billings
   "   St Lawrence   Schooner armed Capt Dundafs
   "   Magdalene   "   "   "   Callder
   "   Gaspee   Capt Allen
   "   Hope   "   Dawson

Oct. 1.   This day the Troops came ashore — the
14th & 29th Regm^t and 2 companies of the 29th with
a company of Artillery — they marched into ye
Common.   Colo Dalrymple summoned the Select
Men.   they all met & did not think themselves

obliged to take Cognisance for their being Quartered in Town so that the 29th pitched their Tents in the Common the 14th got into Fanewill Hall & part of the 59th at Robt Gordons Stores.

Oct. 2. I went to the Coffee House to pay a visit to Mr Edington & was most smartly accosted by Capt Dundass in the following words — " Ha John are you there — Dammy I expected to have heard of your being hanged before now, for Dammy You deserve it " upon which I made reply " Surely Capt Dundafs, you're Joking "— upon which he answered " No "— Damn him if he was, for you are a Damn Incendiary & I shall see you hanged in your Shoes — & repeated the same — upon which I say to him " Then you are in earnest are you, I was in hopes you were joking "— " No " he repeated " Damn you, I am in earnest, I tell you. You are an Incendiary & I hope to see you hanged yet in your shoes." I took notice who were present as it was spoke about Twelve of Clock at Noon. Mr Forrest, Mr Phillip Dumaresque, Mr Geo. Brinley & several officers of the Army who I did not know in the Coffee Room & entry way — I thought it Prudent not to take any Notice of it just then but came home to dinner.

Oct. 5. After Dinner a Committee from the Grand Lodge Bro. Richd Gridley, Bro. Jenkins & Bro. John Cutler — they Presented me the Commission from the Duke of Beaufort appointing me Grand Master of No America — afterwards I met the Select men & spent the evening at the Charitable Society & an hour at the Coffee House.

Oct. 7.   Let one of my houses to Capt Ohara yesterday & the other this day to Major Furlong — both at £20 Ster'g per annum.

Oct. 10.   Last night some Villains cut the Frame of the Guard House so as to Render it useless. some people make Light of this affair, but I think the scoundrels that did it ought to be severely punished & I wish they may be found out.

Oct. 14.   I went to the Funeral of Old Mrs Skinner & was a bearer.

Oct. 15.   General Gage arr'd from New York at Major Byards at Roxbury.   The regiments were under arms & made a Good Appearance.   The General with his attendants came into Town ab^o four P.M.   The Artillery saluted with 17 Guns. They passed & marched along the Front of both Regiments & Capt Wilsons two Companies who were formed in the Center.

Oct. 16.   This morning I waited on Colo. Robertson who came with Gen. Gage.   He received me very Politely.   I had a full hour's discourse with him ab^o the troops.   I find him to be a Gentleman of Great Abilities & very cool & dispassionate.   I took a walk & met Gen. Gage & Colo. Dalrymple. Gen. Gage engaged me to wait on him tomorrow morning.

Oct. 20.   This day the Sheriff got into the Factory House.

Oct. 22.   Waited on Colo. Maitland Adj't Gen.

to provide a Division for the King's Gunpowder in the Magazine. This forenoon was held a General Court Martial on a soldier of the 14th who deserted. Colo. Dalrymple sat a President. I also attended Gen. Gage & Colo Robertson.

23 Oct. The Honble John Temple Esq Child was Christened this forenoon at our Church. The Sponsors were Gen[l] Gage, Rob[t] Temple Esq[r] & his Lady — by the name of Greenville.

Oct. 28. Spent part of the evening with the Grand Lodge. They agreed to Install the Grand Master on Wednesday the 23rd of Nov. & ordered the Secretary to write a letter to our Brother the Rev[d] Mr. Bass of Newbury on the occasion.

Oct. 29. This day the Troops went from Fanewill Hall into the Barracks. The Select men met about an affair of Cap[t] Wilson's, they were all present but referred it until Monday.

1 Nov. Tuesday the first of November a fine morning WW Dined at home with M[r]. Inman M[rs] Rowe & Sucky — this day Cap[t] Willson was carried before Justice Dana for some Drunken Behaviour & bound over to the Sessions Spent part of the Evening at the Coffee house with James Otis & John Erving John Dennie, Henderson Inches Solo Davis Nich Boylston James Warden W[m] Mollineux & the Remainder at Cap[t] M[c]Nealls with him, his Lady his Daughter General Gage Colo Robertson Colo Maitland Colo Dalrymple Colo Kerr Major Gambell Major Small Major Sheriff Cap[t] Kimball Cap[t] Matrin Cap[t] Preston M[r] Mills M[r]

Leigh M[r] Forrest M[r] Cromwell D[r] Pettigrew Cap[t]
Molesworth Major Vafsall & Lady, M[r] Lavicount
& Lady — M[r] Dumaresq & wife M[r] Arch[d] M Neall
& wife & three Daughters — Two Miss Martins
M[rs] Rowe Sucky Inman Cap[t] W[m] Handfield M[rs]
Handfield M[rs] Billy Gould Brigg[r] Royall Miss
Polly Royal & Miss Gardner.

9 Nov.   Wednesday   A Dull heavy morng WS°
dined at home with Cap[t] Molesworth of the 29th
Cap[t] Bracket & M[r] Leight of the 14th M[r] Inman
M[rs] Rowe & Sucky   Spent part of the evening at
the Coffee house with Joshua Winslow Treasurer
Gray Tho[s] Gray Edw[d] Payne Ezek[l] Goldthwait Geo
Bethune Melachiar Bourne Will[m] Mollineux John
Erving Nich° Boylston & James Otis   And the
Remainder at home with M[r] Inman M[r] Cromwell
Lady Frankland her sister M[rs] Rowe & Sucky

Tis Reported the Commifsioners Came to Town
this Day.   I saw One of them M[r] Robinson

Nov 10.   This morning Colo. Pomroy arr'd with
part of the Irish Regiments N° 64 & 65 — This
day also the famous Tryal between Mollineux &
Cotton — Snow ab° Eleven of Clock.

Nov. 13.   The Commissioners & their officers all
at church this day — & the first time they have
appeared in Publick — Dr Catherwood arr'd on the
Romney Man of War from Halifax — in her the
Commodore & Lady — also Lord   W[m] Campbell
& Cap[t] Gould — The Doctor gives the Commodor
Hood a great character

Nov. 18.   When I got to my store this morning,

found it Broke open & sundry Goods therein taken way to my great mortification — Spent the evening at the Coffee House with the Grand Lodge, 82 Brethren present

Nov. 19. I carried a fellow before Justice Quincy to night on suspicion of theft, who called his name Tobin — alias Jacobs — who committed him.

Nov. 23. I had the honour & pleasure of being Installed Grand Master of Masons for North America at Concert Hall this morning This was a very solemn Ceremony After the Installation the whole Fraternity proceeded in Order & marched in Procession from Concert Hall round the Town House, accompanied with two Brass Bands of musick, the 59th & 64th Regiments, to Trinity Church, the Revd Mr Walter read Prayers & our Worthy Brother the Revd Mr Bass of Newbury preached from the 21st Chap. St John & part of the 20th Verse After service wee returned in Procession to Concert Hall and dined on an elegant Entertainment provided by a Committee, appointed by the Grand Lodge — there were one hundred thirty four Brethren present — wee spent the afternoon very cheerfully & in good order which did honour to the Craft I came home at Eight of Clock in the evening & spent the evening at home with Dr Catherwood, Mrs Rowe & Sucky

Nov. 24. Gen. Gage & Family went out of Town this morning. I took my leave of the General who behaved very Politely &c.

Nov. 26. I waited on the Commodore who Receiv'd me very politely.

Dec. 1. Thanksgiving Day — I paid a visit to Lord Wm Campbell at Mr Boutineau's, who was going on Board (the Glasgow to sail for Halifax) Dined at Mr Inman's at Cambridge with Dr. Catherwood, Capt O'hara, Mr Robt Temple, Mrs Rowe & Sucky, George & Sally Inman — came home & spent the evening at Capt Solomon Davis' with him, Mrs Davis, Miss Betty Debuke Miss Katy Wendall, Lady Frankland, Mr Cromwell, Mrs Swain, Mr Sheaffe, Mrs Sheaffe, Miss Saky Sheaffe, Mrs Skinner, Miss Penny Winslow, Mr Thomas Brattle & Mr Inman, also Dr. Catherwood.

Dec. 5. Be it remembered that Sir Thos Rich of the Senegal pressed all Capt Dashwood's hands.

Dec. 15. Capt McNeal arr'd from Quebeck who broug^t me a Bill on the Commissioners of the Customs I attended with Capt Watts from twelve till almost three on their High Mightinessesses — this Behaviour of theirs is not only very Insolent but not to be born & for which they may hear more about.

Dec. 25. Sunday & Christmas Day — I dined at home with Mr Thos Brattle, Saml Calef, Mrs Rowe Sucky W^m & Gilbert Speakman & Anthony Lechmere. I pd a visit to Old Mr Gould who is very Ill.

Dec. 27. We celebrated the Feast of St John at Colo Ingersoll's where we had a very elegant dinner & 48 present.

1769

Jan. 6.   We searched McVickers house & found some of my goods that were stole out of my warehouse in November — & sent Stoodly to goal — the other Vickers made his escape.   Dined & supped at Commodore Hood's.

Jan. 10.   This day the King's speech came to hand.   Spent the eve'ng at the Pofsee.   when I came home found the Revd Mr Walter with whom I had two hours Conversation on the Times.

Jan. 19.   Queen's Birthday — three Regiments under arms on the Common 14th — 29th & 64th they made a fine appearance.   Spent the evening at the Assembly for the first time — too much Confusion

Jan. 31.   Last night I was awakened by the cry of Fire   it was the County Goal which was burnt down & the neighbourhood very much in Danger.   The officers & Army behaved extremely clever on this Occasion & ought to have the Publick thanks of this Town.   I can truly say they were the means of saving it — I waited on Brigadier Pomroy & Colo. Kerr & thanked them for their Behaviour.   Attended the Selectmen on the affair of Hollidays.   Attended the Funeral of Master Holbrook.   this afternoon met the Adventurers in the Whale Fishery at the Coffee House

Febry. 1.   Yesterday three of the Prisoners were examined before the Bench of Justices for the Sessions for setting fire to the Goal, their names —

Abel Badger of this Town, a Great Rogue — one
Donnelly, a soldier & one Man Michael — all very
bad Fellows

Febry 2.   The Revd Mr Forbes married to Miss
Dolly Murray this day at Brush Hill.

Febry 7.   I went to James Smith Esq at Brush
Hill & dined there with him Mrs Smith, the Rev^d
Mr Forbes Mrs Forbes, Mr Clark, Mr Robt Gould,
Mrs Gould, Miss Betty & Sally Gould, Mr Inman,
Mrs Rowe & Sucky   After dinner Mad^m Belcher &
daughter paid them a visit —

Febry 9.   The harbour all froze in.   People
came from the Castle on the Ice.

Feb. 14.   I went this morning in the Sleigh to
Cambridge & din'd at Mr Inman

Mar. 6.   Dined at Major Cunningham's, with
him, his two sons — all his officers of his Company, the Rev^d Dr Elliot — Mr Henderson Inches,
Mr John Adams Lawyer — Mr Thomas Trot Senr
& jun^r Mr George Trot & Mr Baker.   Spent the
eve'ng at Mrs Cordis with the Fire Club.

Mar 7.   This forenoon Capt McKowan's ship
was seized by the Custom House officers.

Mar. 13.   Town Meeting.   I desired my Friends
not to vote for me as Selectman & in Consequence
was not Chose, but Mr Jonathan Mason was Chose
in my Room.   In the afternoon I went to Town
Meeting.   Mr Saml Adams affair came on & the
prayer of his Petition Granted, which appears to
be a very wrong step in the Town, & what they,
I am afraid will repent.

Mar. 14. This forenoon the Superior Court met in the New Court House & made a splendid appearance.

Mar. 15. Spent the evening at the Assembly with the Governour, Commodore, General, Colo. Kerr Colo. Lesly, Major Furlong, Major Fleming, Major Fordyce. A Great Number of Officers of the Navy & Army & Gentlemen & Ladies of the Town, that it was a Brilliant Assembly & very Good Dancing.

Mar. 16. Attended the Superior Court this afternoon ab° Mr Thomas's Briggs Hallowells' affairs. Spent the evening at the Fife Major's Concert at Concert Hall — there was a large genteel Company & the best Musick I have heard performed there After I came home wee were alarmed by the cry of Fire which happened at Henderson Inches — but, Thank God, it did very little Damage.

Mar. 19. Just heard of the death of my Friend Colo Henry Vafsall of Cambridge who died Fryday night.

22. Mar. Wednesday very Cold Blows hard N. West dined at Mr Inman at Cambridge with him Mr Cromwell Lady Frankland Mrs Harding Miss Mollie Wethered Mrs Rowe & George Inman in the afternoon I went to the Funerall of Henry Vafsall Esqr. I was a Pallholder together with General Brattle Colo Phipps Jos Lee Esqr Richd Letchmore Esq & Robt Temple Esq it was a very handsome Funerall & a Great Number of People & Carriages, came to Town in the Evening & spent the Evening

at the Pofsee with Rufus Greene Benj Greene Thos
Foster Saml Swift Jno Box James Richardson Willm
Henshaw Francis Johnnot Wm Coffin & John
Avery.

I laid a Wager of a Beaver Hat with Sam Swift
that Mr George Ruggles married his Present Wife
after the year 1737

Mar. 23. I sent out the Tickets to invite the
Charitable Society this morning   I sold my Schooner
Suky to Capt. Billings   This afternoon I attended
the Superior Court Mr Thos Thomas' action against
Briggs Hallowell came on & the Jury Brought in a
Verdict £329.. 4.. 9 in favour of M Thomas

Mar. 26. Mr Forbes of the 29th Regiment
preached a most excellent discourse   This Mr
Forbes is a most delightful & charming preacher.

Mar. 28. Dined at Colo. Ingersolls with the
Members of the Charitable Society — Present John
Rowe Treas. His Excellency Gov. Barnard Colo.
Pomroy, Commodore Hood J^{no} Apthorp Stephen
Greenleaf — Wm Coffin Senr John Greene Nath.
Greene Jos Greene, Danl Hubbard, Henry Loyd,
Jon Simpson, Mr Inman John Box Senr John Box
jun^r, The Revd Mr Troutbeck, The Revd Mr Win-
slow, The Revd Mr Walter, The Revd Mr Palmer &
the Revd Mr Byles   We had a fine Salmon for
Dinner —

Mar. 29. Spent the Evening at the Assembly
which was a very Brilliant one.

Apr. 2. I went to church both forenoon &
afternoon & acted as Warden for the first time.

Apr. 6.   After dinner I took a Ride to Milton, came to Town & spent the eve'ng at Colo Ingersolls

Apr. 9.   About eleven Mrs Rowe & I went to Cambridge wee dined at Mrs Vassall's with her, Dr Russell Mrs Fanewill Senr, Miss Polly Betume, Wm Vassall, his Lady, his Daughter, Mr Inman & Suky Inman   In the afternoon wee went to church — Mrs Vassall Mrs Rowe & myself stood Sponsors for Dr Russell's child named Penelope   After church wee returned to Mistress Vassall's & drank tea & coffee.

Apr. 11.   Dined at the Coffee House with the Proprietors of Long Wharff — Andrew Oliver Esq., Arnold Wells, Mr Habejah Savage Mr Jos. Henderson, Mr Gillam Phillips, John Phillips Mr Saml Hewes, Capt Benj^{m} Waldo, Mr Oliver Wendall Capt Job Prince, Dr Whitworth, Mr Boutineau, Jos. Winslow Esq, Mr J^{no} Powell, Robt Jenkins Thos Savage, Capt James Dalton, John Hancock & myself.

Apr. 12.   Some letters of Govr Barnard to the Earl of Hilsborough are sent over by Mr Bollan which makes great noise & censure.   Spent the evening at the Assembly, a very large Company — Govr absent.

Apr. 20.   Capt Parker arrivd from Glasgow in A Short Passage of Twenty two days.

Apr. 21.   Capt Molesworth of the 29th carried off Miss Suky Sheaffe to Hampton — I met the Merchants at Fanewill Hall this afternoon.

Apr. 24.   Mr Hooper of Marblehead came to

town & brings the melancholly acc^t of Lieut. Paxton being killed in endeavoring to Press some hands of Mr Hooper's Brigg, Capt Poor fr Cadiz.

May 6. Settled with Mrs Speakman ab^o the Land near the Stillhouse — I went out of Town & called on M^r & Mrs Payson & M^r & Mrs Jones & dined at Mr Voses at Milton Bridge.

May 7. I went again to see M^r & Mrs Payson who I found in very deplorable circumstances.

May 8th. I sold my Stillhouse &c to Colo Jackson for the sum of £886.13.4.

May 14. After church there was a contribution for the Widow of the Late Revd Mr Hooper, the sum was £319.13.9 equal to £42.13 & 3^d Lawful Money — this I think with Private Donations may be equal to the sum voted her last year, at least I hope so.

May 31. Election Day.

June 1. The Governour Negatived eleven counsellors — James Boudoin, Brigg^r Brattle, Jos. Henshaw, Mr Foster, Mr Greenleaf, Colo. James Otis, Colo. Bowers, Mr Saunders, Colo. Gerrish, & Mr Walter Spooner.

June 3. Went with Mr James Perkins & Mr Saml Calef to Spot Pond a fishing — we were joyned by Major Vassall & Mr Thompson of Medford — Wee had very great luck — I never saw such large Perch. before Caught there, many of them ab^o 12 inches.

June 4. King's birthday — All the Men of War in harbour fired 21 guns each.

June 5.   Washing day.   Dined at Fanewill with
the Govern^r & Council & the Artillery Company.
Spent the evening at the Concert Hall with a very
Brilliant company of Gentlemen & Ladies — a fine
Ball, excellent Musick & a good large Plumb Cake.

June 7.   I rose very early & went to Cambridge with Colo. Robertson, Dr Catherwood, Major
Golthwait, Lord George Gordon, Mrs Rowe & Sucky
& breakfasted at Mr Inman's — Afterwards I went
with the same Company to the College with M^r
Winthrop who was very obliging & shew us the
Apparatus which is very Elegant, also the Library.

June 10.   Capt Hall arrivd from London.   Great
News.

June 14.   Sent for Dr. Loyd to have my Tooth
drawn & had not Resolution to go thro' the Opera-
tion.   This day Power & others were on Tryal for
their Conduct on board the Rose Man of War.
their Behaviour was very Couragious & I think
very Right.

June 15.   The 14th Regim^t were Reviewed by
Genl McKay   they Behaved extremely Clever &
were much Admired & were much Approv'd by the
General.   The Govr Adjourned the General Court.
After dinner M^rs R & I took a Ride round Jamaica
Pond where wee had the Melancholly Sight of
Maj^r Byard's Ruins.

June 19.   Began to mow the Pasture.

June 20.   Let my Sloop St John for One Hun-
dred & Fifty Dollars to go to Halifax & back.
This day the 29th Regiment were Reviewed.   They
Really made A fine Appearance.

June 21.   Tis said that Govr Barnard has dismissed G. Brattle from being Col. of his Regim^t.

June 24.   St John's Day.   Very hot.   Dined at the King's Arms on Boston Neck with the Free Masons.   A very Elegant Dinner.   Present (41 Brethren).

July 5.   I waited on Commodore Hood to Visit the Schools in Boston & dined with the Select Men Overseers of the Poor, The Rev^{ds} Dr. Byles, Mr Mather, Dr. Elliot, Mr Bowen, Mr Walley Mr Howard, The Commodore, Colo. Brattle Mr James Otis, Eze^l Golthwait, Maj^r Cunningham Colo. Marshall, Mr Nich. Boylston, Major Lovell Mr James Lovell, Master Hunt, Master Proctor Master Holbrook, Capt Job Prince, Mr Ed^w Carnes Mr Robt Jenkins Jr & Mr Wm Ivers.   A very Genteel Entertainment.

July 6.   The Small Pox broke out in Several Families.

July 8.   When I came home I found Capt Robt Lyndsay at Our Hous being arrivd on the Vipers Sloop of Warr from N^o Carolina, his brother Capt John Lyndsay (& others).

July 15.   Last night Mr John Temple & Mr Flucker had a Quarrel attended with Blows in the town-house ob^o the Dialogues.

July 16.   The Governor Prorogued the General Court yesterday untill the 10 Jan next.

July 21.   This afternoon Mrs Rachel Willson, the Famous Quaker preacher, preached in Fanewill Hall to at Least Twelve hundred people.   She seems to be a Woman of Good Understanding.

Spent the evening at home with Mr John Lyndsay, Mrs Rowe & Sucky.

July 24. Met the Merchant's Committee at the Coffee House, present — Thos Cushing, John Hancock, Wm Phillips, Edwd Payne & myself.

July 28. I went to Mr Charles Harrison's Funerall.

July 31. Rainy weather. Lightning & thunder. Two vessels sunk at Hancock's wharf. In the evening I went to hear Mr Douglass Lecture on heads. he Performed well.

Aug. 1. This forenoon Capt Thompson in the Rippon, Man of War — for England & Govr Barnard went home in him. The Flag hoisted on Liberty Tree — the Bells Ringing — Great Joy to the People. A Great Bonfire in King St & on Fort Hill.

Aug 2. I went with Capt Caldwell, Mr George, Mrs Rowe & Sucky in Capt Caldwell's Cutter up Cambridge River — wee landed near the Bridge & dined at Mr Inman's

Aug. 4. Dined at John Champney's on a Pigy with the following Company — John Hancock, James Otis, John Adams, Wm Coffin Senr, Robt Auchmooty, Sam. Swift, Francis Johnnot, Hugh McDaniel Wm Read, Henry Laughton, Benj Kent, Tuthill Hubbard, Henderson Inches, John Cutler Thom^s Amory & Peter Johnnot We sunk the Box at my Wharf this noon and were very Lucky — I attended the Merchants Meeting this afternoon who gave me a pretty tight Lecture ab° the Importation

of some Porter on board Jarvis — I wish the Porter
had not been Imported as tis like to make an
Uneasiness   Last evening died my Friend Mr James
Smith at Milton.

Aug. 6.   This morning died my old Friend Capt
James Forbes

Aug. 7.   In the afternoon attended the Funerall
of Mr James Smith

Aug. 8.   I was a Bearer to my Old Friend Capt
Forbes together with John Erving Senr, James
Murray Jonathan Simpson, John Erving Ju^r & M^r
Inman   The Freemasons walk'd in form & made a
very handsome Appearance

Aug. 10.   On Tuesday Mr Wm Coffin Senr, myself & Mrs Rowe stood sponsors for Mr Walter's
Son William

Aug. 12.   I dined on invitation from Capt Caldwell of the Rose on Noddles Island

Aug. 14.   The Sons of Liberty met at Liberty
Tree & dined at Robinson's at Dorchester — they
contained 139 Carriages on their Return   Mr Hancock preceeded the Company & Mr Otis Brought up
the Rear   Spend part of the eve'ng at the Pofsee &
was greatly surprised to find when I came home my
Old Friend Mr John Lane at Our house   He came
in the Nafsau very unexpected.

Sept. 3rd.   I paid a visit to Mrs Walter & my God-
son this afternoon

Sept. 5.   I got up at two of Clock this morning
to take a view of the Comet which hath made his
Appearance from twelve until three in the morning

for five Nights preceeding — it appeared very Large & its Tail very Long   In the eve'ng an Affray happened at the Coffeehouse between M[r] Robinson the Commissioner & James Otis Esq — it's said Otis is much bruised.

Sept. 6.   I find the Inhabitants greatly alarmed at the Usage M[r] Otis met with — tis generally thought he was very Rascally treated — this afternoon the Sheriff took W[m] Brown Esq formerly of Salem for being accessary in Beating M[r] Otis — he was Carried to Fanewill Hall & examined before Justice Dana & Justice Pemberton & followed by a Great Number of People — I believe about Two Thousand — M[r] Murray was there & used Roughly by the People

Sept. 8.   A very Great Storm — it looks like the Tail of a hurricane

Sept. 9.   I rose early & found the Storm had done great damage among the Shipping, Wharfs & other parts of the Town.

Sept. 18.   M[r] Hallowell Launcht his Ship this Day

Sept. 25.   This afternoon I attended the Funerall of Miss Sarah Calef & was a Bearer with Treasurer Gray Tho[s] Gray, Sam[l] Adams, Benj[n] Fanewill Jun[r] & M[r] Sam[l] Hews.

Sept. 26.   In the afternoon I attended M[r] Henderson Inches wife's Funeral & was a Bearer together with Tho[s] Cushing Esq[r], Dr. Sprague, M[r] Isaac Smith M[r] Johnathan Mason & M[r] Tho[s] Russell.

Sept. 28. Dined at his honor the Lieu^t Governor with him, his two Daughters, his two sons Thomas & Elisha, Mr Harris a Gentleman from St Christopher's, M^r —— & Mr Paxton two of the Commissioners, for the first time since their arrival I have been in their Company & which I did not know now.

Sept. 30. This day the Custom house officers made a large Seizure from Capt John Homer who I take to be a very honest Good man & for which I am very sorry should happen at this time.

Oct. 3. This morning the Merchants met at Fanewill Hall to consider what measures should be taken about Capt Bryants cargo.

Oct. 4. This day there was a Town Meeting & the Transactions are agreed to be published to-morrow.

Oct. 8. I did not go to Church this forenoon as I was oblig'd to attend Capt Jacobson who sailed for London his Passengers Mr Harrison, Mrs Smith & Capt Courance & Betty Murray.

Oct. 9. Spent the afternoon & evening at Mrs Cordis' with Robt Goulds Creditors & Mr J. Lane proposed to pay Robt Goulds Cred^ts after a Long debate 15 / in the Pound, payable in four years.

Oct. 10. Dined at home on the finest Haunch of Venison I ever saw. My worthy Friend Jos Winslow Esqr died yesterday

Oct. 14. Mr Tol Brought me home a New Coat & Breeches.

Oct. 19. Mr Jos. Loring married to Night by Mr Walter to Miss Betty Lloyde.

Oct. 24.   An affray happened at the So' Guards between M[r] Ness of the 14th & M[r] Pierrepoint which has made some Considerable Noise about Town.

Oct. 25.   King's accession of the throne & the Tenth Year of his Majesty's Reign.

Oct. 26.   The Vestry of Trinity Church met this day & settled all the Affairs of S[d] Church — M[rs] Rowe had the misfortune to sprain her ancle this day.

Oct. 28.   M[r] M—— Publication that appeared to Day has Given Great uneasiness & this evening he was spoke to by Cap[t] Dashwood — Some people getting aroused he got into Ezek[l] Price's office & from thence fired a Pistol & wounded a Grenadier of the 29th Regiment in the Arm.   Warrants were Issued out to secure him but he could not be found. In the evening a large Mob Assembled & got hold of one George Greyer an informer who they stript naked & painted him all over with Tar & then covered him with Feathers & put him in a Cart & carried him thro' all the main Streets of the Town huzzaring &c and at nine dismissed him — this matter occasioned much terror &c in some fearfull People among the Inhabitants — When this happened I was with the Pofsee.

Nov. 6.   Monday — The People have behaved Well, being Pope Day.

Nov. 21.   The Superior Court met today. Judge Lynde gave the charge to the Grand Jury.

Nov. 25.   I sent Cato on board the Rose Man of War, this morning

Nov. 27. My Birth Day being fifty four years old. Snows this morning for the second time.

Dec. 6. Afternoon at the Funerall of the Revd Mr Checkly & this evening at the Charitable Society.

Dec. 7. I attended the Funerall of my Friend Saml Cary Esqr who was buried from his Brother Richards at Charlestown. I was a Bearer together with John Erving Senr Esq John Avery Esq Mr John Powell Capt Henly of Charlestown & Robt Temple Esq. Twas a handsome Funeral

Dec. 18. Spent the evening at the Coffee House with the Committee of Merch^{ts} Present Thos Cushing, Isaac Smith Edwd Payne Wm Mollineaux, Henderson Inches Wm Greenlief Samuel Dashwood Wm Whitwell Wm Phillips John Barrat & Jon^n Mason

Dec. 19. Spent the afternoon at Colo Ingersolls with Mr Blake & Savage ab^o the Forge at Hardwick

Dec. 22. This morning Mr John Dennie of Cambridge lost his house by Fire for which I am very sorry.

Dec. 27. St. John's Day. Dind at Colo Ingersolls with the Brotherhood.

1770

Jan'y 1. This afternoon the Committee of Merchants came to waite on me about Mr Wm Sheaffe's affair. Deacon Phillips, Wm Dennie, Wm Greenleaf Wm Mollineaux & John Ruddock Esq. This day we distributed the Poor's money —

Jan'y 4. Spent the eve'ng at Mr Robt Gould's to see the Celebration of the Marriage between Mr John Baker Brimmer & Miss Betty Gould.

Jan'y 9. Dined at home with His Honor the Lieut. Govern^r his Brother Foster Hutchinson Esq, Colo. Dalrymple Capt Caldwell, Mr Nich^o Boylston, Mr Inman, Mr John Lane & Mrs Rowe.

Jan'y 17. Spent the afternoon at the Merch^ts Meeting at Fanewill Hall & part of the eve'ng at the Coffee House This Day the Body of Merchants visited Mr Wm Jackson

Jan'y 18. The Merchants met again this day & the whole Body as they are called visited the sons of his Honor Mr Theophilus Lillie, Mr John Taylor, Mr Wm Jackson again & Mr Nath. Rogers. they adjourned until tomorrow, Ten of Clock.

Jan'y 19. The harbour froze in. The Merchants met again to Day. Messrs Hutchinsons agreed to deliver up

Jan'y 23. The Trade met again today at Fanewill Hall which highly displeased the Lieut. Governour who sent the Sheriff & ordered them to disperse which they took no notice of. Colo. Dalrymple, I believe, ordered his Regiment to keep

MRS. JOHN LINZEE

("Sucky" Inman)

under Arms all night — the Body voted said Colo. Dalrymple should be cashiered.

Jan'y 25. The Harbour full of ice. I took a Ride over the Neck in the Sleigh.

Jan'y 29. I went to Cambridge & dined at Mr Inmans. Mr J. Lane Read us the Diverting Farce, the Mayor of Garrets.

Feb'y 9. Spent the evening at Colo John Ingersolls on Arbitration between Hugh Tarbut & Benj Caldwell.

Feb'y 21. Mrs Rowe to please Sucky made a Dance & entertainment which was a Genteel One.

Feb. 24. Snow & Hail. Smart Thunder & Lightning ab° Ten of Clock, very uncommon at this season.

Feb. 26. This afternoon the Boy that was killed by Richardson was buried. I am very sure two thousand people attended his Funerall.

Mar. 2. Spent the afternoon on a visit to Mr Henderson Inches & Lady, where we found Mr Harrison of London Mr Jsaac Smith M^r Ed Payne Mr John Timmins Mr Inman Mrs Rowe & Sucky, Mrs George Brinley Mrs Louder Miss Betty Inches & two or three young Ladies whom I didn't know.

Mar. 3. A Quarrel between some of the 29th Regim^t & the Ropemakers — yesterday & today.

Mar. 5. This night the 29th Regim^t on Duty. A Quarrel between the soldiers & Inhabitants. The Bells Rung A Great Number Assembled in King Street. A Party of the 29th under the Command of Capt Preston fired on the People — they

killed five — wounded several others, particularly
M[r] Ed[w] Payne in his Right Arm. Cap[t] Preston
bears a good Character — he was taken in the night
& Committed also seven more of the 29th — the
inhabitants are greatly enraged & not without
Reason.

Mar. 6. Most all the Town in Uproar & Confusion. The Gov[r] & Council met. The Cryer
went about to warn a Town Meeting at Eleven of
Clock. The Inhabitants met at Fanewill Hall,
they chose a Respectable Committee to wait on his
Honor the Lieut. Governour to desire the Troops
might be removed from the Town — Upon which
he Consulted Colo. Dalrymple & Colo. Kerr — the
Lieut. Governour Returned for answer that the
29th Regim[t] should go to the Castle & the 14th
Regim[t] Remain in Town. Afternoon the Inhabitants met at the Old South Meeting House & after
some Debate they unanimously Voted not to accept
the Lieut Governour's Proposals but Chose another
Committee of Seven to wait on him again & Insist
on all the Troops Being Removed from the Town
& without this is Complyed with it would not be
Satisfactory to the Inhabitants. The Committee
went & Returned that His Honor would Order both
Regiments to the Castle & Colo. Dalrymple consented to it — this gave Great Joy to the Inhabitants & I believe a General Satisfaction — so that
they went from the Meeting very Peaceably to
their Habitations.

Mar. 7. A Military Watch tonight.

Mar. 8.   I attended the Funeral of the four Unhappy People that were killed on Monday last. Such a Concourse of People I never saw before — I believe Ten or Twelve thousand.   One Corps with their Relations followed the other & then the Select Men & Inhabitants.   A Military Watch again tonight.

Mar. 9.   I went & paid a visit to Capt Preston in Goal who I found in much better spirits than I expected.   Military watch.

Mar. 10.   Yesterday two Companies of the 29th went to the Castle & four companies more went this day.   Still a Military watch.

Mar. 15.   This morning I settled a Long Dispute between Colo. Jones & Mr Millins.   Spent the afternoon with the Town Committee, myself Chairman John Ruddock Esq, Isaac Smith, Wm Dennie & Mr Timothy Fitch.

Mar. 16.   Mr Otis got into a mad Freak to night & broke a great many windows in the Town House. All the 14th Regiment are gone to the Castle the Last of them this day.   Capt Robson & Capt Miller both sailed for London this forenoon, in Capt Robson, Mr Robinson one of the Board of Commissioners went Passenger

Mar. 17.   This afternoon another of the unhappy Sufferers was Buried from Fanewill Hall — The General Court sitting at Cambridge which will be the Cause of a Quarrel between the Lieu^t Governour & the House of Representatives.

Mar. 18.   I was glad to find the Colo. Dalrymple was pleased with the answers to his Letters by Return of the Express.

Mar. 19.   Town meeting again today.   The Town voted a vessel to be hired to carry home dispatches & Capt Dashwood offered himself a Candidate to Carry them.

Mar 21.   This Day Mr Lock was installed President of Cambridge   The Superior Court met according to Adjournment

Mar. 23.   In the evening I went to the Concert Hall to hear Mr Joan read the Beggars Opera & sing the Songs.   He read but indifferently but Sung in Taste.   there were upwards one hundred people there.

Mar. 28.   My Goddaughter Miss Bella Sheaff dyed.

April 2.   I attended the Funeral of my old Acquaintance Brother Hugh McDaniel & was one of his Bearers   The Brotherhood walked in Procession before the Corps & made a handsome Appearance.

April 9.   Dined on Boston Neck at Bracketts with Ezek^l Golthwait, Jos. Golthwait, Solo. Davis, Capt Fenton, James Perkins, Joshua Winslow & Mr Inman.   Part of our Dinner was Buffalo Stakes which was very Tender.   Sir Thos Rich & John Allen Esq paid us a visit this afternoon.

April 16.   In the forenoon I attended Trinity Church Affairs as usual.

April 17.   Our Hannah dyed this day.

April 18.   Mr Hancock was Chosen Speaker of

the House pro Tempore & negatived by the Lieut
Governour   Colo. Warren was Chose in his Room
& approved.

April 19.   I attended the Funerall of Hannah
this afternoon.

April 20.   I attended the meeting of the Trade
as it is Called — they passed a Vote I did not like.
The Infamous Richardson on Tryal today.

April 21.   Richardson was found Guilty by the
Jury.   I attended the Merchants Meeting this forenoon.

April 22.   This afternoon Mr Otis behaved very
madly, firing Guns out of his Window that Caused
a Large Number of People to assemble about him.

April 24.   Capt Scot Brings an acc^t of the Repeal
of the Duties on Glass, Oyl Paper & painters Colours but the Duty on Tea still Remains.   Tis said
our Lieut Governour is made Governour — he negatived Cushing as Commissary Generall

April 25.   Merchants Meeting.   I attended.   I
was to my Great Mortification chose a Committeeman.   Meeting adj'd.

April 26.   Attended Merchants Meeting.   I did
not approve much of their Proceedings — think
them too severe.

Aprill 28.   The Revd Mr Walter's Child was
buried this afternoon   Mr George Erving's wife
died last evening.

May 8.   This day the Town of Boston Chose
Representatives

The Honble James Boudoin Esq. 439
"   "   John Hancock   "   511
            Thos Cushing   "   510
            Saml Adams   "   510
number of votes 513.

May 9. This Day Mr Adams of Roxbury preached the Dudleian Lecture — Mr Bleners went to Woodstock this morning on business for me.

May 10. Spent the evening at the Coffee House with the Proprietors of Point Shirley, John Hancock Esq., J^no Baker, Nat. Holmes, Ezech^l Golthwait & Thos Golthwait.

May 11. Dined at home with Sir Thos Rich, Mr Pashaw, a Gentleman in the Navy a Rushian Mr John Lane, Mr Inman, Mrs R. & Sucky — Spent the evening at the Coffee House with the Proprietors of Point Shirley, James Pitt Esq, John Hancock, John Baker, Ezekl Golthwait, Thos Golthwait, Nat. Holmes, Danl Hubbard & Charles Sigourney — agreed to go to the Point next Fryday.

May 17. This morning the 29th Regiment Marched from the Caftle to Providence.

May 18. Just as I was going to bed there was a very great Hallooing in the street & a mob of upwards a thousand people — it seems they had got an informer & put him in a Cart, covered with Tar & Feathers & so exhibited him thro' the Streets.

May 19. This morning James swept our Chimneys.

May 23. Sandwich — Wee rose early & set out for Mashby an Indian Town — Wee took a Guide,

one Mr Fowler — wee reached Jos. Ashers, a Native.
Wee fished there, found it a wild place — Wee had
Good Sport — from thence wee went to Mr Crocker's
the Tavern — wee dined there & wee were joyned by
Capt Solo. Davis, Mr Calef, Mr Brattle & the Rev-
erend Mr Hawley, the Indian Minister who I take
to be a Clever man — there were two young Ladies
Daughters of Mr Crocker, Miss Betty & Miss Sally
— very Clever & Genteel   from this we Returned
to Sandwich — we spent the evening & supped at
Mr Fessenden's — We slept at Mr Newcombs —
very Good Beds — We passed by the most Beautiful Pond, named Wakely.

May 24.   Wee Rose early & set out for Plymouth
— Stopt at Ellis & from thence got to the monu-
ment where we stopt at Isaac Jeffreys, an Indian &
a preacher to the Indians — his Squaw had a neat
Wigwam — I slept an hour there.   We dined there
after dinner I went down to the River & Caught
Ten Trout — The Largest I ever saw several of
them eighteen Inches in Length.   From thence we
returned to Plymouth & spent the evening at
Edward Winslows.

May 29.   King's Restoration — This afternoon
an Ox was carried thro' the streets in Triumph to
be exhibited tomorrow.

May 30.   Election kept at Cambridge.   This
day an Ox was Roasted whole on the Common — a
Great many People attended & a Large Company
dined at Fanewil Hall.

May 31.   Convention of the Ministers today —
Dr. Cooper preached at Dr Sewall's Meeting House.

June 4. Artillery Election — dined at Fanewill Hall with the Lieut Governour, his Majesty's Council & the Gentlemen Officers of the Artillery & a Great Number of other Gentlemen — Afternoon I went to Mr Hancock's & saw the Ceremony of Investing the New Officers of the Artillery — Capt Heath of Roxbury, Capt Martin, Gay Lieut. & Jonas Clark ensign — the Company made a pretty appearance & exercised well — Spent part of the evening with the House of Representatives at the Province House in Drinking his Majesty's Health — A Great many Gentlemen attended this Publick mark of Loyalty to his Majesty & Family.

June 6. Town meeting. Mr John Adams was Chose a Member for the Town.

June 14. In the afternoon I pd The Lieut Governor a visit at his seat at Milton.

July 9. Yesterday was discovered the Black Caterpillar which devours everything before it — they march from the North East direct S° West.

July 10. Dry weather — The caterpillars increase.

July 18. This was the first Day the new President made his appearance in Publick.

July 22. Capt Smith of the Nassau arrived from London & gives an acc^t of the Prorogation of the Parliament the 20th of May without Repealing the Duty on Tea — the people I hope will have Virtue enough never to make use of it as Long as the Duty is demanded.

July 24. This afternoon " The Body " as they

are called met & just before some of them Proceeded
through the streets with Dr Young at their head
with Three Flags Flying, Drums Beating & a
french Horn — Thos Baker carried one of them
for which he is much Blamed by me — The meeting today will I believe prove very Predjudicial to
the Merchants & Trade of the Town of Boston.

July 26.   The Govr offered me the Colonial
Commission —

Aug 4.   I & Mrs Rowe paid a visit to Colin Campbell Esq & Lady

Aug 14.   The Revd Mr Whitfield came to Town
this day — A Large Party of the Sons of Liberty
dined this day at the House of Thos Carnes at
Dorchester.

Aug. 16.   Mr Whitfield preached at the Old
North yesterday first Time — after dinner I went to
Dr Sewall's meeting house & heard Mr Whitfield
preach from the 9^h Chap. of Zachariah & 12 Verse
"Turn Ye to the Strong Hold Ye Prisoners, of
Hope   I liked his Discourse.

Aug. 17.   Mr Whitfield Preached at (New
North) Dr Elliots this morning.

Aug 18.   Mr Whitfield preached this morning
at Mr Pemberton's.

Aug 20.   Mr Whitfield preached at New North,
Dr Elliots.

Aug 21.   Mr Whitfield preached this morning
at Dr Sewalls.

Aug 22.   Mr Whitfield preached again this
morning at Dr Sewall's.

Aug 23.   Mr Whitfield preached at New North.

Aug 24.   In the forenoon I went to Old Dr Sewell's meeting & heard Mr Whitfield preach from 22^d Chap. St Matthews & 11. 12 & 13 Verses — this was in my opinion a Clever Discourse.

Aug 26.   I have been married twenty seven year yesterday.

Aug 28.   Mr Whitfield preached yesterday at Cambridge, this day at Charlestown.

Aug 29.   Mr Whitfield preached at Old South.

Aug 30.   Mr Whitfield preached at New North.

Aug. 31.   Mr Whitfield preached at Jamaica Plain.

Sept 1.   Mr Whitfield preached at Milton this day.

Sept 2.   Mr Whitfield preached at Roxbury this day

Sept 3.   Mr Whitfield preached at Old South

Sept 4.   Mr Whitfield set out for Portsmouth — I should have gone to Point Shirley with the proprietors but was very Busy.

Sept 5.   I attended the Merch^ts Meeting at Fanewill Hall I attended the Funerall of Mr Fitch Pool yesterday in the afternoon.

Sept 10.   This day the Council set & the Lieut Governour delivered up the Castle unto Colo Dalrymple by express order from his Majesty in Council.   I spent the evening at the Coffee House with the Merchants — Present 24.

Sept 11.   I spent the forenoon at the Coffee House with the Merchants, present 93

Sept 12.   I spent the evening with the Merchants at the Coffee House, present 74.

Sept 13.   Spent the afternoon at Fanewill Hall with the Body as they are called — Capt Scot arrivd from London 7 weeks passage

Sept 14.   I attended the Merchants Meeting this forenoon.   Present 51.   I spent the afternoon at Fanewill Hall with the Body as they are called.

Sept 15.   This forenoon I attended the Merchants Meeting at Mr Cordis there were present 64 I also attended the Body at Fanewill Hall & they came to a Conclusion to Forward a Letter to the Trade at Philadelphia.

Sept 19.   Young Thatcher was ordained this day.

Sept 24.   After Dinner I attended the Proprietors of Long Wharf.

Sept 25.   Mr Inman set out for Newport with Sucky & Katy Wendall.   Spent the evening at the Pofsee all present except J. Richardson who buried his Mother this afternoon.

Sept 28.   Sir Thos Rich arrivd this day from Hallifax.   The Viper Capt Porter Returnd from a Cruise   The St John Capt Murray from Hallifax The Bristol Packet Capt Skinner from St Jubes Capt Fellows from London.

Sept 30.   The Revd Mr Whitfield died suddenly this morning at Newberry, much Lamented.   Capt Hussey arrivd from the Streights.

Oct 3.   This Day Council & house are to have a fast at Cambridge.   Mr Appleton & Mr Cook are to preach.

Oct 4.   I attended the Funerall of Coll° Jarvis.

Oct 5.   Afternoon I went with M[r] John Cutler & viewed the Organ (of Trinity) & gave him the key of the Organ

Oct 6.   M[r] Inman came home from Newport to-day & brought Sally Winslow & Sucky

Oct 9.   I went on Board the Rose with Cap[t] Caldwell from thence to the Cafsell & from thence on board the Romney & dined with Comm[n] Hood his Lady, his Son, Major Butler of the 60[h], Major Powell of the 38[h], Dr Pertersby, M[r] Thomas & M[r] West.   I returned & spent the evening with the Committee of Merchants at the Coffee House, Henderson Inches J[no] Amory Ed[w] Payne, Isaac Smith & myself.   Cap[t] John Linzee arrivd in the Beaver from Hallifax.

Oct. 10.   This morning arrivd Cap[t] Davis from London & Comm° Gambier from England & Maderia in the Salisbury.   I spent the afternoon with the Merchants at the Coffee House.

Oct. 11.   Spent the evening at the Coffee House on an Arbitration between Tho[s] Flucker & M[r] Clark of Milton, W[m] Phillips Jos Barrett & myself Referees.

Oct. 12.   I paid Comm° Gambier a visit this morning & dind at home with Comm° Hood & Lady, Cap[t] Jno Linzee M[r] Inman M[rs] Rowe Sucky & Sally Inman & Cap[t] Bellew.   Attended the Merch[ts] Meeting Present 72.

Oct. 13.   The Salisbury Man of War came up to the Wharff this Day.

Oct. 14.   The Boston Man of Warr Capt Parker came up.

Oct. 15.   The Rose & Senegall came up the Harbour.

Oct. 16.   I dined at home with Capt John Lynzee, Mr Gregory Townsend Mrs Rowe Sucky & Sally Inman & Antony Letchmere & spent the evening at home with Capt John Lynzee etc. The Gibralter Man of Warr Capt Bond arrivd from England

Oct. 18.   Spent the evening at home with Capt John Linzee Mrs Rowe, Sucky and Sally Inman.

Oct. 19.   I dined at home with the following Company Capt Barclay of the Salisbury, Capt Hide Parker of the Boston, Capt Benjn Caldwell of the Rose, Capt Bond of the Gibraltar, Sir Thos Rich of the Senegall, Capt John Lynzee of the Beaver, Colo. Dalrymple & Capt Mason of the 14th Reg^t, Mr Inman, Mrs Rowe & Sucky Inman — Spent the afternoon & evening at home with the same company

Oct. 20.   The Highest Tide I ever saw — it has done great Damages to the Wharffs, Storehouses & vast Quantitys of Lumber Wood &c a Drift — Quantitys of Salt washed out. Several People have lost Sugars — Several vessels drove ashore from their Anchors. Even Storehouses set adrift   After noon I paid a visit & found my Wharff & stores had escaped better than I expected.

Oct. 21.   Afternoon I went to King's Chapel — M^r. Troutbeck had his Daughter Christened. I

stood Godfather Mrs Gould & Mrs Rogers God-
mothers — the Child's name Elizabeth.[1]

Oct. 23.   The Judges of the Superior Court met
today and ordered the Trialls of Capt Preston tomorrow.

Oct. 25.   The King's Ascension to the Throne.
The whole Fleet the Castle & Batterys fired on this
Occasion, the Comm^e first, then every Capt accord-
ing to Seniority — Capt Preston still on Triall

Oct. 29.   Capt Preston Still on Tryall.   The
Judges gave their Opinion in his favor.   The Jurys
verdict not Guilty.

Nov. 18.   Great Talk of a Spanish War & of
Report of the Plague being Broke out in the Island
of Hispaniola.

Nov. 20.   A Ship & a Schooner arrivd from Hispaniola were ordered to perform Quarantine.

Dec. 5.   This Day The Tryall of the Soldiers
ended (after five days trial in the Superior Court)
Six of them were acquitted & two were found
Guilty of Manslaughter.

Dec. 9.   Mr Properts pay commences as Organist from this day at £40 Sterl^g pr Annum.

Dec. 12.   Capt Linzee Brought the Beaver into
my Dock & graved her, the Commodore being well
pleased.

Dec. 14.   The Beaver got Docked & well out
this evening.

----

[1] A miniature of this Elizabeth Troutbeck, afterwards
Mrs. Bows, is in the possession of Mr. Rowe's great-grand-
niece.

Dec. 25.   Christmas Day — I dined at home
with Capt John Linzee Mr John Lane, Dr Miller
Joseph Golthwait Mr Inman, Mrs Rowe, Miss Lucy
Flucker[1] & Sucky Inman — The same Company
staid & spent the afternoon & evening & wee were
very Cheerfull.

Dec. 26.   Spent the evening at Mr Lewis Deblois
with him & his new wife & a very Large Company
too many to enumerate — a very Genteel Entertainment.

1771

Jan. 3.   Spent the evening at Concert Hall where
there was a Concert performed by Hartley, Morgan
& others — after the Concert a Dance   the Commodore & all the Captains of the Navy here, were
there & Colo Dalrymple & fifty or sixty Gentlemen
& the same number of Ladies Present —

Jan. 4.   Spent the evening at the Concert Room
at an Afsembly.   A very Large & respectable
afsembly it was.

Jan. 18.   The Queens Birth Day, fine weather,
Guns firing Jovial Day — Spent the Evening at
Concert Hall with a very Grand Assembly, Gov-
ernour, Lieut. Govr Commodore, Colonel, Captains
of the Navy & Army, Commissioners, all the Best
People in town — A General Coalition so that
Harmony Peace & Friendship will once more be

[1] Miss Lucy Flucker was afterwards the wife of General
Knox.

Established in Boston — Very Good Dancing & Good Musick but very Bad Wine & Punch.

Jan. 29. Spent an hour with Mr James Otis who I found in a gloomy way

March 4. My worthy Friend Nat Bethune died this morning, also Mrs Inches.[1]

March 6. I attended the Funerall of Mrs Sarah Inches & was a Bearer with Isaac Smith, Sam Austin Thos Rufsell Jona. Mason & Eben^r Storer.

Mar. 7. I attended the Funerall of my worthy Friend Nat. Bethune & was a Bearer with James Boutineau Thos Flucker Jos. Green Nich^o Boylston & Solomon Davis

Mar. 8. Arrivd from London Our Ship Boscawen Capt Robson & the Marquis of Rockingham, Capt Whitwood both from London

Mar. 9. The Chaplain Mr Mofsely of the Salisbury was taken in an Apoplectick fit yesterday which hindered him coming to our house.

Mar. 11. Blustering weather Snow & sleet. Town meeting for the Choice of Officers — I attended on Purpose to oblige my Friend Ezek^l Goldthwait Esqr

Mar. 14. The Govern^r Commission Read today also the Lieut. Govern^{rs} the Company that waited on the Govern^r were Gentlemen of Reputation & the Best Fortunes — I spent the evening at the Assembly which was very Brilliant

---

[1] From the opening of the Diary Mr. Rowe had passed every Sunday evening, almost without exception, at Mr. Nat. Bethune's.

March 15. Afternoon the Merchants met at the British Coffee House to prepare an Address to the Governour — Present Rich[d] Clark, Jos. Green, myself, John Erving Geo. Erving, Tho[s] Gray, Henderson Inches, Edw[d] Payne Melabiah Bourne, Dan[l] Hubbard, Ezek[l] Golthwait John Dennie, John Amory & Solomon Davis — & spent the evening there with most of the same Company — when I came home I found M[r] J. Lane & M[r] Propert who supped & diverted us all the evening by playing on Sucky's Spinnet & Joyned by M[r] J. Lane in singing — Propert is a fine hand.

Mar. 18. The Merchants waited on his Excellency, The Govern[r] with their Address — Present 106.

Mar. 19. I Launched my Brigg Sucky at Walker's this day.

Mar. 28. This Day The French Boy & a Charcoal Fellow stood in the Pillory. The French Boy was to have been whipt but the Populous hindered the Sheriff doing his duty.

Mar. 30. A Brigg.[a] Cap[t] Hosey arrived this day from Liverpool in 51 days brings an acc[t] that matters were accommodated between the Contending Powers. I had a letter from Quebeck that tells me of an Horrid Assasination on my Brother.

Mar. 31. The News I Receivd ab[o] My Brother prevented my Going out this Day

April 1. I attended the Wardens & Vestry of Trinity Church this morning Afternoon the Funerall of General Shirley.

April 2. Easter Tuesday. I dined with the members of the Charitable Society at Colo. Ingersolls in King Street. Present Myself, Ralph Inman, J^{no} Apthorp, Govr Hutchinson, Commo. Gambier, Mr J^{no} Lane, Rufus Greene, Nat Greene, J^{no} Greene, Benjn Greene Joseph Greene, Dan Hubbard, Robt Jenkins, J^{no} Box John Box J^r, Wm Coffin, John Haskins, J^{no} Cutler Gilb^t Deblois, Richd Green, Stephen Greenleaf & the ministers — Dr Byles, Mr Winslow, Mr Walter Mr Fogg & Mr Mosely.

April 3. This day the Genl Court meets at Cambridge. The Governour was met by the Gentlemen of Cambridge & escorted to the College where there was an Oration spoke in Latin by one of the students.

Aprill 7. After Church the Vestry met ab° Dr Byles affairs. Capt Scot arrivd from London & brought the news of Mrs Eustis Death — who is greatly Lamented Capt Airy arrivd from a Whaling Voyage has bad Luck

Aprill 9. This Forenoon Our Vestry met at Our house ab° Dr Byles affairs.

Aprill 10. Afternoon I attended the Creditors of Mr Caleb Loring at the Coffee House. I dind & suppd on Salmon for the first time.

Aprill 16. The Wid° Green Mr Townsend Mrs Townsend Mrs Benjn Green junr Mrs Rogers Miss Betty Gould & the Revd Mr Walter spent the afternoon with us.

Aprill 18. The Boscawen Capt Robson saild for Hallifax this morning & Capt Whitwood sailed for

Barbadoes in him Mr Sober & Mrs Sober went Paſsengers.

Aprill 19.   Capt Stratsburg paid us a visit this
afternoon & is a Chearfull Old Gentleman.

Aprill 25.   (Plymouth) Set out for the Mano-
ment Ponds   Wee Reachd Isaac Jeffrys the Indian
Parsons Wigwam   wee were joynd by Pelham &
Edwd Winslow junr^r wee were disappointed in our
Diversions, the water been very high & the Ponds
not drawn off — wee stayd the Day & had but poo
Luck.

Aprill 29.   I dind on board the Salisbury Man
of Warr with the Gentlemen of the Wardrobe.

Aprill 30.   I attended Mrs Taylor's Funerall &
met the Proprietors of Long Wharff at the Coffee
House

May 3.   Spent the Evening at the Aſsembly a
very Grand one Sixty-eight Ladies & forty-five
Gentlemen

May 6.   The Boston Capt Parker, the Mermaid
Capt Smith, the Rose Capt Caldwell, the Senegal
Capt Thompson & all the Transports arrivd from
Hallifax with the 64^h & 65^h Regiments in this
Harbour.

May 7.   I attended Town Meeting for the
Choice of Representatives — Mr Otis, Mr Cushing,
Mr Saml Adams & Mr Hancock were Chose by a
Great Majority.

May 9.   I Rose very early this morning & found
Capt Hall arrived from London — Andrew Brimmer,
Thos Palfrey, Mr Grey came Passengers — they

Bring an acc^t of the Lord Mayor & Alderman
Oliver being Put in the Tower —

May 16.   Afternoon I went over to Dorchester
with Mr Brattle to a new place he has hird & I
think a very agreeable Rural Spot.

May 19.   Capt Barthlet arrivd in the St John
from James River Virginia   Royall Tyler Died —
Mr Price the Picture man died on Fryday

May 21.   I attended the Funerall of Old M^r
Wm Price — he was buried under Trinity Church.

May 22.   I attended the Funerall of Royall
Tyler Esqr — his bearers were John Erving Esqr
Generall Brattle, James Rufsell Esqr Saml Dexter
Esqr John Barrat & Mr Wm Whitwell.

May 26.   Sunday — There was a Collection for
Mrs Hooper the sum was £29.7.9 Lawfull money.

May 27.   Capt John Linzee arrivd in the Beaver
from Antigua & paid us a Visit.

June 4.   King's   Birthday — The   Governour
made a Dinner for the King's Officers at the Coffee
house — Spent the evening at Concert Hall at
Comm^e Gambier's Ball which was very Brilliant —
A Great Company & very Good — too many to
enumerate —

June 10.   I went to Needham with Greg Townsend, James Perkins Capt Fenton & Harry.   Wee
Stopt & dind at Coolidges Watertown who keeps
a Clean House from thence to Bullard's wee suppd,
spent the evening & slept there.

June 11.   Wee fishd again no Great Sport —
Wee din'd at Bullard's from thence came home to

Boston, was Caught in a very hard Shower of Rain
much Lighting & Thunder. Wet to Skin. I was
called up by Major Fleming on a Particular Affair
between Capt Linzee & Lieut Sharp Marine officer
of the Salisbury

June 12. They began to mow my Pasture yesterday.

June 16. There were three seizures made, some
Tea at Plymouth, A schooner from St Peters with
Brandy, Wine &c — another Schooner that short
entered her Cargoe of Molasses belonging to M^r
Forster of Cape Anne. These affairs give great
Uneasiness & tis believed will Raise the Minds of
the People. The mowers made an end of mowing
my Pasture yesterday.

June 17. Another Sloop was Seized this Day
from St Peters by Capt Parker of the Boston Man
of War.

June 20. Capt Brown saild for Oporto in my
New Briggatine Sucky this morning.

June 21. I dind at Cambridge at Mr Inman's
with him   Govern^r Hutchinson Commo Gambier
Mrs Gambier Mrs James Gambier Colo Phipps M^{rs}
Phipps, Major Vafsall Mrs Vafsall Colo. Oliver M^{rs}
Oliver Mrs Rowe George & Sucky Inman & Sally
Gould. Spent the evening at home with Capt
John Linzee (& others) My Coachman was thrown
from his horse & hurt himself.

June 25. I dind at Mr Brackets with the Free
Masons at the Celebration of St John — present 32.

July 5. After Dinner I took a Ride over to

Dorchester with Mrs Rowe.   The Generall Court
Prorogued this day.

July 12.   After Dinner I paid a visit to M^{rs}
Smith who Came to Town last Night & came Pafsenger in the Mast Ship two of her nieces came
with her — afterwards I took a Ride to Dorchester
with Capt John Linzee — Wee went to Savine Hill
— wee met Miss Atherton a Smart, Clever Girl.

July 16.   I dind at Brackets in School St with
Mr Williams of Maryland Mr Glover of Leeds
Yorkshire Henry Loyd, Bishop Barrett Thos Amory
John Amory Jonathan Amory Mr Inman, Nat.
Coffin & Willm Coffin junr.   The Beaver Man of
Warr, Capt Linzee saild this day.

July 17.   Commencement Day — I rose very
early & wrote until I could not write any more for
the Pain of my head.   I went to Cambridge & dined
with Mr Inman — after Dinner I went to Colo.
Murrays Room in the New College where there was
a Large Company, the Govern^r Council & too many
to enumerate — I staid till six.

July 22.   I waited on Mr John Lane who sailed
for London in the Ship Boscawen Capt Robson,
also Mr Mills of Newhaven.   I dind at home with
Capt Fenton Mr Inman, Mrs Smith Mrs Rowe, George
& Sucky Inman & Anthony Lechmere — after Din-
ner Mr Inman Introduced his Design to Mrs Smith.

July 24.   Last night the mob Routed the
Whores at the House of Joseph Henderson at
Olivers Dock.

July 25.   Attended the Tryall between James
Otis & Mr Robinson

July 26. The Tryall of Mr Otis against Mr Robinson finished the Jury found £2000 Ster^g damages in favor of the Plaintiff.

July 27. I spent the evening at home with Capt John Linzee who is just come in, Mrs Rowe & Sucky.

July 30. I went this morning about some Particular Bufsiness with Mr Shrimp^t Hutchinson & paid a visit to my Friend Old Mr Gould who I found very Ill.

Aug. 6. In the afternoon I went on board the Commodore's Ship the Salisbury by Invitation from him with the following Company (then follow 61 names) Wee all spent the evening had a fine entertainment & the Genteelest supper I ever saw.

Aug. 9. The Tamar Man of Warr Capt Charles Hay arrivd from England he came out in Company with the Captain, Adm^l John Montague, the Lively & Swan Men of Warr

Aug. 12. Admirall Montague in the Captain & Capt Talbot in the Lively arrivd from England — I dind on board the Beaver with Capt John Linzee, Capt Caldwell, Colo. Dalrymple, Capt Barckly, Capt Blair & Mr Holwell. The Commodore & all his Captains went on board the Admirall to pay their Compliments

Aug. 13. I went on board the Captain Man of Warr to pay a visit to Admiral Montague who Received me very Politely.

Aug. 14. Capt Skimmer arrivd from Lisbon having 8 weeks pafsage.

Aug. 15. The Beaver Man of War, Capt John Linzee sailed this day to find out Cashier's Ledge.

Aug. 16. Afternoon Mr Inman & Mrs Rowe paid a visit to Mrs Smith over to Golthwait's. Mr Inman came home well pleased & agreed on his Plan of Matrimony —

Aug. 17. I am very Busy in Sending Provisions off to the Ships.

Aug. 19. I was taken very Ill in the Night. I sent to Dr. Perkins who advisd me to stay at home. I did all Day.

Aug. 24. Capt Jarvis arrived from London & the Canso arm'd Ship in the Service of the Government under the Direction of Saml Holland Esqr fr Plym° in England

Aug 25.   Mr Burnet a Midshipman of the Beaver Brings an acc^t of Capt Jn° Linzees finding Cashier's Ledge.

Aug 27. I had a Considerable Conversation with Mr Atkinson the Admiralls secretary. The Beaver, Capt John Linzee Returned from a cruise.

Sept. 1. My Brother in Law Mr Inman was Published this morning to Mrs Smith at the King's Chapell.

Sept 3. Young Mr Gore died very suddenly this day.

Sept 4. I dined on board the Beaver, Capt John Linzee. The Beaver people made a Seizure for wh. I am sorry.

Sep^t 5 My Whale Sloop Polly, Capt Airy arrived this day with 150 Barrells.

RALPH INMAN, Esq.

Sept 22. The Kings Accession to the Throne.

Sept 26. About eleven my Brother in Law Ralph Inman was married at the Seat of Mr Ezek^l Golthwait to Mrs Smith. the Ceremony was Performed by the Revd Mr Caner. after marriage we all went except Dr Caner to Mr Inman's. We dined there & were Joyned by the Revd Mr Serjeant, Mr John Inman & Mr Thos Hooper. The Company was very Chearfull. I spent the evening there with Mr Inman, Mrs Inman, George Sucky & Sally Inman Mrs Rowe & Sally Gould. We slept there.

Sept 27. Came to Boston, Returned to Cambridge with Capt Linzee & dined at Mr Inmans with him & Mrs Inman etc.

Sept 29. I did not go to Church this morning being engaged with Mr Mich^l Everet who is just going to sea in the Viper.

Oct 14. The Beaver Man of War Capt John Linzee sailed on a Cruise this day

Oct. 20. Capt Bryant arrived from London in whom my Kinsman Mr Jacob Rowe of Exeter came passenger.

Oct 23. I went to Cambridge with Cousin Jacob Rowe & din'd at Mr Inman's.

Nov. 1. I dined at Mr Henderson Inches'. After Dinner we went over to Brackets & see a Yorkshire man stand upon a horse's Back & Gallop him full Speed, afterwards upon two Horses & after that on Three, he endeavoured to make all them gallop as fast as he could. then he mounted a single Horse & Run him full speed & while Running he Jumped off & on three severall times.

Nov. 2.   The Hope, Schooner arrived with her seizure.

Nov 7.   After dinner I was called upon to go to the Coffee house to see Sir Thos Rich who was under arrest at the Suit of Capt Cookson for a protested bill.

Nov 16.   The Printers of the Massachusetts Spy was sent for by the Govr & Councill this day.   they ordered the King's Attorney to Prosecute them. Our Henry Smith left us yesterday.

Nov 25.   We took in our ̶wood :   20 cord of Mr Hatch.

Nov 27.   This Day I am fifty six years of age.

Nov 29.   Yesterday morning died very suddenly my old Friend Wm Sheaffe.   The Commissioners have appointed William Waterhouse in the Room of Mr Sheaffe.

Dec 2.   Spent the evening at the Fire Club at Colo. Ingersolls with Treas. Gray, Master Lovell, Jos. Green, Solo. Davis Geo Bethune, Melabiah Bourne, Thos Flucker, Benj^a Fanewill John Dennie, Mr Inman.   We voted in Mr Thos Boylston a member.

Dec 7.   Mr Edward Payne had a Quantity of Malaga Wine seized in the Heron by Sheppard.

Dec 11.   John Dennie & Tim^o Folger made Justices yesterday.   I attended the Funerall of Mrs Storer this afternoon.

Dec 13.   Mr Thompson went into my house opposite me the 11th Instant at £30 p annum.

Dec 17.   This Day Mr Thompson took the House

CAPT. JOHN LINZEE

over the way at 100 Doll^s pr Annum for six months.
I deliv'd him the key.

Dec 25. Christmas Day. excessive cold weather,
the ink freezes — I went to Church this forenoon.
We gathered £318.6/ old tenor which was more
than I expected being very Cold & few People at
Church.

Dec 26. Still very cold — Capt Stephen Davis
in my Sloop Polly sailed for Madeira this day —
Mr Henderson Inches was married this eve'ng to
Miss Bettsy Brimner.

Dec. 27. St John's Day — I dined at Colo. Ingersolls with the Brethren 41 Present.

1772

Primo Jany. I attended the Distribution of the
Poor money at the Church. Din'd & Spent the
evening at home with Capt John Linzee Mr Mrs Inman, Sucky & Sally Inman also Mrs Rowe.

Jany 8. I paid a visit to see Old Mr Gould who
is very Ill. Capt Linzee & Sucky gone to Cambridge.

Jany 9. My Worthy Friend Old Mr Gould
Died.

Jany 13. I Attended as a Relation The Funerall
of my Old Friend Mr John Gould, a Great Number
of Gentlemen & others attended.

Jany 16. Spent part of the evening at the
Coffee House on an Arbitration between the Underwriters of the N^o End & Pain Newman of Newberry, myself, John Avery & John Scollay.

Jany 17. Mr Inmans birth Day Mrs Rowe & Sucky gone to Cambridge.

Jan 22. The Trial of Wm Tyng came on this day for Treble Damages.

Jan 26. Mr Walter read prayers & preached. A most charming Discourse. I spent an hour or two with Robt Gould & perused his Uncles' Last Will & Testament.

Jan 27. Judge Auchmooty told in his Decree against Wm Tyng.

Jan 30. Spent the evening at the Assembly Present 44 Gentlemen 53 Ladies.

Feby 2. Wee have Rec'd the Bad news Robt Gould's Sloop was cast away on Plum Island Fryday night.

Feby 5. Mr Golthwait told us of a Conference between him & Mollineaux, very extraordinary wanting Mr G. to destroy Josiah Quincy & Benjn Kent.

Feb'y 9. Several Vessells Blown off are heard off at Antigua & Statia.

Feb 12. I attended the Funerall of Miss Polly Wethered & was a Bearer together with Dr Gardner James Pitts Peter Chardon Shrimpton Hutchinson & Major Vafsall.

Feb 13. Mr John Wendall was buried this afternoon. Spent the evening at the Afsembly There was a Clever Company.

Feb 15. I attended the Funerall of Mrs Miller Sister to Wm Vafsall Esq and was a Bearer

Feb 16. I paid a Visit to Robt Gould who has

got the Gout   came home & spent the evening with Capt Solo. Davis Capt Linzee Mrs Rowe & Sucky. ab° Ten of Clock Mrs Davis & Katy Wendall came to Our house.

Feb 17. Very Smart Cold. The Ink Freezes as I write.

Feb. 19. The Superior Court met yesterday & made a Good Figure. they were attended by a Great Number of Gentlemen, the Governor, Admiral & many more.

Feb. 22. The Beaver's Gunner Quelch & Capt Linzee's Clark have had an Affray. the Gunner has wounded the Clark.

Mar 5. A Town meeting this morning. they adjourned to Dr Sewall's Meeting house where there was an Oration spoke by Dr Warren on the memory of this day Two Year. tis said upwards of four thousand People were present. There was an Exhibition at Mrs Clappams in Kings Street this evening. A great many Spectators.

Mar 7. The Treasurer's (Gray) Birthday, aged Sixty years. he says he was very Brisk this morning.

Mar 9. Town meeting this day — The Petitions of the Lieu^t Governour Mr Hubbard & Dr Gardiner were Dismissed   Also Mr Payson's & Mr Mollineux. Two new Select Men Saml Austin & Colo. Marshall in the Room of Mr Inches & Mr Mason. I got excused from Being a Fire Ward.

Mar 10. I attended Town Meeting this Forenoon. Large Debates on the affairs of Mr Mollineaux.

Mar 26.   I attended the Funerall of Mr Ethoridge
& was a Bearer with Francis Johnnot Capt Par-
tridge Capt Dogget Mr Hews & Mr Ruggles the
Carpenter. The Glasgow Man of Warr Capt
Maltby arriv'd from England. Last from Lisbon.
Mrs Grace Gardner Buried too night.

Mar 27.   Capt Linzee saild in the Beaver. (From
Jan'y 1st there is scarcely a day when the Diary
does not record his dining or spending the evening
at Mr Rowe's & oftener both).

I spent the former Part of the Evening at Colo.
Ingersolls with John Hancock, Treas^r Gray Thos
Gray Ezek^l Goldthwait Solo. Davis Wm Davis, W^m
Coffin, jun^r, Arnold Wells Tuthill Hubbard & Jos.
Scot. The Treasurer told a story ab^o Capt Tyng
sending his Irish man to buy cheese etc. The Re-
mainder at home with Capt Linzee Mrs Rowe &
Sucky

April 1.   This morning ab^o four of Clock The
Town was alarmed by a fire which Broke Out in the
Front Room of the British Coffee house — it was
very lucky our Engines got the Better of it Soon.

Aprill 2.   Fast Day.   Mr Walter read prayers &
preached a very Clever & pertnent sermon. After
(dinner) Capt Linzee Came in being Return'd in
the Beaver very Leaky. Capt Higginson, Capt
Callahan Capt Jenkins arriv'd from London and a
Great number of Other Vessels from Different parts
it snows very fast & blows hard at North East.

April 3.   Thos Symms Shut up Yesterday.

Aprill 4.   Young Robt Jarvis arrivd in Geo.

Ervings Schooner from London, Capt Folger in Thos Boylston's Ship from London, Capt Wood in Mr Hancock's Brigg^n was Cast away on Point Allerton & another Brigg^n near the same place from the West Indies both in the Storms yesterday.

Aprill 6. Capt Jarvis arrivd in 27 Days from London — Sir Thos Rich Passenger in Jarvis. The Admirall visited the Fleet to Day.

Aprill 8. The General Court met at Cambridge this day. Mr Hancock is Chosen Speaker & approved.

Aprill 11. Capt Davis arrivd in my Sloop Polly from Madeira

Aprill 17. The Treasurer, Commissary & Import officer were Chose this day & the same as last Year — Mr Gray — Mr Cushing — Mr Russell.

Aprill 18. Lewis Turner died very Suddenly.

Aprill 20. Monday. I went to Church this morning to Chose Church officers which were the same as Last Year.

Aprill 23. I attended the Merch^{ts} Meeting. Brigg^r Brattle Major Hawley & John Hancock were Chose Commifsioners to Treat with New York Government.

May 7. The Representatives for Boston were Elected Yesterday John Hancock, Thos Cushing, Mr Saml Adams & Mr Wm Phillips

May 10. I went to church this morning Mr Thompson of Scituate Read prayers & preached from 6th Chap. to the Romans 16th Verse Afternoon I went to church. Mr Thompson read prayers & preached from 6th Chap. of the Prophet Hosea & 6th Verse. Both these sermons were honestly designed but very lengthy.

May 19.   Old Dana the Lawyer was buried this morning. Wm Shephard the Searcher died this morning.

May 27.   The following Gentlemen were Elected Counsellors for the ensuing year —

Sam Danforth	Esq	Thos Saunders	Esq
Wm Brattle	"	Stephen Hall	"
Harrison Gray	"	J^{no} Hancock	"
Sam Dexter	"	John Erving	"
Benj Greenleaf	"	Thos Hubbard	"
Tim° Woodbridge	"	James Pitts	"
Isaac Royall	"	Artemus Ward	"
James Boudoin	"	Caleb Cushing	"
James Russell	"	Sam Phillips	"

PLY^{MO} COLONY.

James   Otis — Wm Sever — Walt^r Spooner & Jerahmiel Bower Esqr.

PROVINCE OF MAYNE.

Nat Sparhawk, John Bradbury, Jeremiah Powell Esqrs.

AT LARGE.

John Humphreys, George Leonard jun'r Esqrs.

For Sagadahock — James Gowen Esq. The Governour consented to the Choice of all the Gentlemen except Jerahmiel Bowers. Mr Hancock declined taking his Seat at the Board.

June 4.   Kings Birth Day.   Colo. Erving made
his appearance at the Head of his Regim^t — the
Grenadiers looked very well.   Major Paddock's
Company behaved very Clever.   I attended the
Governour &c at the Council Chamber.   I spent
the evening at Concert Hall where there was a Ball,
a great Company there the Admiral & Gent^m of
the Navy & too many to enumerate.

June 5.   I went to Richards with Thos Knight,
Jos. Green & J^{no} Williams   wee fished   wee had
but middling Luck.   Thos Knight caught Twenty
Two Trout.   I sent the Admirall a Dozen of Trout
& Perch.

June 10.   The Admiral told me that Capt Dunnisin was wounded & his Vessel burnt at Providence.

June 16.   I rose very early & set out for Ipswitch with Saml Calef & Jack Williams — on acc^t of
a Law Suit I have with Nich^o Tracy.   We Stopt
at Lynn & Salem & Reached Ipswitch before
Dinner.   We Dined at Treadwells with Dr Smith
& Mr Miller both of Newbery Port.   Afternoon I
attended the Court & spent the evening at Treadwells with Mr Marston of M'head & Mr Calef.

June 17.   Attended Court.   dined at Treadwell's
with Colo. Lee of M'head, Epps Sargeant of Gloster,
Mr Adams the Lawyer & Mr Calef.

June 18.   I attended Court & agreed to Refer
my Action to Benjn Greenleaf of Newberry Port,
Mr Thos King of M'head & Job Prince in Boston.

June 19.   Wee went to Flax Pond, wee fished
there, wee had the Best Sport I ever was at, wee

caught very near a hundred Weight of Fish & the Largest Perch I ever saw there.

June 24. St. John's Day. Dr Warren & his Lodge walked in procession to Dr Byles' Church where a sermon was Preached by Mr Saml Fairweather. I dined with the Lodges under my Care at Brother Bracketts. Present 38.

June 27. Dr Church & others petitioned me to be set off to Another Lodge.

June 29. I began to mow the Pasture this day.

July 7. Colo. Hancock turned out this forenoon with the Cadet Company — they made a Good Figure & behaved very well throughout the whole of the exercise. The whole Regiment appeared in the Common this afternoon, also Major Paddock's Company — the whole behaved much Better than usual.

July 10. We were alarmed in the Night by the Turf in the Common behind the Powder House being on Fire.

July 15. I went to Cambridge it being Commencement Day. I attended the Ceremony in the forenoon. I dined at Col. Murray's son's Room with Col^o Murray Col^o Saltonstall Judge Sewall, Colo. Oliver Saml Quincy Mr Pease of Newport, Mr Richd Letchmere, Major Vassall Mr Gooding of Salem, Dr Russell of Concord, Mr Flagg, Mr Sam Fitch, Mr Archer a Gen^t of Lisbon, Mr Archibald Mr Neal, Mr Abram Savage, Mr Balch, Mr Phillip Dumaresque Mr Jos. Russell, Mr Forrest, Mr Greg. Townsend, Capt Fenton Mr Joseph Green, Mr John

Cotton, Mr Thos Brinley & Mr Danl Murray.   After Dinner wee were visited by the Governour & Councill, Admirall Montague & a Great many other Gentlemen — too many to enumerate.   I paid a visit to Mr Jona Williams' Son & also Dr Whitworth Son, both which took their Degree.

·July 16.   I went early to Mr Inman's who made the Genteelest Entertainment I ever saw on acc^t of his son George taking his Degree yesterday — he had Three hundred forty seven Gentlemen & Ladies dined.   Two hundred & Ten at one Table — amongst the Company The Govr & Family, The Lieut Governour & Family, The Admirall & Family & all the Remainder, Gentlemen & Ladies of Character & Reputation.   The whole was conducted with much Ease & Pleasure & all Joyned in making each other Happy — such an Entertainment has not been made in New England before on any Occasion.   I came to Town say Cambridge & went to the Ball at the Town House, where most of the Company went to Dance — they were all very happy & Cheerful & the whole was conducted to the General Satisfaction of all present.   I returned to Mr Inman's & slept there.   Mr J^{no} Inman met a misfortune at Cambridge.

July 21.   This day ab^o noon Sumners Shop was Burnt down.

July 26.   After church the Church Wardens & Vestry met about some alteration in Our Church. I was sorry to see the Gentlemen so Indifferent ab^o it.

July 28. Dr. Heron came to look at my leg which I hurted on Saturday last.

Aug. 6. This morning Mr Hancock, Dr Cooper Mr Brattle, Mr Tuthill Hubbard, Mr Saml Calef, Mr Winthrop of Cambridge Mr Nich° Bowes & Capt Hood went from Boston in the Providence Packet to visit the Eastern Parts of this Province and also on a Party of Pleasure. My Servant Henry Smith & Davis the Barber Man went with them as attendants. This forenoon Capt Jordan removed into the Foge Man of War from the Kingfisher & Capt Lobb Resumed the Command of the King Fisher Sloop. the Guns of the Fleet were fired on this Occasion

Aug 9. I dont go out being Confined by the Wound in my Leg the Doctor cannot at present dry it up.

Aug 10. Dr Peterson came with Dr Heron to see my Leg.

Aug 11. Dr Peterson came with Dr Heron to see my Leg.

Aug 14. Capt Linzee arrivd in the Beaver Man of Warr from Rhode Island. Capt Linzee came ashore to pay us a visit who staid the afternoon & spent the evening with Mrs Rowe myself & Sucky.

Aug 22. Mr Severance Clarkson of New York paid me a visit also Mr Richd Swanwick of Philadelphia Sucky Inman gone to Cambridge with her father & her mother & Capt Linzee

Aug 23. I am still unable to go to church

altho' the Doctor says my Leg is much better. Mr Hancock & his Party arrived here yesterday from the Eastward

Aug 25. Capt Linzee's horse was Brought home last Saturday. The Superfines Superior Court sat to Day. Dr Heron Drefsed my Leg with Tincture of Myrrh.

Aug. 26. Capt Linzee was taken last night at Mr Inman's at the Suit of Clark & Nightingale. I waited on Mr Reeves about this affairr.

Aug 27. I have been much engaged ab^o Capt Linzee's business with the Board. I sent Thos Hooper to Rhode Island on Purpose. My Leg much Better thank God & in a fair way.

Aug 28. The Sheriff in Quest after Capt Linzee & Col. Brattle was going to raise the Militia. The Rising Sun Lodge consecrated.

Aug 31. Capt Linzee was arrested on the Mulatto affair.

Sept 1. I went to Mr Inman's to see my Dear Sucky Inman married to Capt John Linzee. the Revd Mr Walter performed the Ceremony. Present The Admiral, Mrs Montague, Mr George & Miss Sophie Montague, Mr Inman, Mrs Inman George, Sucky & Sally Inman. The Revd Mr Troutbeck, Mrs Troutbeck, The Revd Mr Walter, Mrs Walter, The Revd Mr Serjeant, Capt Linzee, Mr Robt Gould, Mrs Gould, John Inman, George Inman, Miss Polly & Miss Anna Murray Miss Howard, Miss Hannah Speakman, myself & Mrs Rowe. Wee all dined there.

Sept 2. I gave Capt Linzee a Letter with Orders to draw on me every New Years Day Twenty Pounds Sterling, taking the money of Messrs Lane Son & Fraser for my acc^t.

Sept 4. Capt Linzee sailed this forenoon & carried my Dear Sucky with him, I wish them happy together. Mr Inman, Mrs Inman George & Sally went down in the Beaver as far as the Lighthouse with Capt & Mrs Linzee & took their leave of Sucky. 'tis a fair wind. My Leg is much better tonight.

Sept 6. I sent Antony to Judge Sewall at Cambridge on business of Importance ab^o Capt Linzee's matter.

Sept 23. My Negro Marcellus was Brought home this eve'ng much hurt.

Sept 24. Mr Thos Palmer took my house this Day

Sept 25. I got all the Fellows taken up that abused Marcellus & tryd them before Justice Quincy. the Justice ordered them to Goal.

Sept 28. George Inman went to Herman & Andrew Brimmer's this day.

Oct 1. I waited on Wm Vafsall Esqr — about his son Henry.

Oct 6. Capt Wm Brown arr'd in the Sucky from Bristol. Capt Airy in the Sloop Polly from Whaling having met Bad Weather & an unsuccessfull Voyage.

Oct 19. After Dinner Capt Freeman Brought in my Kinsman Jack Rowe Son of my Brother

Jacob of Quebeck. he came in Capt Wies. I am glad he is come. He is Upwards of seven Year Old.

Oct 26. Colo. Hancock with his Company appeared under Arms Yesterday being the King's Accession to the Throne & the 13th Year of his Majesty's Reign.

Oct 28. Town Meeting to Day ab^o the Judges Salary.

Oct 30. Mr Murray & Family also Thos Hooper sailed this day for Cape Fear.

Oct 31. After Dinner I rode over to Brackets where I spent an hour with Treas. Gray & John Cotton & we were Joyned by James Otis who had been to wait on Govr Hutchinson as a Committee man from the Town of Boston. Mr Propert sent me the Key of the Organ at Trinity Church. I sent for Mr John Cutler & delivered him the Key.

Nov 2. I attended Mr John Adams this morning about Colo. Lee's affair. Town meeting this afternoon.

Nov 10. I set out in Paddocks Coach for Salem with Madame Apthorp, Mr Gilb^t Deblois, Mr Inman & Mrs Inman & Mrs Rowe & Capt Jacobson & Jack Rowe in my chaise. We went all Round thro Cambridge & dined at Martins. we got to Salem ab^o four of Clock. We spent the Evening at the Revd Mr Nicholls where we were Joyned by Old Mr Nickolls, his Lady, his Son & Daughter, Mr Fisher the Collector, Mr Joseph Douse & Several Young Gentlemen under the Care of Mr Nickolls'.

Nov 11.   We breakfasted at Goodhews &
stoped at Mr Nickolls I left my Kinsman Jack
Rowe there to school.   We set out for home we
dined at Martins.   we got to Cambridge, we left
Mr Inman, Mrs Inman & Capt Jacobson there.   We
got safe to Boston.

Nov 16.   The Admirall sent for me this morning & told me ab° the Fresh Beef Contract extend-
ing to New England & demanded a supply for the
Ships at Rhode Island.

Nov. 17.   We have an acc^t of a Pirate on the
Coast this day.   The Lively Man of War is fitting
to go in search of her.

Nov 21.   Mr Bacon is come to Town from
Barnstaple & says the Man is in Goal ab° the
Piracy.   The Story is very Intricate.

Nov 22.   The man was Brought to Town from
Barnstaple this evening & examined before the
Govr, Admiral Montague & others Relating the Piracy.   they Committed him to Goal, Strong Suspi-
cions against him.

Nov 24.   Capt Jenkins arrived from London &
bro^t news of the Beaver being safe arrived at Portsmouth.

Nov 27.   My Birth Day I am this day Fifty seven
years old

Nov. 28.   The Lively Capt Talbot Returned from
a Cruize into Nantasket Roads.   No Further acc^t of
any Pirate.

Primo Dec.   George Inman has got the measles
& Jack Rowe has had them at Salem & got well

Dec. 3. Thanksgiving Day. I dined at home with Capt Jacobson & Mrs Rowe & spent the afternoon & evening at home with Capt Jacobson, Mrs Rowe & Geo. Inman.

Dec 7. I dined at home with the Revd Mr Walter & Mr Serjeant a young Gentleman from Andover that's a Candidate for an Assistant to Mr Walter. he Read Prayers in the Church this morning to several of us that wee might Judge of His Voice & I think he has a pleasant & agreeable Voice.

Dec 14. Geo Inman set out for Norwitch. A very Busy Day with mee this Day.

Dec 16. The man that is supposed to have Committed the Piracy was arraigned this Day—before The Governour, Lieut Govr, The Secretary of the Province, The Admirall The Judge of Admiralty, Mr Fisher the Collector of Salem, Mr Waldo, The Collector of Falmouth Casco Bay.

Dec 18. Terry took my new Black Colt away to Day to break.

Dec 24. This morning ab^o one of Clock wee were alarmed by Fire. it was a large Barn burnt down & Mr Saml Wells house much Damaged & in Great Danger.

Dec 25. Christmas Day. Mr Walter Read Prayers & preached a sensible metaphysical sermon for Christmas from 3rd Chap. Timothy 16th Verse. We collected ab^o four hundred pounds Old Tendr for the Poor.

1773

Jany 5.   I spent the afternoon with the Proprietors of Long Wharf at the Coffee House.   Present. The Lieut-Governour Mr Oliver, Mr Arnold Wells, Mr Wm Powell, Capt Dalton, Mr And^r Phillips Mr John Savage, Deacon Grant, John Hancock Esq & Job Prince.

Jan 7.   A Fire broke out at the Foot of the Rope Walk, it Consumed Mr Russell's house, Mr Calfs' Tanhouse & a Carpenter's Shop, also other Damage to the Neighbourhood.   James Richardson called on me ab^o the affair of Thos Symms, which I signed.

Jan 18.   The coldest night this season.   The Queens Birthday   I spent the evening at Concert Hall at a very Brilliant Ball, upwards of Two hundred Gentlemen & Ladies.

Jan 21.   The House voted the Judges Salary this Day Chief Justice £300 p ann̄, the others £250.

Jan 22.   The House Read an Answer to the Governour's Speech Twice this Forenoon, a very lengthy Speech.

Jan 26.   I sold the Hannah, Capt Jarvis to Thos Russell & Capt Dunn for nine hundred Guineas this day — The Sessions set this day on the Petition ab^o Our Goal.

Jan 31.   After church Mr Erving, young Mr Loring, Mr Walter & myself had a long talk ab^o the Revd Mr Coombs of Philadelphia as an Assistant for us.

Feb 3.   I went to the Concert at the Coffee

House of Mr Propert's — very fine Musick & Good
Performers.

Feb'y 8. This morning my Brigg sailed for So
Carolina Capt Skinner, young Josiah Quincy went
Passenger

Feb 17. Spent the Evening at the Coffee House
with a Great number of Gentlemen & Ladies being
Mr Poperts Concert.

Febry 18. I attended all Day at the Superior
Court to hear the Tryall between the Proprietors of
the Long Wharf & Geo. Minot — The Proprietors
lost their Cause.

Febry 21. A fire Broke out this morning between two & three of Clock in Mr Sumner's Shop at
the Bottom of Cole Lane — it Burnt several Dwelling Houses & Shops. The Coldest Day this winter — the Ink & everything else freezes. The
weather so very cold Mr Walter did not preach this
morning

Febry 22. The coldest night ever known. New
Moon —

Feb'ry 24. After Dinner Mr Ezek Golthwait
came to Our house ab^o the settlement of Jack Linzee's affairs.

March 1. Afternoon I spent at Faneuill Hall with
the Committee ab^o Lighting the Lamps. Present
myself, Henderson Inches, Wm Phillips, Benjn
Austin & Mr Appleton.

March 5. Dr Church performed an Oration at
Dr Sewall's meeting. The Judges say to Great
Acceptance — This evening an Exhibition in M^{rs}

Clapham's Balcony.   A Great Concourse of People in King's St of all sorts & a large Number to remember the 5th of March 1770 assembled at M[rs] Claphams —

March 8.   Town Meeting for the Choice of Officers.

March 16.   I went to Brush Hill & dined with M[r] & M[rs] Inman Madam Belcher, M[rs] Belcher, M[rs] Jones, Sally Inman, Cap[t] Jacobson, M[rs] Rowe, Ezeck[l] Golthwait, M[rs] Golthwait, Anna & Betty Murray — Wee were very merry.

March 19.   Antony went to Newport this morning in Browns Stage.

March 20.   The Lieut Governour's Lady was Buried this evening.

March 22.   Afternoon the new Court house took Fire but did no Great Damage.

March 23.   I attended the Funeral of my Friend Cap[t] Hay of the Tamar Man of War.   The order of Procession as follows

The Band of the 64 Regiment.

The Officers & the Marines of the Navy.

The Clergymen of the Town.

The Doctors Peterson & White — full mourning.

The Corps & Bearers — Cap[ts] Loring, Talbot, Symonds, Jordan, Howe & Crosse —

The Admirall, The Governour, M[r] Atkinson, Sec[try]

The Commissioners M[r] Hulton, M[r] Paxton, M[r] Birch, M[r] Hallowell

Lieutenants of the Navy Two & Two

Officers of the Army   "   "   "

The Midshipmen   "   "   "

The Warrant Officers   "   "   "

The Gentlemen Inhabitants of the Town — The
Coaches Chariots & other Carriages — Such a Multitude & Concourse of People I never saw before together. The Corps was preceded with Solemn
Musick to the Chapel & after service was performed
was Interred under the Chapel —

March 28. The King's Chapel was shut up this
Day. the Rev^d Dr Caner & Mr Troutbeck are both
confined.

April 4. A fire Broke out at the North End &
burnt two shops & Sandiman's Meetinghouse.

April 5. Several Stores on the Long Wharff
Broke Open on Saturday night & Last night.

April 6. I went to see an Ox at Dimond More-
tons which was Bred by Mr Baker of Westborough
which weighed 2587 pounds — 5 foot 8 inches
high.

April 15. The Swan Man of War Capt Aiken
arr'd from Rhode Island & this day a Court Martial
was held on board the Captain Man of War to Try
the Lieutenant of the Cruizer for Neglect of Duty.
dismissed the Service.

Aprill 17. This morning I was taken very Ill
& obliged to send for Dr. Perkins. I Continued in
Great Pain all Day & all Night.

Aprill 18. I still continue in Great Pain. the
Doctor has made an Apothecary Shop in my Stomach.

Aprill 19.   I have still much Pain & continue So all Day

Aprill 20.   Still in Pain & grown weak

Aprill 21.   I felt Better this morning but have yet a Little Pain.   & I eat a Little Veal for the First time, am not yet quite Well.   I am much obliged to numbers of my Friends who have been kind enough to visit me in this Sickness.   Ezek^l Goldthwait Jos Golthwait Mr Meredith Greg. Townsend Wm Coffin John Coffin Solo Davis, Tuthill Hubbard, The Revd Mr Walter, Colo. Erving, Capt Jacobson Capt Jarvis, Mr Ingersol, Richd Greene Nathl Barber Bro. Fitch.   I slept Tolerable to Night.

Aprill 22.   Am still in Great Pain.   after dinner I took a Ride in the Carriage Round the Little Square.   when I Returned found much Pain.   I took a Little Geneva of mint ab^o Ten of Clock, it Relieved me

Aprill 23.   I Rode out & felt much Better but still weak.   I dind Below for the first Time

Aprill 25.   Being still unwell I did not get Abroad this Day

Aprill 29.   After Dinner I went to settle the Town Treasurers acc^{tts} present Thos Gray J^{no} Amory Major Davis myself.

Aprill 30.   I dind at home with Mr Meredith, Mr Inman Mrs Rowe Geo Inman & Anthony — wee had a Pike w^d 5^{lbs} 10^{oz} — very fine.

Primo May.   I went to Chapell this morning & stood Godfather for Mr Gib^t Deblois Son together

with Mrs Rowe & Mr Inman. It was Baptized by
the Revd Mr Fairweather and Named Ralph. I
dind at Mr Deblois with him Mrs Deblois his three
Sons Stephen Willm & Jack — The Revd Mr Fairweather Mr Inman Mrs Inman Geo Inman Madam
Apthorp Mrs Snow & Mrs Rowe.

May 2. I dind at home with The Revd Mr Sar-
jent of Cambridge on Calf.

May 4. Mr Meredith went out of Town today.
This afternoon wee met ab^o the Lamps Present myself Deacon Phillips Mr Henderson Inches Mr Appleton Deacon Storer Benj^m Austin.

May 5. Mr Townsend & myself caught five
dozen & eight fine Trout (at Pembroke.)

There was a Town meeting this day at Boston
the four Old Representatives were Chosen. John
Hancock, Thos Cushing, Samuell Adams & W^m
Phillips.

May 8. Wee had very fine Trout which I Caught
at Pembrook for Dinner. I sent Mrs Montague Six
Large Ones.

May 10. I met the Committee ab^o the Lamps,
at the Coffee house Present myself, Wm Phillips,
Benj^{mn} Austin Mr Storer & Mr Appleton.

This day I let my house over the way for
£26.13.4 pr annum he to paper the Rooms at his
Own Expense.

May 11. I attended Town meeting — my Old
Bookeeper James Perkins was buried this afternoon.

May 13. I waited on the Committee ab^o Lighting the Lamps.

May 14. Town meeting this afternoon I attended.

May 18. Attended the Committee ab° fixing the Lamps — We finished the North part of the Town No 1 — 2 — 3 — 4 — 5 Divisions. Present myself, Deacon Phillips Deacon Storer, Tho[s] Gray, M[r] Appleton, Major Daws to which were the Gentlemen of the Several Wards M[r] J[no] Brown, M[r] John Leach M[r] Paul Revere M[r] Ed[w] Procter M[r] Tho[s] Hitchum.

May 19. The Rev[d] M[r] How was ordained at the late M[r] Cheeklys meeting this afternoon.

May 22. I went with James Perkins, Henry Laughton & Sam[l] Calef to Natick Pond — wee were Joyned by Tuthill Hubbard & Joshua Blanchard & wee fished there   wee had Good Sport — Wee caught upwards of Ten doz[n] Pickerell & Perch — the Boats in very Bad order & Leaky — Our Commissioners Returned home last night from the Congress of New York — ab° the Line which was held at Hartford — they have adjusted the affair to the Satisfaction of the Government. Gov[r] Hutchinson, Gen[l] Brattle, Colo Hancock & Major Hawley.

May 23. After church M[r] Walter desired a Conversation with me & M[r] Erving about M[r] Pickering of Portsmouth.

May 24. This day I went with the Committee ab° the Lamps to view the Wards N[os] 6, 7 & 8 which we finished. Present myself, M[r] Storer, Henderson Inches, W[m] Phillips, Benj[n] Austin, Nat Appleton also John Basset Cap[t] Bradford Joseph Jackson, Cap[t] John Homer Cap[t] Job Prince & in

the afternoon Dan¹ Hubbard John Amory Major
Paddock, Deacon Church, John Sweetzer & Thoˢ
Amory.

May 26. General Election. The following Gentlemen were Chose his Majesty's Council.

Sam¹ Danforth	Esq	Sam Phillips	Esq
James Boudoin	"	John Winthrop	"
Sam Dexter	"	John Adams	"
Caleb Cushing	"	John Erving	"
Humphrey Hobson	"	James Pitts	"
William Phillips	"	Benjⁿ Greenleaf	"
Isaac Royall	"	John Hancock	"
James Russell	"	John Whitcomb	"
Artemas Ward	"		

Colony of Plymouth

James Otis, Wᵐ Sever, Walter Spooner, Jeremiah
Bowers

for Sagadohock, Wᵐ Brattle Esq

for the Province of the Mayne

Jeremiah Powell, Jedediah Prebble James Gowan
At Large. James Humphreys, Geo. Leonard junʳ
The Governour negatived Wᵐ Phillips, John
Adams & Jerahmiel Bowers — Jnᵒ Hancock & John
Whitcomb declined going up.

May 27. Two of the Commissioners were very
much abused yesterday when they came out from
the Publick Dinner at Concert Hall, Mʳ Hulton &
Mʳ Hallowell. Wᵐ Mollineux, Wᵐ Dennie, Paul
Revere & several others were the Principal Actors.

May 28. I attended the Select Men in order to
get my Sloop St John up.

May 29. I rose very early this morning in order to get Hunter away. afterward I went to Richards a fishing with Tuthill Hubbard, James Perkins, Sam[l] Calef & W[m] Davis. After I came home I heard of his Majesty's Store Ship having Caught fire & was burnt with all the Stores in her. it put the Inhabitants of the Town Into Great Consternation for Fear of a Large Quantity of Powder being on board. They tow'd her to Noddles Island.

Capt Hood arrivd from London with the Small Pox on board

June 4. King's Birthday aged 35. Colo. Hancock & Company of Cadets, Major Paddock & Artillery, Colo. Erving & the Regiment, Colo. Phipps & Company all made their appearance in the Common — Such a Quantity or Rather Multitude of People as Spectators I never saw before. they behaved very well.

June 8. I rose very early & set out with Duncan for Wrentham on a Party with Admirall Montague. I stopt at Richards & at Robin's Walpole & at eleven I reached Wrentham. I went a fishing with the Admiral & Cap[t] Jordan. Wee caught a great many but very small. I dined at Mann's Tavern with Admiral & M[rs] Montague, Cap[t] & M[rs] Jordan, Cap[t] George Montague Miss Sophia Montague, Maj[r] Musgrave, Miss Blake. Wee spent the afternoon & evening. wee all slept there.

June 9. I rose very early & went afishing with the Admiral. The Admiral caught 173 Perch.

June 12. Letters from Sucky.

June 19. I got in Most Part of my Hay to Day

June 24. I attended the Brethren at their Feast at Bracketts on Boston Neck. Present myself, The worshipfull Dr Warren who favoured the Lodges with his Company (& 46 Brethren) We spent the Day agreeably & very Chearfull.

July 5. J^{no} Inman went to Mendon after the Willders — both villains.

July 7. The Select Men & other Gentlemen of the Town were to visit the schools.

July 13. I went to Milton & paid a visit to Govr Hutchinson.

July 25. The Rev^d Dr Cooper's Meeting House, Built new, was Preached in for the First time this day.

July 28. Went with Mrs Rowe to Salem — We stopt at Newalls Lynn from thence to Flax Pond — I fished there. I had very good sport — We reached Salem, we dined at Goodhew's Tavern — Afternoon we paid a visit to Revd Mr Nicholls & Jack Rowe.

July 29. Went with Mr Inman & Duncan to Flax Pond — When we came there we found James Perkins & Saml Calef — We dined under the Trees there & were joyned by Mrs Inman, Sally Inman, Mrs Rowe, the Revd Mr Nicholls, Jack Rowe, Jack Coffin & Lewis Deblois — We were merry there — On our way home we met Mrs Fisher of Salem & Miss Peggy Douse at Lynn — The Ladies Nicholls drank Tea Together — Yesterday Ansell Nickerson's Triall for Piracy begun, not yet over — his Judges are the Govr Mr Hutchinson. Lieut Govr

Andrew Oliver Esq, Admirall Montague Secretary of this Province Mr Flucker, Mr Dudley Collector of Newport, Mr Fisher Collector of Salem Robt Auchmooty Esqr Judge of Admiralty, Geo Jefrey Counsellor New Hampshire.

Aug. 6. The Tryall of Ansell Nickerson was over this forenoon. He was acquitted contrary to Generall expectation.

Aug 14. This day the Sons of Liberty held their Annual Feast at Roxbury in the Training Field by John Williams — there were upwards of four hundred that dined there.

Aug 15. Mr Walter read Prayers & Preached. A very Serious Good Discourse — Mr Walter Shines more & more in his preaching.

Aug 22. After dinner I went to church — Mr Walter read prayers & preached a very moving & Pathetick Discourse from the 32 Chap. Book of Deut. & 29^h Verse — this sermon was occasioned by the Death of four of his Parishioners vizt Charles Hammock, Mr Mortimer, his Wife, his Brother — who all Died in this week — Mr Walter is so Good a man that my Pen cannot Describe his Virtues — Mr Lynch, Mrs Lynch & Mrs Rowe went to hear the Indian Minister Oatum preach at Mr Moorhead's Meeting.

28 Aug. Saturday I rose very early this morning & went with Admiral Montagu Capt Williams of the Advice & Duncan to Menotomy Pond — Wee dind at the Tavern Mr Weathersbys & wee were Joynd by the following Company — Mrs Mon-

tagu, Miss Montagu George Montagu James Montagu Lady Frankland Mr Cromwell, Richd Letchmere Mrs Letchmere Miss Letchmere Mr Jonathan Simpson Mrs Simpson Miss Simpson Mr Inman Mrs Inman Geo Inman Sally Inman Commiſsioner Hulton Mrs Hulton Secretary Flucker Mrs Flucker Miss Flucker Lucy Flucker Sally Flucker Mr Harrison the Collector of the Customs Capt Tho' Symonds Commandor, the Captain Capt Campbell that Commands the Marines Major Musgrave of the 64th Regiment, Miss Bettsy Coffin Daughter of Nath Coffin Dr White Surgeon of the Hospitall, Mrs Rowe & Mr Atkinson who made this Entertainment — Wee were very Jolly I Came home & spent the Evening at home with Mrs Rowe & Geo Inman Miss Mary Green Daughter of Rufus Green died this morning much Lamented — The Admirall Capt Williams & I had very Poor Luck the fish very small.

Sept 2.   Yesterday was Suckys Wedding Day. Jack Rowe came to Town Yesterday.

Sept 7.   I attended the Town's Committee at Faneuill Hall on the Lamp Affair — Present myself, Wm Phillips, Benjn Austin, Eben Storer, Henderson Inches & Nat Appleton.   Mrs Rowe went to Cambridge, Sally Inman being much out of order with a very bad Throat, Ulcerated.

Sept 8.   This afternoon Mr Bates performed for the first Time horsemanship — A great many People attended him.

Sept 10.   Sally Inman is very Ill.

Sept 11.   The Packet arrivd   Letters from Sucky.   Sally Inman continues very Ill.

Sept 13.   The Doctor gives my Dear Sally Inman over.   I staid all night there with Mrs Rowe.

Sept 14.   Wee are all in Great Affliction.   The Dear Sally Inman Departed about One of Clock this morning.   She is gone to the Realms of Joy.   I came to Town & met M^r & Mrs Deblois & Brought them back to consult about Sallys Funerall.

Sept 15.   I went this day with Great Sorrow to Mr Inman's to attend the Funerall of my Dear Sally Inman who was buried in the afternoon ab° four of Clock, attended by a Great Number of Friends too many to enumerate with upwards of Forty Carriages & abundance of Spectators.   She was a most Amiable Girl & belov'd by All — her Bearers were Sam Perkins, Antony Letchmere, Jonathan Williams Wm Coffin, young Borland & young Fenton.

Sept 21.   Went with Capt Robertson & Duncan to Dedham, Mr Woodwards afishing — we fished there had very Great Luck we caught upwards Twenty Dozen of Large Perch.   John Inman was married this evening to Capt Haskins Daughter Miss Sally — a very Clever Young Lady.

Sept 22.   King's Coronation — Colo. Erving & Regim^t made their appearance, Colo. Hancock & Co & Major Paddock — I dined at Deacon Jones on Turtle by Invitation.

Sept 24.   Spent Part of the Afternoon at Fanewill Hall with the Town Committee ab° the Lamps.

Sept 26.   Mr Walter read prayers & preached

from 34th Psalm & the 11th 12th 13th & 14th verses.
This sermon was adapted & directed to the Youth
& I think very cleverly handled.

Oct 4. I visited the Admiral this morning &
settled the acc^{ts} for July & August Navy Matters
with Mr Atkinson.

Oct 5. This morning the Gentlemen of the
Vestry belonging to Trinity Church met at my
house & also Mr Parker from Portsmouth — Present Stephen Greenleaf Jon^a Simpson, Dan Hubbard,
Geo Bethune John Cutler Henry Laughton, Rufus
Greene, $Benj^n$ Green, myself & Johnson Jackson —
we went to Church & heard Mr Parker Read several Chapters which he did with Propriety & had a
Good Voice — he was much liked — Afternoon
Mr Parker Mrs Rowe & myself went to see Bates
Performance in Horsemanship t'is a smart, active &
strong man & does every thing to General Acceptance — The Vestry adj^{nd} too Thursday 10 of Clock.

Oct. 7. Dr Bundle from Hopkinton came to
Our house ab^o the Little Farm there that was Capt
Ellis' — he says he pays eighteen Pounds a year for
it & offered me three hundred & Ten pounds for
it — The Church Wardens, Vestry & Heirs of M^r
Thos Greene Deceased met according to Adjournment about the Choice of Mr Parker — they were
all of them for him. Mr Goldthwaits Son in Law
Williams dyed this night.

Oct 10. We had a Vestry meeting after Service
ab^o the settlement of Mr Parker — There was a
Duel fought between Capt Maltby of the Glasgow

Man of War & Lieu^t Finney of the Marines on Noddles Island Yesterday — Lieu^t Finney is wounded in the Breast & t'is thought mortally.

Oct. 18.   Mr Finlay from Quebeck paid me a visit.

Oct 21.   Levi Ames was hanged this afternoon — many Thousand Spectators attended the Execution — I dind at home with Mr Finlay of Quebeck.

Oct 25.   King's Accession to the Throne — The Cadets Under Arms — General Muster at Cambridge.

Nov 2.   This morning the Revd Mr Walter & Mr Parker paid me a visit on affairs of our Church — When I got abroad I found an advertisement stuck up at almost every Corner as Follows

" To the Freemen of this & the neighboring Towns Gen^{tlm}, you are desired to meet at Liberty Tree this day at Twelve of Clock at noon, then & there to hear the Persons to whom the Tea is shipped by the East India Company, make a publick Resignation of their Office as Consignees upon Oath & also swear that they will re-ship any Tea that may be Consigned to them by said Company by the first Vessell sailing for London." Boston Nov. 3rd 1773 — O. C. Secretary.

Nov 3.   This day the Inhabitants of the Town are alarmed Occasioned by the advertisement of yesterday — The Gentlemen to whom the Tea was Supposed to be Consigned did not obey the Summons & make their Appearance at Liberty Tree, upon which the Sons of Liberty appointed a Com-

mittee to go & wait on them to know their Determi-
nation, upon which the Committee with a large
Concourse of People went from Liberty Tree to the
store of Mr Richd Clark & Sons at the Bottom of
King Street where they found Mr Richd Clark,
Mr Benjn Faneuil the Governour, two Sons, M^r
Jos Winslow of Marshfield who are the Gentlemen
These Teas are supposed to be Consigned to.
There were several of their Friends there with them,
Colo. Hatch of Dorchester, Judge Lee of Cambridge, Mr Nat Cary, Mr Thos Laughton, & many
others — Mr Mollineux as Chairman of this Com-
mittee Read to them a Paper & produced another
which they Required them to sign &c — Mr Rich^d
Clark & the other Gentlemen gave them for answer
— they would not Comply with their Request or
words to that purpose — this was an Unexpected
answer to them & has given them much Displeasure
The principal People that accompanied Mr Mollineux were as Follows — Mr Saml Adams, M^r W^m
Dennie, Mr John Pitts, Colo. Heath of Roxbury, Dr
Church, Dr Warren, Dr Young, Capt J^{no} Matchet,
Capt Hopkins, Nat Barker, Gabriel Johnnot, Ezek^l
Cheever & about five hundred more as near as I
could guess — The same pieces was posted up this day
as yesterday with this addition — Shew me the Man
that dare take this down — I spent the evening at
the Bunch of Grapes, Colo. Ingersoll with Treas.
Gray, Thos Gray, James Warden, Nat Cary, Geo.
Erving. Melabiah Bourne. Jos. Scot, Jos. Blanchard Thos Brattle, Tuth. Hubbard, Jos. Winslow,

Jos. Golthwait John Cotton, Solo Davis, Edwd
Davis, Wm Davis & Saml Quincy.

Nov 4.   The Town very Quiet this day — I dined
at Bracketts on Boston Neck on Turtle & Spent the
evening at the Possee.   Thos Palmer Esq had his
Ball to Night at Concert Hall.

Nov 5.   This day there is to be a Town Meeting
— Mr Palmer's Ball was very Brilliant, there were
Upwards of Two hundred Gentlemen & Ladies —
Very quiet for a Pope Night.

Nov 6.   Town Meeting again this forenoon.

Nov 11.   The Geese flew to the S°ward yesterday.

Nov 12.   The Govr sent Colo. Hancock an order
for Him to hold his Company in Readiness.

Nov. 17.   This morning Capt Scot arrived from
London   he Brings advice that Hall, Loring, Coffin
& Bruce are to Bring the Tea from the East India
Company — this a measure that is Generally dis-
approved & will Remain a Great Occasion of Dis-
agreement between England & America.

Nov. 18.   Last night a Considerable Body of
People paraded thro' the Streets & attacked the
House of Mr Richd Clark   One of his Family fired
a Gun from the House but luckily did not Hurt —
they Broke all his Windows & Window Frames —
but very little other Damage — This morning a
Town Meeting was called on this & the Tea Affair
— Another Committee Chose — the Gentlemen to
whom the Tea is Consigned are still Resolved to
Pursue such orders as they may receive.

Nov. 19.   This day the Gentlemen to whom the

Tea is Consigned Petitioned the Governour & Council Relative their affairs.

Nov 21.   Letters from Dear Sucky Inman.

Nov 23.   The Governour & Council met this morning on the Tea Matters.

Nov 25.   Thanksgiving — Mr Walter read prayers & preached a most charming Sermon Suitable to this Order of Government from the 92^{sc} Psalm 21st 22^{sc} Verses.

Nov 27.   This day is my Birthday — I am fifty eight years old — I am at present very hearty & strong — but in my knees — Rather Feeble. I bless God for all his Mercies to me.

Nov 28.   Sunday — This morning was Bro^t me a threatening letter Signed Determined which is on File — This agitated my mind & I did not go to Church — Capt Hall arr'd fr. London — Great Noise ab^o the Tea on board Capt Hall.

Nov 29.   This morning there were Papers stuck up to the following Purpose " Friends, Brethren, Countrymen ! " That worst of Plagues The Detestable Tea, ship'd for this Port by the East India Company is now arriv'd in this harbour, the Hour of Destruction or manly Opposition to the Machinations of Tyranny Stares you in the Face : every Friend to his Country to himself & to Posterity is now called upon to meet at Fanewill Hall at nine of Clock this Day (at which time the Bells will begin to Ring) to make a United & Successful Resistance to this last worst & most Destructive Measure of Administration."

Boston Novr 29, 1773.

In consequence of the above notification about one thousand People met at Faneuill Hall where they past a Vote that they would at all events Return this Tea — from Faneuill Hall they adjourn'd to the Old South Meeting. Afternoon they met again & adjourn'd until the morning — there were in the meeting this afternoon ab° Twenty five hundred People as near as I could guess.

Nov 30. The Body met again this morning. The Govr sent them a message advising them to depart on their Perill — they took but little notice of the message — they met again this afternoon. I told them that I had purchased a Cargo for Capt Bruce' Ship, that it was on the wharff & that Capt Bruce when he arrived would apply to the Body & that I would endeavour to prevail on him to act with Reason in this Affair & that I was very sorry he had any Tea on Board — & which is very True for it hath given me great Uneasiness. I staid some time at the Meeting & was Chose a Committee Man much against my will but I dare not say a word. After Dinner I was sent for by the Body by Two Messengers John Ingersoll & Jos. Eyres. This was at the motion of Mr Hancock. I wish he had Omitted it.

Dec 1. Met the Committee, present Sam Adams, J^{no} Hancock, Jonathan Williams & myself.

Dec 2. Capt Bruce arriv'd this morning from London.

Dec 3. This morning Capt Bruce & I were sent for by the Committee Relative the Tea on board

him they ordered him to Griffins Wharff & gave
him the same Directions as to Capt Hall.

Dec 6. Spent the evening at Col. Ingersoll's
with " The Five Club " Present, Dr Wm Loyd, M^r
Geo Bethune, Mr Timo Fitch, Mr Secretary Flucker,
Mr Treas. Gray, Mr Thos Boylston, Colo. Solomon
Davis, Mr Melabiah Bourn, myself & Mr Inman.
Mr John Brown Voted a member. The Rev^d M^r
Morehead was buried this afternoon his Bearers
were, Dr Pemberton, Dr Elliot, Mr Bacon, Dr
Mather, Mr Stillman, Mr Lathrop. A Great Con-
course of People attended this Funeral.

Dec 7.   Afternoon I attended the Funeral of M^r
Robt Jenkins he being a Brother was Buried in
Form, the Masons of the Several Lodges walking in
Procession with their Jewels & White Aprons. I
was Pallholder with Bro. Price, Bro. Warren, Bro.
Box, Bro. Cutler & Bro. McNeal.

Dec 8. Capt Coffin arrived in Nantasket Road
with the Small Pox & part of the Tea.

Dec 11. This forenoon a Committee was sent to
me ab^o Bruce's Ship, Dr Warren, Wm Mollineux,
John Potts, to know when she would be unloaded
& many other Questions.

Dec 14. The Body of the people met at Dr
Sewall's meeting.

Dec 15. An acc^t came this evening that Young
Capt Loring was cast away on the Back of Cape
Cod last Friday.

Dec 16. I being a little Unwell staid at home
all Day & all the evening. The Body meeting in

the Forenoon adjourn'd until afternoon.   Broke up
at Dark.   Several Things passed between Mr Rotch
& them.   A number of People appearing in Indian
Dresses went on board the three Ships Hall, Bruce
& Coffin, they opened the Hatches, hoisted out the
Tea & flung it overboard — this might I believe
have been prevented.   I am sincerely sorry for the
Event.   Tis said near two thousand People were
present at this affair.

Dec 17.   I am still unwell & staid at home all
day.   My New Ship, the Montague, was launched
this day at Walker's Yard.

Dec 18.   Miss Betty Inches was buried this afternoon.   The affair of Destroying the Tea makes
Great Noise in the Town.   Tis a Disastrous Affair
& some People are much Alarmed.   I can truly
say, I know nothing of the Matter nor who were
concerned in it.   I would rather have lost five hundred Guineas than Bruce should have taken any
of this Tea on board his Ship.

Dec 20.   My nephew Jack came to Town from
Salem this afternoon.

Dec 25.   Christmas Day.   I went to Church this
morning.   Mr Walter read prayers & preached a
most excellent sermon.   We collected in old tenor
£400–8/ for the Benefit of the Poor.

Dec 26.   Exceeding windy & stormy — its Blown
down many Turrets & done Damage among the
Shipping at Long Wharff & Tillstons & Blown off
the Tiles from my house.

Dec 27.   St John's Day.   I dined at Colo. Ingersoll's with the Brethren Free Masons under my Jurisdiction (Present 34)

Dec 31. The People of Charlestown collected what Tea they could find in The Town & burnt it in the View of a thousand Spectators. There was found in the House of One Withington of Dorchester about half a Chest of Tea — the People gathered together & took the Tea, Brought it into the Common of Boston & Burnt it this night about eleven of Clock   This is supposed to be part of the Tea that was taken out of the Ships & floated over to Dorchester.

1774

Jan'y 7. I paid Admiral Montague a visit this morning & found him very Angry, I think without Reason, be that as it may if he is Angry he may be pleased again &c. I wish the Good Wishes of All Mankind — & should Esteem his Favour but as for his Business — that dont give me any Concern he has taken it away with° Just Cause.

Jan. 8. I met the Committee about the Lamps.

Jan 9. Cap⁴ Hall sailed this day for London. Passengers Francis Rotch John Whitworth Billy Threer & Young & Willson.

Jan 15. Afternoon I went to Church. M⁵ Walter read prayers & preached a most Delightful Discourse & exceedingly well delivered.

Jan. 17. I dined at Childs' in Roxbury at the Peacock. The Inferior Court sat this day.

Jan. 19. I attended the Carpenter & Blacksmith

in marking out the places the Lamps are to be fixed.

Jan 20. This Forenoon the Selectmen & the Committee for the Lamps met at Faneuill Hall. Present

SELECTMEN

John Scollay	Thos Marshall
Saml Austin	Tim^o Newall
Oliver Wendall	John Pitts

COMMITTEE

John Rowe	Henderson Inches
Benjn Austin	Thos Gray
Wm Phillips	Thos Dawes
Eben Stores	

We consulted on the method of lighting them & had a long Conference with Mr Smith for that Purpose.

Jan 21. We Received Letters from Sucky this day by Capt Agness who has been arr'd from London a month. rec'd letters from my Bro Jacob Rowe & Mr Meredith from Quebec pr Capt Huter McKneil who came over the Lakes.

Jan. 23. Sunday. Severe cold. The Ink Freezes as I write — very Bad Travelling — no Post in. I did not go abroad this forenoon. Afternoon I went to Church. Mr Walter read prayers & preached. Mr Walter handled this Subject with Great Propriety & made a very Good Sermon. The People say that Last night was the Coldest of any for thirty years past — it froze all the way from the

South End down to Castle William, also almost the whole harbour.

Jan 24.   A Little snow fell in the Night.   Afternoon I drove Mrs Foster Round the Little Square.

Jan 25.   John Malcom having done some violence to a man with a Sword, enraged the Multitude that they took him & put him into a Cart, Tarr'd & feathered him — carrying thro' the principal Streets of This Town with a halter about him, from thence to the Gallows & Returned thro' the Main Street making Great Noise & Huzzaing.   I did not see the numbers attending but tis supposed by the People that did, there were upwards of twelve hundred people — tis said that Malcom behaved with Great Fortitude & Resolution.   This was looked upon by me & every Sober man as an act of outrageous Violence & when several of the Inhabitants applyed to a particular Justice to Exert his Authority & suppress & they would support him in the execution of his Duty, he Refused. B. N.

Jan 26.   A Great Concourse of People were in Quest of the Infamous Richardson this night — they could not find him, very lucky for him.

Jan 27.   The General Court met yesterday.   The Governour's speech much admired.

Jan 28.   I spent the Evening at Colo. Ingersoll's with the Brethren of the Several Lodges in Boston under my Direction, being on a very amiable & good Design so as to make the Fraternity more Uniform & Reputable.   Present Myself G. M. Henry Price

P. G. M. Abram Savage S. G. W. Sam Fitch
J. G. W. Tho[s] Brown G. Secretary John Box
T. G. W. John Cutler P. G. W. (& thirty Brethren).

We adjourned to this day fortnight & chose a
Committee to prepare a Draft.

Feb 1.   I met the Lamp Committee this forenoon
at the Selectmen's Room.

Feb 2.   The Charitable Society meeting this
evening.   No person but Nat Greene & myself.

Feb 3.   The General Court went thro' the Choice
of Officers for the ensuing Year this Day.   I met
the Lamp Committee this forenoon.

Feb 7.   I met the Lamp Committee this forenoon.

Feb. 8.   The Judges of the Superior Court Returned their Answers to the House this day.
Judge Trowbridge Judge Ropes, Judge Foster
Hutchinson & Judge Cushing are willing to Receive
their Salaries as Granted them by the General
Court & relinquish their Grants from the Crown.
The Chief Justice Peter Oliver Esq[r] has Received
Part of his money as Salary granted him by the
Crown already & will not Relinquish that Grant,
therefore the House voted his Answer not satisfactory.   The Rev[d] Dr Cooper of this Town was yesterday Chosen President of the College.

Feb 10.   The Corporation of the College at Cambridge met this forenoon in the Council Chamber
to fix on Dr Cooper as their President but he
refused accepting the Choice as President of that

College — to the great Joy & Satisfaction of his Parishioners.

Feb 11. I spent the Beginning of the evening at Colo. Ingersolls with the members of the Grand Lodge. Present Myself G. M. John Box P. G. W. Abram Savage S. G. W. Sam. Fitch J. G. W. Thomas Brown Grand Secretary, our Brother Brattle of Cambridge (& 25 Brethren).

The House of Assembly passed several Resolves against the Conduct of the Chief Justice Peter Oliver Esq which may be fully seen in the Fleets & Edes & Gills Papers — & tis my opinion they'l Repent of their Resolutions — they are in Direct Opposition to Government at home.

Feb. 15. The Superior Court met & adjourned untill this day week upon the Acc^t of the Chief Justice Peter Oliver. I dined at home with the following Gent^m Colo James Warren of Plymouth Mr Nat. Graham of Charlestown Colo. William Tyng of Falmouth Casco Capt Wm Heath of Roxbury Major David Ingersoll of G^t Barrington Mr Saml Adams of Boston Capt Thos Gardner of Cambridge also Mrs Rowe & Geo Inman. After Dinner I took a ride with Mrs Rowe over the Neck. Very good sleighing.

Feb. 19. Yesterday the whole House presented in a Body a Remonstrance to the Govr Relating to the Chief Justice Mr Oliver.

Feby 21. Mrs Hubbard buried this afternoon.

Feb. 22. This day the Superior Court adjourned too June which has given Great Uneasiness. Old Mr Boylston buried this afternoon.

Feb 23.   I dined at home with The Hon'ble
John Hancock Esq. Major Joseph Hawley of North-
ampton, Mr Robt I. Paine of Taunton, Mr John
Pickering of Salem, Jedediah Prebble of Falm°
Casco Bay, Mr Isaac Lathrop of Plymouth The
Hon'ble Wm Sever of Kingston, Mr Gorham of
Charlestown M^r & Mrs Inman, Mrs Rowe & Geo.
Inman.

Feb 25.   I spent the Evening at Colo. Ingersoll's
with the Brethren of the Grand Lodge over special
Matters.

Feby 27.   Jack Clark his wife & Miss Curtifs
are in Town f^r Providence.

Mar. 3.   Last evening The Lamps were Lighted
for the first time — they Burnt Tolerable Well.

His Honour the Lieu^t Governour Andrew Oliver
Esq died this morning — Anno Estatis 68.

Mar 5.   Mr Hancock delivered An Oration this
day at Dr Sewalls Meeting house to the Greatest
Number of People that ever met on the Occasion.
I tryd to get in but could not.   Some Gentlemen
speak of the Oration with Great Applause.

Mar 6.   Capt Gorham arr'd in the Brigg Fortune from London having nine weeks Passage.   Our
Bell on Trinity got cracked this day.

Mar 7.   This night an Exhibition was Put on M^{rs}
Clappam's Balcony which drew the attention of
most·of the Inhabitants.

Mar 8.   Last evening The Tea Brought by Capt
Gorham in the Brigg Fortune was destroyed.   This
afternoon his Honour the Lieu^t Governour An-

drew Oliver Esq was Buried as Follows. Colo.
Hancock with his Company of Cadets & Colo.
Erving with the officers of his Regim^t preceded the
Corps — Colo. Hancock's Comp^y under Arms. The
Bearers were — Judge Danforth, Judge Hutchinson, Treasurer Gray James Russell Esq, Mr Secretary Flucker, Foster Hutchinson Esq. Then Followed the Family, next in order should have
the Council & house of Assembly but thro some
Blunder the Admirall & his Core followed the
Family & Relations, next them Colo. Lesly of the
64 Regiment & his Core, then the Gentlemen of
this & the Neighboring Towns which were very
few. Then followed the Coaches & chariots
amounting to Twenty, then the Chaises amounting to Ten. Minute Guns were fired from the S^o
Battery. Such a Concourse or rather Multitude of
Spectators I never saw at any Funeral here before.

Thro some misunderstanding or Blunder the Gentlemen of the Councill did not attend this Funerall
& very few of the House of Representatives. There
was, after Colo. Hancock's Company had fired &
the Funerall over, as the Relations were Returning,
Some Rude Behaviour.

Mar 10. The Governour Prorogued the General
Court yesterday to the 13th April next.

Mar 12. Capt Solo. Davis & I had a few words
ab^o Trifles — he was wrong. I took him up a little
too Quick. I am sorry, as I believe him honest but
too Volatile.

Mar 13. Afternoon I went to Church. M^r

Walter read prayers & preached a very Sensible Discourse & well delivered. Dr. John Green Lord Bishop of Lincoln treats on this Subject very delightfully in his Treatise under the Title of Improvement of the Mind.

Mar 14.   Town Meeting this day.

Mar 15.   Town Meeting again this day. I attended.

Mar 16.   I spent the evening at Bro. Prince Lodge with him, Bro Salter, Bro Benj Jackson his Wardens (& 21 Brethren).

Mar 21.   The Gentlemen of the Lamp Committee met this morning at Faneuill Hall.

Mar 22.   I spent the evening at Faneuill with the Committee & a Number of Merchants.

Mar 24.   The Committee ab° the Lamps met this morning.   We finished our Drafts.

Mar 25.   I attended the Committee for Filling up the Town Dock.

March 29.   I had a Long Conversation with Tristram Dalton on the insurance affairs.

Mar 30.   Town Meeting this morning. I was Chose Moderator.   We delivered in Our Reports Respecting the erecting & fixing up the Lamps in the Town.   Accepted.   The Town agreed with Garvin Brown for the Clock on the South Meeting house.

Mar 31.   This afternoon my Brother Jacob Rowe came to town from Quebeck.

Apr 3.   After church the Gentlemen vestry met.

Apr 4. The Church Wardens Vestry & Proprietors of Trinity Church met this forenoon on affairs of the Church. Present, Myself, John Erving, Esq, James Boutineau, Dan. Hubbard, Mr Rufus Green, Wm Coffin, James Perkins, Johnson Jackson, John Cutler, Richard Greene, Stephen Greenleaf, John Head, Daniel Crosby, Mr And. Fane^l Phillips Mr Erving & Mr Hubbard were Chose Wardens.

Apr 7. I met the Gent^n Proprietors of Long Wharf at Colo. Ingersoll's. We did the Usual Business of the Meeting & Chose Capt Wm Fleet Wharfinger for the ensuing year.

8 Aprill. I Rose early & went down to my Wharff & there had a Long Conversation with Admirr^l Montague. After Dinner I attended Town Meeting. Capt Hood in Mr Hancock's Ship sail'd yesterday for London.

10 Aprill. Bro Jacob & Little Jack gone to Cambridge. After Church a Vestry. Present Mr Erving & Mr Hubbard the Wardens, Mr Boutman Mr Geo Bethune Mr Rufus Greene Mr Johnson Jackson, Mr Wm Coffin Mr Jon^a Simpson Mr Henry Laughlin Mr James Perkins Mr John Cutler The Revd Mr Walter myself.

11 Aprill. My Bro Jacob & Jack Rowe gone to Salem.

14 Aprill. Mr Mrs Inman were God Father & God Mother for John Head's Child. Christened this afternoon.

Apr 15. The Famous Dr Latham who has been

at Salem innoculating came to Town last evening. My Brother Jacob got home this evening from Cape Ann.

Apr 17.   After church Mr Henry Knox & Miss Lucy Flucker paid us a visit.

Apr 18.   This day the Admirall made his son George Montague Post & gave him the Command of the Foye in the Room of Capt Jordan who has Liberty to go home.   he also made old Mr Thornborough Master & Commander.   The Court Martial set this day to Try Lieu^t Rogers on board the Active the Cap^ts as Follows, Capt Talbot of the Active President Capt Thos Simonds of the Captain, Capt Jordan of the Foye Capt Ayscough of the Swan & Capt Geo. Montague of the Kingfisher. The Result we shall soon know.   I dind at home with Dr Latham, Commodore Loring etc.

Apr 19.   The Result of the Court Martial on Lieu^t Rogers is Severe — he being Broke & Dismissed the Service.   Capt Folger arrivd from London in six weeks.

Apr 24.   The Post, Mr Peter Mumpford brings an acc^t that the Tea Ship is arr'd from Antigua to New York last Monday at Sandy Hook.   The Swan Man of War Capt Ayscough sailed from hence this morning for New York.

Apr 28.   I met the Committee ab° the Granary. Present Mr Ezeck^l Golthwait, Ed^wd Payne Wm Whitwell & myself.   Mr Thos. Lee paid me a visit.

Apr 29.   The Committee on the Affair of the Granary met this morning.   We were attended by

Col⁰ Leverett & Mʳ David Jeffries Messʳˢ Willders paid me a visit this morning.

Apr 30. After Dinner came to our house Mʳ Willson a Gentleman from Sheffield in Yorkshire who has been taken in Grossly by Edmᵈ Quincy. This evening the York Paper Brings an account of the Destruction of Eighteen Boxes of Tea belonging to Capᵗ Chambers.

May 3. My Brother Jacob went to Cape Ann yesterday.

May 8. Letters from Mʳˢ Linzee pr. the Post that came by the Packet.

May 10. The Annual Town Meeting. the four old Representatives were Chosen, Samˡ Adams, John Hancock, Wᵐ Phillips & Thoˢ Cushing. they were almost unanimously chosen. The Harmony Capᵗ Shayler arrived from London & brings the Severest Act ever was Penned against the Town of Boston.

May 13. Town Meeting this day relating to the Distressing Situation of this Town occasioned by a Late Act of Parliament for Blocking up the Harbour of Boston which is & will be a Great Evill — at present there is no Describing the Circumstances. The Lively, Man of Warr, Capᵗ Bishop is arrived this day & has Brought out Genˡ Gage, our New Governour. God Grant his Instructions be not severe as I think him to be a Very Good Man.

This day I rec'd a Large Pacquet by Capᵗ Smith from Liverpool from the proprietors of Campo Bello,. John Lyon, Walter Kerfoot, Roger Rogerson, Samˡ Johnson, Rowland Hunter.

May 14. Spent most part of the Day with the Town Committee at the Representatives Room. Present, Sam¹ Adams, Myself, John Adams, Thoˢ Cushing, Wᵐ Phillips, Henderson Inches, Wᵐ Mollineux & Dr Warren.

15 May. After Church Mʳ Robins Purser of the Lively, with Mʳ McKinnerly Master of the Lively and his wife & Child came to pay us a visit, they being Recommended by Capᵗ Jnᵒ Linzee & Sucky.

May 16. I spent Both parts of the Day with the Towns Committee at the Town House. Pressent, Sam¹ Adams, John Adams, Josiah Quincy junʳ, Wᵐ Phillips, Henderson Inches, Wᵐ Mollineux, Thoˢ Cushing, Myself. Capᵗ Hall arr'd from London — in him came Passengers, Our Assistant the Revᵈ Mʳ Parker, Mʳ Francis Rotch & Mʳ Willᵐ Palfrey.

May 17. This morning Gen¹ Gage Our New Governour landed from the Castle after having breakfasted with Admiral Montague on board the Captain Man of Warr — he was saluted by the Castle & the Captain Man of Warr & Rec'd at the Long Wharf by Colo. Hancock's Company of Cadets. The Regiment was under arms in King street. The Company of Grenadiers made a good appearance. Capᵗ Paddock's Company of Artillery & Colo. Phipps Company of Guards were also under arms in King street. He came to the Town House, had his Commission Read by the Secretary & took the Usual Oaths — from thence he was escorted to Faneuill Hall where a good Dinner by his Majesty's Council. There were but very few Gentlemen of the Town asked to dine there.

May 18. I waited on Genl Gage this morning who Received me very Cordially. The Town met by adjournment this day. I was so Busy I could not attend.

May 21. On my way home I met with Mr Willson who desired me to go to Henry Quincy's which I did, ab^o his affairs & found he had been treated very Ill.

May 22. Afternoon I went to Church. Mr Walter read Prayers & Mr Parker preached for the first Time from 123rd Psalm, 1^{rst} Verse. A sensible Good Discourse & very well delivered for his First Time of Preaching. After church Henry Knox & Lucy Flucker paid us a visit.

May 24. The Merchants met at the Town House on Business of Importance.

May 25. General Election. I attended & went to Meeting this morning. The Revd Gad Hitchcock of Pembroke preached a high Discourse suitable to his Party fr Proverbs 29th v. 2nd. The Following Gentlemen were Chose his Majesty's Council for the year ensuing.

FOR THE COLONY OF THE MASSACHUSETTS BAY.

Saml Danforth Esq		Benj Greenleaf Esq	
John Erving	"	Caleb Cushing	"
James Bowdoin	"	Saml Phillips	"
James Pitts	"	Artemas Ward	"
Saml Dexter	"	J^{no} Winthrop	"

*Wm Phillips   Esq   *Richd Derby jun^r Esq
*John Adams   "   *Mich^l Farley   "
*James Prescott "   *Benj Austin   "
*Thos Donaldson "   *Morton Quincy   "

FOR THE LATE COLONY OF PLYMOUTH

James Otis,   Walter Spooner
Wm Sever,   *Jeremiah Bowers Esqr

FOR THE LATE PROVINCE OF MAINE

Jeremiah Prebble,   *Enoch Freeman Esqr
Jedediah Prebble,

For Sagadathock — *Benj^m Chatbourne Esqr.

At Large — George Leonard jun^r Esq. *Jedediah Foster.

The Gentlemen with this (*) mark were not of the Council last year. Before the Election of Counsellors Letters were Received from the Honble Isaac Royall & James Gowan Esq^{rs} Resigning their Seats at the Board. The List of Counsellors chosen yesterday being this day agreeable to the Direction of the Royal Charter presented to his Excellency the Governour — his Excellency was pleased to Consent to the Election of the Gentlemen aforementioned except, James Boudoin Esq, Wm Phillips, Esq, Thos Donaldson, Esq. Jerahmiel Bowers, Saml Dexter, John Adams, Michael Farley, Enoch Freeman, John Winthrop, James Prescott, Benjⁿ Austin, Jedediah Foster.

May 29. The Kings Restoration. The Admirall has now Stationed all his Ships.

The Tartar behind the Castle. Capt Meadows.

The Mercury in Nantasket.   Capt McCartney

The Tamar at the Mouth of Broad Sound. Capt Thornborough.

The Lively at the Channel of Gov^n Island.   Capt Bishop.

The Magdalen at Point Shirley.   Capt Collins.

The Canceaux between the Two Ferrys, Winnissimet & Charlestown.   Capt. Mowat.

The Halifax at Winnissimmet.   Capt Heath.

The Captain between Long Wharf & Hancock's Wharf.   The Flag Ship.

The St John Capt Grant at —

May 30.   I paid the General a visit this morning. Town Meeting.   Nothing done but Harangue.

May 31.   The Minerva Capt Calahan is gone Below to take in Govr Hutchinson, his Son Elisha Hutchinson & his Daughter Miss Peggy Hutchinson who are going Passengers as is Miss Polly Murray.   My Bro^r. & Jack Rowe gone to Salem.

June 1.   This is the last day any Vessel can enter this Harbour until this Fatal Act of Parliament is Repealed.   Poor Unhappy Boston.   God knows only thy wretched Fate.   I see nothing but misery will attend thy Inhabitants.

June 2.   I met the Gentlemen Merch^{ts} at the West Side of the Court House in Boston.   While wee were in the Meeting Capt Williamson arrived at Marblehead from Bristoll & Brought with him Another Act of Parliament for the Better Regulating The Province of the Massachusetts Bay which Act strikes the very Charter Granted to this Province by King William & Queen Mary — & is, or will be, productive with many Evils to the advancement of this, his Majesty's Province & sour the minds of most of the Inhabitants thereof. I am afraid of the Consequences that this Act will Produce. I wish for Harmony & Peace between Great Britain Our Mother Country & the Colonies — but the Time is far off. The People have done amiss & no sober man can vindicate their Conduct but the Revenge of the Ministry is too severe.

June 3. Spent the evening at Deacon Jones' with the Following Merchants — John Amory, Jonathan Amory, Saml Barrat, Henderson Inches, John Timmins, Eben^r Storer, Wm Whitwell, Edwd Payne, Henry Bromfield & myself. We adjrd untill Monday eve'ng

June 6. Artillery Election. Brigg^r Brattle did the Honours of the Day in the Absence of his Excellency Govr Gage.

June 7. There was a Grand Ball at Salem last Evening as an Entertainment to Genl Gage, his Officers, the Commissioners of the Customs & many others.

June 8. The Committee of Merchants waited on Genl Gage with their address.

Treas^r Gray, Thos Gray, J^{ho} Erving, Geo. Erving, Richd Lechmere, John Timmins, Jos. Winslow, Frank Green, James Forest, James Anderson.

June 10. The Transports with the 4th Regiment are arrived from Southampton this morning. Mr Atkinson & Mr Williams the Storekeeper are arrivd in the Sally Schooner from Hallifax.

June 12. Afternoon I went to church. Mr Weeks of Marblehead read Prayers & Mr Parker preached from 4th Chap. Book of Exodus & 11th Verse. this was most sensible Discourse & extremely well delivered, being the Second Sermon Mr Parker preached in Our Church since his arrival. After church I walked Round the Wharffs. tis impossible to describe the Distressed Situation of this Poor Town — not one Topsail Merchantman to be seen.

June 14. This is the Last day any vessel can depart this Harbour. Boston, thy Fate is very distressing! The Fourth Regiment landed this morning & pitched their Tents in the Common by the Pound — a number of Spectators to see them.

June 15. The forty third Regiment Landed this morning & pitched their Tents in the Common near the Workhouse on that Plain. This evening the Tradesmen of the Town met to Consult on the Distress of this Place. There were upwards of eight hundred at this meeting. they did nothing being much Divided in Sentiment.

June 16. I went this morning to see my kinsman Jacob Rowe who I found very Ill and very Dangerous. After dinner I spent an hour with J^{no} Adams & Josiah Quincy Junr.

June 17. A General Town Meeting this forenoon. they Chose Mee Moderator. I was much engaged & therefore did not accept. The People at present seem very averse to Accommodate Matters. I think they will Repent of their Behaviour, sooner or later. The Governour Disolved the Assembly this day. The Gen¹ Court Chose a Committee of five to go to the General Congress — James Bowdoin, Jnº Adams, Sam¹ Adams, The Speaker & Mʳ Payne of Taunton.

June 19. I went to see Jacob Rowe at the North End who I found very ill.

June 21. My kinsman Jacob Rowe died last night between ten & eleven of Clock in a convulsion Fit — this morning I attended about his affairs.

June 22. Afternoon I attended the Funeral of my kinsman Jacob Rowe, he was buried under Trinity Church in my Tomb. One of the Transports with part of the 5ᵗʰ Regimᵗ on Board arrived here.

June 23. I began to mow our Pasture yesterday & this day.

June 27. Town Meeting, the Hall so full they adjournd to the Old South Meeting — the Debates were for & against the Committee of Correspondence very warm on both sides, it lasted all day & adjournd until tomorrow 10 of Clock. The Speakers in behalf of the Committee were Sam¹ Adams, Dr Warren, Wᵐ Mollineux, Josiah Quincy junʳ, Dr Young, Benjⁿ Kent. The Speakers against the Behaviour of the Committee were Treasʳ Gray, Thos Gray, Sam¹ Elliot, Sam¹ Barrat, John Amory, Edwᵈ Payne, Francis Greene, Ezeck¹ Golthwait.

June 28. The Town met again at the Old South Meeting. The Debates very warm on both sides — I think are wrong. I mean the Committee are wrong in the matter. The Merchants have taken up against them, they have in my Opinion exceeded

their Power & the Motion was Put that they
should be dismissed. the Gentlemen that made &
supported this Motion could not Obtain their Vote,
the Majority were four to One against them. this
affair will cause much evil one against the other. I
wish for Peace in this Town I fear the Consequences.
I dind at the Peacock on Turtle with (43 Ladies & Gentlemen) Wee spent the afternoon very
agreeably & were very merry.

July 1. The Preston Man of Warr with Admirall
Graves came into this harbour this day, as did several Transport Ships with the Remainder of the 5ʰ
& 38ʰ Regiments on board. Lord Percy is with
them.

July 4. The 38ʰ Regiment Landed this day &
pitched their Tents in the Common. I paid Admirall Montague a visit this mornᵍ.

July 5. The 5ʰ Regiment landed this day &
pitched their Tents in the Common. Admiral Montague Lady & Miss Sophie Montague paid us a visit
this morning & took leave of us being just on their
departure for England.

July 6. Mʳ Humphreys left my house this day &
Major Clerk of the 43ʳᵈ Regiment went into it at
100 Dollars pʳ annum.

July 7. The Captain Man of Warr with the Admiral on board saluted Admirall Graves but the
wind died away they did not sail. The Generall
visited the Troops in the Common this Forenoon.

July 8. I heard of the Bad Behaviour of the
People of Marlborough. its said that the Speak-

mans were Concerned, if it Proves so, they have not only behaved Ill but contrary to my Sentiments & forfeited my Regard in future for them.

July 9.   Capt Willm Brown of my Brigg Sucky came to Town this evening from Salem.   He arrivd there from London a few days ago.

July 10.   I went to Church this morning.   Mr Parker Read Prayers & Mr Walter Preached.   A very Good & Serious Discourse & well adapted to our Present Situation.   Colo. Cleveland that commands the Train of Artillery came to Town from New York.

July 12.   Last Night Mrs Skinner Dyed, she was a Good Woman, much Lamented, a Great Loss to her Distressed Children being Ten in Number & most of them very Young.   Capt Dove arr'd from S^o Carolina at Salem with Rice as a present from Sundry Gentlemen there for this Place.

July 13.   Attended the Funerall of Mrs Skinner & was a Bearer.

July 14.   This Day a fast is Recommended by Some of the Ministers on Acc^t of the Miserable Situation of this Town.   I cannot Reconcile this measure & should much Rather the People would do Justice & Recommend the Payment for the Tea instead of losing a Day by fasting.

July 15.   I called on Thos Golthwait & went with him & David Duncan to Salem.   Wee Breakfasted at Newall's Lynn.   I did my Business at The Town of Salem.   I dined with the Revd Mr Nicholls' & his 14 Scholars.   he Keeps them under strict or-

der & Decorum. After dinner I stoped at Flax
Pond & caught Two dozen of Perch from the Rocks.
I Returned to Town & found my Dear Mrs Rowe in
a most melancholly & distressed Situation. She
with Mrs Inman had been to the Funeral of Gilb^{t}
Deblois Child & Returning home in the Carriage the
Horses took Fright & Run away, oversett the Carriage, I Believe has Bruised them very much. M^{rs}
Rowe is so much frightened & so very much Over-
come that she does not know the Event & at Present
is in a very Dangerous State. Dr Lloyd & Dr
Church attend her. I am in Good hopes she will
soon mend. Our house is full of Visitors on the
Occasion — twas very lucky I Returned this evening.
Mr Inman, Mrs Inman, Dr Lloyd & Mrs Gould
stay all night. We are in Great Trouble & distress. God Grant she may be better in the
morning.

July 16. My Dear Mrs Rowe I think is somewhat
Better, tho' still very Ill, her Case is very hazardous.
Dr Lloyd gives great attention to her — he is very
good. My Friends are very kind & attentive to
my Dear Dear Mrs Rowe, I keep home all Day, I
cannot leave her. Miss Patty Green watches with
her tonight — at Ten of Clock the Doc^{tr} thinks she
is Better, ab^{o} six The Dr gave her some annodine
Drops. She was before that very weak.

July 17. Dr. Lloyd thinks my Dear Mrs Rowe
much better. She has had a tolerable night. I
staid at home all day. Our house much Crowded
with Company to see my Dear Mrs Rowe — this

afternoon she appears to Grow Better. Mrs Cutler is kind & watches with Mrs Rowe this night.

July 18. I think Mrs Rowe not so well this morning. She is very weak & Feeble altho' she seemed to sleep well to night. I staid at home all Day. Mrs Rowe continues very weak, altho' Dr Lloyd thinks her much better. I rec^d^ a letter from Mr Richd Letchmere dated this day giving an acc^t^ of Mr Trollet's Death at Lancaster, also heard of my Old Friend Capt Thos Gerry of Marblehead being Dead. Mrs Inman is so kind & obliging as to watch with Mrs Rowe tonight.

July 19. My Dear Mrs Rowe is very weak this morning her Medicines are too Strong for her feeble Constitution. I think her still hazardous. Mrs Rowe much better this afternoon. Peggy Cragin watches too night.

July 20. This day is the Annual Commencement Day but the Distressed Situation of the Town & Province prevents it being kept Publick as usual. Mrs Rowe has had a Good Night & is Mending.

July 22. Mrs Rowe growing Better for which I & all her Friends Rejoice. I dined at home with her alone. She eat some Dinner with Appetite.

July 23. Mrs Rowe grows better by Degrees but slowly.

July 25. Mrs Rowe growing Better. After Dinner My Bro^r^ Jacob set out for Quebeck.

July 27. A Quarrel happened last night between some of the Towns People & some Officers of the Army. Town Meeting yesterday I did not attend.

July 29.   Dr Lloyd & Dr White paid Mrs Rowe
a visit.   Afternoon I went with Mrs Rowe over the
Neck Round the Little Square.

July 30.   After Breakfast I went again with
Mrs Rowe in the Carriage over the Neck Round the
Little Square.

Aug 7.   The Scarborough Man of Warr, Capt
J. Chadds arr'd yesterday from England.   She left
Plym° the last Port.   A letter from Sucky to M^rs
Rowe by Mr Holt who is Lieu^t of the Scarborough.
The York Transports are arrived & the Regi-
ment of Welsh Fusileers on board them.   The
Transports from Halifax with the 59th Regiment
are also arr'd & the Tamar Sloop Capt Thornbor-
ough, their Convoy.

Aug 8.   Mrs Rowe growing better dayley.
When I came to the Store I Found my Friend M^r
Meredith from Quebeck.   My Friend Joe Jackson
died this morning.

Aug 9.   This morning the 23rd Regiment or
Royal Welsh Fusileers Landed & encamped on
Fort Hill — they made a very Good Appearance.

Ten of his Majesty's Council were Sworn in yesterday at Salem.

Thos Oliver Esq Lieu^t Govr & President of the
Council John Eving jun^r Esq. James Boutineau
Esq. Foster Hutchinson Esq. Harrison Gray Treas^r
of the Province Isaac Winslow Esq of Roxbury
Joseph Lee Esqr of Cambridge Joshua Loring,
Capt^t in his Majesty's Navy.   Mr Pepperell of
Roxbury, Thos Flucker Secretary of the Province.

Aug 10. The Artillery from New York landed this morning & encamped on the Common. I went to the Funerall of Joe Jackson & was a Bearer.

Aug 17. The following is a list of the Gentlemen appointed by his Majesty Capt Counsellors of this Province agreeable to the late Act of Parliament.

Thos Oliver Lieut Govr Thos Flucker Secretary of the Province.

Peter Oliver Chief Justice of the Province.

Foster Hutchinson Judge of the Superior Court.

Thos Hutchinson   "   "   " Inferior   "

Harrison Gray, Treas^r of the Province.

Saml Danforth Esq Judge of Probate.

James Russell Import Officer.

Timothy Ruggles, A Salary from the Crown.

Jos. Lee   Judge of the Inferior Court, Middlesex.

Willm Brown   "   "   " Superior   " .

Andrew Oliver   "   "   " Inferior   " Essex

Josiah Edson   "   "   "   "   " Plymouth

Joshua Loring Capt of his Majesty's Navy.

Jerry Powell Judge of the Inferior Court, York.

John Erving jun^r Isaac Winslow, Israel Williams Geo Watson, Nat Ray Thomas, Timothy Woodbridge William Vassall, Joseph Green, Jam^s Boutineau Richd Letchmere, John Worthington Timothy Paine, Wm Pepperell, Jo^ha Simpson, John Murray,

Daniel Leonard, Tho⁵ Palmer, Isaac Royall, Robᵗ Hooper, Abijah Willard, John Erving senʳ.

Aug 21 A Vessel arrived from Falmouth at Marblehead brings advice of Govʳ Hutchinson's arrival in England, having a short Passage from hence.

Aug 22. A Report that Daniel Leonard Esq one of the Counsellors at Taunton was obliged to leave the Town of Taunton. On Thursday last the following Gentlemen were sworn in his Majesty's Council & took the Oaths Requisite to Qualify them for their seats at the Council Board —

Samuel Danforth	Esq	of	Cambridge.
Peter Oliver	"	of	Middleborough
Richard Letchmere	"	"	Boston
Jonathan Simpson	"	"	"
Josiah Edson	"	"	Bridgewater
Nathˡ Ray Thomas	"	"	Marshfield
Tim° Ruggles	"	"	Hardwicke
Tim° Paine	"	"	Worcester
Abijah Willard	"	"	Lancaster
Tho⁵ Hutchinson junʳ	"	"	Milton
John Murray	"	"	Rutland
Daniel Leonard	"	"	Taunton
Geo. Watson	"	"	Plymouth

Sept 1. This morning a Letter was picked up wrote by Genˡ Brattle to Genˡ Gage & the Genˡ in Consequence sent a Party of Two hundred men under the Command of Colo. Mattison & took the Gunpowder belonging to the Province from the Arsenal on Quarry Hill & brought it from thence

in the Transport Boats to the Castle. This Letter has exasperated the Country People against Brattle so that he now takes Refuge in Boston.

Sept 2. A Great Number of People from the Country are Collected at Waltham, Watertown & Cambridge Occasioned as tis Reported from the Behaviour of Gen¹ Brattle. The People seem to be Frightened & afraid of its Consequences. The General has Reinforced the Entrance at the Neck. Commissioner Hallowell has been Insulted in his way through Cambridge — he fled for shelter to this Town. This evening appeared a Flimsey Recantation from Gen¹ Brattle.

Sept 3. The People at Cambridge mostly dis-spersed & gone home The General sent four field pieces to Boston Neck.

Sept 4. This morning Mʳ Parker read Prayers & Preached from 25th Chap. St. Matthew & 29ᵗʰ verse & afternoon from 65th Chap. St. Matthew & part of the 9ᵗʰ verse — both these Discourses were very Clever & much liked. Several Gentlemen of Distinction were at Our Church — Peter Oliver Esq Chief Justice, Judge Brown of Salem, Jonᵃ Sewall Esq Attorney General, Wᵐ Pepperell Esq & a great many others too many to particularize.

Sept. 5. The Lively at her Moorings above Charlestown Ferry The Camceaux at her moorings in Gallows Bay.

Sept. 6. The Diligence, Schooner, Capᵗ Knight arrived from England with Dispatches for the Gen¹ & Admirrall. Seven sail of Transports sailed for

Quebeck & Three or more for New York & Philadelphia.   John Inman goes to Salem this morning.

Sept. 7.   The General has Doubled the Guards
at the Neck & I believe designs to Fortify it.

Sept. 9.   This morning a Soldier of the 65th Regiment which had three times deserted was shot in
the Common.

Sept. 10.   The 59th Regim[t] came from Salem &
encamped on the West Side of Boston Neck.

Sept. 14.   Church Convention. I went to Chapel,
Dr Caner Read Prayers & M[r] Serjeant of Cambridge
preached a sensible Short Sermon on the Occasion.
The General & his Aide de Camps, the Admirall &
Lady & the Cap[t] of the Preston with the Navy
Officers of the Day, The Commissioners, many of
the Council the High Sheriff & many other Gentlemen & Ladies attended.   This night some of the
officers of the Navy came & spiked up the Guns of
the North Battery.   A Ridiculous Manœuvre.

Sept. 22.   This day is the Anniversary of his
Majesty's Accession to the Throne.   I went to the
Councill Chamber with the Govern[r], Admirall &
many other Gentlemen to drink the King's Health
& many other Loyal Toasts.

Oct. 2.   Sunday.   The Proprietors met after
Church & gave Our Old Broken Bell to the Min-
ister & Church Wardens of Norwitch Church in
Connecticut.

Oct. 6.   A Large Fire hap'ned at Salem last
Night.   Dr Whitaker's Meeting house & eighteen
houses were Destroyed.

Oct. 11.   A number of Deputys met at Concord this day.   Capt Callahan arrivd from London at Salem.   Severall Passengers among the Rest Geo. Inman.

Oct. 13.   Capt Wallace arrived this morning in the Rose, Man of Warr from Newfoundland & Brought Two Companys of the 65th Regiment with him Capt Sinclair & Capt John McKay.

Oct 18.   This day an Audacious Villain attacked Colo. Cleveland & Capt Montrasor Snapped Pistolls at Both of. them & wounded Colo. Cleveland with his Own Ranger.

Oct 19.   The Fellow that attacked Colo. Cleveland & Capt Montrasor was brought from Cambridge & Committed to our Goal — his name is Dyer.

Oct 22.   Mr Mollineaux died suddenly this morning.

Oct 23.   Genl Huldimand arr'd here from New York with the 47th Regiment & part of the Royal Irish, the 18th Regim^t this morning with some Officers of Distinction.   There was a Vestry after Church ab^o altering the Time of Morning Service & admitting the 59th Regiment to come to Church as also the 5th Regim^t.

Oct 24.   This afternoon Willm Mollineux was buried — he has been famous among the Sons of Liberty.   Many Things are attributed to him & tis believed he was first Leader of Dirty Matters. A Great Concourse of People attended his Funeral — his Bearers were Old Mr Erving, Mr Jam^s Bowdoin,

Mr Pitts, Mr Thos Boylston, Capt^t John Bradford & Mr Wm Dennis.

Nov. 2.   Yesterday Brother Box died.

Nov. 3.   I attended the Funeral of Brother Box & was a Bearer together with James Pitts Esq, Dr Silv^r Gardiner Mr Chardon, Mr Henderson Inches & Mr Gilbert Deblois. It was a handsome Funerall. The Free Masons walked in Proper Form.

Nov. 5.   The pope made a Poor Appearance to Day. The people Behaved well. The Inscription was Unity & No Popery.

Nov. 9.   Our Delegates Returned to Town from Philadelphia. I went to Salem this morning & did my Business there.

Nov. 15.   The 47th Regiment & part of the Royal Irish landed this day & the Regim^{ts} from the Common went in Barracks. Little Jack Rowe went to Salem yesterday with Mr Nicholls.

Nov. 17.   My Worthy Friend Thos Gray Esq died at Hingham of the Wounds he Rec^d from his Fall sometime Past — this day ab^o Twelve oClock. Capt Sheppard arrived from London & brings advice that the Parliament was disolved & writs Issued for a New Parliament to meet the 24th November.

Nov. 19.   I attended the Funerall of my Worthy Friend Thos. Gray Esqr.

Nov. 27.   This is my Birth Day & I am fifty nine years Old. I am Thank God pretty well in Health.

Dec. 4.   Capt Brown is just arrived from London at Salem in the Sucky

Dec. 5.   I rose early this morning & went to Salem with Mr Edwd Church & Duncan — we stop'd at Lynn at Newhalls & dined at Goodhew's Tavern, Salem.   The Committee attended me ab^o Browns Cargoe, after some Conversation we Settled the affair.

Dec. 6.   Very Bad Travelling on the Salem Road.

Dec. 17.   The Asia & Boyne, Men of Warr came this morning up against the Town & anchored between the Long Wharff & Hancocks.   I attended the Funeral of Mr Maturin, the Generall's Secretary.

The Procession as Follows

first part of the 4th Regiment Under Arms

then the Band of Musick

then the Clergy — then the Corps

then the Generall & his Family

then the 4th Regiment without Arms

then the Officers of the Army & afterwards the Gentlemen of the Town.

Dec 18.   A Serjeant of the 47th Regiment was buried this evening — he Being a Mason there were 152 Brethren followed the Corps & the whole 47th Regim^t

Dec 27.   St John's Day.   I celebrated the Feast at Colo. Ingersoll's with the Following Brethren (23)

1775

9 Jan'y. Mr Inman Mrs Inman gone to Marlborough.

10 Jan'y. Capt Maltby of the Glasgow Man of Warr was try'd this day by a Court Martial on board the Somerset & suspended.

11 Jan'y. Jack Rowe went to Mr Nicholls to School this day.

14 Jan'y. Mr Lyell came to Town this day from Nantucket being Landed there out of a Brigg he Came in Passenger from London.

Jan'y 18. This being the Queens birthday it was Celebrated by Drinking their Majesty's Health at the Town house. The Picquet Guards from all the Regiments fired three vollies. The Castle & Batteries & all the Fleet Fired a Royal Salute. Geo Inman was taken ill this day & keeps his Chamber.

Jan 21. An Affray happened between the Officers & the Town House Watch last evening which makes Great Uneasiness in Town.

Jan 24. A Detachment from each Regim^t went on board Capt Thos Graves & are bound to Marshfield under the Command of Capt Ballfour of the 4th Regiment in order to keep the People there Quiet & Peaceable. This morning also was a Court of Enquiry about the matter of the Affray between the officers & the Watchmen — the Court adjourned until tomorrow morning

Jan 27.   This day the Smallpox was discovered at the House of John Barthlet the Taylor.

Jan 31.   This day the King's Speech is come to Town from Marblehead in a Vessel of Mr Ornes from Falmouth.   he takes notice of the Behaviour of the Colonies & particularly this Province — his Remarks are very Just.

Feb'y 12.   Mr Lysle the Solicitor in the Customs died at Mrs Arthur's.

Mar 6.   This Day Dr Warren dl'd an oration at Dr Sewall's Meeting.   I did not hear him.

March 8.   Frank Johnnot died this morning.

Mar. 9.   This morning a Country Fellow who had Bought a Gun from one of the Soldiers was punished by them in the Modern Taste of Tarring & Feathering & carried in a Cart through the main Streets of the Town.

Mar 15.   This day an Oration was delivered by a Dirty Scoundrel from Mrs Cordis' Balcony wherein many Characters were Unfairly Represented & much abused & mine among the Rest.

Mar 16.   This day is kept by many People as a Publick Fast, which gives Great Umbrage to a Great Many People which do not pay any Regard to it & I think they are not Right because they say the Order does not originate under the Direction of Good Government, yet it can no harm.

Mar 17.   This Being St Patrick's the officers in Number ab° Sixty walked in Procession with a Chosen Band of Musick to Kings Chapel where a Sermon was Preached by the Revd Mr Nicholls.

They Returned in the same manner & Dined at Colo. Ingersoll's in King Street.

Mar 18. The Letters by the Jan'y Packet came to hand.

Mar 20. A Quarrel between Wm Davis & Willm Bowes this day.

Mar 25. Afternoon the Generall sent for me to see a letter I received from Thos Griffith.

Aprill 3. Lieu^t Jackson of the 5th Reg^{mt} was buried this day.

April 16. After Dinner I went down Clark's Wharff to meet Capt Linzee & Sucky who arrived from Spithead & Falmouth in the Falcon Sloop. I brought them home & their little Son Saml Hood Linzee.

Aprill 17. Our house full of visitors all day.

April 19. Last night the Grenadiers & Light Companies belonging to the several Regiments in this Town were ferry'd over Charles River & landed on Phipps Farm in Cambridge from whence they Proceeded on their way to Concord, where they arrived early this day. On their march they had a Skirmish with some Country People at Lexington. The First Brigade commanded by Lord Percy with Two pieces of Artillery set off from this Town this morning about Ten of Clock as a Reinforcement which with the Grenadiers & Light Infantry made about eighteen hundred men. The People in the Country had notice of this movement early in the Night. Alarm Guns were fired thro' the Country & Expresses sent off to the Different Towns so that very early this

morning large Numbers from all Parts of the Coun-
try were Assembled. A General Battle ensued
which from what I can learn was Supported with
Great Spirit on both Sides & continued untill the
Kings Troops got back to Charlestown which was
near Sunset. Numbers are killed & wounded on
Both Sides. Capt Linzee & Capt Collins in two
Small Armed Vessels were ordered up Charles River
to Bring off the Troops to Boston but Lord Percy
& General Smith thought Proper to encamp on
Bunker's Hill this Night — this Unhappy affair is a
Shocking Introduction to all the Miseries of a Civil
War.

April 20. The General sent some more Troops
to Charlestown last night & this morning, so that
Lord Percy & the Troops under his Command Returned to Town. This night some People ab° Two
hundred Attacked Capt Linzee in the Armed
Schooner a little Below Cambridge Bridge. he gave
them a Warm Reception so that they thought
proper to Retreat with the Loss of some men. Tis
said many thousands of Country People are at Roxbury & in the neighborhood. The People in Town
are alarmed & the entrenchments on Boston Neck
double Guarded   Mrs Linzee din'd at the Admirall's.

April 21. The Reinforcement that was sent to
Charlestown by the Genl are Returned too & the
64th Regim^t that was at the Castle are now in Boston
Town House. All Business at an end & all Com-
munication Stop'd between the Town & Country.
No Fresh Provisions of any kind brought to this

market so that Boston is in a most Distressed Condition. This afternoon Several Gentlemen met with the Selectmen to Consult on Our Situation & chose a Committee to draft a Memorial to Genl Gage — vizt — The Selectmen, James Bowdoin, Henderson Inches, Alex Hill, Edward Payne & Jos Barrett — they adjourn'd until tomorrow Ten of Clock.

April 22. The Same Company met & Reported upon which the Inhabitants were called together. After much Debate & some Amendments they Passed two Votes which were presented to the General by the same Committee & on delivery they asked the General to Grant their Prayer — he in some measure Complyed but made some other Proposalls. Mr Nicholls sent Jack home last night & Broke up his School.

April 23. The Inhabitants met again this morning & after some Debate they came into the Generall's Measures — which was to deliver up their Arms to be deposited in the hands of the Select Men & such of the Inhabitants as had a mind to leave the Town might go with their Effects. This evening news was Brought that Capt Brown was Stop'd at Charlestown in his way by the Country People.

April 24. I Rose very early & got away Mr Nun, John Inman, Mr Sparks, Thos Knights, Jos. Taylor & John Head on board Mr Sheriff's Sloop for Salem. Between one & Two Capt Brown got to Town. I soon despatched him. This day the Inhabitants carried in their Arms. The number 2674

Geo Inman had two very Severe fits too night, I thought very dangerous.

April 26.   John Inman is come to Town & tells me that my Brigg^n Sucky sailed from Marblehead yesterday towards night — in her went the following Passengers Lieut Nun, Mr Sparks, Jos. Taylor, Thos Knight, John Headt, Mr Sherlock, Young Paine of Worcester, Mrs Brown & her Child.   Mr Sheriff sent upwards of 40 Sheep into Our Pastures this day.

April 27.   The General has given Leave for All People to leave the Town that Choose with their Effects.

April 28.   This day I apply'd to get a Pass to go out with my Effects but could not prevail.

April 30.   I went to church this morning.   Mr Parker read Prayers & Mr Walter preached a very serious Discourse on Our Present Distressing Situation from the 7th Chap. Ecclesiastes & part of the 14th Verse   "In the Day of Adversity, consider."

May 1.   Capt Linzee & Sucky & Little Saml Hood sailed this morning in the Falcon Sloop.

May 2.   The post is in.   Bad News from New York.   Dr Wm Saml Johnson & Colo. Wallcot are Come to Town on Special Business with the Generall from the Colony of Connecticut.

May 3.   Mr Inman went to the Lines to see Mrs Inman — he had some Conversation with her.

May 5.   The Inhabitants Flocking out of Town. Some Transports arrived from Halifax with four Companies of the 65th Regiment.

May 10.   William Vassall & all his Family, together with Tim° Fitch & family, Tho⁸ Brattle & many others went off this morning.

May 17.   About eight of Clock a Terrible Fire Broke Out in the Barracks on Treat's Wharf Occupied by the 65ᵗʰ Regiment — it was Occasioned by Accident or rather from Great Carelessness — it destroyed 33 Stores on Dock Square.   Mine was in Great Danger, I thought it so & therefore removed great part of my Effects from thence — it continued until half past One with Progress.   The Officers Behaved very well.   The Clothing of 4 Companies belonging to the 47ᵗʰ Regiment was burnt & some Fire Arms Lost.

May 18.   The People in General very Busy in Collecting the Effects that were Saved out of the Fire.

May 21.   A Party was sent under the Command of Mʳ Jarvis of the 43ʳᵈ to Grape Island to Bring off some Cattle & Hay, the Country People being very numerous kept a Brisk Fire on them so that they were Obliged to Return without Effecting their design.   One Marine wounded.   Two Transports from Deptford with Recruits & one with Marines from Plym° arrived this day.

May 24.   Yesterday the Merlin Sloop of War, Capᵗ Duddington arr'd & Some Transports with Part of the 14ᵗʰ Regimᵗ & one Transport with Light Horse.

May 25.   The Ceberus Man of War, Capᵗ Chad arrived from Spithead — in this Ship The Generals Bourgoyne, How & Clynton came Passengers.

May 28. A Continual Firing all night on Nortons Island between the Provincials & Marines & Sailors. Severall Marines & Sailors killed & wounded & tis supposed the Provincials lost many. The Diana Schooner, Capt Thos Graves, is Burnt.

May 29. Twenty Sheep & Lambs have been killed this night in my Pasture.

May 30. Last night the Country People Burnt one House & several Barns on Norton's Island — & the Dwelling House & Store this forenoon.

Our Two Girls Peggy & Becky went away this day.

(Vol. XII. of the Diary is missing and inside the cover of Vol. XIII. is written : —

" from June to Decemb^r is mislaid or taken away out of My Store ")

Dec. 25. Christmas Day. Mr Walter read prayers & Mr Parker preached a very Good Sermon from 2^d Chap. St Luke's Gospel & 14th Verse.

The money gathered for the Use of the Poor of this Church am° to Sixty Dollars.

Dec. 27. I dined at Home with Capt Linzee, Mrs Linzee Little Saml Hood who is two years old this day, Mr Inman Mrs Inman Geo Inman Mrs Rowe & Jack Rowe

Dec. 29. The Busy Body Acted tonight.

Dec. 30. Admiral Shouldham arrived in Nantasket Road in the Chatham, Man of Warr, Capt Rayner Several Ships with part of the 17th Regim^t from Cork arrived in the harbour. The Scarborough Capt Barclay & severall Transports are sailed today on a Secret Expedition.

Dec. 31. Thus endeth the Year 1775, a most fatal year for this Part of America.

The Niger, Mann of Warr, Capt Talbot is arrived in Nantasket Road & has brought the King's Speech dated the 26 October.

1776

7 Jany. Capt Linzee behav'd very cruelly to me. I shall not forget it.

12 Jan'y. I paid Adm^l Shouldham a Visit this morning who is a Genteel man & Received me Politely. Dined at home with Mrs Rowe Jack Rowe & Little Sammy

13 Jany. This morning a Soldier of the 59th Regm^t was hang'd for Thieving

Jan. 17. I sold my Brigg, Bristol Packet to Capt Grant this morning for £490 Ster'g Bill for acc^t of 2 Gent'^{n} in London.

Jan. 18. Mrs Linzee & George paid us a visit & took their Leave — perhaps Forever.

The Centurion, Man of Warr, Capt Brathwait arrived in Nantasket from England.

Jan. 19. The Julius Cæsar sail'd for England In this Ship Mrs Oliver & Family Mrs Wentworth & some others went Passengers.

Jan. 20. This day The Falcon, Capt Linzee, sailed — he took with him Mrs Linzee, Little Sam & Hannah. I sincerely wish their Prosperity & Happiness. With the Falcon sailed the Mercury, in her Genl Clynton is Passenger & Mr Reeves the Gen$^{l's}$ Secretary Several Transports went with them with the Light Infantry of the 4th & 44th Regiment. They are Gone on some Expedition to the Southward.

Jan. 21. Some Good Person Put in Mr Parker's hands, a Quantity of Provisions, Wood & Coals to be distributed for the Poor of Trinity Church.

Jan. 22. This evening The Tragedy Tamarlane to which was added the Blockade of Boston was performed at Faneuill Hall.

Jan. 24. Its Generally believed that Genl Carleton has given Montgomery & Arnold a very severe Drubbing at Quebeck.

Jan. 25. Two Vessels are said to be taken this day in Our Bay & carried into Plymouth.

Feb. 1. The Preston Man of Warr, under sail. Also The Canceaux & Trident, Transport — in this Ship Sir Wm Pepperell & Family were Passengers.

Feb. 2. Tis Reported that Capt Dawson has destroyed the Schooner Privateer, Capt Manley, that was fitted out at Plymouth — Admir^l Graves left Nantasket this morning with his Fleet.

Feb. 4. Capt George Montague of the Fewey, Man of Warr sent in a Sloop from Dartmouth Laden with Wood for Marblehead — very Acceptable.

Feb. 5. The Troops at Charlestown got four Cattle this morning which were sent out for a Decoy they lost one man & had another very much

Wounded Sir Henry Callder Commanded. Mrs Robt Gould much out of order.

Feb. 9. Tis Reported that Capt Banks has hoisted the Broad Pendant on board the Renown Man of Warr.

Feb. 11. Some plan for an Expedition was projected last night, tis Supposed the Alteration of the Weather put a stop to it. Mrs Gould continues very ill.

Feb. 14. This morning a party of the King's Troops burnt the Houses on Dorchester Neck & brought off seven prisoners.

Feb. 17. Capt Dawson has brought in several prizes.

Feb. 23. Poor Mrs Gould died this morning.

Feb. 24. Last Evening The Wonder of Wonders was acted & generally approved of. I waited on Genl Howe this morning ab° Spooner & Church's affairs.

Feb'y 26. Attended the Funerall of Dear Mrs Gould. Her Bearers were Dr Loyd Henry Laighton Greg. Townsend Eze^k Golthwait Danl Hubbard & James Perkins.

Mar. 1. Blows fresh. My Brigg Sucky went down in Order to Proceed to Oporto.

Mar. 3. This Night The People from the Battery at Phipps Farm threw Many Shells in Town which put the Inhabitants in great Fear & they have done Damage to many Houses Particularly Sherburn Fitch's Geo Erving's & Courtney's the Taylor

Mar 4.   All the Preceding Night the Town
had been fired at by the People with° from Every
Quarter   I dont hear of much Damage being done.
The Guns from Cobler's Hill on Charlestown side
have thrown their shot the farthest in Town, one
of them struck Wheatley's in King's Street.

Mar 5.   This morning wee Perceived a Battery
Erected on the Hill on Dorchester Neck — this
has alarmed us very much — ab° 12 the Generall
sent off Six Regiments — perhaps this day or
tomorrow determines the Fate of this truly distressed Place.   All night Both sides kept a Con-
tinuall Fire.   Six men of the 22nd are wounded
in a house at the S° End.   One Boy lost his Leg.
A very Severe Storm it Blew down my Rail Fences
Both sides the Front of the House.

Mar 6.   This Morning the Country People has
thrown a Strong Work — on another Place on the
Neck at Dorchester Neck.   Gen[l] Howe has ordered
the Troops ashore again & tis now out of Doubt
that Gen[l] Howe will leave this Town with his
Troops &c — which has put The Inhabitants of
this Town into Great Disorder, Confusion & much
Distress.   The Firing has ceased this day.

Mar 7.   The Troops & Inhabitants very Busy
in Getting all the Goods & Effects on board the
Shipping in the Harbour — tis Impossible to describe the Distress of this Unfortunate Town.
Gen[l] Robinson pd mee a Visit

Mar 8.   My Situation has almost Distressed me.
John Inman, Archy McNeil & Duncan are deter-

mined to Leave me. God send me Comfort in
my Old Age. I try to do what Business I can but
am. Disappointed & nothing but Cruelty & Ingrati-
tude falls to My Lot. I spend the Day & Evening
with my Dear Mrs Rowe Richd Green & John
Haskins

Mar 9. This day Genl Robinson pressed the
Ship Minerva into the Service — nothing but
hurry & Confusion, every Person striving to get
out of this Place. A Great Deal of Firing on
both sides this night.

Mar 10. Capt Dawson is Returned with Two
Vessels — he has had a severe Brush with four
Privateers. A Proclamation came out from Genl
Howe this day, a very severe one, on some People.
John Inman went on board this day with his
Wife — he has in his Possession three Watches
of mine & sundry Pieces of Checks which were to
be made into Shirts — Jos. Golthwait, Mrs Winslow
went on board — he has carried off Cap^n Linzee's
horse with° Paying for him.

Mar 11. This morning I Rose very early &
very luckily went to my warehouse — when I
came there I found Mr Crian Brush with an Order
& party from the Genl who were just going to
Break Open the Warehouse which I prevented
by sending for the Keys & Opening the Doors.
They took from me to the Value of Twenty Two
hundred & Sixty Pounds Sterling according to
the best Calculations I could make, in Linens,
Checks, Cloths & Woolens. This Party behaved

very Insolently & with Great Rapacity & I am
very well Convinced, exceeding their orders to a
Great Degree. They stole many things &
plundered my Store. Words cannot Describe it.
This Party consisted of Mr Blasswitch who was
one of the Canceaux People, Mr Brush, The provost Mr Cunningham, a Refugee, Mr Welsh the
Provost Deputy — a man nam^d Hill & ab^o fifteen
Soldiers with others. I Remained all day in the
Store but could not hinder their Destruction of
my Goods. This day I got a piece of Bread &
one Draft of Flip. They are making the utmost
Speed to get away & carrying Ammunition, Cannon & everything they can away, taking all things
they meet with, never asking who is Owner or
whose Property — making havock in every house
& Destruction of all kinds of Furniture. There
never was such Destruction & Outrage committed
any day before this. Many other People have
suffered the same Fate as wee, Particularly M^r
Saml Austin, Mr John Scollay, Capt Partridge,
Capt Dashwood, Mr Cyrus Baldwin, The Widow
Newman.

Mar 12. A Continual Fire from Both sides this
night. They are hurrying off all their Provisions
& destroying & mangling all Navigation, also Large
Quantitys of Salt & other things they heave into
the Sea & scuttle the stores. The Inhabitants are
greatly terrified & alarmed for Fear of Greater Evils
when the Troops leave this distressed Place. I got
Crean Brush' Rec^t for the Goods taken from me but

dont expect much Good from it tho' several Gentlemen say they will be my Friends in this affair.

Mar. 13. The Confusion still continues & Plun-
dering of Houses &c Increasing. Gen¹ Robinson
paid me a visit & eat a morsel of Provisions together
with Richᵈ Green, Mʳˢ Rowe & Jack. The Sailors
from the Ships have Broke open my stores on my
wharff & plundered them. this was done at Noon
this day. This morning a house was burnt at the
North End, whether set on Fire on Purpose or from
accident seems uncertain. A Considerable Number
of Cannon fired in the night from Both Sides.
The Country People throwing up more entrenchments &c on Dorchester Neck.

Mar 14. This night much damage has been done
to Many houses & stores in this Town & many valuable articles stolen & Destroyed. Stole out of Wᵐ
Perry's Store a Quantity of Tea, Rum & Sugar to the
value of £120 Sterling. Mʳ Sam¹ Quincy's house
broke & great Destruction. The Revᵈ Mʳ Walter's,
also the Revᵈ Dr Caner's & many others

Mar 15. This night my store on the Long
Wharff broke open & almost a hhd of sugar & a
hogshead of ware stole. Twas expected The Troops
would have embarked this night but they still Remain in Town — after dinner Capᵗ Haskins gave me
Notice that several officers were in Mʳˢ Hooper's
House committing Violence & breaking everything
left. they Broke a Looking Glass over the Chimney which cost Twenty Guineas — such Barbarous
Treatment is too much for the most Patient man to
bear.

Mar 16. The Troops are getting everything in order to depart. My store on Long Wharff broke open again this night — the Behaviour of the Soldiers is too bad — tis almost Impossible to believe it. Two officers of the 5th came to me ı ıʳ Wine. they wanted to be Trusted, I refused them — since I have heard nothing only they Damned me & swore they would take it by Force. One of them nam'd Russell of the 5th Regiment, the Other I dont know.

Mar 17. St Patrick's. The Provincials are throwing up a Battery on Nook Hill on Dorchester Neck which has occasioned much Firing this night This morning the Troops evacuated the Town & went on board the Transports at & about Long Wharff. they sailed & got most part of them into King Road. About Noon Gen[l] Putnam & some Troops came into Town to the Great Joy of the Inhabitants that Remained behind.

Mar 18. The Town very quiet this night. Several of my Friends came to see me from the Country.

Mar 19. Numbers of People belonging to Boston are daily coming in. Gen[l] Washington & his Retinue were in Town yesterday, I did not hear of it otherwise should have paid my Respects & waited on him. This afternoon the King's Troops burnt the Blockhouse at the Castle & the Continental Troops are throwing up a Battery on Fort Hill — most all the Ships are gone from King Road into Nantasket Road.

Mar 20. They Burnt the Barracks & houses at the Castle this afternoon & destroyed everything they could on the Island & blew up the Fortifications all around it.

Mar 22. I dined at home with Genl Putnam, Genl Greene, Mr Inman, Mrs Inman, Mrs Forbes, Mrs Rowe & Jack after Dinner Colo. Gridley, Mr Chase, Both Mr Webbs & several other officers came to the house.

Mar 23. Some Fire below Nantasket Road I take it to be a Transport set on Fire to destroy her.

Mar 24. Afternoon I went to Church. Mr Parker Read prayers & preached a very Good Sermon & considering the distressing Time a Good Many People at Church. A Transport was burnt last night in the Lighthouse Channel.

Mar 25. The Fleet still in Nantasket Road. A Great Many of the Ships in Nantasket sailed this afternoon.

Mar 26. I waited on Genl Greene this morning with Mr Baker ab^o some Iron on my Wharff. After dinner I went with Mr. Parker & paid My Respects to Generall Washington who Received us very Politely.

Mar 27. This afternoon all the Fleet sailed from Nantasket Road but three which is supposed to be Men of Warr.

Mar 28. This day The General Court made a handsome Entertainment at Capt Marston's that now lives in Colo. Ingersoll's house, for Genl

Washington & the other Generalls of the United Colonies & the Rev^d Dr. Elliot preached at Dr. Chauncey's meeting a Sermon on the Occasion giving a History of what has hapind in Town during the Siege. I dined with Twenty four Gentlemen at Watermans Tavern in Roxbury all Free Masons by Invitation.

Mar 29. A Town Meeting this day at Dr. Champney's Meeting house. The old officers of the Town were chose. Mr Thos Rufsell & his Brother paid me a Visit this afternoon Mr Richd Greene's wife came to Town.

Mar 31. I gave Genl Washington an Invitation to dine who Returned me a very Polite Answer. Severall Regiments under orders to march to the Southward from Prospect & Winter Hills.

Apr 4. A Town Meeting this day at Dr. Champney's Meeting House. Mr Kent Moderator. Mr Parker slept in his house this night. He gives me £26–13–4 P Annum.

Apr 5. Genl Washington & Lady & Family set Out Yesterday also Genl Gates to the Southward. News of Jolly Allen being ashore at Cape Cod & Twenty six Other Passengers.

Apr 6. Capt Manley is come to Town & brings the acc^t of his Taking Crean Brush, Wm Jackson & Seventy other Passengers in a Brigg bound with The Fleet. This Vessell tis said has Twenty five Thousand pounds Sterling on board in English Goods & other Merchandise — among the Prisoners is a Serjeant & 12 men of the King's Troops.

Apr 7. Mrs Hooper came to Town. She is in a most Distressed Situation. The Proprietors of Trinity Church met after Church. Present Twelve Persons.

April 8. I attended the Church Meeting this morning & was Chose Warden with Danl Hubbard. Afternoon I went by invitation of Brother Webb to attend the Funeral of the Remains of Dr. Warren & went accordingly to the Council Chamber with a Design to Attend & Walk in Procession with the Lodges under my Jurisdiction with our Proper Jewells & Cloathing but to my great mortification was very much Insulted by some furious & hot Persons with° the Least Provocation one of Brethren thought it most Prudent for me to Retire. I accordingly did so — this has caused some Uneasy Reflections in my mind as I am not Conscious to myself of doing anything Prejudicial to the Cause of America either by will or deed.

The Corps of Dr. Warren was Carried into Chapell Dr. Cooper prayed & Mr Provoz Morton delivered an Oration on the Occasion. There was a handsome Procession of the Craft with Two Companies of Soldiers.

There is a Confirmation of Crean Brush & Wm Jackson being taken & also my Negro Fellow Adam.

Apr 10. I attended the proprietors of Trinity Church this morning on Mr Parker's affairs. I see Mr Jos. Wentworth & had some Conversation with him ab° Capt Manley's Capture. My Worthy Friend

Benj Green was taken Out of this Troublesome World this afternoon.

Apr 12. This morning came an acc^t of Brymers Brigg being taken in the Bay by some Whale Boats under the Command of Capt Fletcher & carried into Hingham   Tis said the vessel taken by Thatcher is very Valuable & belongs to Bristol.   Crean Brush & Wm Jackson are Brought to Boston.

Aprill 13. Martin Brimmer & Mr Dalton of Newberry Port paid us a visit

Apr 14. I staid at home all Day   Our Church shut up   Mr Parker gone to Newberry Port & Mr Bass expected to Town who Disapointed him.

I had a long Conversation with Mr Mumpford ab° my affairs at Newport.

Apr 17. Several People taken up this day & carried to Goal.   Dr Whitworth, his Son, Wm Perry one Edwards & others.

Apr 18. This morning The persons that were taken up were carried over to Dorchester & there examined by a Court appointed by the General Court for that Purpose   they examined Wm Perry & Edwards & ordered them to Goal   the Rest they kept all night there.   Mrs Handing buried this afternoon.   Her Bearers were Saml Austin Henry Bromfield Tutthill Hubbard, Oliver Wendall & Deacon Stores.

Apr. 19. Dr. Whitworth examined this day & admitted to Bail.

Apr. 24. My Old Friend Capt Solo Davis came to Town & pd me a visit.

May 1. My Dear Little Fellow & Kinsman Jack taken very ill.

May 2. The Justices are still sitting — Jack still unwell.

May 3. Dr Whitworth & Son Committed to Close Goal My Dear Little Jack very Ill.

May 4. Jack very Ill. Dr Lloyd is afraid of him. The Justices adjourned until Wednesday week.

May 7. Jack growing Better & I hope out of Danger. Severall Parties have been for Severall Days on Noddles Island throwing up Breastworks &c for a Fort.

May 8. This morning Mr Hammonds Plough began to Plough up the Pasture. Two Briggs, one from Cork, the other from the Western Islands taken by Capt Tucker in Manley's Schooner & carried into Lynn. Jack growing Better

May 15. This day the Justices met again as adjourned. they summoned Geo Lush, Dr Danforth, Mr Prout & Hopestill Capan.

May 16. A poor Woman was found drown'd at the foot of the Common — a melancholly Specta-cle. A daughter of Mr Grant's.

May 17. This is a Fast Day appointed by the Continental Congress throughout the Colonies. This morning was Brought into this Harbour thro Point Shirley Gut a Large Ship loaded with Ordnance Stores — 1500 whole & 4 half Barrels Gunpowder, 1000 Stands of Arms, a large Quantity of Entrenching Tools & many other Stores — this Vessell came last from Cork under the Direction & Convoy of the Greyhound Man of Warr, Capt Dixon — she was taken by Capt Mugford in a Schooner from Beverly

May 21.   Bad News from Quebeck. Some Boats from the Men of Warr in Nantasket Road attacked Capt Mugford — they were obliged to quit her — Mr Mugford & another man was killed.   tis supposed several were lost out of the Boats — one Marine found Dead & one Barge with Ten Oars

May 22.   The Army from Quebeck is Retired from before it.   the acc^t Imperfect.

May 23.   Town Meeting for the Choice of Representatives   they Chose Twelve —

Wm Phillips	J^{no} Brown	Benjn Austin
Wm Cooper	John Pitts	Wm Powell
Oliver Wendall	Nat Appleton	Arnold Wells
David Jeffries	Jos. Gardner	Caleb Davis

May 24.   They Chose two Representatives in the Room of Arnold Wells Esq & Wm Powell vizt Henry Hill & Saml Allen Otis.   Din'd at home with M^r & Mrs Inman, Mrs Forbes Mrs Rowe & Jack.

May 27.   Town Meeting again this Morning.

May 28.   Town Meeting again this Morning.

May 31.   Jack went to Mr Payson yesterday (Chelsea)

June 2.   Tis said Dr Church came to Town last evening.

June 4.   Dr Church was confined this evening.

June 8.   One of the Men of Warr has Brought into Nantasket the Privateer Brigga^e Yankey Hero commanded by Capt Tracey who Behaved very well. Some Privateers from Marblehead have Brought in a Ship from England with 95 Soldiers Cloathing & Provisions. Mostly Highlanders, Scotch.

June 9. One Ship from Jamaica Bro^t into Dartmouth, another from thence into Cape Ann. Both of these Large Ships & Valuable.

June 11. A Flag of Truce went from Town on board the Renown,— Mr White of Marblehead & Mr Martin Brimmer. Comm^e Banks treated them very Politely.

June 12. A hand Bill is sent about containing Interesting news from the Continental Army in Canada

June 14. An expedition went forward against the Ships in Nantasket Road — three separate Bodies are on Long Island. one on Pedruk's Island & another on Nantafket. they have driven the Ships from Nantafket Road. Comm° Banks its said Burnt the House on Georges Island the Lighthouse & the House on Lighthouse Island.

June 15. I have been very busy all this morning in finding out some Persons that have wickedly & Maliciously spread a false Report about me & have had them before Justice Hill & have got the first of them to Acknowledge it to be a lye & she hath signed a Declaration which I hope will Satisfy & Clear my Innocence.

June 17. Two Ships with Highlanders taken by the Privateers, among them is Colo. Campbell.

June 18. Another Ship with Highlanders taken.

June 22.   The Continental affairs appear in Canada very unfavourable

June 23.   There have been Twelve Sail of Ships in Our Bay this day, one of them is Judged to be a Friggate.

June 24.   Thirteen Ships have been in the Bay again this day.   they stand off & on & about four Leagues distance from the Light house.

June 25.   I dined at Capt Marstons with the Brethren of the Lodges under my Direction.   Present 13.   Bro. Marston gave us a Good Dinner. The Ships still in the Bay & plying from N^o to S^o as yesterday.   The Highland officers & Soldiers are sent out of Town to Mendon Reading & Lunenburg.

June 29.   No Sight of the Ships This morning.

July 7.   Capt Henry Johnson has sent in a Ship from Jamaica a Three Decker very Valuable & another from Antigua with Rum — 419 hogh'ds.

July 8.   I attended the Committee ab^o the Goods Retaken by Capt Manly.

July 11.   Young Shaw Brought Ten Indians from the Misimiche & St John's Tribe.   they are come to negotiate some Business with the General Court & are the Head men of their Tribes.   A Report in Town that Lord Howe has been spoke with — tis said his Designs are to settle the present Unhappy Disputes that subsist between G. Britain & the United Colonies.

July 13.   I attended the Gentlemen Sufferers by Crean Brush   Tis said by Mr Mumpford the Post that Independency was declared the 4th Instant at Philadephia   A Generall Inoculation in This Town for the Small Pox.

July 17.   There is an acc[t] from New York of Two Men of Warr & some Tender being got up beyond the City.   The Phœnix, Cap[t] Parker & Rose, Cap[t] Wallace.

July 18.   This day Independency was Declared in Boston from the Balcony of the Council Chamber.   A great Confusion in Town.

July 20.   This Evening Advertisements were put up for the Inhabitants to meet on Monday next at Ten in the morning in the Common.

July 21.   I went to Church this morning.   M[r] Parker omitted the petitions in the Liturgy for the King & Royal Family thinking it Prudent.

July 22.   I Rose very early & went with M[r] Parker, Phillip Jarvis & Turner for Portsmouth. Wee stopt at Lynn at Newalls   from thence wee Reached Danvers, we dined at Piemonts with Sam[l] Ruggles, his Bro[r] & John Lovell — from thence to Ipswitch wee Stop'ed at Treadwells from thence thro' Newberry & over the Ferry thro' Salisbury & to Hampton Falls.   Wee put up at Sandburns, we supp'd & slept there.   This house I Recommend for Good.   The People very Obliging.   Wee were smoak'd at Charlestown Ferry but passed at Newberry Bridge.

July 23.   Wee Rose early, wee Breakfasted, wee set out from Sandburns.   Wee went through Hampton & thro' North Hills from thence to

Greenland & from thence to Portsmouth. Wee put up at Mr Slaver's — afternoon wee went to the store to look after Our Goods & went & visited the Man of Warr & several other Places — particularly the Fort. I have met many of my Old Acquaintances. Wee met Capt Nat Douse on the Road this morning.

July 24. After Breakfast wee set about dividing our Goods & were very Diligent. I dined at Old Judge Parker's with him, his Son, the Sheriff his son, the Revd Mr Parker his Daughter Mrs Hale, his Grand Daughter Miss Adams & Colo. Leveret.

July 25. We Rose & attended the Division of Our Goods   wee were very Diligent — after Dinner the Claimants for their Goods Met Mr Wentworth their Agent at Tilton's & discoursed about the further pursuit of this affair. Mr Wentworth behaved well.

July 26. Wee set out from Portsmouth — wee reached Sandburn's — wee Breakfasted — wee set out from thence to Salisbury Point — wee crossed the Ferry — wee went to Tristran Dalton's Esq at Newberry Old Town — wee dined with him, Mrs Dalton & Miss Becky Hooper. This Seat of Mr. Dalton's is most Delightfully situated & has the most Extensive Prospect I ever saw particularly of the River Merrimack & the Sea beyond Newberry Port & Hampton Beach. Wee set out from Mr Daltons & stopt at Mr Jackson's where wee met many Old Friends — from thence wee went thro Rowly & W Ipswitch. We stopt at Treadwells — wee went from thence & called on Judge Lynds at Ipswitch Hamlet & from thence to Piemonts at Danvers — we supp'd spent the evening & slept there — a Good House.

July 27. Wee set out & Reached Newall at Lynn. Wee Breakfasted there & were Joyn'd by Mr Brick of Dartmouth — wee set out from Newall's wee passed thro' Mallden, Medford & Charlestown & got home ab° Ten of Clock, after a Pleasant Journey.

July 30. I dined at home with Capt Annet who Runs in here & was taken in the Ship Queen of England belonging to my Friend Jos. Squires of Plymouth laden with Provisions for the Genl How's Army

Primo Aug. This day is appointed by the Congress as a Fast to be Observed throughout the Colonies.

Aug 4. This is Mrs Rowe's birth Day. She is this day 51 years old & very hearty & well.

Aug 5. Richard Green set out this morning for Brookfield for 4 Months Exile

James Perkins for 4 Months to Medfield
Nat Cary   "   "   "   " Dedham
John Timmins ". 2   "   " Waltham
Thos Amory   " 2   "   "   "
Wm Perry   " 4   "   " Medfield
Nat Brinley   "   "   "   " Framingham

Aug 9. A Ship Brought in Portsmouth from Tortola & another sent in here from the Granades both very valuable.

Aug 10.   The Owners of the Goods met at the Royal Exchange this day.

Aug 11.   After service Mr Parker Read the Proclamation of Independence.

Aug 14.   This day the Sons of Liberty kept the Remembrance of it at John Marston's in King's Street.

Aug 17.   After Dinner Mr Warner & I set out for Portsmouth over the Ferry, from thence to Newalls, Lynn, from thence to Piemonts.

Aug 18.   Wee went through Beverly, Wenham Ipswich, from thence to Rowley — wee Stopt at Paysons, wee Reached Newberry Port, stopt at Davenport's & dined with Mr Nat Tracey.   We went to Church & heard Mr Bass Preach — after Church I paid a visit to Colo Ingersoll & went over the Ferry thro' Salisbury, over the Line & Reached Sandburns at Hampton.   Wee had the Pleasure of the Company of Mr Ware president of the Councill who is a man of understanding.

Aug 19.   Set out from Sandburns, wee stopt at Greenland at Mr Fulsoms, from thence to Portsmouth.   I paid a visit to several of my Friends particularly Mark Wentworth & his lady & Mrs Fisher

Aug 20.   We expected our Tryall this morning. put off untill tomorrow   A Large Ship from the Bay of Honduras is sent in here.

Aug 21.   This morning Our Tryall came on. after Dinner I attended the Court.   Our Attorney Mr Lovell deserves Praise & is a Gentleman of Merit

& so is Mr Pickering who pleaded as Advocate for the Captors & Against us   They had not time to finish & adjourn'd untill the morning.

Aug 22.   Our Tryall came on again.   The Cause was given to the Jury by Dr Brackett who is Judge of Admiralty.   This afternoon the Jury Brought in their Verdict in Our Favour — vizt that the Capture was not within the Act & that the Claimants ought to have their Goods Restored. This Verdict is disliked by Capt Manly &c & therefore he intends to move for an Appeal.   I dined at my Worthy Friend Mark Wentworth's.

Aug 23.   I with the Rest of the Claimants have try'ed to settle this affair with the Agent & Capt Manly but to no Purpose

Aug 26.   Yesterday was our Wedding Day — we have been married thirty Three Years.

Aug. 28.   Mr Saml Adams & Colo. Whipple of Portsmouth came to Town from Philadelphia this morning.   The Claimants met this Forenoon.   they chose a Committee to Report their Cause to Saml Adams Esq — Myself, Mr Saml Austin Capt Saml Partridge.

Aug 31.   The post says that General Howe has landed some of his Troops on Long Island near Flat Bush & that some Skirmishes had taken Place.

Sept 4.   Jack Rowe went to Chelsea this morning.

Sept 5.   I attended the Court of Admiralty in Boston Judge Pickering   Severall skirmishes be-

tween the Two Armies at Long Island.   Lord Sterling & Gen[1] Sullivan are missing.

Sept 7.   Tis said the Continental Troops have
left Long Island.

Sept 8.   Several West India men carried into
Providence by the Continental vesssels.

Sept 14.   Tis said by the Post, M[r] Mumpford,
that the Continentals have appointed three Gentlemen from their Body to hold Conference with Lord
Howe & his Brother Generall Howe, viz[t]

Benj[n] Franklynn Esq Philadelphia

M[r] Rutledge of S[o] Carolina

M[r] John Adams of Massachusetts Bay in New England Braintree.

Sept 17.   Yesterday the Independent Company
made their appearance in the Common under the
Command of Colo. Jackson & were Reviewed by
some of the Council & Gen[1] Ward & a Number of
other Gentlemen

Sept 20.   The Continental Troops evacuated New
York on Sunday

Sept 21.   The Post confirms the account of the
Army evacuating the City of New York.

Sept 24.   Went to Watertown with Cap[t] Jos.
Cunningham, M[r] Parker & M[r] Warner.   I had some
Business with the Council   I dined at M[rs] Coolidge's with twelve Gentlemen   Very Bad News
from Gen[1] Washington.   The Connecticut Militia
behaved very badly & much to their Discredit in an
action that hap'ned at harlem in New York the 16th
Instant.

Sept 25.   Robt Temple is come to Town   by him we hear from Geo Inman Capt Linzee Mrs Linzee

Sept 29.   People from New York bring Acc^ts of One third part of that City being destroy'd by Fire on Fryday night the 20th September — tis not yet ascertained how it hap'ned

Oct 4.   A Ship with Light Horse on board is sent into Salem by Capt Lowter

Oct 6.   I sent my Old Mare to Mr Beals Pasture yesterday.

Oct 13.   A valuable prize is sent into Casco Bay by Capt Lee out of Newberry Port.

Oct 15.   The Post says that three Men of Warr & some tenders are passed by Fort Washington having taken severall Gallies on their Way.

Oct 24.   Tis said the King's Troops have landed at Frogs Point near Westchester.

Oct 27.   Sunday.   The Revd Mr Parker was Published this day to Miss Nancy Cutler for the first Time.

Nov 4.   A very valuable prize brought in here bound from London to Hallifax

Nov. 17.   Turner came from Portsmouth & Brought three Waggon Loads of Goods with him. I went to Church this morning.   Mr Parker preached.   A good sermon & suitable to the Solemnity of the Occasion — being Sacrament Day.

(Vol. XIV. of the Diary from Nov. 18, 1776, to Aug. 13, 1778, is missing.)

1778

Aug 13.   An English Fleet appear'd off Rhode Island.   The French Admiral Count D'Estang is gone in Quest of them this hap'ned on Tuesday.

Aug 14.   Mr Payson Brought Jack home this morning — a sad accident hap'ned unto him. Some Boys were out a Shooting one of them named Barthlet's Gun went off accidentally & shot Jack thro' his Coat & Lodged at Least thirty shot in his Right Arm — tis a Great Mercy he escaped with Life.

Aug 15.   Great Damages in the Country & Town by the late Storm especially to the Corn, Fruit & Apples.   Count D'Estang's Fleet not Returned this morning.

Aug 17.   This is Mr Parker's birth Day, he being now 33 years old.

Aug 20.   This day Count D'Estang's Fleet Returned to their Station off Newport — tis said they have taken a Friggate & a Bombketch.

Aug 22.   A French Man of Warr of 74 Guns is got into Nantasket having had a Brush with an English 64 Gun Ship.   The French Captain is Wounded.

Aug 24.   An acc^t of Count D'Estang's Fleet leaving Newport harbour bound to Boston on Saturday last.

Aug 26.   Genl Hancock Returnd.

Aug 28.   This morning the French fleet came

to an anchor in Nantasket Road Some of them dismasted.

Aug 30. The Count D'Estang came with his Retinue on Shore yesterday & dined with Gen[l] Hancock. Two Friggates seen in Our Bay this afternoon, supposed to be English

Aug 31. An Express from Plymouth this morning giving an acc[t] of a Fleet of Twenty Sails in our Bay. Several Prizes are arrived also Cap[t] Skimmer's Brigg from a Cruise — poor Skimmer was killed the 3rd this month in an Engagement with a Letter of Marque Brigg which they made a Prize of.

Primo Sept. The Fleet appearing again in Our Bay has alarmed the People that the whole of the Militia are Ordered under Arms. Gen[l] Sullivan & his whole Army have Retired from Rhode Island having had a smart engagement with the British troops there under the Command of Gen[l] Peggot.

Sept 2. Several People taken up & put on board the Prize Ship, Particularly M[r] Shirley & Cap[t] Callahan The Militia under arms again twice this day & a Constant Guard kept up. I met the Proprietors of Point Shirley this day. The French Admiral wants to be accommodated with the Houses for an Hospitall for his People upwards of 700 being sick of the Scurvey.

Sept 7. The English have sent a Party to Bedford & Burnt it on Saturday night together with the Shipping & Stores in that harbour. Jack Rowe went to Chelsea this morning.

Sept 10.   I dined at home with the Honble Jery Powell President of Our Council & Mrs Rowe.

Sept 11.   High Training this day.   Genl Hancock Treated the Council & all his officers, many other Gentlemen at Capt Marston's.   The Dinner was very Clever   I dined there.

Sept 13.   The Rev^d Dr. Elliot dyed this morning, much lamented.

Sept. 20.   Mr Parker preached a very Serious & Good sermon — he mentioned the Character of that Good & Worthy man the Revd Dr Elliot.

Sept 22.   We have heard this Day from George Sucky & the Children who are well at New York.

Sept 23.   The Count D'Estang with his officers &c made a Grand Appearance yesterday — they paid a visit to the General Court & were escorted by a Committee from Both Houses on their Landing at the Long Wharf.

Sept 25.   The Count DEstang dined with the Councill & house this day

Sept 26.   Count D'Estang din'd with Genl Heath this day.

Oct 3.   This afternoon I Purchased a pair of Horses.

Oct 6.   I dined at home with the Chevalier DeBorde, Monsr Gondclose, Admiral's Secretary, Mr Holker, Colo. Baddock & Mrs Rowe.   We have try'd our New Horses   they prove very well.

Oct 13.   Many Prizes arriv'd here at Salem & Newberry Port.

Oct 20.   Colo. Revere Bro^t me a Letter from

Sam¹ Gould who is arrived in a Cartell from New York. This morning my Negro Marcellus made his appearance in our Kitchen & a very Frightfull one it was.

Oct 24. I dined at Mʳ Holkers — with him Capᵗ Landy of the Alliance, Capᵗ Ingersoll of the Dean, Colo. Adam Babcock Mʳ Thoˢ Cushing, Mʳ Thoˢ Cushing junʳ, General Warren & Mʳ Martin Brimmer. Mʳ Inman Mʳˢ Inman & Mʳˢ Haskins set out for Providence.

Oct 29. Genˡ Hancock Invited all the Gentlemen of the French Fleet to a Grand Ball at Concert Hall. Many Gentlemen & Ladies of the Town were there & made a Good Appearance.

Oct 30. The Council with a Number of Other Gentlemen dined on board The Languedock, Count DEstang.

Nov 1st. My Negro Man Marcellus died this day.

Nov 5. The Count DEstang sailed yesterday from this Port. A Good Deal of Snow fell this day. This Evening came news that the Somerset Man of Warr was cast away on the back of Cape Cod.

Nov 6ᵗʰ. Genˡ Gates came to Town this day from Hartford.

Nov 7. The Brigg Peace & Harmony sail'd yesterday & return'd.

Nov. 8ᵗʰ. Sunday. Mʳ Selby had a Collection this afternoon. it amounted £97. very handsome. I went to pay my Compliments to Genˡ Gates this day.

Nov 10. M^r & Mrs Inman & Mrs Haskins returned from their Journey & spent the evening with us together with Betty Murray.

Nov 12. A Gentleman & an Indian came from Quebeck thro — the Eastern Country by Land & bro^t me a letter from my Bro^r Jacob.

Nov 14. A great Number of the Somerset's Men are come to town from Cape Cod.

Nov 17. Town Meeting this day ab° Capt Pepper & Young Francis Johnnot.

Nov 25. Wee had a Vestry this afternoon at Mr Parkers.

Nov 29. A Seaman by name Herring belonging to Chagford in England came to our house & told me many things about my Relatives & Friends there, which pleased me.

Dec 3. I saw Dr Watson of the Somerset that was Cast away on the Back of Cape Cod. he is very much out of health

Dec 5. Mr Sandford from Bedford brings us the Bad News of Our Brigg Peace & Harmony, Capt Lawrence being taken & by Chance is got into Bedford.

Decem 7. Capt Solo Davis & Mr Warner Returned from Portsmouth having bought the Briggatine.

Dec. 9. Our New Brigg got ashore & overset coming round from Portsmouth, on the Devil's Back.

Dec. 19. A notification appeared yesterday at the Town House threatening some People which Bo^t flour at Vendue.

Dec 25.   Christmas Day.   The Coldest morning as by the Thermometer for 40 years — a thin Congregation.   The Collection for the Poor at our Church was £154.

Dec 26.   A very heavy Storm of Snow all day — it has been colder for these last five Days than at any one time a Great many Years.

Dec 28.   A Sermon was Preached this day by Mr Howard at the Old Brick at the Request of St Andrew's Lodge & the money Collected given to the Poor.

Dec 29.   In a storm last Saturday four oxen, one man & one Horse were froze to Death on Boston Neck & Sunday other Persons in different Places.

Dec 31.   The General Arnold Privateer is lost in the late Storm at Plymouth & upwards of eighty of the crew Perished also the General Starks Privateer at Nantucket & upwards of Twenty of their Crew Perished

1779

Jan 10.   A very melancholly affair hap'nd last evening.   Mr Benjⁿ Andrews, a worthy Good Man Shot himself by mere accident.

Jan 13.   A Town Meeting this morning.   The Inhabitants of this Town are in Great Distress for want of Corn, Flour &c   A Committee of Nine were Chosen to consult the best methods to be taken for their Immediate Relief.   John Brown John Rowe

Tho⁸ Malley Wᵐ Foster, Wᵐ Cooper Nat Appleton
Nat Noyes Samˡ Barrett & Tho⁸ Wallace With
Ezeˡ Price.

Jan 16. Town Meeting again this morning. A
Committee of Eighteen were Chosen to provide
Corn, flour etc for the Poor & distressed Inhabitants of This Town. We met this afternoon &
adjourned until Monday 11 of Clock.

Jan'y 18. I attended this morning the Committee.

Jan 20. I attended Town Meeting this morning. The calling in two emissions of money occasions much uneasiness.

Jan'y 27. Town meeting this morning. Mʳˢ
Allyn Otis was buried this afternoon.

13 Feby. Jack Rowe came from Chelsea this
morning.

16 Feb'y. Mʳ Payson came to see me on Jack's
affair. I am very uneasy about it. I din'd at
Mʳ Cottons by invitation of Colo. Badcock.

19 Feb'y. The Committee for purchasing Flour
met this afternoon at Fanewill Hall.

21 Feb'y. A contribution at Church 643 Dolls
John Temple's Child was Christened this afternoon
by the name of Angela.

24 Feb'y. The Committee met this morning &
apply'd to Government ab° the Distressed Situation
of this Town.

27 Feb'y. I din'd at Col. Marstons by Invitation of the Sieur Duvaluais Consul of France
with 54 Gentlemen The Committee sat all Day.

Primo Mar. Jack Rowe went to Chelsea. The Committee sat all day. The Gener¹ Court adjourn'd this Day.

Mar 5. Town Meeting this morning. Mʳ Tudor d'ld an oration at the Old Brick Meeting — afternoon I attended the Committee.

Mar 6. I attended the Committee all this morning — a Considerable Skirmish in the Jerseys between a Party sent out from New York & Generall Maxwells the advantage in favour of Gen¹ Maxwell.

Mar 7. My store was broke open last night & a Considerable Quantity of Goods Stolen to the value of abº Two Thousand Pounds as near as I can Guess.

Mar 8. Sam¹ Gould & James Liswall watched at my Store this Night. Annual Town Meeting.

10 March. Town Meeting all Day

12 March. Mʳ Moore & his wife came yesterday to live at our house.

16 March. The Revᵈ Mʳ Payson paid us a visit this morning.

22 March. This is Sucky Linzee's birth Day 25 years old.

23 March. Colonel Badcock married to Miss Polly Hubbard this evening.

26 March. Many vessels Cast away in the late Storms & severall taken in the Bay.

27 March. The Committee met this morning.

Mar 29. The Thief taken up that stole my Sails & Committed.

April 6. Tuesday. I went to Church this morning & stood Sponsor for John Haskins Son — is named Ralph. The Charitable Society met at my house.

Aprill 10. M[r] Parker's Child was Christened by the name Elizabeth. Sponsors M[r] Greenleaf, M[rs] Inman & M[rs] Amory.

Apr 16. The Continental Friggate Warren, Cap[t] John Hopkins arrived in Port. She in Company with the Queen of France & Ranger have taken bound from New York to Georgia.

The Ship Jason, Cap[t] Potterfield 20 Guns 150 Men
Ship Maria   16 " & 84 "
Privateer Schooner Hibernian   8 " & 45 "

Briggs Patriot, Prince Frederick, Batchelor & Schooner — Transports — all Laden with Stores.

A Bonfire & Great Rejoicings on this Occasion.

May 1. I din'd at Martin Brimmers with him M[rs] Brimmer Herman & Andrew Brimmer Rich[d] Green & M[r] Inman.

May 5. This Day Town Meeting, the following Gentlemen were Chosen Representatives —

John Hancock Sam[l] Adams, Thomas Dawes, Tho[s] Walley, W[m] Tudor, Caleb Davis & Gustavus Fellows.

May 6. M[r] Van Ranselear paid me a Visit this morning.

May 26. Election Day. I went to Meeting this morning. M[r] Stillman preached. The Choice of Councillors not finished this evening.

Primo June. I dined at Stephen Cleverly's with

him, Miss Sally & Young Stephen Cleverly, Mr Parker, Capt Haskins & Richd Green — they all went with Mr Parker a Haymaking.

June 13. Sunday. After Church the Proprietors met — they voted our Church Vacated by Mr Walter — 12 Yeas 4 Nays

June 15. I began to mow my Pasture this morning Merchants Meeting

June 19. Merchants Meeting Dissolved. Every day this week my Time has been taken up with the Merchants part of the Hay got in.

June 20. Sunday. Mr Parker was Chosen the Incumbent Minister of Trinity Church this afternoon. Voters Present 23.

June 22. Good News from the Southward. I got all my Hay in yesterday

June 24. St John's Day I dined at Deacon Jones with the Free Masons their Number 46. I spent the Day very Cheerfully.

June 29. The Caterpillars appear in Our Pasture & all over the Pastures in Boston.

July 2. The Caterpillars are most of them gone Out of the Pasture

July 8. Bad Accounts from New Haven in Connecticut State. Mrs Rowe din'd at Brush Hill.

July 9. Town Meeting this morning Saml Adams Moderator Several Prizes arr'd yesterday at Salem & Marblehead.

July 11. Sunday. Mr Parker Read the Address of Congress.

July 12. A Furious Press this morning to Man

the Fleet.   The Delegates from the Trading Towns
met this morning.

July 13.   Bad Intelligence from Connecticut.   I
devoted my Whole Time this day with the Delegates
fr. the Trading Towns.

July 15.   A Body meeting this Day.   Dr Rand
before them & Examined.   The Remainder of the
Fleet got into Nantasket Road this day so that
they are now Ready for Sea.

All knowledge of John Rowe's private life ends
with the Diary.

He was a member of the House of Representatives in 1784, and the following entry is copied
from the Journal of the House, March 17 of that
year : —

" Mr Rowe moved the House that leave be given
to hang up the representation of a Cod Fish in the
room where the House sits, as a memorial of the
importance of the Cod-Fishery to the welfare of
the Commonwealth as had been used formerly.
The said motion having been seconded, the ques-
tion was put, and leave given for the purpose
aforesaid."

It is probable, though no positive record has
been found, that, when in 1785 the town of Mery-
field (my rye field) changed its name to Rowe, the
change was made in honor of John Rowe.   Tradition says that he promised to give the town a bell
on that occasion, which promise was never fulfilled,
perhaps because at that time there was nowhere to

hang the bell, and his death followed two years
after. In Fleet's Almanack and Register for 1787
is the following: "J. Rowe Esq obt 17th Feb 1787
Etat anæ — 72 — Gratitude demands a Tear."

ACTION OF GRAND LODGE ON JOHN ROWE'S DEATH

At a meeting of members of the Grand Lodge
at Brother Sam Dunns house Feb 17, 1787

Present

R. W. Richard Gridly	D. G. M.
" John Cutler	S. G. W.
W. Nathaniel Patten	M. M. Lodge
" Charles Sigourney	G. S.
" Samuel Dunn	M. St (John's) Lodge

" Joseph Coolidge & Sam Gridly Wardens

" Mungo Mackay } Past G. Officers
Samuel Parkman }

Whereas it has pleased Almighty God to take
hence our dear & well beloved Grand Master John
Rowe Esqr the G. Lodge desirous of Manifesting
their Respect & Affection for him agree to Attend
his funeral in due form and that the several Lodges
of this Town & Charlestown be Invited to Attend
on the same sorrowful Occasion and

Voted that Wp Brother Cutler, Gardner & Patten be a Committee to wait on Mrs Rowe to know if
tis agreeable to her that The Free Masons walk in
Procession at the funeral and Voted, That they together with Brother Price Mackay & Dunn be a

Committee to Arrange & Superintend the Funeral Procession.

Voted, That the Committee furnish Two doz Aprons Two dozen Pair Gloves which the Treasurer is directed to pay for.

NOTE FROM Mʀꜱ JOHN ROWE TO GRAND LODGE

Mʳˢ Rowe & Mʳ John Rowe (nephew) present their most respectful Compliments to Mʳ Cutler & the other Officers & Brethren of the Grand Lodge & beg them to accept their most grateful acknowledgements for their respect shown at the interment of Mʳ Rowe their late Grand Master & to assure them they retain a grateful sense of Their attention to his memory. And as Mʳˢ & Mʳ Rowe have not the pleasure of an acquaintance with the Masters & Officers of the other Lodges that attended at the funeral they beg the favour of Mʳ Cutler that he will be so kind as to communicate to them in their names their particular thanks for the polite & respectful Behaviour shewn by the Brethren on this mournful occasion ; & they request that Mʳ Cutler will do this in the manner he thinks most proper.

Pᴏɴᴅ Sᴛʀᴇᴇᴛ 22ɴᴅ Feb. 1787

ROWE ESTATE AT MILTON

Bought from Gov. Belcher's Heirs in 1781

EXTRACTS

LETTER BOOK OF JOHN ROWE

SEPT 1759 — 1762 MAY

To MR JOHN AMIEL   BOSTON Sept. 7th 1759
    Sir

We have Rec'd sundry Letters from you Relating to Capt Doggett's Voyage. Inclosed is the acc^tts Relating to the same, pr Good Management there was but —— old Tenor Sunk, besides the Goods we sent you, for your acc^t. I hope you'l have Better Luck in Time to Come — especially as we have now a good Prospect. I refer you to the Bearer for News; at Present tis Uncertain whether Genl Wolff will force the french to a Capitulation at Canada, if he dont all their whole Country will be Destroyed; both Upper & Lower Towns at Quebeck was Destroyd when the Last Vefsell came away. The Consequence will be Worse to them than their Keeping Possession of their Inland Country. Mrs Amiel is well but Trollet has the Gout, all your friends here are Glad that you have so Good a Prospect before you. I hope your

friends will Continue their Business. Believe me
that I will Continue your Real Friend

JOHN ROWE

To Dr Thoˢ Wood   Boston Sept 11ᵗʰ 1759
    Revᵈ Sir
    I Received your favor of the 9ᵗʰ last month &
note its Contents & find that you got your discharge from all your Debts by act of Insolvency in
England; how far a Debt that was Contracted in
the plantations, will take effect, by said Insolvency
or take place, I leave you to Judge. . . . It seems
that providence will again take place in yʳ favor &
by your attention to Industrious application to
Business you will have it in your power pretty
soon to discharge your debts & pay your Creditors. I wish with you that happy period may
arrive, as your disposition by your Letter, will
operate in their behalf and be no doubt the Greatest Satisfaction to an Honest mind. dont take
this as advice but only to Remind you that the
money we lent you was, at that [time] a Good
act of business to you, and that it had not the
Expected design, it was not the Loss then Esteemd
by you, and we are sorry the Event prov'd not so
favorable to you, this we think is Just Reasoning
& we Cannot help thinking we ought to stand the
first in your thoughts — and no doubt you will be
of our opinion and make us payment as soon as
your ability will let you.

To be sure it will give us pleasure to see you & Congratulate you on your smiles of Fortune and as far as prudence directs, we shall on all Occasions be Ready to do you any Good Office. In the meantime we wish you the success of your Labours & Remain with Compliments to Mrs Wood, Your very humble Servts

JOHN ROWE *for himself & Ralph Inman*

To JACOB ROWE   BOSTON Sept 20th 1759
Dr Brother

I had your letters of the 3^d 9th & 11th June to all which I gave answer. I hear fr Capt Barthlett you are well at your station in the Camp & I hope you will make it worth your attention & when you have fixd with Mr Goldthrop please to acquaint me. I Endeavored to get a Camp Bed to send but in short did not know where to send it nor where your situation was — as soon as you are fixt for the winter Quarters anything you wish for I'll Send you. I will send you two Quintails of the Best Fish to the Care of Mr William Clark pr first Opportunity after this.

If you winter at Louisburg, let Capt Sam : Mackay of Genl Hobsons Regiment know you are my Brother, he writes me, I may expect Letters from Mr Shay the Contractor, which I shall be glad off; if you have any acquaintance with him give my Compliments & tell him any of his Commands will be Executed with Great pleasure. . . . I send you

Inclosed the last Newspapers they are of no Consequence. Whether Gen¹ Amherst will make any further progress at present seems very uncertain. Mʳˢ Rowe Mʳ Inman & wife are all well & wish you Success. no letters from the West of England since you went away — nor have I been yet able to examine or go to Cape Ann on your affairs but Intend it, as soon as the next Convoy for England is gone. I Remain

> Yʳ affectionate brother

> > JOHN ROWE

My Compliments to Mʳ Goldthrop.

> > > BOSTON Sept 20th 1759

Revᵈ Sir

I have your favour of the 7ᵗʰ July last & thank you for your favouring me with Such Intelligence. I hope we shall be able to Maintain our Ground up the River & I doubt not, but Mʳ Amherst goes forward, altogether Succeed — as soon as the Situation of my affairs will enable me, I will do the piece of Service you Requird which will take place before the departure of our fleet for England, meantime I Remain

> Yʳ most hum. Servt

> > JOHN ROWE

BOSTON Sept 24th 1759

To Mᴿ PHILIP CUYLER, NEW YORK
  Sir

I have your favour of the 17ᵗʰ pr post — observe
what Mʳ Stillwell says, as yet I have no Letters, but
whenever I see Capᵗ Stoddard depend ont I'll make
him pay both them Fellows ballance of their Shares.
If you had sent the Skins pr Wimble who arrivd
yesterday they would have Sold Immediately no
person has any in town but Mʳ Rhoades & his are
very Ordinary. I will speak to Mʳ Trumbel this
day for the frames you Order'd & also for the Rid-
ing Chaise which I Guess may be handsom for
twenty five pounds York money, both these I will
Get made with all Speed Messʳˢ Watts & Moss
were unluckily taken pr a privateer mannd with
Montreal French that came out of the Gut of
Canso. I am very sorry for them, they have nothing Insured — they are both gone in two privateers
fitted out at Hallifax, they write me they intend
to go to the Head Quarters where these French
Rascalls came from & Endeavor to at least get their
own property. I wish them Success & think they
stand a Tolerable Chance. I wish you Joy of the
Glorious News Obtained by prince Ferdinand over
the French near the Borders of Hanover. I refer
you to prints for particulars tho they are not altogether compleat — this action hapen'd to be gain'd
in the most Critical time & is more Consequence to
our affairs than anything that has taken place this
Ward, for had the french Succeeded all the Elec-

torates of Hanover Hessee etc would have remained
in possession of them or destroy'd; wee are to have
Great Rejoicings here on the Occasion & I wish
we may have another Occasion on the Surrender of
Quebeck. I remain Sir

Your very humble Servt

JOHN ROWE

To MR PHILLIP CUYLER   BOSTON Jan' 5 1760
    Sir
    Inclos'd is bill lading for the Riding Chair I
have got made for you pr Mr Paddock, I wish it
may get safe to your hands & prove to your Like-
ing.   I dont know the expense of it yet but I
shall send it with the cost of the Frames which will
come pr Wimble. . .
    The bearer Capt Jarvis belongs to me & if you
can do him any Services 'twill oblige me.   I wish
you the Compliments of the Season & am

Sir your Friend & humb^{le} Sev^t

JOHN ROWE.

To JAMES OTIS ESQ^R   BOSTON Oct 1rst 1759
    Sir
    As you are going to plym° have taken the
Liberty to Inclose you perez Tillson Acc^t by which
you'l see the Ballance in my favour is £387.9.
Lawful money, this ought to have been discharged
by him some years past.   As I thought the money

in his hands was Secure have omitted urging payment, now I begin to doubt his ability, therefore
by the favour you'l get as much as you Can & if
possible security for the Remainder, which he can
by no means think hard in me to Insist on, as the
Time he has already had is too long . . . your prudence will direct you in what method to proceed;
by Enquiring of your Brother M[r] Warren how his
affairs stand & whatever you do will be Justify'd by

Sir your very hum[l] Servt

JOHN ROWE

P.S.   Treasury notes will do as well as money.

BOSTON Oct 30th 1759

To CAP[T] EDW[D] CAHILL LONDON
    Sir

As the french have Lost Quebeck & in Consequence of that Canada must fall, its now become
the General Opinion that peace will take place,
if you Continue your Resolution of seeing Boston
& intend to keep in the London Trade I shall hold
any part of a ship with you in comp[y] with Mess[rs]
Lane & Booth.   I think I have no Occasion to tell
you that if there is any Oyl or freight going I
have Interest enough to get it — pr this Convoy
I have two Vessells, Namely Hunter I own all myself, any good offices you do him will be kindly
Receiv'd, also the principal part of Dashwood &
your good offices will also be acceptable to him.

Mrs Rowe has wrote you at Large & I dont know whether I am indebted or not for sundries sent Mrs Rowe if I am you must call on Messrs Lane & Booth for payment. I wish you all Imaginable Happiness & Remain

Y^r assur'd friend

J. ROWE

BOSTON Oct 30th 1759.

To Capt Samuel Dashwood

Sir

You have already Receiv'd Orders from Jno Rowe Relative to your proceeding in the Ship this is to tell you that pr Case you should miss of your Convoy (which you must at all events keep with if possible) & should be taken, you have our Liberty to Ransom the Vessell & Cargo for any sum short of Eighteen hundred pounds ster^g & even that sum Rather than omit it, but no further & this shall be your Justification

from your friends

JOHN ROWE

JOS & WM ROTCH, *for*
Themselves & Timothy Folger.

A copy of the above I have rec^d which I promise to follow

SAM^{LL} DASHWOOD

To MR SAMUEL HORNER   BOSTON, Jan'y 4th 1760
    Sir

I wrote you pr Capt Binney advising that my
Brother Rowe had Chartered his Vessell from New
York to some port in Ireland & have now given
a few lines to Capt Jarvis who goes master (by the
Desire of Brother Rowe) who writes you by same
conveyance, to Desire you will Render him all the
good offices in your power for the good of the
Voyage & as you mention'd you Could give a Vessell freight to America she will be in good season
for it provided the Master Thinks it will be preferable to a Load of Salt from Liverpool, who is to
consult you upon it — what money you supply the
Master with his Bills will be Honour'd & your good
Service to him.

    Shall be gratefully acknowledg'd by
        Your Esteem'd friend & Servt

                        RALPH INMAN

                        BOSTON Jan'y 11th 1760
To CAP^T MICHAEL DALTON NEWBURY
    Sir

Upon Receipt of your Letter of 3rd Curr^t I waited
on Capt Pryce who immediately got into a passion
& produc'd a Letter from Admiral Saunders' Secretary Relating to Capt Pryce' Cable & anchor,
upon which I produced the Certificate, who swore
he would not Receive it, upon which I went away
— another interview much to same purpose & once
more — nothing done.

This morning I went again, Capt Gwynn hapn'd
to be present & after some talk wee settled it & I
hope to your approbation, he Insisted on the Cable
to be value at 257 which Capt Gwynn & [I] consented too & so tis settled & I have pd him as pr
his Receipt 19.15.1^{ster} When I came to pay him
your Guineas he ask'd if they were weight. I told
him they were the Guineas Rec^d from you they
hapen'd to prove very deficient, that set him a swear-
ing again. Says he, " I'll be damnd if Dalton has
not pickt up all the light Guineas he could find in
Newbury &c "— however enough of this — on the
Back of this stands a memorandum of what I pd &
what I rec^d. I assure you had it not been to have
served you, he should not have made me run after
him so often. I cannot at present secure a Certificate neither do I expect it, he seems very angry with
Capt Pike for telling him, as he says, Lies. I shall
always endeavor to serve you but hope on no such
occasion again

        & Remain Sir

           Yr Friend & very hum^l Servt

             JOHN ROWE

                         BOSTON 4 Feby 1769

To MR DAVID VANHORNE AT NEW YORK
    Dr Sir
    . . . As to the note of hand I Got of Mr Benjn
Brandon on your acc^t it was George Mills note,
which I have now in my Possession he is gone from

hence Sometime in the Service of the Government
but at what place I cannot exactly tell, so that there
is no hope of Getting any Mahogany Tables or
Desks on acc^t of that not till he Returns & I fear
but Little or nothing when he does, he is very Poor
has no Stock nor I believe any Tools, however I'll
keep a look out for him — & get anything I can
for you . . .

To Mrs MARY TOLCHER   BOSTON 23rd Feb'y 1760
      Dear Sister
    I wrote you sometime ago pr the purser of
the Man of Warr who belongs to plymouth wherein
I told you of my health & which thank God Continues.   I also wish You Joy & happiness in your
new State of Life which I hope your prudence will
always Contribute too.   As it pleas'd God to take
our Dear parent from us & the house is now the
property of us all, you seem desirous to know what
is to be done with it.   Brother Robins wrote me
he could obtain a hundred pounds for it.   I
thought it so Inconsiderable a price, that I wrote
him I would give that price or more for it &
order'd my Friends in London to pay you three
parts on a proper Deed being Executed to me &
when compleated for Bro. Robins to take care of
it on my acc^t but I Confess I could not Imagine he
had —— for it himself especially at that price, not
that I care much about it but I Dont like this small
price — nor will I part with my own or Bro^r

Jacobs' which is now my property, the first Leisure
I have I will write to Uncle Hawker my full sentiments about it.   I think Bro^r Robins might have
answer'd my letter on this acc^t pray give my love
to him & Sister Robins.   It will always give me
pleasure to hear from you & every other Relative.
shall Be Glad to know if uncle John is still alive.
Brother Jacob is now at Quebeck & in Good Business being assistant to Daniel Weir Esqr Commissary General.   Pray give my Compliments to your
Husband & I remain with Esteem, Dear Sister, your
very affectionate Brother.

BOSTON March 1st 1760

To FRIEND CHRISTO HUSSEY AT NEWBURYPORT

I must desire you to Send me pr very first good
opportunity, Two Quintals of the Largest & best
fish you Can get, it is for a particular friend & I
must beg your Care about it . . . please to tell
your Bro^r Obed that I have got Mr Fitch to sign
their Charter party which they Sent up & please to
ask Mr Barker & him how they come not to let me
know that they had sent the old Sloop Hannah to
the mount.   I hear she is arriv'd there, but dont
know whether she is Coming or not, so that if I
had an Inclination to Insure my part, I am at a
Loss about, if they had mentioned it t'woud have
[been] more agreeable.

I Shall be glad to hear from you ab^o this old
Sloop whether She is coming direct back or not &

any Service I can do for you please to give notice
to   Y^r Friend

JOHN ROWE

Callo, in my Snow is cast away   Hunter Dashwood Jacobson are arrivd & I believe the other
Ships that went with that Convoy.

To Capt Cahill   BOSTON Mar 3rd 1760
     Dear Sir
     I Confirm the proceeding copy of my Last &
have Nothing farther to say on that Head. M^r
Greens Snow is arriv'd, but Sherrard nor Bradford
dont yet appear; be Kind Enough to purchase for
me, a Book wrote pr Capt Gardner Giving a particular acc^t of the expedition to Martinico & Guadaloupe. all your friends here are Well.
     I Remain
          Dr Sir your very humb^l Servt

JOHN ROWE

To Colo Preble   BOSTON March 17th 1760
     Sir,
     I Rece'd your Letter of the 5th March & see the
Indians have an Inclination to make terms of Peace,
I dont know what directions you'l have from the
Government but guess t'will be peaceable News for
the Indians. I have sent the Articles you wrote
for & shall at any time be glad to send any Articles

I have or you may want & any orders you send I
will fullfill

I Remain Sir yr friend & very humb^le Servt
to Command

JOHN ROWE

To MR Peter Hubbert   Boston Mar 24th 1760
Sir

. . . .

P.S. We have had the Preceeding Week Such
Terrible Fires: the News Paper will give you an
acc^t, the Last of which was very Terrible Indeed.
Such Devastation in so short a Time was hardly
ever known. I am a Sufferer among the Rest, but
thank God, not so much as to Give mee any Uneasiness. it has Consum'd upwards of Two hundred Houses, Stores & Shops

Boston April 15th 1760
To MR Phillip Cuyler New York
Sir

I have your favour of the 31st March pr Capt
Wimble. As to the Frames they are not yet done,
Mr Cumber promises you shall not fail of them pr
Return of Wimble. as to Tea it is now worth
from a Dollar to 51. . . . The Calamity that has
hapen'd to the Town by fire is very great. I lost
some Goods at my Store at Oliver's Dock, but
nothing of Consequence to make mee uneasy.
This will be deliver'd you pr Mr John Gould who

takes New York in his Way to England. Shall
Esteem it a favour you make him free of your City.
I shall on all Occasion Shew you, I am

Sir, your very hum̃ Servt

JOHN ROWE

To JACOB ROWE   BOSTON April 21st 1760
    Bro^r Jacob
    I Rece'd your favour of the 6th Sept & 1st Nov
Last, am very glad you have got into Business with
Mr Wyer. I wrote you many Letters pr Sundry
Vessells that Return'd here again.
    I would have put in hand a vessell for your place
had I any Vessell of my own at home, but as I had
not, did not care to charter any & I am much
afraid the Gentleman that has order'd this Cargoe
pr Capt Cushion will not find his Acc^t in it, There
are at Least Thirty sail gone & going from hence
& a Great Quantity from all other places on the
Continent. I have sent you one Cask of oporto,
one Cask of Lemons & one Barrell of W. I. Rum
& I have wrote Mr Wyer an answer to his Letter &
offer'd him my Services here, I Cannot at present
say Any Thing particular ab° your affairs as I have
not been at Cape Ann, but as there will be Opportunity you shall hear — no news from the West of
England, n̊or from London — we have had a
Terrible Fire hapen'd at Boston in which I was a
Sufferer at Oliver's Dock, the Newspapers will fully
acquaint you the Situation of what was burnt, such

a Melancholy & Dismal Burning was never yet
seen in any part of this Continent The wind blew
very hard at North West and the Fury of the
flames is beyond Conception; I have been oblig'd
to pay Quincy your Obligation ab° two months
past I shall pay Mr Webb & Mr Beachum M^r
Sherburne & Jos. Rhodes are yet unpaid, why did
you not mention these affairs I suppose you forgot
it — as there will be opportunity now from Quebeck
let me hear from you & I shall do you all the Service in my power; the Bearer, Capt Cushion, Capt
Forbes & myself have Chartered for Acc^t of M^r
Ogilvy, if you can do Cushion any service t'will not
be amiss.

I send the Coppy for Capt Nickolls & Remain

Your very affectionate Brother

JOHN ROWE

To Capt Cushing   BOSTON April 24th 1760

Sir

The Sloop Charming Molly which we have
Charter'd, Being Ready to Sail, its Our desire you
proceed immediately to Hallifax — you are then to
apply to Mr Jeremiah Condy Russell & take from
him Such Goods as he shall put on board you &
proceed Immediately to Quebeck and there Deliver
your Cargoe to Mr James Ogilvy Merch^t There.
If Mr Russell should Be departed from Hallifax,
you are then to proceed Immediately to Quebeck
with° him & there deliver your Cargo to said M^r

James Ogilvy & when you are unloaded, then you to follow such orders as you Receive from him for your proceedings afterwards.

We wish you a Good Voyage & am

Yrs Friends

JAM FORBES

JOHN ROWE

To MR FRANCIS ROBINS   BOSTON May 1760
    Dr Brother

A few days ago, came to hand your Letter of the first of October via Londⁿ pr Capt^t Sherrard who was blown of the Coast & had a Long Passage — the Contents thereof I duly note.

Please to Look into your former Letters Respecting the House & you'l find that you tell me you were offer'd a hundred pounds for it, which price I Could by no means consent to take & in Consequence thereof I told you I would take it myself at that Rate, & I supposing you Consented thereto, then Messrs Lane & Booth were to pay you & my Bro Joseph & Mrs Tolcher your Shares on a deed being properly accredited by you all & Left in their Care; now I perceive by your Letter, that you are willing to part with your Three Shares for thirty pounds sterl'g each & if my Sister Mrs Tolcher will part with her share, then you may get a deed executed properly by yrself, Bro. Jos & her, under the Direction of Uncle Hawker. Let it be done Authentick & then Lodg'd with Messrs Lane &

Booth Merch^ts in London, who have orders when
this is done, to answer your bills on them for my
acc^t, namely sixty pounds sterl^g to you for yours &
Brother Joseph's Shares & thirty pounds more to
Mr Tolcher for sister Mary's share — please to
observe that Bro^r Jacob is now at Quebeck with
Daniel Weir Esqr Commissary General, this place is
worth him Two Hundred pounds sterl^g per annum,
nothing has given me more pleasure than to be able
to assist him in procuring this place & many other
Good offices &c   Capt Thomas Farr, is the Bearer
of this to London, I hope he will arrive in safety
as he is a person of your acquaintance, I thought
proper to Show him a power Jacob Left with me
to settle this affair, so that you have no Occassion
to trouble yrself, only in executing a deed in my
name for your three shares & send me a copy that
I may get his executed here at his Return as the
Redemption of his Lies without Dispute in me.   I
think Mrs Tolcher can have no objection & I do it
on no other Acct than to keep it in the Family,
Rather than it shall be sold to a Stranger — when
this is compleatedLet Mr Brown the present Ten-
nant Remain in it & you take the care of it the
same as if it was your own & Receive from him the
Rent as Usual, only Let it be done in my name &
for my Acc^t. I have drawn a bill on my Bro^r
Joseph for thirty three pounds six shillings & 8^d
being for Jacob's share of the Legacy Left him
pr his Aunt Bradford which now is become due
& which I presume he will pay. . . . I think he

might have had Opportunitys enough to give me a
Line on the affairs of the Family there's no excuse
for him because he was taught to write before I
left home. . . . I am very sorry to hear you are so
great a Sufferer by Geo. Conde I Fancy that Spark
has troubl'd his heart more ab^t Religious Politicks
than Business. I see a scandalous Pamphlet of his
which has made great noise & Clamour here — being
well adapted for this Meridian — the Gentleman M^r
Sylvester that had the care of Grace Knowling'
money is now dead & his executers Live on
Shelter Ilend.   I will when there is any opportunity write to them on her Acc^t & you may depend on't if I succeed will Remit it to her immediately & as soon as I know ab^t it, will advise you
in Course.   I cant now give Mrs Wilcocks any Intelligence ab^t her Son's Family but next post I will
mention to my friend Mr Vanhorne at New York
& get him to Enquire ab^t them I think they are in
some Remote town in the Jersey Government.
I am glad to hear your little Family are well & I
thank my sister for her many Letters, you will make
my Love & Compliments Acceptable to her — you'l
please to show my Uncle Hawker this Letter to
whom I have wrote on this occasion & Correspond
with Messrs Lane & Booth thereon.

    Mrs Rowe Joyns with me in Sincere Love & affec-
tion to you & Sister &

        I Remain y^r Affectionate Bro^r

             JOHN ROWE

BOSTON May 5th 1760

To JOHN HAWKER ESQ EXETER

Hon^d Sir

It is a Long time since I had the pleasure to write
you & having not a Line from you you'l please to
excuse it. I often Try'd to get Mr Jos Gerrish to
do some what in the affair of Mr Upcolis but Could
not prevail, he had nothing then to pay, & went off
to Hallifax in Debt he is now there & store Keeper
to his Majesty's Navy & by the best advices, he is
in a good way so that if he Returns you may yet
stand a Chance to get something, should he Return
depend ont I will Oblige him to settle this Account.
I have lately Rece'd a Letter from Bro^r Robins, he
tells me he is willing to part with his share & my
Bro^r Joseph in the House Left us per Our deceas'd
Parents, in Consequence of which I have wrote him
that I will take it & give him his Price & I will also
take my Sister Molly's at the same rate & for that
purpose have order'd my friends Messrs Lane &
Booth of Lond° to pay him for his two shares & my
Sister Molly for her share as soon as the writings
are compleated & lodg'd in the aforesaid Gentle-
mens' hands & therefore this Conveyance cannot be
Regularly made without your assistance, which I
must desire you to see done in a Right & Authentick way. Bro^r Jacob is now assistant to Daniel
Wyer Esqr Commissary Generall at Quebeck & his
place is in worth at Least Two hundred pounds
Sterl^g per annum, it gives me Great Satisfaction that
I have been able so well to Provide for him; he has

left me his power of attorney to settle this affair
which I have shown to Bearer of this Capt Farr
who is an Exeter Man & who will, if you should
not be otherwise Satisfy'd, Convince you thereof,
so that there is no Occasion of his name in the
Deed or Release. I shall on all occasions be glad
to hear from you & of your Familys welfare, in the
meantime please to accept of my best Regards &
give my compliments to my Aunt & Cousins. I
Remain, Hon^d Sir

Your affectionate Kinsman
& very hum^e Servt
JOHN ROWE

To MR ALEX^R COBDEN   BOSTON May 12th 1760
    Sir
    Your favour of the 5th Curr^t is now before me,
I am much Obligd to you for the Care of Mr Barrons Letter, it gives me pleasure to tell you, that
Mr Barrons was Restored to his office without any
Solicitation thro' his friends &c, a footing that no
moves of Mr L. ill nature will effect him & I guess
the old Gentleman will Repent his Cruel Treatment

Sir
Your very hum Servt
JOHN ROWE

BOSTON May 12th 1760

To THE Hon^{BLE} Brig^{R} Gen^{ALL} Burton at Quebeck
    Sir,
    . . . I have a Letter dat^{d} 8th March from London
& from a Gentle^{n} well acquainted in Governm^{t}
affairs, he says a peace is at no great Distance, all
parties seem to be tired of the expense of the warr
& the King of Prussia affairs seems not to be in that
favorable state, we would wish them. You have
Enclosed the latest Newspaper from New York
which Contains what news the Packett Brg^{t} from
England. . . .
            I am, Sir, your very Hum^{le} Servt

                                JOHN ROWE

To Mess^{RS} Reed & Pettit   BOSTON May 19th 1760
    Gent^{n}
    . . . to come pr any other Vessels & then Stop in
y^{r} hands till you hear further from mee for Wee have
very Disagreeable Acc^{ts} from Quebeck & the Chance
of Loosing it is very Great   God Grant it may be
otherwise.
    I much fear a General Battle took place between
Monsr Lane who Commanded eleven thousand
French Canadians & Indians & our Commanding
officer Mj^{r} Murray the 28th Last Month, he had but
twenty seven hundred — this Small Body made the
French give Way but they were Caught & a Great
Many Men Kill'd & Wounded. I Know of hardly
one Officer of ours that was Engaged but Receiv'd

Wounds or Were Killed.   Among the last is Coll.
Hufsey, a brave Good Officer   this was a fatal
affair — had the G——l kept in his Lines   There
could have been no Danger or if Lord Colvil is
not up before the Town by this time or Before,
its Generally thought its Gone.   Tis a Melancholly
affair that Such Brave Fellows Must Submit, if you
hear nothing more of this affair Let it be only Communicated to Your Best Friends & You'l Oblige
Gent[n]

Your Very Hum[l] Serv[t]

J. ROWE

Boston May 29th 1760

To Friend Jos. Rotch New Bedford
    Sir

I am now going to Load the Snow Devonshire,
Hugh Hunter for London, it will much oblige me
for Your Friendship in assisting me with Fifty Tons
of Oyl on Freight and I shall also be Glad if you
Can purchase me a hundred Barrells.   I will pay you
to your Content what you Generally have from other
people.   I Remain

Y[r] friend to Serve

JOHN ROWE

To Alex[r] Cobden Esq[r]   Boston May 26th 1760
    Sir

I have yours of the 19th   I am oblig'd to you for
putting my Letters directed to Mess[rs] Lane &
Booth into the Tourists Bagg.

As to the sentiments of the Commissioner of the Customs in Regard to the Conduct of their Officer in America ab[t] Clearing Sugar from the mount &c, he is silent about but I Conclude when he says every Matter will be settled to his Satisfaction, that that affair will be Included for I have good Reason to think the Surveyor General has wrote to the Commissioners on that very Subject, at the Departure of M[r] Barrons which was Like to have made some puzzle at home; as I expect to have a Larger & better Acc[t] from him pr Cap[t] Evers who is dayley expected, it may then be in my power to Satisfy you more Clearly in this matter. As soon as I have it you shall hear further from

Sir, Your very hum Serv[t]

JOHN ROWE

BOSTON June 2[d] 1760

To Cap[T] Edw[D] Cahill London

D[r] Sir

I have your favour of 29th March & 10th April pr Cap[t] Watts & Cap[t] Willson. Am very glad to find your Business of Such Consequence & that it will prevent your further Progress on the Risque of the Seas & when anything offers that I can Contribute to your Business I shall do it with Pleasure. I thank Fortune who has been kind to my Endeavours that I shall not enlarge or even wish for more Business than I have at present & a Great Deal of what I do on my own Acc[t], I shall Cut short by degrees. Am sorry there is like to be any difficulty

about Sam¹ Marshalls Bills but be it as it will, I
shall be Contented. I shall send the Devonshire
Capᵗ Hunter for London, by whom I shall again
write you. I shall on all Occasions, Show you I
Remain,
        Dʳ Sir
                Your Friend & Hum Servᵗ
                            JOHN ROWE

Mʳˢ Rowe is much obligd to you for the Care of
her Stays etc.

                            BOSTON June 2ᵈ 1760
TO MESSʳˢ LANE & BOOTH [his London Corre-
    spondent]
        Gentˡᵐ
    ... Mʳ Hooper is much obligd to you for the
Care of his Teeth & if he should have any farther
Occasion, he will follow your directions. ... I am
much surprizd to find Capᵗ Browns Bill protested —
he is now gone to Qeubeck, I hope he may escape
the fate of Warr, if so I am safe, But as our present Situation in that Quarter is very precarious, I
look on it an Equal Chance whether an Officer
Lives or Dies. A Great Havock of Both Officers &
men has lately taken place there; however I thank
you for taking the Bills up & paying it for my
honor ... nothing I think occasions more at
present, save only that I Remain & am on all occasions — Dr Sirs
        Your assured Friend & hum Servᵗ
                            JOHN ROWE

To Major Currie   BOSTON June 8th 1760
     Dr Sir
     According to Your Expectation & my Own Capt
Arthur Brown's bill is protested & I have now In-
closd it for My Namesake Mr Roe the Change
thereof is at foot of this. I must beg your Care
to get this Settled. His other bills of one hundred
& twenty will also be protested & what he has in the
Agents hands is only about Forty pounds. How he
could be so Imprudent to draw bills & have no Effects
& never give Advice is a mystery to mee.
     I shall always be glad to Render you or Friends
any Good Offices & Remain
                    Dr Sir, your very hum Servt
                                   JOHN ROWE

     I had almost forgot to tell you that M^r fisher is
appointed Agent for the 28th Reg^t this Advice is
from my Friends Messrs Lane & Booth of London
the 12th April

To Messrs Reeds & Petit   BOSTON June 16th 1760
     Gent^m
     I am just Return'd from a Journey so that have
only time to tell you I found your several favours
. . . Every hour wee expect an Acc^t from the River,
tis high time that some of the trading vessells Return'd I am in hopes We shall have good news
but I must confess I am still afraid If anything
Occurs you shall hear further
                    from Gent^lm
                         Your very hum Servt
                                   JOHN ROWE

Boston June 30th 1760

To David Wier Esq at Quebeck with the Forces

Dr Sir

. . . It gives me Great pleasure to find my Brother's Behaviour has merited your approbation & that you have given him part of your Profits, be assur'd Sir, I will always with Gratitude endeavour to Return you Such Good offices as lies in my Power here meantime I Remain, waiting your further Commands   Dr Sir

Your very hum Servt

JOHN ROWE

The Invoice of Garden Seeds is Inclos'd

To Capt Wm Dunbar   Boston July 2d 1760

Dear Sir

I Rec^d your favour of the 23^d May . . . I have all along taken Care of Serjeant Bell's Children & shall follow his further directions Relating to them . . . I rejoice with you in the Success of the Garrison the officers that were taken on the 23^d April are all Return'd in a flag of Truce from Montreal to Albany except Colo. Young who is Still at Montreal

I Remain, your very hum Servt

JOHN ROWE

To Jacob Rowe   Boston July 3ᵈ 1760
        Dʳ Brother
    I Received both your Letters of the 30ᵗʰ April
pr the Racehorse & if Mʳ Anderson had Come here
I should have Shown him all the Civilities I could
both on his & your Accᵗ . . . I thank you for your
Advices about Both Battles & am Glad your fears
are at an End, as yours of the 17ᵗʰ & 18ᵗʰ May ad-
vises — the Friends of Wᵐ Fayerweather Return
you their thanks for your advice about him, as to
John Malcolm the method of his Behaviour seems
not to be much Regretted. By the Best Accᵗ I can
get of the Brittannia is that She was one of the
Five Ships sent down the River, at the Beginning
of the Siege last year & in Consequence therof
burnt, but this may prove a Mistake & if it should
& you should find her Claim her for my Accᵗ & this
shall be your Justification I have made your Re-
spectfull Compliments acceptable to your friends
who all are very glad to hear of your welfare. . . .
It will always give me pleasure to do you any good
office as I have wrote you pr Capt Cushion & in the
course of this year it may suit my affairs better to
advance than at the Juncture ; I will fullfill any
orders that you send in Conjunction with Mʳ Wier
& you may see I will advance the cash which I pay
every shilling down for in Molasses. I dare say Mʳ
Wier will not let me Remain long out of it. Tis
Great pleasure to me to hear your good behaviour
has merited your friends Esteem & Countenance.
Let me beg you to Continue Stedfast in your good

Progress & my good offices shall be always a pleasure to you & myself. . . . I shall take care of Serjeants' Bells Children, which at present are very well & I have ever since the Death of their mother put them into good Care, one of them is at Mr Collsons my Neighbour and the other under the care of Mrs Serjeant who I pay 40/ a week for his Board. I Believe Mr Hawkings will go to Quebeck, if so I shall send them both by him & write Mr Bell at Large. . . . I every day expect Bartlett from Bristol, its very probable I shall send him up with a Cargoe from hence for its Impossible to persuade any of these people to take any Live Stock on Freight. . . . Mrs Rowe Joyns with me in Sincere Regard & I Remain

Yr affectionate Brother

JOHN ROWE

To Messrs Lane & Booth   Boston July 4th 1760
    Gent^{ln}

. . . I have just Rec^d the first Bills for Quebeck for three hundred pounds ster^g which I shall send pr Capt Hunter & I hope a Considerable Sum more, that Garrison is now out of Danger the Enemy having Rais'd the Siege from Before that place & gone off with the Loss of all their Ammunition, Stores & all Utensils.

Being all that offers at present from

Gent^{ln} your very hum Servt

JOHN ROWE

BOSTON July 14th 1760

Capt Hunter as it will oblige you, you may bring me from your young Milliner a fashionable round Cap handerchief & Ruffles of fine plain Muslin & a Cheap India mount fan.

Things to be Brought for Mrs Rowe (pr Capt Hunter)

2 Doz^n of Blue & White China plates
1 p^r Black Sattin Shoes
1 pair Pink Sattin Shoes
2 pounds of Green Tea
2 Long Brushes
2 Baskets of Salt
One Glass Lamp to fit the top sent
2 Shillings worth of French Chalk.

BOSTON 16th 1760

To CAP^T EDW^D CAHILL LONDON
    Sir
    . . . Our Old Friend Gunter is at Rest, he·has Left the Bulk of his Estate to Charitable Uses in the City of Gloster which is Some Chagrin to Some of his Friends. All the Rest of Our Friends are at present well & a Great many going this day to Commencement which you know is a high Frollick in this Country. I shall make One of the party with Mrs Rowe who Joyns with mee in Sincere Regards.
                I am

BOSTON July 25th 1760

To DAVᴰ WIER ESQ WITH THE FORCES IN CANADA
  Dʳ Sir

... A young fellow from Quebeck from Louisburg brings an Accᵗ of Sundry Vessells being
taken going to Quebeck which has started the
premio of Insurance to 10 pr Cent which I was
Oblig'd to give on this Vessell & hope you'l approve therof as I could not on any Terms get it
done Cheaper.   I shall send Ten Hogsheads more of
Molasses & a Quantity of Corn if to be had, at
present its very Dear & Scarce.   I hope you'l approve of my dividing your Interest in Several Vessells — at present there's nothing new here.   Genˡ
Amherst was at Oswego when the last advice Came
from thence, which is now about a fortnight past.

  I shall on all Occasions of Service Shew you
    I am, Dʳ Sir
            Your very hum Servᵗ
                JOHN ROWE

BOSTON August 5th 1760

To MESSʳˢ JOHN JAMIESON & SON
  Gentˡᵐ

... Building at present seems to be dear, which
is in some part Occasion'd by our Carpenters going
with the Army to Build Vessells Battoes &C, so
that I dont advise you to be concern'd this year,
if we Should Succeed in our further Operations in
Canada, tis probable the Warr here will Cease & in

Consequence the people will then get Steady at their Labour which will be of Great Service to the Article of Building. . . .

Scotch & English goods are at present very Dull, but its a Season of the year that Our Trades generally Slack. . . .

I shall give Attention to y^r Interests & I Remain Gent^{ln}

Your very hum Servt

JOHN ROWE

To Messrs Lane & Booth   Boston August 8th 1760
Gent^{ln}

. . . I think you are very Right in not Sending any goods very Late & especially in Friggate Built Ships, they Cannot Beat to Windward Like a small Galley Built Ship which are the only Vessells to Come on this Coast. If I Can get one of them built to my mind, I dare say she shall answer the purpose design'd

Govr Bernard has a Son in London which is to Come out with Capt Hunter. I shall esteem it a favour you'll Shew him any Civilities & Recommend it to Capt Hunter to have a Regard to him & Treat him as a Gentleman.

Our fears ab^t Quebeck for this year, are at an End — & I belive Genl Murray is now at Montreal, if he is not, he has got a Second Drubbing.

I must beg your Attention to Send the Devonshire out in the Fall. I am not afraid of her going off the Coast, the Cap[t] is well acquainted and Such Vessells as his are vastly Preferable to Such Ships as Bradford's & Sherrard's.   This is at present what offers from Gentlemen

Your very hum Serv[t]

J ROWE

To THE SAME   BOSTON Aug. 9th 1760
     Gentlemen
     . . . Please to send me a pair of Netts for Horses, Let them be Large.

& You'l Oblige, Gent[ln]

Your very hum Serv[t]

JOHN ROWE

To CAP[T] EZEKIEL CUSHING   BOSTON, Aug 27th 1760
     Sir
     We are very sorry to hear of Your Misfortune in being taken, its very unlucky both for you & ourselves.   Wee desire you'll Immediately Send Us your protest that Wee may Recover what Insurance Wee have made on the Gen[tln's] Acc[t] Wee Loaded you for.
     Wee desire you'll not fail doing this as soon as you Receive this Letter & forward it by a good & safe hand & you'll oblige

Your hum Serv[ts]

JAMES FORBES

JOHN ROWE

To ——

Worthy Sir

I have taken the Liberty to write you Several
Letters which have been forwarded as Opportunity
Offer'd — have now taken the Liberty to tell you
that Our prospect in Canada is Great. Gen¹ Murray Since he Left Quebeck, has had a Battle & has
got the Best of it & is at Troy River.   Colo. Haviland who went from Crown point is Landed on one
part of Nut Island with all his Troops.   he Lost
Capᵗ Legg & seven others of the Train in Landing — no other of the Troops Suffer'd much.   Gen¹
Amherst Certainly Left Oswego in the Divisions.
The Hon¹ the Colo Haldiman with the first, the
7ᵗʰ this Month, Marched the Tenth with the main
Body & was follow'd by Colo Gage the Eleventh —
and there's a Report he was within a few days
march of Montreal. Some people among us believe it & the time may admit of it, if there's no
Obstructions in his way   Wee every day expect to
hear that their Country is surrender'd   as soon as
the Happy Event Comes, you shall be sure to have
as Early Intelligence as I can give you & at all
times Shall think myself happy in giving you
pleasure   being, Dʳ Sir

Yʳ Most Obedᵗ hum Servᵗ

JOHN ROWE

To MR Sam Sheppard   Boston Sept 11th 1760
    Sir

... We are in great Spirits here expecting all
Canada will Submit to his Majesty's Arms. Our
Generalls are far Advanc'd into the heart of the
Enemies Country.

                    I Remain Sir
                Your most hum Servt

                            J ROWE

To Jacob Rowe   Boston Sept 14th 1760
    Dear Bro^r

... I wish Capt Cushing had arriv'd that you
might have had the things I sent you but he
was taken & carried into the Bay of Chalons &
is just come home. You may depend on my taking the Greatest Care of your affairs at Cape
Ann, but my Business has not yet permitted me
to Look very Closely into them   I purpose a
Journey there very soon & shall then fix a Method
to bring the people you have to do with, to do
you Justice. Some of your Debts, I know I shall
Receive. As it's probable Canada must Surrender
you'll send me as early as you can, a memorandum of what will answer & I will Endeavor to send
it.

    I hope as you are gone with the Army that God
will protect you & Return you in Safety. Let me
hear from you by all opportunity & give my Com-

pliments to Mr Wier. I shall write you again pr
Capt.   Y^r affectionate Bro^r

JOHN ROWE

Mrs Rowe is well & desires
to be kindly Remember'd

To Dan^L Gibbs Esq   Boston Sept 10th 1760
    Sir

I just have Rec'd yours of the 29th past & have
waited on Mr Prat whose Opinion is that Vessells
& men ought to pay what Damage is Sustained
partially, as a fishing Voyage is on a different
Situation than a Merch^{ts} Voyage however upon the
whole I would Advise You to Settle this Affair
Amicably, as all these Cases depend on the Temper
& disposition of One Man, say — Judge of Admiralty & by Enquiring among Mr Bethune &
other friends about your Case, they seem to think
otherwise than Mr Prat has Advis'd you & me, &
think that all Accidents must take their Fate — it
will be necessary for Capt Haskell & Crew, if they
go to Sea, to Leave a power with you or some other
friend — if you purpose to pursue it. I shall
always be glad to Serve You & Remain Dr Sir

Yr assur'd Friend

JOHN ROWE

Boston Sept 14th 1760

To Friends Joseph & Wm Rotch New Bedford
The Oyl you are to Ship on board the John

Galley, Capt Jarvis for London, together with Two hundred Barrels I am to have of you, I shall be glad to have it as soon as possible & the Quantity on my Acc^t, I desire it may be of the Pale Sort or Bank Oyl. The Reason I desire this to be soon up, will be a Benefit to Both you & myself, for there is a Convoy appointed for the mast fleet which will be here in this month & may depart from portsmouth by the Middle or Twentieth of Oct so that your Insurance will make a great saving by Proceeding with this Convoy — which is his Majesty's Ship the Crown, Capt Mead, of 40 Guns.   I am with Esteem

Y^r Friend to Serve

JOHN ROWE

To FRANCIS ROBINS EXETER   BOSTON Sept 16th 1760
   Bro^r Robins
   Sir

This I send by our Townsman Capt Jam^s Luke who I hope will arrive with you in Safety.   I have taken the Liberty to Send you a Dozⁿ Bottles of West India Rum which I beg your Acceptance of. Bro^r Jacob is now in Canada, Commissary of his Majestys detachment under Generall Murray, his Behaviour has gain'd him the Esteem of the officers of that Body & Mr Wier the Commissary General writes me very much in his favour, so that I hope he is well provided for   his place is worth at Least Two hundred pounds Sterl^g per Ann.   Our forces

are now in possession of all Canada which is a
Glorious Conquest & I pray God, if a peace it may
not be Restor'd to the French if it should We
Shall always, on this Continent, be under Continual
Alarms from the Villanous Canadians & Barbarous
Indians. I thank God am Well & so is Mrs Rowe
who Joyns with me in Sincere Regard to you &
Sister Robins. Let me hear from you as Oppor-
tunity Presents & you'll oblige.

Dr Sir

Your affectionate Friend & Bro^r

JOHN ROWE

Boston Sep^t 19 1760

To Mr Harry Roe at Quebeck

Dr Sir

This day I Rec'd your favour of the 18th Aug &
am much oblig'd to you for your Intelligence of the
Situation of the Army & am glad you got up Safe,
altho you had a Long Passage. Pray give my Compliments to Mrs Peggy Lydias & assure her that any
Commands of hers will be Cheerfully & faithfully
executed.

I am sorry the Tobacco Turn'd out so poorly but
twas the best could be had in Boston. Indeed
there was no other at that time. It will always give
me pleasure to send anything for yourself or your
Regiment. I sent Brigg^r Burton a hhd of very good
Beer for Capt Harris in the Armed Schooner who I
hear is arriv'd at Quebeck, as to the Cyder it was

Really forgetfullness but as soon as I Know where
your Regiment is fix'd for the Winter, you Shall
have the Barrell with Interest. You'l please to let
me hear from you as often as opportunity offers &
if you should See Jacob my Bro^r I hope you'll get
acquainted.

We have News over the Lakes that Montreal &
all Canada Surrendered the 8th this month tho' it
dont come authenticated, yet tis Generally Believ'd.
Who Knows if this be True but your Regiment may
Winter in Boston Which will give mee pleasure.
You'l please to give my Compliments to Genl Bur-
ton & tell him I am always Ready to fullfill his
Commands & I Remain with Sincere Regards

Dr Harry

Your affectionate Friend & hum Servt

JOHN ROWE

To MR JOHN HOLMES JUN^R BOSTON Sep^t 22 1760
    Sir

Last Night the post from New York brought me
y^r Letter of the 10th July. I am Very Sorry you
have Lost y^r Bro^r in Law, Mr David Hillman jun^r
but you must content y^{o}self as all mankind must
Sooner or Later pay the Sam Debt. tis of Great
Comfort to you that Mrs Hillman Keeps up her Spirits in So Extraordinary a manner. I take notice
that you carry on Business with Mr John James
Herts in the woolen way . . . when you think proper
to favour me with your Commands I'll execute them

with pleasure but I Cant at Present Say there's any Great prospect for the Sale of Woolens from the West of England in this part of America, as Canada is now in possession of the English if We still hold it, I mean when peace is Concluded, I Guess it will be of Great Consequence to Your Business. This I thought Necessary to mention to you & if any vessel is bound to Quebeck from Exeter or Topsham,— you cannot fail of a market. My Bro Jacob Rowe is there & Commissary of Provisions, he will be able to dispose of them for you & will be Ready to Receive y^r Commission on your telling him I Recommend you to him—or if you Should Conclude to send any here, I'll Endeavour to do my Best for you, at present I have a great Quantity of goods on hand & more Business than I can well manage that I dare not venture many on my Acc^t . . .   I am glad you & your Spouse have got over y^r Indisposition & hope you'll Continue your Health. The Bearer Capt Luke is Just on Departure that you'l excuse my Adding at present anything more

only that I am—Sir

Your very hum Servant

J. ROWE

To ——   BOSTON Sept 11th 1760
    Worthy Sir
    Annext is a Coppy of what I wrote for Capt Bartlett via Bristol. According to my Promise I

now —— You that Gen[l] Amherst has taken Legolet, but was oblig'd to wait Six days before that
Small Garrison Surrendered ab° five hundred are
made prisoners of warr which are now at Albany
the Last Acc[ts] from Gen[l] Amherst are, that he was
at the Rapids, which I take to be ab° 30 Leagues
from Montreal Cap[t] Loring Lost his ship in En-
gaging the fleet at Legolet & seven hundred men,
himself slightly wounded.

Colo. Haviland has got possession of Nut Island
the Garrison under command of Boucanville deserted it, Leaving everything behind them, it was
well stocked with provisions & upwards a hundred
head of Cattle, a vast Quantity of Ammunition,
Storages & upwards of Seventy Cannon, Great part
of them Brass, tis not Certain he is pass'd St
John's but its Commonly Reported & by Numbers
believ'd. Colo. Thomas of the Provincials is Left to
Garrison Nut Island with four hundred of General
Ruggles Provincials The Rest are gone forward
Gen[l] Murray is got up to Montreal & there is in-
trenching himself, Proposing to wait the Junction
of Both Gen[l] Amherst & Colo. Haviland which has
no doubt taken place before now. So everything
has a good Aspect & Some of our Boston Politicians seem'd to think their whole country is Sur-
rended. others think M[r] Levi will Risque a Battle
first, tis Said he has Twelve to thirteen thousand
men with him if so, they are Chiefly Canadians.
This is at present what Occurs from Worthy Sir

Your most Obed[t] Serv[t]

JOHN ROWE.

To Dan^L Wier Esq^R   Boston Sept 20 1760
    Sir

    . . . I see Bro^r Jacob was gone up the River & thank
you for your Care of the things I sent him. We
have an Acc^t here that Genl Amherst has all Canada
in Possession by Capitulation, its Generally Believ'd
to be True—thank you for your advice. . . .

To Jacob Rowe   Boston Sept 22nd 1760
    Dr Bro^r.

    I wrote you at Large pr Mr Jeffry & send dupli-
cate pr Capt Noble, since which I have your favour
of the 29th Augst Capt Gay. as I have already wrote
you I will give Attention to your Affairs & think
you might have Spar'd your Reflection. I dare say
you'l have it in your power to do every Body that
Justice you Intend. I have wrote to England &
every day expect an Answer & hope t'will be as I
expect. It gives me great pleasure to hear you
meet the Approbation of the Army in General.
Let me know your destination & I will Assist you
as much as possible. I conclude when my letters
pr Gay, Harris & Bradford are got to hand You will
not suspect I did not Intend any further Correspondence & I Cann't but say I'm a Little vex'd you
should harbour Such a thought. . . . Mr Hancock
will not pay the bills you sent me, therefore you
must get it of the person you had it off. . . .   I
hear the Country has surrendered to General Amherst. So you'l by all means Let me know your
destination. . . .

I must desire the favour of you to Enquire in what manner John Malcolm Left his Sloop, he says he Carried a Frenchman from Quebeck to St Barnaby with Permission for him from Genl Murray, on which Occasion he has Stopt there; if its so, he will [have] Some Grounds to Demand his Insurance but if otherways as tis Reported, that he went there to trade, then he can have no demands, pray be as particular as you Can, as he is Esteem'd here not Altogether so Clever as he Should be, while he was on shore his Mate Run away with his Vessell & was taken. I Intend to write you again pr next Conveyance, meantime I Remain

Your affectionate Bro^r

JOHN ROWE

To MESS^{RS} LANE & BOOTH   BOSTON Sep^t 19 1760
Gen^{tm}

... Our Forces are now in Possession of all Canada which is a Glorious Conquest & I hope when a peace takes place it may not be Restor'd to the French, if it should we shall always on this Continent, especially the Frontiers be under Continual Alarms from the Villanous Canadians & Barbarous Indians. Your Letter of the 12th July pr the Harriet Packet with the Certificate of the Cattle Vessells Return'd protested I have at hand, am very sorry. I Guess t'will be Sometime before Genl Amherst will be able to give Attention to this Affair, his Goodness I know will do us Justice but

t'will take up Time he is now (I believe) at Montreal
making the necessary disposition for winter Quarters.
Instead of the Crown Man of Warr, Lord Colville
has appointed the Winchester & the Crown is
to take a Load of Masts. I Remain with Sincere
Regard
Gen^{tm}, you very hum. Servt

JOHN ROWE

To ——   BOSTON Sept 29th 1760
     Worthy Sir
     I Confirm the preceeding Coppy of my Last in
everything & have further to Add that Gen¹ Amherst took possession of Montreal on the 8ᵗʰ this
month by Capitulation, the same day Gen¹ Murray
Landed on the I'land & Colo Haviland encamp'd the
9ᵗʰ Regiment against the I'land So that the three
Armies met all within a day but the Capitulation
took place with Gen¹ Amherst before Gen¹ Murray
Landed, tho' he knew nothing of the Capitulation.
     General Gage is to Remain at Montreal Gover-
nour Twenty five hundred Regulars — Gen¹ Murray to Return to Montreal & Colo Haviland to
Crownpoint. In coming down the Rapids Gen¹
Amherst Lost 85 men & one officer & upwards of
50 at Legolet. Upon the whole the Conquest is
made without much Loss of men — the Publick
prints will give you the terms of Capitulation, which
is Generally Liked. God Grant that our Affairs on
the Continent may prosper, that the Grand Con-

quest may always Remain the property of Great Britain

M^r P—— has Inflamed the Collector by telling him you wrote home Letters against him & by what I Can find Mr Barrons has wrote to know how it Stands — this I thought Convenient to advise you.

It gave me great pleasure to hear of your Safe Arrival & I hope all your Affairs are Applauded & Still Remain

Y^{rs} on all Occasions

JOHN ROWE

BOSTON Sept 30th 1760

TO MESSRS JOHN JAMESON & SON
    Gentlemen

Annext is a Coppy of what I wrote you Via Bristol. I have only now to Confirm the Same & wish you Joy of the Conquest of all Canada. This is a most Glorious Event & I hope every Borough in the Kingdom will present Memorials to His Majesty that he will not Consent to its being delivered at the peace, whenever it Shall happen.

I Say the Keeping this Country will be of more Service to the Manufactures of Great Britain than all the Rest of the Trade of that Kind in the Kingdom & that in the Course of Fifty Years. All the Trade from hence are Writing their Friends on the Occasion, So that I hope you'll excuse my Freedom — be Assur'd Gentlemen, that any Commands of yours will be executed with Pleasure

by Gen^{tm} Your very hum. Servt

JOHN ROWE

To Dan^L Wier Esq^R Boston Oct. 2nd 1760
    Dr Sir

... As there will be Communication over Land by Way of Crownpoint, I shall Esteem it a favour when you have any further Commands you'l write that way, especially when your River is Shut up.

Here is Glorious news of Prince Ferdinand's gaining a Compleat victory over the French & is without all Doubt True.

            I Remain, Dr Sir
                Your very hum Servt
                        JOHN ROWE

To Jacob Rowe   Boston Oct 6th 1760
    Dr Bro^r

On the other side is Coppy of my Last, Since with° any of your favours, I have the Less to add. ... Next Monday I set out for Cape Ann & at my Return will write you the exact Situation of your affairs. Mrs Rowe is well & Desires to be Remember'd to you. I have no Letter from the West [of England] since my Last therefore cannot give you any Acc^t Relative to y^r affairs there. Mr William Handfield is Come to town from Montreal in Ten days, he tells me you were well & gone to Quebeck, so that I Guess this will meet you there. Let me hear from you by all opportunitys which will much Oblige me ...

                Your affectionate Bro^r
                        JOHN ROWE

To Mess^{RS} Lane & Booth   Boston Oct 5th 1760
    Gent^m

I was in hopes to have Compleated Capt Jarvis Ship lading to have come home with this Convoy but very Unlucky the Winds have Continued Easterly for three Weeks, which have Kept out the Nantucket men & brought the Man of Warr from Hallifax . . .

. . . The Crown Man of War is now near Portsm° & is not to Come Home this Convoy but to take in Masts between Decks & have her upper Deck Clear, So that if She Departs in a month or thereabout Jarvis shall wait for her but if Longer, he shall Come with° her. . . .

            I Remain Gent^m
                Your very hum Servt
                    JOHN ROWE

Capt Jacobson has two q^{ts} of meat fish on board him directed for Lord Barrington, pray be kind enough to Let one of your Servants See it Safe deliver'd & you'l oblige yrs as before.

To Jacob Rowe   Boston Decr 1760
    Bro^r Jacob

. . . I have been Lately indisposed that cannot Say anything certain as to Your Cape Ann affairs & had I been well have had no time to go there. I have this day been Talking with Your Friend Gibbs & I expect Daniel Rogers to Town every day, so that before I have another opportunity to write, I shall be able to give you a fresh Acc thereof.

I have Coppy of Bro^r Robins Letter to Messrs Lane & Booth which I send you Enclose which determines the affair of the Bills & the house.   As I expect Messrs Lane & Booth next Letters will bring me an Acc^t that the Deed is executed in my name, then I say I shall give Credit for your Share thereof.

I am Really Surpris'd at Bro^r Jos : Behaviour he has had not only the Benefit of the Estate of Uncle Jos at Chagford but also what Remain'd of Aunt Bradford's & most of Uncle Andrew's & for him to Refuse this Draft is very Cruel & I think he deserves no pity & such an unmannerly man I think I never met with, he has not even once thought of writing.   I can never forgive him unless he has Lost the use of his Right hand.

[Jacob Rowe's Son Jack later married Daniel Rogers's daughter Esther.]

BOSTON Jan'y 30 1761
To FRANCIS ROBINS ESQ EXETER
    Dr Bro^r
I have Just at Hand your Letter of the 15 Sept. Last dated at Branscomb & Since that I have a Letter from Messrs Lane & Booth ab^o the House with their Acc^t of what they have p^d thereon which I presume you have Rec^d from them.   I should

have been glad of another Letter from you but
suppose I am soon to expect it. I conclude the
Deed &c are done Authentically & as they are in
Mr Lanes hands I will let them Remain there for
the present.

It Grieves me to have Such an Acc^t of Bro^r
Joseph's Situation, if he was not Able Immediately
to Discharge the Bill for Jacobs Ballance, I think
he might have Said the bill was good & that he
Intended to have paid it when in his power. as
this is Bro^r Jacob's affair & he Really wants this
money, I must beg Your Intention either to get it
p^d or get him to give Security for it to pay it with
Interest at Some Distant time. Messrs Lane &
Booth have still the Bill in their Possession. It
gives me Pleasure to find you, my Sister & Family
are in good Health. You will Let my Sister know
that I Intend her a Long Letter, the first Leisure
time I Can Conveniently Spare. I beg she'll now
accept of my Kind Love & Compliments. I have
wrote a Long Letter to Sister Tolcher in Answer to
One from her I have sent it now Inclos'd to you
Open that you may peruse it then Seal it & forward it to her at plymouth — as it Contains Some
plan that may be Generally Beneficial to the Family,
I was willing you should see it. I cannot answer
for what Effect may take place from it, but if it
Could be Introduced by a person that has any
Influence on Uncle John it might be of Service. I
am sure tis Reasonable.

I have been Blessed with a great Share of Health

& as much Business as I can well Accomplish.
Sometimes attended with Good & Sometimes bad
Success, upon the whole God has Blessed my At-
tention & Endeavours.   Let me now tell you that
I am very well as is Mrs Rowe & both of us Joyne
in hearty Wishes for Your own & Your Family's
health & prosperity & that I Remain
Your Sincere & affectionate Bro^r & most hum̃ Servt

JOHN ROWE

To Mrs Mary Tolcher   Boston Jan'y 18th 1761
    Dr Sister
    I had the pleasure to Receive your favor of the
17th Novr pr Capt Hulmy a day or two ago, am
Extremely Glad to hear of your Health & welfare
& that you are all pleased ab° the House.   God
Knows whether ever I shall See it or not   be that
as it will, I hope it may Remain in Our Family.
Bro^r Robins will take care to see it kept in good
Repair.   I should have been pleased to have had a
Letter from him.   Jacob was well at Quebeck ab°
a month [ago] & is now in a good way to make a
Good Deal of money   I hope his Generous Disposi-
tion may not get the Better of his prudence.
    I thank you for your Intelligence about the
Friends at Chagford & Observe the Joy, that has
taken place there at Holly Street, I cannot say it
gives me any pleasure that the Family Estate
should be out of its Right Channels, as I find its
Like now to do, I would have made a proposal to

the Old Gentleman my namesake, Could I have
Introduced it in person or even by a Friend of
which — I'll Signify my Plan now to you & if you
can be of any Service in this affair, I shall think
myself Happy. I dont know a Better Man to
Communicate it to do than the Revd Mr Hayter my
Schoolfellow.

I presume when my Uncle John was married to
Miss Burdall some Settlement was made to her
Advantage, which was I Guess some one of his
Estates or More & as he now has a daughter married & a grandchild, provision no doubt must be
made for that, notwithstanding this I say the Estate
May Still be Kept in the Family who to be Sure
have the Best & Legal Right to it — for in Liew
of what this Settlement was or is to be, only Let
the Estate be Left progressively to the Family &
not divided — I'll find the Money to pay the
Widdow & the Heirs of Hers Let the Sum be
more or Less, this is a proposal which I am sure
Mrs Rowe nor none of his Friends can Object too.
Unless my Uncle should take it in his Head to Cut
the Family altogether off — now if this could be
so Manag'd by any Person who has any Prevalence
with my Uncle, it would be of Great Advantage
to my Bro Jos Children &c, as to myself you may
plainly Discover that I can have No Benefit by it,
having no Children but my view is to Stop if Possible the Ancient Estate at Least of Holly Street
from departing from the name of Rowe — I shall
only say that your Judgment & prudence in Con-

ducting this matter may be of Service. I am sorry
to hear Bro[r] Joseph has had so much Trouble with
my Uncle Andr[w] Estate. I hope he will soon get
the Better of it, its a hardship on him to pay £50
pr Ann to his Widdow, however, my Uncle
Andrews Design was good & well dispos'd to his
Kinsfolks — all but myself who thank God dont
want it   however a Little Notice I think might have
been Taken. Some of these Old Fogrums, who I
may say only pursue a Gropish disposition, never
Consider the Vivacitys of youth & nature & its
when once they are Fix'd, I suppose tis Harder to
Break their Views as tis to Stop a Hog that Runs
Right forward. We have Just Rec'd the Advice
of the King's Death & as you Say Great Joy must
fill the Breast of Every Englishman to have a
prince Born among them to Sit on the throne.

You'l please to give my Compliments to M[r]
Tolcher & believe me that I Remain D[r] Sister

Your affectionate Bro[r]

J. ROWE

P.S. Added the 30th
I send this Inclos'd to Bro[r] Robins who I have
the pleasure of a Letter from this Day.

[Nearly one hundred years later, in 1852–3, about
£800 of the above-mentioned estate would have
come to the last surviving son and daughter of Jacob
Rowe through the death of " Uncle John's " grand-
daughter, Miss Southmead, who died unmarried;

but they being both over eighty years of age, and having all that they needed, relinquished their share in favor of the cousins in England.]

BOSTON Jan'y 6th 1761

To CAP^T EDW^D CAHILL LONDON
  Dr Sir

I wrote some Letters pr Capt Hunter & Capt Dashwood both which are taken   its Unlucky for me to have them both taken altho' I Lose nothing in fact.   Yet as the prospect was good tis a Disappointment . . . Mrs Rowe gives her Compliments & will be glad to know if Messrs Lane & Booth have pd you for the Sundrys you have been so kind as to send her from time to time & I take it very kind your Sending the papers & Magazines, they Divert an hour or Two every week.   I shall be glad to hear how Govr Pownall is Like to Fare whether he goes to So Carolina or what he is doing at Lond°.   I shall always esteem yr Commands & am with Truth your Sincere Friend &

most humble Servant

JOHN ROWE

To HIS EXCELLENCY MAJ^R GEN. AMHERST
  Sir

Mr Joseph Green Merchant & Owner of the Ship Squirrell employ'd both years as a Transport in his Maj^{ty} Service being now a Bankrupt & absconded,

having first appointed John Rowe Esqr & myself
Assignees to Receive & Dispose of his Effects for
the Sole Benefit of his Creditors, Among other
Effects Assign'd & made over to us in Trust by
a Lawfull Conveyance, his Certificate for hire due
on his Ship Squirrell which Mr Green expected
from your Excellency & had desired you would be
pleased to forward it under cover to Mr Rowe.
We are now to Request that you would do his
Creditors the favour of Transmitting the Certificate
for the hire due, to us pr post that they may have
the Benefit of y^r am^t in proportion to their Demand.
We are with all possible Respects Your Excellencys

most Obed^t & humble Serv^{ts}

SAM. WENTWORTH — JOHN ROWE

BOSTON Feb 10th 1761

To THOS SAUL Esqr   BOSTON Feb'y 16th 1761
   Dr Sir

I was favour'd with yours from Worster pr Wier
& Shall Let our friends know the Contents   I hope
this will meet you at New York, after I suppose a
Journey of Fatigue.

Yesterday my Brigg^{ne} arriv'd from Bristol in 37
Days — the Capt tells mee that the troops for the
Grand Expedition were disembark'd that is stopt at
Least for the present — the King of Prussia has
made Overtures to the Queen of Hungary which
our prints will acquaint you. I am sorry to tell
you that Charles Apthorp has stop'd Jos Greens

Certificates from taking their due Course for the Money Supply'd Mr Green by Nat Wheelwright — if this matter cannt be Remov'd it will be a heavy Stroke to me. The Instrument is very Strong & I am satisfyed Authentick Enough to Compell any Person (but such Great men as Genl Amherst to fullfill the Contract) & twill be the Greatest hardship for me to Suffer. I should think Charles Apthorp might be soften'd by telling him how matters are Circumstanced — the Real truth is I shall Lose Great part of the value of this Certificate if withheld & I know that Charles will never Let an Old friend Suffer for the Sake of the Contractors, Suppose his Demand be ever so Just you will please to think this as Opportunity presents, & as you find his Pulse Beat, please to Inform mee thereof. My Best Wishes attend you & your Companions to whom my Compliments & Believe me that

I Remain Dr Sir

Your very hum Servt

JOHN ROWE

To Jacob Rowe   Boston March 1^{rst} 1761
  Dr Bro^r

I have already answer'd all yours but one at hand for post of the 27^h Jan'y. Am sorry for the miscarriage of Swathridge, as its a Damage to mee, his Owner Jos. Green is gone off & Considerable in Debt to me, nothing Insur'd on this Vessell. I have wrote Mr Weir a few Lines & Inclos'd his Acc^t Curr^t. the paying money down for molasses & only 5 pr Cent is a poor affair & I hope he will Remit the Ballance if not already done, as I assure you my Business Requires it. . . . I am Sorry Maj^r Currie Should make any Difficulty about Trifles, if he dont Chose to Settle it Amiably don't Insist on it.

The Draft you Sent me for 850 Doll^{rs} on Mr Apthorp & Co is very acceptable & shall be Bro^t to your Credit as you direct.   I wish you may move to Montreal as you expect, twill be much better, as I Imagine . . . am Sorry the Last Madeira was Chilly it all came out of one pipe . . .

There is a son born at Holly street, which Sister Molly writes me has Caus'd great Rejoicings, tis Christened John Rowe (Southmead) which is the Gentleman's name that married my Uncles Daughter.

Bro^r Joseph is in a poor way at Chagford Town he has Losst his wife, is in poor Circumstances & Cannot pay my Draft on your Acc^t for the Ballance of the Legacy due to you.

I Beg you'l have a Strict eye over Capt John Malcom who is a Troublesome Fellow & has Behav'd very Ill to me . . . I have no letters from Colo. Burton nor Lieu^t Roe which I must Admire at. . . . Your Share of the House in England will am^t to near thirty pounds sterl^g which I shall Credit you for exact in your Acc^t. . . . I think I have wrote you fully & shall again Early in the

Spring. all your Friends are well & desire their Compliments &c & I Remain

Your very affectⁿ Bro^r

J ROWE.

To Messrs Hill, Lomar & Hill

Boston March 3rd 1761

Gent^m

The Bearer Capt Proctor being to Return home if he should arrive in Safety with you, I desire you'll Send for him on my Acc^t on his Return Two pipes of the Best Madeira. Let one of them be of the Pale Sort & the other the Deeper Color pray be Carefull that they are the Best & draw on Messrs Lane & Booth of London for the am^t & I shall give these Gentlemen Order to Answer your bills for the same, as usual or if that should not Suit you, you may then draw on me here in favour of Bro^r Inman or any other person & your Draft shall be duly Honoured.

The Last two pipes you sent me were not so good as what I had from you before but Guess it was then owing to the Vintage. These now are order'd for the use of myself & Friends so that you'l be more Care full about them.

My good offices here are at your Commands.

Being Gent^m, your very hum Servt

J. ROWE.

To Mr. David Vanhorne, New York

BOSTON March 31st 1761

D[r] Sir

I Return'd home on Wednesday Last, thank God very well but had a Tedious Journey Occasion'd by having Carriages in Company & Bad Roads — pleas Sir, to accept my Grateful thanks for your Civilitys to me when in New York & I hope M[rs] Vanhorne & Miss Polly will accept my Compliments &c . . . I shall always execute any of your Commands or Friends with Great pleasure & I Remain D[r] Sir

Your very hum Serv[t]

J. ROWE.

To Collo. Williamson   BOSTON, March 31st 1761

Dear Sir

I Return'd to Boston Last Wednesday after a very Tedious Journey the Rhodes being very bad. Upon my Return I enquir'd for M[r] Joy in Your Service but found him not in Boston so presume he is gone — had any Letters been in the post office I should have taken the Liberty to have opened them according to Your directions.

I have had an oppor[y] to see M[r] Spencer who is at present not able to come out of his Room — he has had his neck open'd by the Surgeons several times occasion'd by a Swelling that has taken place there   this matter, I believe, has at present prevented his affair of Matrimony.   You'l please Sir, to accept my most Gratefull thanks for your Kind Civilitys

to me at New York & depend ont that Gratitude
shall always be the Tenor of my Actions. I shall
always esteem Your Commands & shall give Attention thereto when you'l please to honour me with
them, being Dr Sir

Your very hum Servt

J. ROWE.

To Jacob Rowe   Boston, April 10^h 1761

Dear Brother

Since my Last of the 1st March which I sent
under Cares of Mr Appy via New York, I have
your favour of the 20^h & 21st Feb'y — its not in
my power to Send you Either port or Lisbon Wine
being none at market at present — you hint to mee
that the Molasses affair will be soon Settled which
will Certainly Give mee great pleasure as you well
know five pr Cent is not equall to advance of money
so long. . . . I am but got home from a journey to
New York which hinders me from Sending you
some things which I imagine would answer well at
Quebeck but I shall send you some Beer very soon
which will be very Good & the Books you write
for, if its possible to get them. John Malcom has
Brought his Action against the Underwriters for
his Suppos'd Lofs. Wee were credibly told here
that he Carried a Frenchman from Quebeck & went
ashore at St. Barnabus, there he Traded, by that
means Lost his Vessel, if this is true he deviated
from his Policy & in Consquence cann't obtain his

demand but if otherways he will be paid — this matter wants to be clear'd up, which you'l do if you can by first opportunity after Receipt of this.

Inclos'd I Send you a Letter for Lieu^t Roe open which please to Seal & deliver him, you may keep the acc^t in your hands & if the paymaster of their Regm^t will draw for Ster^g money on their Agent in London you may Give a Discharge for the Same. I have Lost more than my Commission for staying so Long out of my money & am determined never to engage any more in Such Affairs. Lieu^t Roe desires it may be settled & I Beg it may be done Mrs Rowe, Mr Inman & Mrs Inman are well & desire to be Remember'd & I Remain, Dr Bro

Yr Affectionate Friend & very hum Servt

J. ROWE.

BOSTON April 10^h 1761

To LIEUT HARRY ROE OF THE 48^H REGM^T AT ST. ANNE'S NEAR TROY RIVER MIDDLE CANADA

Dear Sir,

I had Your favour of the 5^h Feb'y — that you mention to have wrote before never came to hand. I am very glad to hear of your Welfare & Health & hope you'l soon enjoy not only the Name but the Advantage of a Captain's Commission. You'l know long before now that General Burton has got a Regem^t to be form'd from Independant Com panys & Lieu^t Colo. Murray is appointed your Lieu^t Colo.

I am very sorry you Should have occasion to make any Complaint ab° the Stock^{gs} for Sir James Cockburnes Company, You will Know I Bought them & paid the money & twill be a Great Hardship on me to have after so long a time a Demur about them. I must beg the favour the money may be paid by bill of Exchange drawn by your paymaster on the Agent at home & deliver'd to my Bro^r who will discharge the same for my acc^t & send it to me . . . Mrs Rowe, Mr Inman & Wife desire their Compliments & I Remain

Your affectionate Friend

& Very hum Servt

J. ROWE.

BOSTON May 4th 1761

To CAP^T EDW^D CAHILL LONDON

Dear Sir

I have your favour of the 12th Decr now before me & Should have answered it Sooner had not my Business Call'd me to New York which prevented it.

I see you are Great Sufferers in the Insuring Way by the French Privateers, they have not Spar'd mee, having taken Last year Hunters Snow & Jarvis Ship both my Own & Dashwoods Ship One half tho I Really Loose no Great by their being taken, yet tis the Loss of a Good Prospect. . . . I write my Friends Messrs Lane & Booth by this Conveyance to pay you Seventy pounds which I Guess is about what I owe you, if it's more I'll give an order for it. I thank you for your news, Wee are very fond of it here which you know, therefore Newspapers will be always acceptable. My Business at present is as much as I can well Accomplish & shall not puzzle myself again in any Large Concern of Navigation. All your Friends are well except Good Mrs Inman who has been in a poor State of Health Sometime. If peace should take place you have some thoughts of paying us a Visit — be Assur^{ed} Sir, all Your Friends will be glad to see you, more especially Mrs Rowe & your sincere and affectionate Friend

JOHN ROWE

To Jacob Rowe   Boston June primo 1761
     Dear Brother
     I have this post at hand your favours of 18th & 21st April also yr^{s} of 3rd May pr Capt Hoppes — if Swathridge has sav^{d} anything & you or Capt Phillips have the Care Keep it till you hear further from me or Mr Wentworth. I am very Glad Mr Wier has sent me the Remittance of £900 Sterlg which I am Convinced he could not do before. Shall be glad of the Remainder as soon as possible
     My stay & Bussiness at New York prevented my Sending you Some things but I Intend it at first Leisure . . . I dont know how Affairs will operate at Hollystreet but it seems the Ancient Estate is not to Remain in our Family for which I am very Sorry & if I can prevent it, no money shall be wanting to Carry it into Execution.

I thank you for speaking to Capt Stabo — pray get him to forward the Letter as I advised, twill be of great Service to me & I Cannot well Recover the Demand on the Generall without it. However I will endeavour to find Lieu^t Hutchins & get one from him.

I finish'd my Bussiness as well as I could expect at New York, though not altogether to my mind. Please take notice that partnerships are sometimes attended with Great Inconvenience, if you can do without a partner I should think it best unless the prospect is very Great. I hope soon to Receive a Letter from you to Mr Rogers — these Cape Ann Chapps are very Bad & nothing but Law & Goal will suit them. Capt George Darby Commands the Devonshire Man of Warr & is going to Quebeck. I advise you to pay your Compliments to him he is a very good man & Let him know you are my Brother & should he want anything his bills are very good. I am   y^r Affectionate Bro^r

J R

To D$_R$ W^M Catherwood   Boston July 6 1761
      Dear Sir

I have at hand yr favours of 21st & 28th June pr post & am very much pleas'd your Tour to the Jerseys & Philadelphia was so agreeable & that you Like the Country — pray give my Service to your Companion Major Hamilton & tell him any good office he has to be done in Boston, will be done on his Commands. I find you are now on a Party of Pleasure, with Colo. Delaney at Springfield. . . . If you go to Long Island to Spend your Summer, I wish you may Spend it to your Content.

We have no certain acc^t of the full possession of Belle Isle but its Generally Believ'd — The Earl of Egremount, Lord Viscount Stormout & Sr Phillips York are our Plenipotentiaries at the Congress to be held at the Imperial City of Ausberg. God grant their negotiations may fill the Breast of Brittons with Joy. Tis a mistery to us what Generall Amherst is to do with the ships that have been and are now taken up here. I guess that Matter will be Determin'd at the arrival of the packet which was to depar^t from Falmouth ab^o the 20^h May so that she may be in New York by the time this Reaches.

I made your Compliments Acceptable to Colo Vassall who is our Sundays man, where your Company will always be thought a pleasure. I also made your Compliments to Mr Amiel, also Mrs Newton who has the pleasure of her husband just arriv'd from Quebeck, which I guess will be very agreeable after five months absence.

Poor B. Barrons the Collector is Suspend'd by that Old Fogrum Letchmere, the most Malicious thing that perhaps ever was done. I have no Occasions to tell you, whence this arrives. The poor man is not only destitute of £600 Sterlg pr anum but his peace of mind is Broke & his health much Impair'd, he is now Selling all his goods & bound home again to get Restor'd & I assure

MRS. RALPH INMAN
(Susannah Speakman)

you no Reason of Consequence given for Suspending him.

I must now be a Little More Serious, being very sorry to tell you that Last Tuesday died Good Mrs Inman to the Inexpressible Grief of Her Husband, as also her Sister Mrs Rowe & I can venture to say, I Greatly Lament her as a good woman & Friend — but tis the Road we all must go sooner or later & therefore we must Content our Selves.

It will always give me pleasure to hear from you & any Commands will always be taken care off — by Dr Sir,

Your very hum Servt

JOHN ROWE

My Compliments to Mr Wallace

Vessell arriv'd Yesterday in five weeks from England, brings no acc^t of the arrival of Mr Saul. I hope he is not gone to learn French.

To the Same   BOSTON July 27th 1761
    Dr Sir

I should have answer'd your favour on the 13th Curr^t but was out of Town — the Two Trunks & Bedding &c shall be sent pr the True Briton Capt Searl & they shall be Directed to the Care of Our Friend Mr Hugh Wallace, the Charges theron shall let you know I am oblig'd to you for your Good Offices to Major Hamilton and Oliver Delaney & am

Glad to hear the Pittsburgh affair is not to be depended On. Mr Barrows is Like to be a Sacrifice to the Resentmen^t of Old Fogrum & I cannot yet prevail on him to buckle too.   I Pity him — but tis some Measure his own Fault . . . Mr Inman Bears his Loss with fortitude & Mrs Rowe seems more easy than I could expect.   She is well & desires her Compliments   The Packett is not come yet therfore I Conclude all things are at a stand.   Hancock is still taking up Transports to send round to York — pray give my Service to Capt McKay, also to Colo. Elliot & Lady, I should have sent Colo Eliot some Wine for his Journey, but Mrs Rowe, being at that time at Mr Inmans with her Sister who was very Ill, prevented it, which I hope he will excuse.   If you go to Harlum, I hope you'l Spend your time Agreeable to your desire — Mr Jonge is not yet married to Miss Cottnam but is to be very soon.   Elliot of the Royal has taken a Tripp to Hampton with Byard's youngest Daughter & is married.   Burns of the 48th has done the Same with Miss Hicks of Salem, he has ab^o fifteen hundred pounds Sterlg.   I shall take care of your Machine that you left with Dr Crosier & Send it with the other things.   Meantime, I Remain Dr Sir, &c

JOHN ROWE

To Jacob Rowe   Boston July 24th 1761
      Dr Bro^r
    I have already wrote you for this day pr this Conveyance, to which I refer you   Mr Perry has this

Instant dld me your Letter of the 16th June.
Your Draft for 150 Dollars I will pay him to Oblige
you & I hope your New Affair with Mr Walker may
turn out to your Satisfaction, as it will be a pleasure
to me always to hear of your Welfare. I make no
doubt but you will Reimburse me at your Return

I deliver'd your Letter to Mr Tasker & forwarded
both them to Cape Ann. I expect Daniel Rogers
in Town in a day or two when I shall settle with
him — that affair of the Warehouse is a perplext one
& will be attended with some Trouble & Charge.

We have lately Buried poor Mrs Inman therefore
you may Judge of the Distress of him & her Sister
& I am not a Little Troubled — it is a great Loss.
The Inclos'd is from Exeter & your sister Mary was
well ab° six weeks ago.

You'l please to give my Compliments to M^r
Walker your partner, any services I can do you here,
shall be done with pleasure.

I remain, Your affectionate Brother

JOHN ROWE.

To Henry Newton Esq^R   Boston Sept 3rd 1761
    Dr Sir

Yesterday I Rec'd both your Letters of the 14th
& 23rd Augst. I am oblig'd to you for your Regards for me & am glad you think I did as every
Man ought to do in your Situation but no Argu-
ments or Reason will turn a Hog from Running
forward.

I have according to your Request p^d your good
Mother eighty Dollars. . . . I will at all times Send
you anything you order from hence, that I can get
here & shall be very glad to Continue our friendship. Mr Amiel is soon going abroad. I think his
Prospect is good, if the providence Privateers do
but Let him go in the Right path.

I am on all Occasions, Dr Sir,

Your Friend & very hum Servt

JOHN ROWE

To JACOB ROWE   BOSTON Sept 18th 1761
        Dr Brother

Since the foregoing am favor'd with yours of ,8th
& 23^d July & Sept. As to Brandy it will fetch
here a Dollar pr Gallon but if you Send any, it
must be Regularly clear'd — as to Mr Roe's Behaviour, its not only Unjust but Cruel & Neglect-
full, however as he is now at New York, I'll get
him if possible to settle it there. Mrs Rowe is well
pleas'd with your present but it happen'd to Come
just at the Death of her Sister which was Something Unlucky. . . . I am very glad to hear you are
to Remain in the Victualling Office, I assure you it
gives me pleasure. I take notice what you say
ab^o Bro^r William's affairs — as I have given them
Gent^m, he Liv'd with, a Smart Letter, I guess they'll
be silent on his affairs in future. . . . tis very surpriz-
ing Capt Phillips has not transmitted Swathridge's
Acc^t I Cannot Recover the Insurance on him with^o

it all but I shall Run the Risque & Transmit you M[r] Wiers Acc[t] in my Next.

Our Sister Molly was well ab[o] ten months [weeks?] ago & so was all the Rest of the Family.

Let me hear from you as often as Possible which will Oblige, D[r] Brother

Yours affectionately

To THOS. SAUL ESQ[R]   BOSTON, Oct 20[h] 1761

Dear Sir

I have but just Receiv'd your Letter of the 6[h] June, am glad to hear you were so Lucky to get home Safe — thank you for your advices about Belle Isle etc.   I think the British Arms have made a great figure this year which I Conclude will bring on the peace Quicker than expected.   I wish M[r] Pitt &c may hold their Resolution & keep all North America — the Settlement of Nova Scotia goes on very fast & its my Opinion they'll have as much a share in the fishery of America as any other of the provinces & Cap[t] Sam[l] McKay of the 40[h] is Major of the 3rd Battallion of Royal Americans Dr Catherwood was very well two posts since   Twelve Regiments are encamp'd on Stattin Island — the troops are very Healthy & no person knows the Intention of the General.

You will not be disappointed when I tell you that M[r] Benj[n] Barrons is again suspended by M[r] Letchmere, tis a Cruel hardship on him, I dont speak as a party man, but Really as I think.   You will make use of this Intelligence if you Continue your Design of trying for that Birth. Colo Vassall & all Friends & Acquaintances are very well & have desired me to make their Compliments acceptable to You. I Assure you your good & Friendly offices to me shall always & on all Occasions of Service be Sincerely Remember'd

by Dr Sir,

Your most hum Servt

JOHN ROWE.

Boston Oct 19th 1761

To Colo Jedediah Preble at Falmouth [Portland]

Sir

I have now before me your Letter of the 22ⁿ Sep^t Last. When I wrote you my Last Letter I did it out of Good will to you & did not know in what manner to tell you of it without & am fully Sensible you never Intended anything & which the Commisary I believe is fully Convinced off. I shall at all times Render you any Service in my power & had I known of your Vessells Proceding to Philadelphia I should have given some Freight but I had promis'd same to your Son before also some to Another Friend therefore you'l Excuse it this time.[1]

I am Sir, your very hum^l Servt

JOHN ROWE

[1] Jedediah Preble, second, and Jacob Rowe afterwards married sisters Avis & Penelope Phillips, daughters of Captain John and Anne (Engs) Phillips.

To Messrs Lane & Booth   Boston Oct 18th 1761
   Gen^{lm}

I must again Request your Attention with the Comm^r of his Majesty's Navy Respecting the Loss of the Hunter Sloop, Capt Annis, for its out of my power to get the Master try'd by a Court Martial, he is gone from this place & where to find him at present I dont know & even if he was here, there are no Men of Warr nor Officers to Compose a Court Martial & I have try'd all possible means to get him here to go to Hallifax, but to no Effect, therefore I must desire you make another application to the Commissioners of the Navy & I dare say they must get over the Ceremony of Court Martial especially as I have found Capt Stobo at New York who was Passenger on Board him at that time going Express from Generall Wolf to Generall Amherst & I inclose you his Certificate of his Behaviour which Corresponds with his Protest, therefore as this is all the Proof I Can Come at, I hope the Commissioners will not delay the payment Longer. I am on all Occasions Gen^{lm}

your very hum Servt

JOHN ROWE

CERTIFICATE OF CAP^T ROB^T STOBO

These are to Certify all whom it may Concern that I Robert Stobo, Captain in his Majesty's Fifteenth Regiment of Foot, Came Passenger with Capt Annis in the Sloop Hunter from Quebeck

Express from General Wolfe to General Amherst, that on the Passage we were taken by some French Cruisers & Carried into Beaver Harbour from thence we came to Hallifax & that said Captain Annis did all he Cou'd to Keep Clear & Defend said Sloop from being taken. Given under my hand in the Camp on Stattin Island

this 9th of Septr 1761

ROBT STOBO

To Mr Mrs Robins   Boston Oct 19h 1761
        Dr Bror & Sister

I have your Letters of the 26h June & 1st July Last & find you had mine with One Inclos'd for Sister Tolcher — I did not mean to purchase an Estate from Uncle John, all my view was, to pay any Sum he might have Engag'd his Estate for to his present Wife, In order to preserve his Engagements & not let the Ancient Estate go out of the Family Channell, but if this Cannot be done Let it Rest as it shall please him.

I am sorry to find Bror Joseph's Affairs so Encumber'd, Let me know what he has Left Unsold & the value he puts upon his Estate & I then Shall be some Judge of his Designs & what his Intentions are, whether he will dispose of them or not.

I have always thought of paying you a Visit but Mrs Rowe will not Consent to it & therefore I dont at present expect it.   Mrs Rowe Returns her thanks

to M[r] Tolcher & Spouse for Remembering her & I
shall write them very soon.[1]

If it should come peaceable terms I may venture
to give you a Small order in your way but my warehouse is at present overstock'd with all Sorts of
English goods so that I must at present defer it.
I am sorry for the Misfortune of M[r] Joseph Rowe
& more so for his wife, who I was personally acquainted with.   I Cannot venture to give him any
Encouragement, please to give My Service to him
& tell him, I would do him any Service or good
Office in my power, but I Cannot pretend to
Recommed him without being acquainted with
his Abilitys.   the Letter he Sent me is very
Modest & humble, but tis Impossible as I have
said above, to make an Agreement unless he was
on the spott & that is a matter to him so uncertain
that I should think he had better attempt some
Employment among his Friends at home than come
abroad.

M[rs] Rowe is very well & so am I but we have
Lately Lost M[rs] Inman who was Sister to my wife &
the Loss is very great, being without any Exaggera-
tion, a very good & Valuable Woman, therefore the
Loss so much the Heavier; this is the tryall we
all must Bear, but the Loss of a Valuable Friend &
Relation sits Heavier, than a stranger Can well
Imagine.

Pray Remember me to Aunt Bennet & Family &

---

[1] Probably the naming of their infant daughter Hannah for Mrs.
Rowe.

all other Enquiring Friends & be assured that I Remain

> Dr Bro^r & Sister
>
>> Your most affection Bro^r
>>
>>> JOHN ROWE.

To JOSEPH WOODMASS ESQ^R   BOSTON Oct 25th 1761
> Dr Sir

I have already wrote you by this Conveyance to which I Crave Reference & is the Answer to Your favour of the 4th.   I am now to answer Your favour of the 19th Deliver'd me this Minute by Capt Debbege who arriv'd very Luckily Yesterday.   for Last Night we have had a Violent Gale of wind, the Hardest I ever heard, a good Deal of Damage is done at the wharffs, Many Chimneys, Barns Fences &c are blown down, I am afraid of the Consequences at Sea, which at present we Can Only Judge ab°

I shall pay your bill to M^r pantree for 300 Dollars, also your Letter of Creditt to Capt Hays in favour of Mr William Vance. . . .

> I am, Dr Sir
>
>> Yr Very hum. Servt
>>
>>> JOHN ROWE.

To Lieu^t Roe   Boston Oct 26^h 1761

Mr Roe

   Sir

I have Repeated Letters from Mr Vanhorne advising me you want to throw the goods Left at Quebeck on my hands, I protest I Could not have thought you Could have Attempted such a thought. You tell Mr Vanhorne that you never see the goods that was put up for you, pray Sir, Recollect Your memory — was not these goods shipt in your sight in the true Britton, Capt Searle, was they not by your Order put in the Ship Loose & in a Careless Manner & the Reason You Alledged for it was because he could not stow away the same in Casks — did not you then proceed to sea & after having foul weather Return back again in three or four weeks — was not the goods Brought again to my store Loose, was not some of them Missing & some of them Damaged, how can you be so unjust as to say you never saw them.

   Pray Mr Roe have a Little more Care of your Reputation, I must say I did not expect such Treatment from you, as I took much pains to serve & Oblige you.

   Capt Nickolls told me you were willing to pay my demand when Call'd for, I am very sorry to find you have not done it, I must therefore Insist on your doing it, which will very much oblige

            Your very hum Servt

                  JOHN ROWE.

FROM LIEU^T ROE   18^h Aug 1761

Dr Sir

After a Long tedious Passage of 50 days we
Arrived here (Quebeck) safe, but to Our no small
Mortification, found that all the Troops that could
be spared from the Garrison were form'd into Two
Grand Divisions & had gone up the River a week
before we Arriv'd, the first under the Command of
Brigga^{dr} Burton, the Second, Murray, all the Par-
ishes on the South Shore come into them, take the
Oaths & Lay down their Arms; 14 Days ago, the
first Division pass'd Three Rivers, the Second Immediately Followed. Lord Rollo has since come
up with Murray & the Troops from Louisburg —
from our Last Acc^{ts} they were at Anchor at Isle a
Issee (?) waiting a wind to carry them up to M^t
Leal — they have a Noble Train of Artillery tho'
the British Lyon Receiv'd his Drabing on the
Twenty Eight of April, yet he has Recover'd his
Spirits & declares he'll never Couch to a disorderly
Peasantry, unless they Ambuscade him, because the
third time, our Troops are as eager for Battles as
ever.   A Market is established here to which the
french bring in what the Country round produces
& receive in Return, bread, beef flour & Salt.   The
English Merch^{ts} here are not Admitted to trade as
yet with the french.   Your Bro^r I have enquir'd
after, he is well but up the River — our paymaster
was Gone up before wee arriv'd, which Occasions
my want of Bills for Am^t of your Sum.   I expect
him shortly when I shall remit you.   In my next to

you I shall give you an Acc^t of the Compleat Conquest of Canada, I hope so — pray Present my best Compliments to Mrs Rowe, Mr Mrs Inman &

I am, Dr Sir

Your Very hum^b Servt

H. ROE

To MR PETER HUBBERT   BOSTON Novr 12th 1761

Dr Sir

On the 8th Instant I wrote you in Answer to yours pr post, since which have got Insurance on Capt Telighman for £475 a 6 pr Cent — he is now at Martins (?) Vineyard after having met with Very hard Gales of wind and had a Passage there upwards of 30 Days.   I Rec'd a Letter from him this morning, he has lost his Bowsprit & says he is afraid some of his Cargoe is damag'd.   There are upwards of 40 Sail of Vessells at the Vineyard now waiting for a wind to Come Round   You may depend ont I shall always Consider your Interest as my Own

I am &c

To JOSEPH WOODMASS ESQ   BOSTON Nov 19th 1761

Dr Sir

. . . I now Inclose you a Letter for the Honble Mr Belcher which I have from Andrew Oliver Esqr Secretary of Our Province & in it is Inclos'd a

Mediterranean Pass No 2163 Sign'd by the three Lords of the Admiralty Namely Anson, Hunter & Forbes which I have Sign'd a Rec^t for, which you must deliver to the Lieu^t Govr^n & get him to give you a Receipt, which you'l please Transmit to me here that I may Cancell my Rec^t or otherways desire his Honour to Signify by Letter to our Secretary above nam'd that he has Rec^d it . . . This is a favour done for me & I hope its for Your Self or a particular Friend as I was Oblig'd to make Interest therefore — the other Necessary papers are Inclos'd with the Mediterranean. . . .

To HENRY NEWTON   BOSTON Nov 19th 1761
        Dr Sir

I have now before me Your favour of the 22nd Oct^r & have wrote my Friend at Marblehead to purchase me three Quarter Casks of Lisbon, none is to be had in Boston — when I get them come to hand, I will sent you two of them & the other one shall be sent to your good Mother who is very well.

I have Order'd my Friend at Roxbury to Look out for Venison & had one hind Quarter purchas'd but was Oblig'd to make use of it, as the wind & weather has been so wet & damp that twas time it should be Eat.

I am with much Esteem

To MR BANNISTER.   BOSTON, Dec 7^h 1761

Dr Sir

In the first place you'l give me Leave to Return
your many thanks for your Civilityes at Rhode
Island, but I acknowledge you'l say with good
Reason, I should have done it before, hope you'l
Excuse it &c. I now Inclose you a Coppy of the
Invoice of Mr Benjⁿ Booth's Bed which I assure
you is a very Good One & in good order & am
sure twill please Mrs Bannister to whom please to
give my Compliments. We are very well &
Mrs Rowe Joyns with me, with best Respects &c

I Remain Dr Sir

Your most hum Servt

JOHN ROWE.

BOSTON Dec 7th 1761

To Mr DAVID VANHORNE AT NEW YORK

Dr Sir

I Return you many thanks for your Endeavours
to get me Justice done with Mr Roe I hope that
Spark may yet in some part or other of the world be
still Obliged to do me Justice. Be so kind as to
send me Mr Roe's Original on his Acc^t & the Letter
he wrote me from Quebeck. He says that his
friends in New York would pay what he design'd to,
has he Left any Order with any person or was it
Only a put off. I should be glad to know who he
made his Correspondent at New York & whether he
left any such orders or not. I have given Joseph

Greenleaf's note of hand to Mr Otis the Lawyer who
will put it in Suit as you have Order'd

I Remain, Dr Sir

——— ——

BOSTON Dec 20^h 1761

To MESS^{RS} LANE & BOOTH LONDON
   Gent^m

. . . If Messrs Quarrells don't pay the Ballance of
my Acc^t as its stated, you may let them know, I'll
try it here where the proofs are & this they may
depend on if it's not settled by your Next Answer,
for my own Part I Cannot tell what they mean by
such Shuffling . . .   I am very sorry for Edwd Quincy's detention at Bayonne as a Ransomer for the
Ship Prince George, as to Capt Blake if he does suffer he may thank himself for it — it seems to me
that the Gentlemen Concern'd might get that Ransom Settled without making so much difficulty.
We dont know how or in what Situation it Stands
as there are no Letters from the Company of Messrs
Kilby Barnard & Parker who were the Principall
Shippers . . .   I wish you the Compliments of the
Ensuing Season & Remain with Sincere Regards,
Dr Sirs

     Your very hum Servt

       JOHN ROWE.

To JAMES OTIS ESQ BOSTON, Dec 24th 1761
Sir

I Rec^d a Letter from Mr Perez Tillson & he tells me that by your advice you have Brought a Writ in my name against Colo. Doty & him/ & he desires it may be carried on. I have no Objection to it provided it does not Interfere with my Design of Mr Tillson, that can be unjust, if Colo. Doty is Oblig'd to pay one half the Debt that's due me. I dont see any Reason that he should not but whether he's Oblig'd or not Mr Tillson best knows & if the action should fail he must Endemnify me for the Charges

I shall always Render you any Service in my Power & Remain your hum Servt

J. ROWE.

To MR JOHN AMIEL BOSTON Dec 20th 1761
Dr Sir

We have several of your Letters & are Glad to hear of your Safe Arrival & dare say you'l do the best you can for our Interests. We are very glad you have made a good Sale of the Cargo & we shall Insure the Briggatine home again but we hope She will arrive Safe that we may have an Opportunity to Return her to you. You may depend upon our pursuing your Schooner provided it becomes a Peace which will be very soon or otherways a Spanish Warr but I hope the first will take place. Mrs Amiel is in Good Health as are all the Family.

Coll° Inman Joynes in Compliments & I Remain in Behalf of Mr Erwin & myself, Sir

Your very hum. Servt

JOHN ROWE

If it should be a peace we shall get the Schooner you propose built on Purpose for that Trade. There's now no Risque from the providence privateers they are all call'd in from molesting the Mount Trade

To HENRY NEWTON ESQ^R BOSTON Feby 13th 1762

Dr Sir

. . . I have p^d your Good Mama Newton one pound five shillings & 4^d that she p^d for Postage for your Acc^t

I Congratulate you on the Good Success of your Bro^r Thomas.   I spent the Last Evening with Mrs Amiel & the Old Lady.   Mrs Amiel will very soon, I believe make another addition to your Family. The Last news from England seems to portend a Spanish Warr which will be no Service at present to this part of America, should it take place.   Any further Commands Shall Always be executed with great pleasure by Dr Sir

Your very hum Servt

JOHN ROWE.

To Messrs Lane & Booth Boston Feby 24th 1762
  Gentⁿ

. . . I am not surprised at your prudence in Stopping your progress in Shipping so very Largely, therefore I am of a different Opinion from some Sanguine people among us & that is, that the Trade here, especially Last year, had not been Greatly overdrawn. I must think Otherways & you form some Judgment by your Remittances . . .

I am sorry to see a paragraph of your Letter to our friend Thos Green, Relating to the Dispute between Mr Letchmere & Mr Barrons, it gives great Uneasiness to most of us to See the Usage & art, has been made use off to destroy, I must say, an honest man, however, I find truth & virtue cannot withstand the force of Power. Wee find the Merch^{ts} have been pretty Roughly handled in a Representation from our Governour, as you have a Letter from our Committee you'l be able to form a Judgment from it, however, I shall Esteem it a favour you'l do what's necessary to Support our Reputation & Lett me add to get a Coppy of the Governours Representation I Remain

    with Esteem Gentⁿ

To Jacob Rowe   Boston March 29th 1762
  Dr Bro^r

This day is come to hand yours of the 16th Feb'y with your Acc^t of what has passed between us Since

your Residence at Quebeck which I will Examine &
if Right will note in Conformity. . . . Capt Gibbs Our
Mutual Friend died Suddenly about Ten days past.
I dont Send your Acc^t till my Next as I Cannot tell
how Matters Stand at Cape Ann & Nothing will
do but Employing a Lawyer, no purchase, no pay.
As its now Warr with Spain I presume you'l not
have Leave of Departure for Some Time & as your
Situation at Quebeck Seems to be so much to your
Advantage I think your Own Prudence will determine you to Stay as Long as you Can. It gives me
great Pleasure to Find Mr Murray is your Friend.
You will for your Own Reputation cultivate it & by
no means trouble your Self in any disputes that
may happen. As you purpose to go into Business
with what you have Acquir'd, Let me give you this
Advice, give as Little Credit as Possible.

Our Friend Mr Tudor is dead & Mr Freeman has
given a bill on you for His Ballance which also
please to send pr First Opportunity. . . .

Mrs Rowe Joyns with me in our Wishes for your
further Success & I Remain, Dr Jacob

Your affectionate Bro^r

JOHN ROWE.

To D_R CATHERWOOD   BOSTON April 6th 1762
    Dr Sir
I had a Letter from our Friend Dick Willtshire,
who tells me you were well & severall of my Friends

& tis great Joy to most of us that the Reduction of Martinico was Accomplish'd in so Little time & so few men Lost.   I send you by the Opportunity a Letter from Our Friend Woodmass which was destin'd to Reach you at New York.   I had a Letter from Mr Saul per Last Packett, he mentions nothing of seeing New England again.   Hurd is expected in a Ship from London by whom I shall hear further from him.   Yesterday Arriv'd a Vessell from Bristol, the Captain says Admiral Saunders has taken a Galloon worth half a Million, which is Confirm'd.

The Empress of Russia is Dead.

The Spaniards were Marching Three Armies in Three Divisions into the Kingdom of Portugall because the Portugese would not declare Warr against England & the Portugese have made a Demand of Twelve Thousand Land Forces & Twenty Sail — Men of Warr, from us for their Defense. This is a piece of Policy of our Friends The French who think themselves Ill Treated by our not Complying with their Terms of Peace &c The Certificate you got me from Capt Stobo has had the Desired Effect. . . .

You'll be Kind enough to Remember me to all our Friends & believe me that I shall always be Glad to hear from you & of your welfare &

I Remain Dr Sir,

Y^r very hum^b Servt

JOHN ROWE.

To Messrs Lane & Booth   Boston April 6th 1762
    Gen^{tlm}

. . . The Sudden & Unexpected News of the
Spanish Warr has Alarm'd Us here & the Fishery
will not go with the Same Spirit as before & we
that have Large Demands on the Shoreman must
make the Best Settlement we Can. the West Indies will take of Large Quantitys, & a great deal
more than Usual Since Martinico is in our Hands
— the Grenadas, St Lucia St Vincent must of
Consequence Submit. . . . I have made your Sentiments known to my Friends in the Fish Way &
hope they'll Follow your Advice, tis Certainly the
most prudent Way.   I Remain with Sincere Esteem
            Gent^{lm}

                        Boston April 9th 1762

To Mr John Instrow & Co
    Sirs

. . . Your Demand on the Court of Admiralty
is Still Unsettled Occasioned by Andr^w Belcher
Esqr the Register being now Sick & has been ever
Since I had your Demand.   As soon as he gets
abroad, I shall get it settled . . .
            I am Gent^{lm}

Boston April 10th 1762

To Mr Richard Willtshire, Barbadoes
Dr Sir

I am Much Oblig'd to you for your Letter of the 25th Feb'y & more particularly of your Acct of Martinico which turns out pretty near as the General has wrote. I should have been Glad to have Embraced the Opportunity to send you a Vessell but did not think Convenient to Engage in any Further Concern in Navigation especially as the Spaniards have had Independence enough to Cause a Delaration against them & 'tis very probable they'll Repent of it.

Our Navy is now so well train'd to Conquer that it seems very few of their Navigation can Escape us. I am very glad that Mrs Willtshire has got her health again at Bristol. Mr Inman is well & desires his Compliments as does Mrs Rowe.

The Last News from England brings Advice of the Empress of Russia being dead which is presum'd will favour the King of Prussia. Seems as tis said, the Empress pursued her measures out of some personal Pique Shewn her by the King of Prussia & the Duke of Hollstein has always favour'd him as far as prudence would Admit.

Admiral Saunders has taken a Spanish Galloon bound into Cadiz.

The King of Spain seems to take his Revenge by Invading Portugall, this if it takes Effect will stop Large sums of Money being sent to England as usual & when money begins to be scarce in England

twill be Difficult to maintain so Large a Body of
Troops in Germany as are now in the pay of Great
Britton, however the House of Commons promises
to Support His Majesty & tho, Mr Pitt does not
Publickly act, yet the Politicians Say his Schemes
are pursued.   If at any time I can serve you here
I shall do it with pleasure, being with sincere Es-
teem Dr Sir

                              Your very hum Servt
                                   JOHN ROWE.

                                BOSTON April 7th 1762
To MESS^{RS} MAYNE, BOWEN & MAYNE LISBON
       Gen^{lm}
       . . . The Spaniards having publish'd such a Man-
ifesto has Caus'd the Court of Great Brittain very
justly to declare against them & I dont at all doubt
but we shall make them Repent of their Insolence.
Martinico is now in Possession of the English & the
Troops that are now in America, may Easily Conquer Hispaniola which if the Ministers should give
Attention too, may make the Spaniards a little
humbler.   Whenever I see an Opportunity, I shall
Venture a Cargo to Lisbon but at present there is
a poor prospect.   I Remain, Gent^{lm}

                          _____

                                BOSTON April 7th 1762
To MESS^{RS} LANE & BOOTH
       GENL^m
       . . . Mrs Rowe begs the favour you'll procure her
One doz^n of Common Table Cloths, Two pounds of

Green Tea & Four Pair of Black Calamanco Pumps, the Same as the Last you sent from Ridout & Davis & Two pcs of Sheeting of a Middling Price, not very fine nor very Coarse. . . . I Remain, with much Esteem

> Gent^m

> > Yr very true Servt

> > > > JOHN ROWE

BOSTON April 27th 1762

To CAP^T JOSEPH DOMMETT
> Sir

Yesterday Our Government Laid an Embargo on all Provisions & Gunpowder, which we thought proper to Advise you off that you may Regulate the Sales of your Cargoe. . . .

. . . . .

> Your Wife & Family are all Well
> > We are your very hum Serv^{ts}

> > > > JOHN ROWE & CO
> > > > (HENRY BROMFIELD)

To HENRY NEWTON ESQ^R   BOSTON May 22nd 1762
> Dr Sir

. . . I fancy the Spaniards will Repent their precipitate Engagement with the French which has been the Means of us Breaking with them & the English Nation, I believe, was Right to Resent their Behaviour.

Admiral Peacock is certainly arrivd at Barbadoes
with Lord Albermale & Six Thousand Troops,
they are to take a Number more from Martinico
with the ships that can be spar'd to proceed to Havanna. As Havanna or Cuba is a Healthy Island,
the Troops will not Run the Risque of the West
Indies this Summer & Exercise will help their
Health. Your Mamma & Mrs Amiel & Family are
well — the Spanish Warr has Broke up Mr Amiel's
prospects at Monte Christo which I believe would
have been very Beneficial. Mrs Rowe desires her
Respects to you & Mrs Newton & I Remain on all
Occasions, Dr Sir

Your very hum Servt

JOHN ROWE

One of Mr Pococks Fleet took in her Passage
out to Barbadoes a French East Indiaman home-
ward Bound, very Rich

Messrs Lane & Booth   Boston May 30th 1761
    Gent^m
I have just time to tell you your favours of the
5th & 18^h March have this day been delivered me
pr Roger Hale Esqr our New Collector. Your
Recommendation of him to me I much Esteem. I
shall make it my Study to Show him any Civility I
am Capable of & also do him any Good Offices in
my Power. . . .

I have wrote my Bro^r Jacob to forward the Certificate wanted for the half to you & hope with your Application & mine, he will accomplish it to the end desired. . . .
> Gen^tm
> Your very hum Servt
> > JOHN ROWE

INDEX.

Adams families, 25.

Adams, John, 5, 27, 28, 30, 50, 107, 109; member of town's committee to draw instructions for the representatives, 166; 183, 190; chosen a member for the town, 204; 229, 235; chosen councillor and negatived, 245; town's committee, 270; rechosen councillor and negatived, 272; one of committee of five to the General Congress, 276; one of three appointed by the Continentals to hold conference with Lord Howe and General Howe, 318.

Adams, Miss, 314.

Adams, Rev., of Roxbury, 202.

Adams, Samuel, chosen representative, 15; 16, 27; fire ward, 56; chosen clerk of the House, 97; 112; one of committee of General Court, 115; rechosen representative, 162; one of committee of twenty-one to wait on Gov. Bernard, 166; 171, 172; petition granted in town meeting, 183; rechosen representative, 202, 215, 227; waits upon consignees of tea with Sons of Liberty, 253; 263, 270; speaks for Committee of Correspondence in debate in town meeting, 276; 317; rechosen representative, 328.

Affray between the officers and the town house watch, 289.

Agar, Rev. Mr., 91,

Aiken, Capt., of the Swan, man-of-war, 241.

Airy, Capt., 214, 220, 234.

Allen, John, Esq., 200.

Ames, Levi, hanged, 252.

Amherst, Major-gen., 385.

Amiel family, 40.

Amiel, John, 37, 72, 88, 102, 107, 108; and wife, 111, 121; 133, 139, 142, 147, 149, 333, 396, 413, 422.

Amiel, Miss, 52.

Amory family, 25, 47.

Amory, John, 116, 208, 213, 242, 276.

Amory, Jonathan, 116, 122.

Amory, Mrs., sponsor for Mr. Parker's child, 328.

Amory, Thomas, 34; marriage of, 68; 125, 190; two months' exile at Waltham, 315.

Anderson, James, 274.

Andrews, Benjamin, 325.

Andrews, Joseph, 118.

Annet, Capt., 315.

Annis, Capt., 400.

Antrobus, Capt., 63.

Appleton, Nathaniel, 103, 239, 243, 244, 249, 310, 326.

Appleton, Rev. Mr., 130, 207.

Appy, Mr., 371.

Apthorp family, 25, 34.

Apthorp, Charles Ward, 72, 120, 128, 386.

Apthorp, George, 37, 83, 88, 91.

Apthorp, John, and lady, 149, 173, 185, 214.

Apthorp, Madam, 121, 134, 173, 243.

Apthorp, Mr., of Cambridge, 61.

Apthorp, Nathaniel, 149.

Apthorp, Robert, 134, 145.

Apthorp, Thomas, 28, 88, 125, 133, 134, 149, 156.

Apthorp, William, 28.

Artillery election, 83, 98, 133, 204, 274.

Ashburn, Capt., 65, 68, 105, 106, 142, 144.

Ashers, Joseph, 4.

Ashley, John, Esq., 168.

Ashley, Jno., Jr., 168.

Assembly prorogued, 153.

Astor, Mr., 169.

Atherton, Miss, 218.

Atkinson, Mr., admiral's secretary, 220, 240, 249, 251, 274.

Atkinson, Mrs., 175.

Atwood, Capt., 103.

Auchmooty, Rev. Mr., 85, 86, 87.

Auchmooty, Robert, judge of admiralty, 73, 77, 79, 94, 224, 248.

Auchmuty family, 25, 40, 47.
Austin, Benjamin, 243, 244, 249, 260, 272, 310.
Austin, Mr., of Charlestown, 69, 124.
Austin, Samuel, 144, 225, 260, 308, 315.
Avery, John, 35, 69, 171, 195.
Avery, John, Jr., 157.
Ayescough, Capt., 268.
Ayres, Henry, 51, 62, 63, 64, 65, 66.

Babcock, Col. Adam, 323; marriage of, 327.
Bacon, Rev., 27, 236.
Baddock, Col., 322.
Badger, Abel, a great rogue, 183.
Baker, Dr., 149, 183.
Baker, Jno., 202, 305.
Baker, Mr., of Westborough, 240.
Baker, Thomas, 205.
Balch, Mr., 231.
Baldwin, Cyrus, 302.
Balfour, Capt., of the 4th Regiment, 284.
Ball, Capt., 122.
Banks, Capt., of the Renown, 299.
Banks, Commodore, 311.
Bannister, Mr., ejectment suit, 17, 62, 67, 70, 76, 77, 411.
Barber, Nat., 37, 172, 242, 253.
Barbers' insurance office, 171.
Barclay, Capt., of the Salisbury, 209, 219, 297.
Barker, Mr., 344.
Barnard, Rev., of Marblehead, 42, 170.
Barnard, Rev., of Salem, 162.
Barnard, Rev., of Haverhill, 97.
Barnat, John, 78.
Barnes, Capt., 66.
Barnes, Henry, of Marlborough, 131, 137, 148.
Barr, Rev., of Newbury, 178, 180, 316.
Barrat, John, 195, 216.
Barrat, Samuel, 276.
Barrett, Bishop, 218.
Barrington, Lord, 379.
Barrons, Mr. Benjamin, 353, 356, 377, 396, 401, 415.
Barry, Col., toast to, 126.
Barthlet, Capt., 65, 66, 335.
Barthlet, John, the tailor, 290.
Barton, Samuel, 143.
Battery at Phipps' farm, 299.
Battery on Cobler's Hill, Charlestown, 300.
Battery on Fort Hill, 304.

Battery on the hill on Dorchester Neck, 300.
Battery on Nook Hill, Dorchester Neck, 304.
Bayley, Rev., of Kennebeck. 136.
Beachum, Mr., 348.
Beaufort, Duke of, commission from, 176.
Beaver, Capt. Bellew, commander, 166; Capt. ;Billings, commander, 175; Capt. Linzee, commander, 10, 210, 216, 218, 219, 220, 221, 226, 232, 234.
Becky, Miss, at Flax Pond, 83.
Belcher, Andrew, 28, 115; chosen councillor, 132; 409, 417.
Belcher, Mrs. Andrew, 40, 52, 64, 108, 111, 113, 138, 183, 240.
Belcher, Madam, widow of Gov. Jonathan, 40, 52, 64, 108, 111, 113, 138, 183, 240.
Bell, Mr., 361.
Bellew, Capt., of the Beaver, 166.
Bennets, Capt. Moses, 26, 66, 104, 124, 125.
Bernard, or Barnard, Gov., 7, 8, 25, 29, 109, 115, 120; petition to, 165; dissolves the General Court, 168; 185, 186; prorogues the General Court, 189; sails for England in the Rippon, 190.
Bethune, George, member of Fire Club, 36, 37, 83, 84, 116, 151; and wife, 168; 179, 222, 251, 257, 267, 368.
Bethune, Miss Polly, 186.
Bethune, Mr. H., 20, 26.
Bethune, Nathaniel, 63, 78, 80, 87, 127, 135, 163; death of, 212.
Billings, Capt., 175, 185.
Binney, Capt., 341.
Binning, Mr., of Halifax, 61.
Birch, Mr., 145; commissioner, 240.
Bishop, Capt., 63, 71.
Bishop, Capt., commander of the Fortune, man-of-war, 74, 105.
Black Act, The, 64.
Black caterpillar appears, 204, 329.
Blair, Capt., 219.
Blair, Mr., 169.
Blair, Rev. Samuel, 21, 89, 115.
Blake, Capt., 71, 73, 95, 146, 149.
Blake, Joseph, 96.
Blake, Jno., 72.
Blake, Miss, 246.
Blake, Mr., of Hardwick, 137, 146.

Blanchard, Joshua, 244, 253.
Blany's tavern, Roxbury, 48.
Blasswitch, Mr., 302.
Bleners, Mr., 202.
Bliss, Mrs., 97.
Block house and barracks at the castle burnt, 305.
Blodgets, Mr., 124, 142.
Blowers, Miss, 40, 52, 64, 108, 114.
Blythe, Capt., 152.
"Body" The, meets, 196; votes Col. Dalrymple to be cashiered, 197; 204, 207, 256.
Bollan, Mr., 186.
Bond, Capt., of the Gibraltar, 209.
Bonelten, The, Capt. Wallace, 175.
Booth & Lane, Messrs., London correspondents, 71.
Booth, Benjamin, 411.
Borland, 250.
Boston Tea Party, 258.
Bouchee, Miss, 168.
Bourne, Col., of Marblehead, 59, 76, 77, 173.
Bourne, Melatiah, member of Fire Club, 36, 52, 69; one of committee about loaf sugar, 70; and wife, 87; 88; member of town's committee, 144; one of committee of nine, 153; 155, 160; one of committee of twenty-one to wait on Gov. Bernard, 166; 179; merchants prepare an address to the governor, 213; 222, 253, 257.
Bourne, Peter, 74.
Boutineau, James, Surveyor-general, 6, 25, 29; member of Fire Club, 36; 52, 63, 67, 69, 73, 76; one of town's committee, 80; 87, 116; one of the proprietors of Long Wharf, 158; 159, 162, 181, 186, 212, 267; chosen one of his Majesty's councillors, 281.
Boutineau, Miss Nancy, 140.
Boudoin, or Bowdoin, James, 5, 25, 45, 52, 87, 169; chosen councillor and negatived, 187; chosen representative, 202; re-chosen councillor, 228, 245, 271; one of the bearers at Mollineux's funeral, 286.
Bowdoin, Mrs., 121.
Bowen, Rev., 92.
Bowen, William, 169, 171.
Bowers, Col., of Swanzey, 99, 100, 102; three times chosen councillor and negatived, 98, 163, 187.

Bowers, Jerahmiel, of Marblehead, 59, 77; chosen councillor five times and five times negatived by the governor, once being the only gentleman negatived, 98, 133, 228, 245, 272.
Bowers, William, 125.
Bowes, Nicholas, 49, 232.
Bowes, William, 174, 291.
Box, John, member of the "Possee," 35, 72, 87, 169, 185, 214, 262, 263. Death and funeral of, 287.
Box, John, Jr., 72, 185, 214.
Boylston families, 25, 47.
Boylston, John, 37, 62, 68, 88, 89, 116, 138, 139, 143, 169; sails for England, 173.
Boylston, Nicholas, 28, 29, 36, 37, 52, 68, 69, 87, 88, 116, 148, 178, 179, 189, 196, 212.
Boylston; "Old Mr.," funeral of, 263.
Boylston, Thomas, 36; chosen on committee at Merchants' meeting, 153; 155; made member of the Fire Club, 222; 227, 257; one of the bearers at Mollineux' funeral, 287.
Bracket, Capt., 179.
Bracket's, in School Street, 127, 218.
Bracket's tavern at Braintree, 27, 31, 50, 80, 81, 106, 107, 129, 130, 160, 161.
Brackett, Dr., judge of admiralty, 317.
Bracketts', on Boston Neck, 200, 217, 221, 230, 247, 254.
Bradbury, John, 98, 133; councillor for the province of Mayne, 228.
Braddocks, Ebenezer, 135.
Bradford, 'Col., or Capt., John, 31, 127, 244, 287.
Bradford, Gamaliel, 98.
Brandon, Benjamin, 342.
Brass, Capt., 140.
Brathwait, Capt., of Centurion, man-of-war, 297.
Brattle, Brig.-gen., 28, 44, 184, 187, 216, 244, 263, 274, 284.
Brattle, Col. G., 94, 98, 99, 124, 172, 189, 295.
Brattle, Thomas, 30, 38, 48, 51, 116, 125, 127, 132, 133, 147, 156, 168, 174, 181, 203, 232, 253.
Brattle, William, 98; chosen councillor, 132, 228, 245.
Bray, the baker, 121.
Brayley, Capt., 100.

Breck, Samuel, "Recollections," 12.

Brett, Capt., 167.

Brick, Mr., of Dartmouth, 315.

Brimhall, Miss Polly, 53.

Brimmer, Andrew, 25, 119, 215, 234, 328.

Brimmer, Herman, 328.

Brimmer, John Baker, marriage of, 196.

Brimmer, Martin, 308, 311, 323; and Mrs. Brimmer, 328.

Brimmer, Miss Betsy, marriage of, 223.

Brinley, George, 133; and wife, 174; 176.

Brinley, Nathaniel, four months' exile to Framingham, 315.

Brinley, Thomas, funeral of, 73.

Brinley, Thomas, 231.

British coffee house, Mrs. Cordis's tavern, 159, 213.

Bromage, Capt., from St. Kitts, in twenty-four days, 158.

Bromfield, Henry, 76, 274, 308, 421.

Brown, Bottle, 134.

Brown, Capt. Arthur, 358.

Brown, Capt. William, 64, 163, 217, 234, 278, 287, 293.

Brown, Garvin, the town agrees with, for the clock on the South Meeting-house, 266.

Brown, John, member of Fire Club, 36, 138, 244, 257, 310, 326.

Brown, Rev., of Cohasset, 98.

Brown, Rev., of Portsmouth, 164.

Brown, Thomas, 30, 114, 262, 263.

Brown, William, of Salem, representative, 168, 192; judge of Superior Court, 282; 284.

Bruce, Capt., 55, 71, 90, 254, 256, 258.

Brush, Crian, 301, 302, 306, 312.

Brush Hill, 39, 77, 79, 105, 113, 139, 240.

Bryant, Capt., 91, 125.

Bryant, Jno., 116, 125.

Bryant's tavern, Sudbury, 50.

Bryce, Capt., 119.

Buffam, Samuel, 123.

Bulfinch, Dr,, 29; and wife, 121, 149, 173.

Bullard, Mrs., 85.

Bullard's tavern at Natick, 50, 85, 101, 166, 216.

Bunch of Grapes tavern (Col. Ingersoll's), 118, 119, 146, 153, 160, 185, 214, 226, 253, 258, 291; (Capt. Marston's) entertainment by the General Court for Gen. Washington and other generals of the United Colonies, 305; 312, 326.

Buntin, Capt., 111.

Burdall, Miss, 383.

Burgoin, Mr., and lady, 139.

Búrk, effigy of, 89.

Burnet, Mr., midshipman, 220.

Burton, Brig.-gen., letter to, 354; 388.

Butler, 63.

Butler, major of the 60th Regiment, 208.

Byard, Major Robert, 41, 118, 120, 123; and lady, 134, 149; 177, 188.

Byard, William, 41.

Byles, Rev. Mather, 29, 128, 169, 185, 214.

Byles, Rev. Dr., son of Rev. Mather, 230.

Cadets, Hancock's, 24, 60, 246, 252, 265, 270.

Cahill, Capt. Edward, 339, 345, 356, 362, 384, 393.

Cahoon, Capt., 91.

Calahan, Capt., of the Minerva, 273; takes in Gov. Hutchinson and family, 286, 322.

Caldwell, Capt. Robert, 28, 68, 190, 191, 196, 209, 215, 219.

Caldwell, Benjamin, 197.

Calef, Capt., 66, 104, 144.

Calef, Dr. John, of Ipswitch, 133, 167.

Calef, Miss Sarah, funeral of, 192.

Calef, Samuel, 48, 51, 63, 80, 81, 83, 86, 87, 90, 96, 97, 100, 107, 108, 112, 121, 125, 129, 134, 135, 161, 162, 163, 166, 173, 181, 187, 203, 229, 244, 246, 247.

Campbell, Colin, Esq., and lady, 28, 205.

Campbell, Lord and Lady William, 31, 179, 181.

Campbell, Col., 312.

Campbell, Mrs. Elizabeth, born Murray; second marriage, James Smith; third marriage, Ralph Inman, 39 (see Mrs. Elizabeth Inman).

Caner, Rev. Dr., 29, 136, 221, 241, 285, 303.

Capan, Hopestill, 309.

Carghill, Lieut., 120.

Carnes, Edward, 189.

Cary, Nathaniel, 75, 253; goes into exile, 315.

Cast, Dr., 125.

Cathcart, Capt., 103.
Catherwood,Dr., 38, 180, 181, 188, 395, 416.
Ceberus, The, man-of-war, Capt. Chad, 295.
Centurion, man-of-war, 297.
Chadds, Capt. J., 281, 295.
Chambers, Capt., 269.
Champney's, Dr., meeting-house, 306.
Champney's, John (the Turk's Head), Dorchester, 48, 62, 106, 127, 190.
Chandler, Col. John, of Worcester, 30, 45, 83, 98, 132, 149.
Chandler, Mrs. and Miss Dolly, 131.
Chardon, Mr. Peter, 224, 281, 287.
Charitable lecture, 109.
Charitable society, 14, 65, 80, 84, 99, 145, 146, 152, 169, 185, 195.
Charity, James, 72.
Chatham, The Earle of, 126, 156.
Chatham, The, man-of-war, 296.
Chauncey, Dr., 21, 29, 92, 103, 130, 172, 306.
Checkley, Rev., funeral of, 195.
Checkly, Rev. Samuel, Jr., funeral of, 157, 244.
Cheever, Ezekiel, 253.
Childs, Roxbury (the Peacock), 259, 277.
Chilmark, Matthew Mayhew, 168.
Chipman, Jno., 67.
Churches:
  Trinity, Revs. Hooper,Walter, and Parker, 16, 20, 24, 32, 34, 72, 76, 159, 213, 329, etc.
  King's Chapel, Revs. Troutbeck and Caner, 20, 39, 209, 220; shut up, 241.
  Old North (Christ Church), Dr. Byles, son of Rev. Mather, 22.
  New North, Dr. Eliot, 22.
  Old South, Dr. Sewall, 22, 83, 155.
  New South, Mr. Checkly (Church Green), 92.
  Old Brick Meeting (First Church), Dr. Chauncey, 83, 325, 327.
  Rev. John Moorhead's, in Long Lane, afterwards Federal Street, now the Arlington Street, 257.
  Brattle Street, Rev. Dr. Cooper, rebuilt and preached in for the first time, 247.

Churches (continued): —
  West Church, Revs. Jonathan Mayhew and Simeon Howard, 21, 130.
  Hollis Street, Rev. Mather Byles, 230.
Church's, Edward, wife, funeral of, 91.
Church, Edward, 288.
Church, Dr., 230, 239, 253, 310.
Church, Deacon, 245.
Clappam, Mrs., 120, 225, 240.
Clark, Andrew, 37.
Clark, Christopher, 72.
Clark, Jack, and wife, 264.
Clark, Jonas, 71.
Clark, Miss Anna, 52, 108, 114.
Clark, Rev., of Lexington, 164.
Clark, Richard, 116; & Sons, teas consigned to, 253; 254.
Clark, William, 335.
Clarkson, Severance, 232.
Clergymen: —
  Adams, Rev., of Roxbury, 202.
  Agar, Rev., 91.
  Appleton, Rev., 130, 207.
  Auchmooty, Rev., 85, 86, 87.
  Bacon, Rev., 27, 236.
  Barnard, Rev., of Marblehead, 42, 170.
  Barnard, Rev., of Salem, 162.
  Barnard, Rev., of Haverhill, 97.
  Bass, Rev., of Newberry, 178, 180, 316.
  Bayley, Rev., of Kennebeck, 136.
  Blair, Rev. Samuel, 115.
  Bowen, Rev., 92.
  Brown, Rev., of Cohasset, 98.
  Brown, Rev., of Portsmouth, 164.
  Bulfinch, Rev. Dr., 29, 121, 149, 173.
  Byles, Rev. Mather, 29, 128, 169, 185, 214.
  Byles, Rev. Dr., son of Rev. Mather, 230.
  Caner, Rev. Dr., 29, 136, 221, 241, 285, 303.
  Champney, Rev. Dr., 306.
  Chauncy, Rev. Dr., 21, 29, 92, 103, 130, 172, 306.
  Checkly, Rev., 92, 195.
  Checkly, Rev. Samuel, Jr., 157.
  Clark, Rev., of Lexington, 164.
  Cook, Rev., 207.
  Coombs, Rev., of Philadelphia, 238.
  Cooper, Rev. Dr., 48, 103, 164, 203, 232, 247, 262, 307.

Clergymen (*continued*): —
Elliot, Rev. Dr., 28, 103, 109, 183, 189, 205, 257, 306, 322.
Fairweather, Rev. Samuel, of Narragansett, 230, 243.
Fogg, Rev., 214.
Forbes, Rev. John, 183, 185.
Gay, Rev., of Hingham, 103, 130.
Gilchrist, Rev., of Salem, 136.
Graves, Rev., of Providence, 136.
Graves, Rev., of New London, 136.
Greaton, Rev., of Boston, 136.
Hawley, Rev., an Indian minister, 203.
Hitchcock, Rev. Gad, of Pembroke, 271.
How, Rev., 244.
Howard, Rev. Simeon, 169, 325.
Hunt, Rev., 27.
Mather, Rev. Samuel, 130, 169, 172, 189, 257.
Mayhew, Rev., 21; death of, and funeral, 103.
Moorhead, Rev., 21. 248; funeral of, 257.
Nicholls, Rev., of Salem, 13, 14, 235, 247, 278, 287, 290.
Occum, Rev., 248.
Palmer, Rev., 185.
Parker, Rev., 19–329.
Payson, Rev. Phillips, of Chelsea, 14, 320, 326, 327.
Pemberton, Rev., 21, 115, 205, 257.
Perkins, Rev., of Bridgewater, 130.
Pickering, Rev., of Portsmouth, 244.
Sargeant, Rev., of Cambridge, 140, 160, 164, 221, 233,283.
Sewall, Rev. Dr., 21, 83, 89, 115, 165, 166, 203, 205, 225, 239, 257.
Shute, Rev., of Hingham, 21, 133, 163.
Stillman, Rev., 257, 328.
Thatcher, Rev., 207.
Thompson, Rev., of Scituate, 128, 136, 227.
Townsend, Rev., of Medway, 144.
Turrell, Rev., of Medford, 132.
Usher, Rev., of Bristol, 136.
Walter, Rev. William, 19–303.
Weeks, Rev., of Marblehead, 136, 275.
Whitfield, Rev. George, 21, 22, 205, 206, 207.

Clergymen (*continued*): —
Winslow, Rev. Edward, 40, 45, 87, 128, 136, 185.
Wiswall, Rev., of Casco, 136.
Clerk, Major, of the 43d Regiment, 277.
Cleveland, Col., 278; wounded, 286.
Cleverly, Stephen, dinner at, 328.
Club, Fire, 36, 183, 222, 257.
Club, Merchants', 36.
Club, No. 5, 36, 257.
Club, Wednesday Night, 36, 65, 68.
Clynton, Gen., sails for England, 298.
Cobb, Capt., 45; and wife, 102; 103.
Cobden, Alexander, 353, 355.
Cockle, Mr., suspended, 64.
Cockran, Capt., 67.
Codfish, 330.
Coffin, Capt. Shubael, 95, 115, 254; arrived with part of the tea, 257; tea thrown overboard, 258.
Coffin, John, 242, 247.
Coffin, Miss Bettsy, daughter of Nathaniel, 249.
Coffin, Miss Betty, marriage of, 34, 68, 70.
Coffin, Nathaniel, 218, 249.
Coffin, Richard, 143.
Coffin, William, Sr., 76, 80, 149, 171, 185, 190, 191, 214, 218, 226, 242, 250, 267.
Coffin, William, Jr., 125, 218.
Collins, Capt., 11.
Collson, Mr., 361.
Comet appears Sept. 1st, 1769, 191.
Commissioners to treat with the New York government, Brig. Brattle, Major Hawley, John Hancock, 227.
Committees: —
Grand Committee of Charity, 75.
From the General Court on Excise Act, 76.
Of General Court, 115, 116.
Of Charity (Free Masons), 119.
Of the Sessions of the town about the sale of the town house, 121, 122.
For giving instructions to the representatives on the present difficulties that attend the trade of this town, 147, 166.
Town's committees, 80, 122, 144, 157, 270.

Committees (*continued*): —
Of twenty-one, "to wait upon
Gov. Bernard with an humble petition," 165.
Of seven, to wait upon Hutchinson again, and insist that
all the troops be removed
from the town, 198.
About the granary, 268.
About the lamps, 239–264.
For filling up the town dock,
266.
Of five, chosen by the General
Court to go to the General
Congress, 276.
Of Correspondence, debates
for and against, 276.
Chosen by selectmen and
other gentlemen to draft a
memorial to Gen. Gage, 293.
Of nine, for immediate relief,
325.
Of eighteen, to provide corn,
flour, etc., 326, 327.
Concert Hall, 26, 35, 47, 184, 200,
238, 245, 254; ball by Gen. Hancock to the French Fleet, 323.
Conde, George, 351.
Conell, Capt., Romney, man-of-war, 162.
Conner, Mr., of Madeira, 31.
Conner, Mr., of Teneriffe, 31.
Conway, Gen., 7, 117, 126, 156.
Cook, Rev., 207.
Cook, Robert, 115.
Coolidge's at Watertown Bridge,
48.
Coolidge, Joseph, 331.
Coombs, Rev., of Philadelphia,
238.
Cooper, Dr., 48, 103, 164, 203, 232,
247; chosen President of Harvard and refuses to serve, 262;
307.
Cooper, William, 162, 173, 310.
Copeland, Mr., 108.
Copley, 129.
Copmer, Capt., 138, 143.
Coppinger, Capt., 112.
Corbet, Mr., 163.
Cordis's, Mrs., tavern, British
coffee house, 26, 36, 48, 55, 61,
67, 68, 69, 74, 89, 105, 110, 116,
119, 120, 121, 127, 131, 148, 150;
Merchants' meeting, 155; 158,
160, 169, 179, 183, 186; Merchants' Committee, 190, 202;
Merchants' meeting, 206; 213,
223; fire broke out, 238, 239;
243, 290.
Core, Mr., 108.

Corner, Capt. John, of the
Roundy, 165.
Cottnam, Miss, 398.
Cotton, John, 128, 231, 235.
County Congress, met at Doty's,
Stoughton, 49.
Craddock, Mr., 115.
Crampey's, 161.
Crane, Mr., of the Vineyard, 172.
Crocker, Miss Betty and Miss
Sally, 203.
Crocker's tavern, 203.
Cromwell, Henry, 32, 33, 164, 168,
169, 170, 171, 173, 179, 181, 184,
249.
Cromwell, Frances, 32.
Crook, Mr., of Newport, 104.
Cudworth, Mr., the sheriff, 75.
Cummings, Capt., 138.
Cunningham, Capt. James,
dinner at, 77; 91, 318.
Cunningham, Major, 28, 169;
dinner at, 183; 189.
Currie, Major, 358.
Cushing, Caleb, elected councillor, 228, 245; willing to relinquish his grant from the town,
262; elected councillor, 271.
Cushing, Capt. Ezekiel, 348, 360,
365, 367.
Cushing's, Deacon, in Hingham,
50, 81.
Cushing, Thomas, 15, 25, 27, 30,
44, 47, 80; chosen representative, 82, 93; chosen speaker,
98; rechosen representative,
130; 144, 162; one of committee to present petition to governor, 166; Merchants' Committee, 172, 190; 192; rechosen
representative, 202, 215; commissary, 227; representative,
243, 269; town committee relative to Port Bill, 270; 323.
Cutler, Mrs., 111, 280.
Cutler, Mr. J., 114, 176, 190, 235,
251, 257, 262, 331, 332.
Cutter, J., 72, 87.
Cuyler, Philip, 337, 338, 346.

Dalrymple, Col., 28, 29, 48, 133,
175, 178, 196, 198, 199, 209, 211,
219.
Dalton, Capt. James, 186.
Dalton, Capt. Michael, and wife,
129, 158, 238.
Dalton, Tristram, 45, 46, 171, 266,
308, 314.
Dana, Richard, lawyer, 28, 76;
member of town's committee, 121, 122; member of

committee to give instructions to the representatives, 147, 166; 162; one of the gentlemen chosen to wait on Gov. Bernard, 165; 178, 192.

Danforth, Samuel, 44; seven times chosen member of his Majesty's council, 98, 132, 228, 245, 271, 282, 283.

Darby, Capt. George, Devonshire, man-of-war, 395.

Dashwood, Capt. Samuel, 66, 67, 107, 109, 135, 143, 194, 200, 302, 340, 345, 393.

Davenport's tavern at Newburyport, 316.

Daverson, Sr., Capt., 111.

Davison, Capt., 143.

Davis, Benj., 73, 93, 107, 138.

Davis, Caleb, 310, 328.

Davis, Capt. Solomon, 26, 28, 30, 36, 37, 51, 62, 63, 67, 68, 69, 76, 80, 83, 84, 88, 93, 119, 138, 140, 144, 145, 146, 147, 148, 151, 156, 164; and wife, 168, 169, 173; 178, and wife, 181; 200, 203, 213, 222, 225, 242, 254, 265, 308, 324.

Davis, Capt. Stephen, 82, 89, 124, 143, 208, 223, 227.

Davis, Edward, 73, 107, 116, 125; and wife, 174, 254.

Davis, William, 37, 67, 125, 246, 254, 291.

Davidson, 158, 173.

Dawes, Capt. Thomas, 56, 72, 127, 260, 328.

Dawson, Capt., 298, 299, 301.

Day, Mr., and wife, 163.

Debbege, Capt., 406.

Debert, 125.

Deblois, Gilbert, 120, 214, 235, 243, 250, 279.

Deblois, Lewis, 211, 247.

DeBorde, Chevalier, 322.

Debtors, Act for the relief of insolvent, 75.

Debuke, Miss Betty, 169, 181.

Delaney, Col. Oliver, 396, 397.

Delano, Capt., 55, 131.

Denim, John, 73.

Dennie, John, 28, 36, 37, 69, 74, 148, 178; house burned, 195; 222.

Dennie, William, 196, 245, 253, 287.

Dennison, of New York, 28.

Derby, Richard, Jr., 272.

D'Estang, Count, French admiral, 320, 321, 322, 323.

Dewar, Mr., 41.

Dexter, of Dedham, 98, 115.

Dexter, Samuel, 98, 133, 228, 245, 271, 272.

Diamond, Capt., 70.

Dickinson's, John, "Farmer's Letters," 7.

Doane, Elisha, 65, 172.

Doble, Capt., 26, 124.

Dobson, Capt., 90, 104.

Dogget, Capt., 226, 333.

Dommett, Capt. Joseph, 421.

Donaldson, Thomas, 272.

Donation, Mr. Hancock's, 78.

Doty's tavern, Stoughton, 49, 52, 94, 101, 102, 107, 108, 109, 110, 113, 173, 413.

Douglass, Mother, 61.

Douse, Miss Peggy, 247.

Dove, Capt., 278.

Dowse, Joseph, 37, 45, 65, 77, 79, 103, 121, 143, 235.

Duddington, Capt., Merlin, sloop-of-war, 295.

Dudley, Mr., collector of Newport, 27, 248.

Dumaresque, Philip, 176; and wife, 179.

Dunbar, Capt. William, 359.

Duncan, Capt., 138.

Dundass, Capt., armed schooner, St. Lawrence, 175, 176.

Dunn, Capt. Samuel, 105, 238, 331.

Dunnisin, Capt., 229.

Dupee, Elias, 72.

Duties on glass, etc., 146; repeal of, 201.

Duvalnais, Sieur, consul of France, 326.

Dyer, Miss, 161.

Edes' papers, 263.

Edington, Mr., 176.

Edson, Josiah, judge Inferior Court, Plymouth, 282, 283.

Egremount, The Earl of, 396.

Elliot of the Royal, marriage of, 398.

Elliot, Rev. Dr., 28, 103, 109, 183, 189, 205, 257, 306, 322.

Elliot's, Deacon, corner, 88.

Ellis, Capt., 251.

Ellis's tavern, Plymouth, 203.

Epps, Mrs., 143.

Erving, George, 87, 116, 156, 213, 226, 274, 299; death of Mrs. George Erving, 201.

Erving, John, 29, 37, 69, 76, 85, 98, 118, 138, 141, 148; and lady, 149; 150, 151, 169, 179, 191, 195, 213, 228, 238, 242, 244, 245, 250, 267, 271, 274, 286.

Erving, John, Jr., 79, 86, 87, 116; "wedding Frollick"; 119; 153, 168, 191, 282.
Eustis, Mrs., death of, 214,
Evacuation of Boston, 304.
Everet, Michael, 221.
Eyres, Joseph, 256.

Fairweather, Rev. Samuel, 230. 243.
Falcon, The, Capt. Linzee, 11, 297.
Faneuil, Benjamin, and wife, 168; 192, 222.
Faneuil, Mrs. Benjamin, Sr., 186.
Faneuil Hall, 21, 47, 62, 80, 91, 98, 101, 109, 112, 126, 127, 133, 134, 136, 144, 152; petition to Gov. Bernard, 165; 168, 171; quarterly lecture, 174; 186, 188, 192, 203, 204, 206, 239; one thousand people met about the tea, 256; 260, 266; adjourned to Old South Meeting-house, debates for and against the Committee of Correspondence, 276; 298, 326.
Farley, Michael, 272.
Fayerweather, William, 360.
Fenton, Capt., 200, 216, 230.
Fenton, Mr., Surveyor-general, 151; and Mrs. Fenton, 170; 174.
Fenton, Son of, 250.
Fessenden's, Sandwich, 203.
Finlay, Mr., of Quebeck, 252.
Finney, Lieut., of the marines, 252.
Fire Club, 27, 36, 174, 183, 222.
Fisher, Mr., collector of Salem, 121, 237, 248.
Fisher, Mrs., of Salem, 247, 316.
Fisher's tavern on Charles River, Needham, 50.
Fitch, Samuel, 37, 72, 88, 230, 242, 262, 263.
Fitch, Sherburn, 299.
Fitch, Timothy, 30, 199, 257; and family, 295.
Flagg, James, 120, 123, 230.
Fleming, Major, 184.
Fletcher, Capt., 308.
Flucker, Miss Hannah, 87.
Flucker, Miss Lucy, afterward wife of Gen. Knox, 268, 271.
Flucker, Thomas, Secretary of the Province, 37, 45; and wife, 87; 116; is chosen councillor, 132; 162, 169, 208, 212, 222, 248, 257, 265; rechosen councillor, 281, 282.
Fogg, Rev., 214.

Folger, Capt., 173, 227, 157, 158, 269.
Folger, Timothy, 101, 102, 125, 150, 222.
Folsom's, Greenland, 316.
Forbes, Capt. Edward, 79, 87.
Forbes, Capt. James, 121, 123; death of, and funeral, 191; 348, 349, 365.
Forbes, Capt. Thomas, 102, 105.
Forbes, Mrs. James, funeral of, 107.
Forbes, Rev. John, marriage of, to Dolly Murray, 183; 185.
Ford's, Elisha, tavern in Marshfield, 50.
Fordyce, Major, 184.
Forrest, Mr. James, 125, 156, 175, 176, 178, 230.
Foster, Chillingsworth, Harwitch, 168.
Foster, Deacon, and wife, 118.
Foster, Mrs., 261.
Foster, The Honorable Thomas, 88, 171, 185, 187,
Foster, William, 326.
Fowle, Jacob, Marblehead, 167.
Fowler, Col., 86.
Foxcrafts, Mr., 91.
Frankland, Lady (Agnes Surriage), 32, 33, 53, 164, 168, 169, 170, 171, 173, 179, 181, 184.
Frankland, Sir Charles Henry, 33.
Frankland, Sir Henry, 32.
Frankland, Sir Thomas, 33.
Franklynn, Benjamin, Philadelphia, 318.
Freeman, Capt., 88, 144; brings "Jack" Rowe from Quebeck, 234.
Freeman, Enoch, 272, 416.
Furlong, Major, 177, 184.
Furness' tavern at Shrewsbury, 97, 131, 137.

Gage, Col., 366.
Gage, Gen., 177, 178, 180, 271, 274, 283, 376.
Gardiner's, Gideon, tavern on Boston Neck, 89, 122, 123, 147.
Gardner, Capt., 66; book by, 345.
Gardner, Dr., Jr., 75.
Gardner, Dr. Joseph, 87, 122, 123.
Gardner, Dr. Silvester, 29; settlers for Kennebec, 67; 70, 75, 80, 120; lady and two daughters, 174; 224, 225, 287.
Gardner, George, 72.

Gardner, Jno., 72.
Gardner, Miss., 179.
Gardner, Mrs. Grace, buried, 226.
Gardner, Thomas, of Cambridge, 263.
Gates, Gen., 306, 323.
Gay, Capt., 171.
Gay, Rev., of Hingham, 103, 130.
Gay's tavern in Dedham, 50.
Geneste, Capt. Lewis, 118, 140, 152, 160.
Gerrish, Col. Joseph, of Newberry, 98, 133, 163, 187, 352.
Gerry, Capt. Thomas, of Marblehead, 30, 45, 87; death of, 280.
Gibbs, Daniel, 368, 379.
Giddins, Capt., 103.
Gideon, Capt. John, of the Jamaica, 47, 88, 116.
Gill, Mr., of Boston, 81.
Gill's papers, Fleet's, Edes', and, 263.
Glover, Capt., of Marblehead, 134, 135.
Godfrey's, Widow, tavern at Norton, 109.
Goldthrop, Mr., 335.
Goldthwait, Ezekiel, 27, 39, 50, 62; and wife, 64; 70, 75, 78, 84; and wife and three daughters, 108; 116, 119, 129, 144, 146, 148, 174, 179, 189, 200, 202, 212, 213; Mr. Inman and Mrs. Rowe visit Mrs. Smith at, 220; 224, 226, 239; and wife, dinner at Brush Hill, 240; 242, 268, 290.
Goldthwait family, 25, 40, 53.
Goldthwait, Major Joseph (Westown), 45, 72, 96, 97, 108, 131, 135, 137, 188, 200, 211, 242, 253, 301.
Goldthwait, Thomas, 202, 278.
Gooch, Joseph, 86.
Goodhue's tavern, Salem, 50, 143, 164, 236, 247.
Gooding, Mr., of Salem, 230.
Gordon, Lord George, 188.
Gordon, Robert, 116.
Gorham, Capt., in brig Fortune, tea destroyed, 264.
Gorham, Col., and lady, 120, 121.
Gorham, of Charlestown, 29, 264.
Gould families, 40.
Gould, John, children of, 64.
Gould, Joseph, of Lynn, 105, 121.
Gould, Robert, 37, 64, 68, 70, 73; and Mrs. Gould, 93; 102, 114,
124, 138; dinner at, on turtle, 167; and wife, 174; 181; creditors of, 193; death of, 223; death of Mrs. Gould, 299.
Gould, Robert, nephew, 224; and wife, 233.
Gould, The Misses Betty and Sally, 93, 174. Marriage of, Miss Betty, 196; Sally, 217, 221.
Gould, William, 64, 85, 140; Mrs., William, 171; 175.
Grant, Mr., of Halifax, 28.
Graves, Admiral, 277.
Graves, Capt. Thomas, 289.
Graves, Mrs., 164, 170.
Graves, Mrs. (old), death of, 83.
Gray, Harrison, Treasurer of the Province, 30, 36, 44, 61, 68; and wife, 88; chosen member of his Majesty's council, 98, 132, 228, 281; funeral of Mrs. Gray, 117; 136, 143, 148, 169, 179, 192, 222, 226, 253, 257, 265; one of the merchants to wait on Gen. Gage with an address, 274; 282.
Gray, Harrison, Jr., 156.
Gray, Lewis, 26, 62, 72, 124, 125.
Gray, Thomas, 37, 69, 70, 76, 80, 91, 118, 148, 151, 160, 169, 179, 192, 213, 226, 253, 260, 274; death of, at Hingham, 287.
Greaton's, John (the Greyhound), Roxbury, 48, 100, 102, 135, 136, 167, 168, 172.
Greaton, Rev., of Boston, 136.
Green, Capt. Jerry, 36.
Green, Frank, 274.
Green, Henry, 156.
Green, Joseph, 36, 67, 116, 169, 185, 212, 213, 214, 222, 230, 282, 383, 387.
Green, Miss Chrissy, 97.
Green, Nathaniel, 185, 214.
Greene, Benjamin, 35, 79, 171, 185, 214, 251; death of, 308.
Greene, David, 42, 170.
Greene, Gen., 305.
Greene, John, 131, 185, 214.
Greene, Richard, 242, 267, 303, 315, 328, 329.
Greene, Mrs. Richard, 306.
Greene, Rufus, 35, 73, 79, 171, 185, 214, 254, 267.
Greene, Mrs. Rufus, 42; funeral of, 148.
Greene, Miss Mary, daughter of Rufus, died, 249.
Greene, Thomas, 79, 80; heirs of, 251; 415.
Greene, The Widow, 168.

Greenleaf, Benjamin, 245, 271.
Greenleaf family, 34.
Greenleaf, Miss Betty, 173.
Greenleaf, Sheriff, 74, 119, 121.
Greenleaf, Stephen, 73, 76, 79, 116, 146; and Mrs. Greenleaf, 149; 185, 187, 251, 328.
Greenleaf, William, 145, 195.
Gridley, Col. Richard, 80, 176, 331.
Gridley, Jeremiah, 24, 28, 61, 72, 87, 100, 119, 122, 127, 136; death of, and funeral, 141.
Gridley, Messrs., 25, 27.
Gunter, 362.
Gwynn, Capt., 102, 342.

Haldiman, The Hon. the Col., 366.
Hale, Mrs., daughter of Judge Parker, 314.
Hale, Roger, 422.
Hale, Surveyor-general, 63, 73, 79, 83, 88.
Hall, Andrew, 135.
Hall, Benjamin, Medford, 132.
Hall, Capt., 188, 215, 259.
Hall's, Dr., tavern, Pembroke, 50, 106, 129, 160, 161.
Hall, Stephen, 115, 122, 228.
Hallowell, Benjamin, Jr., 63, 79, 88.
Hallowell, Capt., 150, 167.
Hallowell family, 25, 34, 47.
Hallowell, Mr. Benjamin, Sr., 88, 116, 240, 245.
Hallowell, Robert, 116, 125, 149, 156, 175, 284.
Hallowell, Thomas Briggs, 112, 116, 184, 192.
Hammock, Capt. John, 65.
Hammock, Charles, death of, 248.
Hammond, Mr., 309.
Hancock, John, one of the proprietors of Long Wharf, 6; Capt. Linzee applies to him as Governor for permission for the Penelope to enter the harbor, 12; defeats John Rowe as representative, 15; 27, 28; dinner at Gov. Bernard's, 29; 30, 47, 48; gives a fire engine, 56; 57; committee about Mr. Hancock's donation, 63; dinner at the Governor's, 69; 71; proprietor of Point Shirley, 75; 78; defeated as councillor, 83; one of the selectmen, 90, 92; chosen representative, 93; repeal of the Stamp Act, 95; 98; one of committee on Capt. Daniel Malcolm's affair, 112; one of committee of General Court, 115; present at dinner to Capt. Gideon, 116; dines on board the Thames, 117; several of his houses burned, 122; selectmen's meeting, 118; proprietors of Point Shirley meet, 119, 144; re-elected representative, 130; his Union flag hoisted for the first time, 140; Merchants' meeting chosen to procure the commissions of the Commissioners of Customs, 153; Merchants' Committee, 155; proprietors of Long Wharf meet, 158; re-elected representative, 162; chosen councillor and negatived by the governor, 163; a seizure belonging to him occasions a mob, 165; silver bowl used for first time at Mr. Barber's insurance office, 171; visits Rainsford Island on the province account, 172; proprietors of Long Wharf dine at the coffee house, 186; Merchants' Committee, 190; sons of Liberty dine at Robinson's, 191; chosen speaker of the House pro tem., and negatived by the lieutenant governor, 200; rechosen representative, 202; ceremony of investing new officers of the artillery, 204; 226; chosen speaker and approved, 227; elected councillor, 228; goes with a party of gentlemen to visit the eastern parts of the province, 232; one of the commissioners to the New York Congress, 244; rechosen councillor, 245; he and his cadets parade on the Common king's birthday, 246; king's coronation, 250; is ordered to hold his company in readiness, 254; committee about the tea, 256; delivers an oration at Dr. Sewall's meeting-house, 264; he and his cadets do escort duty at Lieut.-gov. Andrew Oliver's funeral, 265; rechosen representative, 269; he and his cadets receive Gen. Gage, the new governor, at Long Wharf,

270; 320; rechosen representative, 328; gives a ball at Concert Hall to the gentlemen of the French fleet, 323; 374.
Hancock, Madam, 30.
Hancock, Tutor, 170.
Handfield, William, and Mrs., 179; 378.
Handing, Mrs., funeral of, 308.
Hardrigg, Mrs., 175.
Harlow's, Dr., Duxbury, 129, 160.
Harris, Capt., 370.
Harris, Mr., collector of taxes, 71.
Harris, Mr., from St. Christopher's, 193.
Harrison, Charles, funeral of, 190.
Harrison, Joseph, 115, and wife, 148; 150; and wife, 164; 193.
Harrison, Miss Betty, and Mr. Richard, 148.
Harrison, Mr., collector of New Haven, 35, 64, 114, 165.
Harrison, Mr., of London, 197.
Hartley, Mr., 175.
Haskell, Capt., 368.
Haskins, Capt., 329.
Haskins, Mrs., 323.
Hatch, Asa, and Mrs., 96.
Hatch, Capt., 110, 113, 123.
Haviland, Col., 373, 376.
Hawk, Sir Edward, 117.
Hawkes, John, Exeter, Eng., 344, 349, 351.
Hawley, Joseph, 29, 244, 264.
Hawley, Rev., Indian minister, 203.
Hay, Capt. Charles, of Tamar, man-of-war, 219.
Hayden, William, 124.
Head, John, 267, 293, 294.
Heath, Capt. William, of Roxbury, 263.
Heath, Gen., 322.
Heingman, Mr., at Easton, 94.
Henderson, Joseph, 62, 158, 186, 218.
Hendley, Michael, 139.
Henly, Capt., of Charlestown, 195.
Henshaw, Joshua, 42, 112, 144, 145, 165, 170, 172, 187.
Henshaw, William, 35, 185.
Heron, Dr., 232, 233.
Herring, from Chagford, Eng., 324.
Herts, John James, 371.
Hews, Mr., 226.
Hicks, Miss, of Salem, 398.
Hide, Nathaniel, 37.

Higginson, Capt., 226.
Hill, Henry, 122.
Hill, John, 133.
Hill, Lomar & Hill, Messrs., 389.
Hillman, David, Jr., 371.
Hillman, Mrs., 371.
Hitchcock, Rev. Gad, of Pembroke, 271.
Hitchum, Thomas, 244.
Hobson, Gen., 335.
Holbrooke, Mr., 13, 182.
Holker, Mr., 323.
Holland, Samuel, from Plymouth in England, 220.
Holmes, Nathaniel, 75, 119, 144, 145, 146, 202.
Holt, Lieut., of the Scarborough, 281.
Holten, Samuel, member of Congress, 8.
Hood, Capt., 49, 232, 267.
Hood, Commodore, 189, 208.
Hood, Mrs. Samuel, wife of Commodore, 6, 10.
Hooker, Mr., inspector, 161.
Hooper, John, 149.
Hooper, Miss Becky, 314.
Hooper, Miss Polly, 34, 42, 79, 86; marriage of, 149.
Hooper, Mrs., of Marblehead, 129.
Hooper, Mr., of Marblehead, 187.
Hooper, Rev. William, 17, 18, 23, 71; and wife, 79; 86, 90, 92, 93, 95, 111, 112, 113; death and funeral of, 128; 357.
Hooper, Mrs., gratuity £50 for the year, 159; 149, 162, 303.
Hooper, Robert, 42, 76, 116, 283.
Hooper, Thomas, 149.
Hope, Mr., creditors of, 123.
Hopkins, Capt., 125.
Hopkins, Capt. John, of the Continental frigate, Warren, 328.
Hoppes, Capt., 394.
Horner, Samuel, 341.
Hosey, Capt., 213.
How, Rev., ordained, 244.
How's tavern, Marlborough, 131.
Howard, Gen., chancellor of the exchequer, 117, 126.
Howard, Miss, 121, 233.
Howard, Rev., 169, 325.
Howard's tavern at Easton, 107, 113.
Howe, Gen., 317, 318.
Howe, Lord, 312, 318.
Howland's tavern, Plymouth, 50, 106.

Hubbard, Daniel, 80, 125, 145, 169, 185, 202, 213, 214, 245, 267.

Hubbard, Justice, 141.

Hubbard, Miss Polly, marriage of, 327.

Hubbard, Thomas, 98, 132, 162, 169, 225.

Hubbard, Tuthill, 30, 48, 125, 145, 190, 226, 232, 242, 244, 246, 253, 308.

Hubbert, Peter, 346, 409.

Hughes, Samuel, 37, 79; and wife, 88; 116, 118, 127, 134, 135, 158; death of, 162.

Huldimand, Gen., 286.

Hulton, Commissioner, 53, 240, 245; and wife, 249.

Humphreys, Mr., 228.

Hunt, Rev., 27.

Hunter, Capt., 133, 135, 357, 361, 362, 364, 383, 393.

Hunter, Rowland, 269.

Hurd, ——, 417.

Hussey, Stephen, of Nantucket, 123, 143.

Hutchinson, Elisha, 273.

Hutchinson, Foster, 52; and wife, 88; 108, 121, 122, 127, 134, 135, 196, 262, 265, 281, Judge of Superior Court, 282.

Hutchinson, Lieut.-Gov. Thos., 6, 28, 29, 32, 100, 110, 193, 196, 201, 204., 214, 217, 225, 235; Mrs. Hutchinson buried, 240; made governor, 212; 247; sails for England with his son and daughter in the Minerva, Capt. Calahan, 273.

Hutchinson, Madam, funeral of, 75.

Hutchinson, Miss Peggy, 273.

Hutchinson, Shrimpton, 224.

Hutchinson, Thomas, judge of the Inferior Court, 282.

Hutchinson, Thomas, Jr., of Milton, 283.

Inches, family, 25.

Inches, Henderson, 28, 37; on Clement Jackson's affairs, 75; 77; present at dinner to Capt. Gideon, 116; referee, 120; member of "Town's Committee," 144; member of "Committee of Instructions," 147; member of "Committee of Nine," 153; member of "Merchants' Committee," 155; 160; chosen selectman, 163; member of committee of twenty-one, 165; town's com-

mittee, 166; dinner at Major Cunningham's, 183; fire at his house, 184; dinner at John Champney's, 190; funeral of Mrs. Henderson Inches, 192; visit to Mr. Henderson Inches and lady, 197; funeral of Mrs. Sarah Inches, 212; dinner at, 221; marries Miss Bettsy Brimner, 223; member of committee about lighting the lamps, 239, 243, 244, 249; 270; bearer at John Box's funeral, 287.

Inches, Miss Betty, 197; funeral of, 258.

Independency declared in Boston, 313.

Independence Proclamation read at Trinity Church, 316.

Indians from the Misimiche and St. John's tribe come to negotiate business with the General Court, 312.

Ingram, Capt., 135.

Inhabitants, The, carry in their arms to be deposited in the hands of the selectmen, 293.

Inman, George, son of Ralph, 10, 12, 70, 126, 181, 184; his father's second marriage, 221; takes his degree, 231; marriage of his sister Susanna to Capt. Linzee, 233; enters Herman & Andrew Brimner's counting-room, 234; has the measles, 236; goes to Norwitch, 237; 242, 249, 263; seriously ill, 294; sails on Falcon with Capt. and Mrs. Linzee to join the British Army; dies at Granada, W.I., 44; daughters of, 44.

Inman, John, 10, 231, 233, 247; marriage to Sally, daughter of Capt. Haskins, 250; 285, 293, 294, 300.

Inman, Mrs. Elizabeth, born Murray, marries first Thomas Campbell, second becomes second wife of James Smith, 39; 105, 108, 111, 113, 139, 183; sails for England, 193; returns from England with two nieces, 218; third becomes second wife of Ralph Inman, courtship and marriage, 218, 220, 221; godmother to John Head's child, 267; in a carriage accident with Mrs. Rowe, 279; sponsor to Rev. Mr. Parker's child Elizabeth,

438 INDEX

326; meets Mr. Inman at the lines, 294; goes to Providence, 323. (See also "Letters of James Murray, Loyalist.")

Inman, Mrs. Ralph, born Speakman, first wife, 336, 392, 393. Death of 397, 399, 415.

Inman, Ralph, Cambridge, Loyalist, 4; numerous dinners at, 30; lavish ent rtainments at house in Ca dge, standing just behind the site of City Hall, 41. Descendants, 44; dinner at Turk's head on a Barbecue, 64; Christmas, 1764, dines at Mr. Rowe's, 71; one of the proprietors of Point Shirley, 75; dines at Brush Hill with James Smith and wife, 79; falls in getting on his horse, 85; present at a dinner given to Capt. Gideon by the Merchants, 116; goes to Sherburne and Marlborough with James Smith and wife, 132; at wedding of Polly Hooper, 149; returns from Connecticut, 153; dinner at Col. Ingersoll's on the anniversary of the repeal of the Stamp Act, 156; dinner at Greaton's of turtle,168; member of the Charitable Society, 185; dinner at Bracket's on Boston Neck,200; goes to Newport, returns from, 207, 208; Christmas,1770, dines at Mr. Rowe's, 211; dines with the Charitable Society at Col. Ingersoll's, 214; dinner to Gov. Hutchinson, Commodore Gambier, and others, 217; courtship and marriage to Mrs. James Smith, born Murray, 218, 220, 221; birthday, 224; entertainment at Commencement, when his son George takes his degree, 231; marriage of Susanna Inman to Capt. John Linzee, 233; goes in the Beaver as far as the lighthouse, and takes leave of "Sucky," 234; sets out for Salem in Paddock's coach, 235; stands godfather to Gilbert Deblois' son, named "Ralph," 243; dinner at Flax Pond under the trees, 247; dinner at Menotomy Pond, 248; death of his daughter "Sally," 250; present at "No. 5 Club," 257;

goes to Marlborough with Mrs. Inman, 289; goes to the lines to see Mrs. Inman, 294; he and Mrs. Inman dine at Mr. Rowe's, 296, 305, 310; he and Mrs. Inman set out for Providence, 323; return, 329; letter from, 341.

Inman, Sarah, 10, 126, 181, 221, 233, 234; illness and death, 249, 250.

Inman, Susanna (see Linzee).

Inoculation in Boston for the small-pox, 313.

Instant, Mrs., 96.

Ivers, Mr. William, 70, 73, 189.

Ivers, Thomas, 70.

Jackson, Benjamin, 266.

Jackson, Clement, 66, 75, 77; launching at Weymouth, 139.

Jackson, James, 72.

Jackson, Johnson, 267.

Jackson, Joseph, Col., 37; one of selectmen, 90, 122; 166, 244; death of 281; and funeral, 282.

Jackson, Thomas, Sr., 164.

Jackson, William, 72; visited by the body of merchants, 196.

Jacobson, Capt., 66, 91, 101, 105, 134, 138, 166, 167, 174, 236, 242.

Jarvis, Capt., 61, 103, 118, 220, 227, 238, 242.

Jarvis, Robert, 62, 226.

Jeffry, Mr., 374.

Jenkins, Capt., 226, 236.

Jenkins, Mr. Robert, 65; funeral of, 257.

Joan, Mr., 200.

Johnson, Dr. William Samuel, 294.

Johnson, Sam'l, one of the proprietors of Campo Bello, 269.

Johnson's tavern on Lynn Plain, 63.

Johonnot, Andrew, 72.

Johonnot, Francis, member of the Possee, 35; dinner at, 115; 171, 185; dinner at John Champney's "on a Pigy," 190; 226; death of, 290.

Johonnot, Young Francis, 324.

Johonnot, Gabriel, 253.

Johonnot,Peter, 133.

Jones, Col., 199.

Jones, Mrs., 108, 114, 187.

Jones, Mr., 187.

Jones, Nathan, 103, 106.

Jones, Polly, 42.

Jonge, Mr., 398.

Jordan, Capt., transferred from the Kingfisher to the Foge, man-of-war, 232; and Mrs. Jordan, 246; 268.
Jordan, Mr., a gentleman from Barbadoes, 88.
Joy, Mr., 390.

Keen, Trial of, 105.
Kempenfelt, Admiral, 33.
Kendrick's, Capt., tavern on Charles River, 52, 108, 132, 134, 143.
Kent, Benjamin, 27, 190, 224, 276.
Kent, Mr., the lawyer, 75.
Kent's tavern at Dorchester, 102.
Kerfoot, Walter, one of the proprietors of Campo Bello, 269.
Kerr, Col., 35, 182, 184, 198.
Kimball, Mr., 61.
King, Thomas, of Marblehead, 229.
Kingman's tavern at Easton, 101.
Kneeland, Bartholomew, 122.
Knights, Thomas, 99, 100, 120, 160, 161, 229, 293, 294.
Knox, Henry, later Gen., 268, 271.

Lacy, Capt., 72.
Laighton, Henry, 299.
Lamps ·lighted for the first time in Boston, March 2, 1774, 264.
Land Bank, Commissioners of, and the Heirs of Rentham, trial between, 99.
Land Bank scheme, 123, 150.
Lander, Mr., 103.
Lane & Booth, Messrs., letters from, 65, 71; letters to, 357, 361, 364, 375, 379, 400, 412, 415, 418, 420, 422.
Lane, John, 48, 63, 64, 82, 83, 84, 191, 196, 197, 213.
Lapier, Andrew, 72.
Latham, Dr., 267, 268.
Lathrop, Isaac, of Plymouth, 264.
Laughton, Henry, 251.
Laughton, Thomas, 253.
Lavicount, Mr., and wife, 174.
Leaned, Zephaniah, of Rainham, 140.
Leddell, Miss Betsy, 96.
Lee, Col., 63.
Lee, Jerry, 138.
Lee, Joseph, 76; judge of the Inferior Court, Middlesex, 282.

Leight, Mr., of the 14th Regiment, 179.
Leonard, Col. Ephraim, 107.
Leonard, Daniel, of Taunton, sworn in councillor, 283.
Lesly, Col., 35.
Letchmere, Anthony, 181, 250.
Letchmere, Mr., death of, 83.
Letchmere, Mrs. and Miss, 249.
Letchmere, Richard, 249, 274, 280; appointed councillor, 282, 283.
Leveret, Col., 269, 314.
Lewis, Eben, 63, 80.
Lewis, Mrs., 129.
Liberty, Sons of, meet and drink the King's health, 139; 172, 205; annual feast at Roxbury, 248; committee appointed by, to wait on consignees of tea, 253; death of Mollineux of the, 286; 316.
Liberty Tree, 139; two effigies on, 157; 165; flag hoisted on, when Gov. Bernard sailed, 190; meeting of Sons of Liberty at, and dinner at Robinson's, Dorchester, 191; consignees of tea called upon to meet at, 252.
Lillie, Theophilus, 196.
Lincoln, Benjamin, 98.
Linzee, Capt. John, commanding the Beaver, 10; death of, 12; 14, 189, 208, 209; brings the Beaver into dock and graves her, 210; 211; arrives in the Beaver from Antigua, 216; 217; the Beaver sails, 218; 219; returns from a cruise, the Beaver people make a seizure, 220; 221; sails on a cruise, 221; 223; Beaver returns very leaky, 226; arrives in the Beaver from Rhode Island, 232; is taken at the suit of Clark and Nightingale, is arrested on the mulatto affair, marries "Sucky" Inman, 233; sails in the Beaver with his wife, 234; arrives in the Falcon with his wife and little son Samuel Hood, 291; is ordered up Charles River to bring off the troops, 292; sails with his wife and son in the Falcon, 294; dines at Mr. Rowe's on little Samuel Hood's second birthday, Dec. 27, 296; 297; sails in the Falcon with Mrs. Linzee, little Sam and Hannah and George Inman, 297.

Linzee, Rear-admiral Robert, 10, 29, 189.
Linzee, Susanna (Inman), wife of Capt. John Linzee, 10; 84; 85; goes to Commencement, 86; 89, 109, 126, 135, 142, 163; 169; goes to Marlborough, 170; spends the evening at Lady Frankland's, 173; 178, 179, 180, 181; dines at Brush Hill, 183; dines at Mrs. Vassall's, 186; 188; goes up Cambridge River in Capt. Caldwell's cutter, 190; Mrs. Rowe gives dance for, 197; goes to Newport and returns, 207, 208; 209, 211, 217, 218, 219; her father's second marriage, 221; 223; her father's birthday, 224; 225, 226; marriage, 233; sails in the Beaver, 234; letters from, 255, 260; arrives in the Falcon with her husband and little son Samuel Hood, 291; Sails in the Falcon with husband, little Sam and Hannah, 297.
Liswall, James, 327.
Little, Miss Lydia, 130.
Little, Miss Massy, 161.
Little, Miss Polly, 161.
Little's tavern at Kingston, 106, 130.
Lock, Mr., installed President of Cambridge (Harvard), 200.
Logie, Capt., 69, 82.
Longly, Mr., 80.
Loring, Caleb, 214.
Loring, Capt., of one of the tea ships, 254, 257.
Loring, Joshua, marriage of, 193; sworn in councillor, 281.
Louder, Mrs., 197.
Louis, Mr., 101.
Lovell, James, member to Congress from Massachusetts and one of three to present petition to Congress, 8.
Lovell, John, Jr., 106.
Lovell, Master John, member of Fire Club, 36; 101, 313, 316.
Lowell, John, 160.
Loyd, Dr. William, member of Fire Club, 36; 188, 279, 280, 281, 299.
Loyd, Henry, 116.
Loyde, Miss Betty, marriage of, 193.
Lyde, Byfield, 115.
Lyde, Capt., 136.
Lynch, Mr. and Mrs., 248.

Lynds, Judge, at Ipswitch Hamlet, 315.
Lynds, Miss Lydia, 110. (See Mrs. Walter.)
Lyon, John, one of proprietors of Campo Bello, 269.
Lysle, Mr., solicitor in the customs, 290.

McCartney, Capt., of the Mercury, 273.
McClean, Capt., 91.
McDaniel, Hugh, 72, 190; funeral of, 200.
McDonald, Capt., 125.
McGuire, Lawrence and Mary, 140.
McKay, Capt. John, of the 65th Regiment, 286.
Mackay, Capt. Samuel, 172, 335, 398, 401.
McKay, Gen., 188.
Mackay, Mungo, 331.
McKinnerly, master of the Lively, wife and child, 270.
McKintosh, Capt., 76.
Mackintosh's tavern, Needham, 50, 133.
McKneil, Capt. Huter, 260.
McKowan, Capt., ship seized, 183.
McNeal, Archibald, 62, 72, 99, 100, 116, 125, 164; and two daughters, 174; wife and three daughters, 179; 230, 300.
McNeal, John, Capt., wife, son, and daughter, 174; wife and daughter, 178; 181, 257.
McNeal, Mr., of Surrinam, 164.
McNeal, Mrs., 170.
McNeal, the baker, 74.
McVickers, 182.
McWhorter's or McQuarter's tavern, Taunton, 50, 93, 104, 113.
Maitland, Col., Adjutant-general, 177, 178.
Malcom, Capt. Daniel, 111, 125; one of committee of twenty-one to wait on Gov. Bernard, 166; 172.
Malcom, John, 261.
Malcom, Old Mr., 125.
Mallard, Capt., 66.
Mallet, 75.
Malley, Thomas, 326.
Maltby, Capt., of the Glasgow, 226, 251, 289.
Manley, Capt., 306, 307, 312, 317.
Mann's tavern, Wrentham, 50, 246.

Marlet, William, 91.
Marra, Patrick, 140.
Marshall, Capt., 83, 109, 110, 145, 146.
Marshall, Col. Thomas, 169, 171, 189; chosen selectman, 225, 260.
Marshall, Samuel, 357.
Marshman, Capt., 166, 167.
Marston's, Capt., 48. (See Bunch of Grapes tavern.)
Marston, John, 171.
Marston, Mr., of Marblehead, 229.
Martin, Capt., 204.
Martin's tavern, 236.
Martin, The two Misses, 179.
Mason, Capt., of the 14th Regiment, 29, 209.
Mason, Jonathan, 183, 192, 212, 225.
Matchet, Capt. Jonathan, at the North End, 120, 125, 253.
Mather, Rev. Samuel, 130, 169, 172, 189, 257.
Matrin, Capt., 178.
Maturin, John, the general's secretary, funeral of, 288.
Maxwell, Mr., 90.
Maxwell, Gen., 327.
Mayhew, Rev., 21; death of, and funeral, 103.
Meadows, Capt., of the Tartar, 272.
Men-of-war in the harbor, and where stationed, 272.
Mendall, Capt. Paul, 96.
Mercer, of New York, 31.
Merchants' meetings, about loaf sugar duties, 70; 101; choose committee of nine, 152; which reports, 153; agree to the resolutions of the city of New York, 161; 162; present 62, and 60 sign an agreement not to import any goods, 171; 190, 193, 195, 196, 201, 206, 207, 208; prepare an address to the governor, 213; choose commissioners to treat with New York, 227; regulating act, 273; wait on Gen. Gage with address, 274; dissolved, 329.
Meredith, Mr., of Quebec, 242, 243; letters from, 260; arrived in Boston, 281.
Meredith, Sir William, 156.
Millens, Thomas, and wife, 94, 199.
Millens, James, 94.
Miller, Capt., 199.
Miller, Dr., 211.

Miller, Mrs., funeral of, 224.
Miller, Mr., of Newburyport, 229.
Mills, Mr., of New Haven, 148, 178, 218.
Minerva, The, Capt. Calahan, in which Gov. Hutchinson, son, and daughter sail for England, 273.
Minot, Christopher, 79, 85, 88.
Minot, George, 239.
Mitchell, Capt. Thomas, 68, 69, 125.
Molesworth, Capt., 179, 186.
Molineux, William, 36, 37, 76, 88, 116, 148, 150, 151, 169, 178, 179, 196, 224; petition dismissed at town meeting, 225; 245; chairman of committee of Sons of Liberty to wait on consignees of tea, 253; 257, 276; death and funeral of, 286.
Moore, Mr., and wife come to live at Rowe's, 327.
Moorhead, Rev., 21, 248; funeral of, 257.
Montague, Admiral John, 43, 53, 219; and Mrs. Montague, 233; 236, 243, 246, 248; and Mrs. 249; 259, 267, 270; with Mrs. and Miss, pays farewell visit and sails for England, 277.
Montague, Capt. George, 233, 246, 249; made post captain in command of the Foye, 268; 298.
Montague, James, 249.
Montague, Miss Sophie, 233, 246.
Montgomerie, Capt. James, 67, 71.
Montgomerie, Capt. Robert, 66, 105.
Montrasor, Capt., 286.
Morley, Jno., death of, 71.
Mortimer, Mr., 248.
Morton, Provoz, delivered an oration at the funeral of Dr. Warren, 307.
Morton, Silas, 81.
Mosely, chaplain of the Salisbury, 212, 214.
Mowat, Capt., of the Canceaux, 273.
Mugford, Capt., 310.
Mumpford, Mr., the post, 268, 308, 312, 318.
Murray, Anna, daughter of Dr. John, 40, 233, 240.
Murray, Betsey, daughter of James, 40, 97; sails for England, 193; 240, 329.
Murray, Dorothy, daughter of

James, 40, 79, 104, 105, 138, 139, 149; marries Rev. Forbes, 183.

Murray, Capt., of the St. John, 207.

Murray, James, and wife, 40; 105, 111, 116, 129; and wife, 138, 139, 149; 174, 191; roughly used by the people at the time of Robinson and Otis affray, 192; with family sails for Cape Fear, 235.

Murray, Col. John, of Rutland, 30, 42, 43, 45, 96, 97, 98, 218, 230; chosen councillor, 282, 283.

Murray, Daniel, son of Col. John, 43; H. C. 1771, 231.

Murray, Samuel, son of Col. John, 43; H. C. 1772, 230.

Murray, Gen., 364, 366, 369, 373, 376.

Murray, Lieut.-col., 392.

Murray, Major, 354.

Murray, Miss Polly, 233; returns to England, 273.

Musgrave, Major, 246, 249.

Nazro, John, 94, 109, 131.

Ness, Mr., of the 14th Regiment, 194.

Newall's, at Menotomy Pond, 135.

Newall's tavern, at Lynn, 135, 247, 313, 315, 316.

Newall, Timothy, 90, 92, 118, 122, 162, 163, 169, 260.

Newcastle, Duke of, 117.

Newcomb's tavern, Sandwich, 50.

Newell's, Thomas, diary, 58.

Newman, Paine, of Newberry, 223.

Newton, Henry, letters to, 399, 410, 414, 421.

Newton, Mrs., 396.

New York, evacuation of, by Continental troops, 318.

Nicholls, Rev., Salem, 13, 14, 235, 247, 278, 287, 290.

Nichols, Capt. William, 125, 348, 407.

Nichols, Mr., wife, son, and daughter, 235.

Nickerson, Ansell, tried for forgery, 247; acquitted, 248.

Noble, Capt., 374.

Norwood's tavern, Lynn, 50.

Noyes, Nathaniel, 326.

Noyes', Widow, tavern at Stoughtonham, 104, 109, 113.

Occum, Rev., an Indian minister, 21.

Ogilvy, James, 348, 349.

O'hara, Capt., 177, 181.

Oliver, Andrew, judge of the Inferior Court, Essex, 282.

Oliver, Capt. James, 71.

Oliver, Chief Justice Peter, declines to relinquish his grant from the Crown, 262; House of Assembly passes several resolves against his conduct, the whole House presents a remonstrance to the governor, relating to him reappointed chief justice, 263; 282, 284.

Oliver, Col. Thomas, 40, 43, 109; and wife, 217; 230; lieutenant-governor, and president of the council, 281.

Oliver, Lieut.-gov., Andrew, 24; resigns his commission, 89; secretary, 136; one of the proprietors of Long Wharf, 158, 159, 186, 238; 248; death of, 264; funeral, 265; 409.

Oliver, Mrs., and family sail, 297.

Oliver, Miss, 64.

Oman, Capt., 134.

Onslow, Right Hon. Sir Arthur, 117.

Otis, James, 15, 27; and Mrs. Otis, 28; 37, 41, 44, 47, 77; and wife, 88; chosen representative, 93: chosen speaker, 97; one of his Majesty's council and negatived, 98; 99, 112, 115, 116, 125; rechosen as representative, 130; rechosen councillor and negatived, 133; 141, 148, 151; chosen representative, 162; dinner at, 162; chosen councillor and negatived, 163; moderator of town meeting, which adjourned to Dr. Sewall's meeting, 165; chairman of committee of twenty-one to wait on Gov. Barnard, 165; and wife, 168; 169, 171, 178, 179; rechosen and negatived, 187; 189, 190; assaulted by Robinson, 192; breaks windows in the town house, 199; fires guns from his window, 201; 212; chosen representative, 215; trial between him and Robinson, 218, 219; rechosen councillor, 228; waits on Gov. Hutchinson as committeeman for the town of Boston, 235; rechosen councillor, 245, 272; letters to, 338, 413.

Otis, James, Jr., 41.

Otis, Madam, death of, 147.

Otis, Samuel Allen, and wife, 168; chosen representative, 310.

Otis, Mrs. Samuel Allen, funeral of, 326.

Overing, Miss Polly, 87.

Paddock, Major Isaac, 143, 171, 230, 245, 246, 250, 270.

Paine, Robert Treat, 29, 30, 45, 93, 109, 121, 264; one of the committee of five to go to the General Congress, 276.

Paine, Samuel Treat, of Taunton, 125.

Paine, Timothy, chosen, of his Majesty's council, 98, 132, 282, 283.

Paine, Young, of Worcester, 294.

Palfrey, Thomas, 69, 215.

Palfrey, William, 270.

Palmer, Rev., 185.

Palmer, Thomas, 64, 88, 105, 234; gives brilliant ball at Concert Hall, 254; chosen councillor, 283.

Parker, Capt. Hide, of the Boston, 186, 209, 215, 217, of the Phœnix, 313.

Parker, carpenter, 80.

Parker, Daniel, 172.

Parker's, Dr., at Rutland, 96.

Parker, Judge, father of the Rev., of Portsmouth, 314.

Parker, Rev., 18, 19, 20, 251, 252; returns from England and becomes assistant at Trinity Church, 270; preaches for the first time, 271; 275, 305, 307, 308; omits petitions in the liturgy for the king and royal family, 313; 314; reads Declaration of Independence at Trinity Church, 316; 318; banns published for the first time, 319; 320, 322; child christened "Elizabeth," 328; chosen incumbent minister of Trinity Church, the proprietors having voted the church vacated by Mr. Walter, 329.

Parkman, Samuel, 331.

Partridge, Capt. Samuel, 226, 317.

Pashaw, Mr., of the Navy, 202.

Patten, Nathaniel, 331.

Pattershall, Richard, 99.

Paxton, Charles, 63, 79, 88, 105, 145; death of, 187.

Paxton, Mr., one of the commissioners, 192, 240.

Payne (or Paine), Col., of Worcester, 123.

Payne (or Paine), Edward, 37, 70, 80, 112, 116, 118, 120, 144, 145, 147, 155, 160; one of committee of twenty-one to wait on Gov. Bernard, 165; 169, 179, 190, 195; wounded in right arm at time of "Boston Massacre," 198, 208, 213; his Malaga wine seized, 222; one of the committee about the granary, 268; 274, 276, 293.

Payson, Mr., and Mrs., 187; petition dismissed, 225.

Payson, Rev. Phillips, Chelsea, 14, 320, 326, 327.

Payson's tavern, Rowley, 316.

Peacock, Admiral, 422.

Pease, Mr., of Newport, 230.

Peele, Mr., 116.

Peet, Lieut., of the Jamaica, 88.

Pemberton, Rev., 21, 115, 205, 257.

Pemberton, Samuel, 163; one of committee of twenty-one to wait on Gov. Bernard, 166; 172, 192.

Pepper, Capt., 329.

Pepperell, Sir William, and family sail, 298.

Pepperell, William, of Roxbury, 45, 104; sworn in councillor, 281, 282; 284.

Percy, Lord, arrives, 277.

Perkins, Dr. William Lee, 37, 125, 133, 220, 241.

Perkins, James, 37, 69, 79; and wife, 88; 90, 112, 116, 148; and wife, 168; 187, 216, 244, 246, 267, 299; sets out for four months exile at Medfield, 315.

Perkins, James, Rowe's bookkeeper, funeral of, 243.

Perkins, John, 72.

Perkins, Rev., of Bridgewater, 130.

Perkins, Samuel, 250.

Perkins, The Misses Joanna and Betty, 168.

Perry, Ebenezer, 126.

Perry, William, store broken into by the soldiers, 303; is

taken up and carried to jail, 308; sets out for four months' exile at Medfield, 315.

Pertersby, Dr., 208.

Peterson, Dr., 240.

Pettigrew, Dr., 116, 175, 179.

Phillips, Andrew, one of the proprietors of Long Wharf, 238.

Phillips, Capt., 82; and wife, 121; 400.

Phillips, Deacon William, 80, 85, 90, 92, 122, 132; moderator at Merchants' meeting, 152; one of committee of nine, 153; 155, 160, 162, 163, 169, 190, 195, 196, 208; representative for Boston, 227; one of lamp committee, 239; 243, 244; chosen councillor and negatived, 245; 249, chosen representative, 259; 270; rechosen and negatived, 272; chosen representative, 310.

Phillips, Faneuil, 267.

Phillips, Gillam, 79; one of the proprietors of Long Wharf, 158, 186.

Phillips, John, 186.

Phillips, Mary, 155.

Phillips, Miss, daughter of William, 121.

Phillips, Samuel, chosen councillor, 228; rechosen, 245; councillor, 271.

Phipps, Col. David, 41; and wife, 169, 173; 184; and wife, 217; 270.

Pickering, John, of Salem, 29, 80, 264.

Pickering, Judge, of the court of admiralty, 317.

Pickering, Rev., of Portsmouth, 244.

Pickering, Mr., lawyer, 317.

Pickman (or Pitman), Col., 45, 103, 121, 143.

Pidgeon, John, 114, 124, 127.

Piemont's tavern at Danvers, 313, 315, 316.

Pierrepoint, Mr., 192.

Pike, Capt., 342.

Pipon, Mr., 123.

Pitt, Mr., 401, 420.

Pitt, Mr., again in the ministry, 88.

Pitts, James, 75; chosen of his Majesty's council, 98; 116; 119; and wife, 121; rechosen councillor, 133; one of proprietors of Point Shirley, 144, 146; 162,

202, 224; rechosen councillor, 228, 245, 271; 287.

Pitts, John, 253, 287; chosen representative, 310.

Pitts, Miss Betty, 121.

Pomroy, Col., 179, 185.

Pool, Fitch, funeral of, 206.

Poor, Capt., 187.

Port Bill, arrival of, and town meeting relating to, 269.

Porter, Aaron, of Halifax, 69, 145.

Porter, Capt., of the Viper, 207.

Post, Capt., 55.

Potterfield, Capt., of the ship Jason, 328.

Potts, Capt., 77.

Potts, John, 257.

Pourvier, William, 72.

Powell, Jery, chosen of his Majesty's council, 98; rechosen and negatived, 228; rechosen, 245; is made judge of the Inferior Court, York, 282; 322.

Powell, John, 111, 116, 118, 138; one of the proprietors of Long Wharf, 158, 186; 195.

Powell, Major, of the 38th Regiment, 208.

Powell, William, one of the proprietors of Long Wharf, 238; chosen representative, 310.

Pownall, Gov., 385.

Prat, Mrs., 86, 87.

Prat, Miss Bella, 87.

Pratt, Mr., 368.

Pratt's tavern at Needham Bridge, 50, 85.

Prebble, Jeremiah, chosen councillor, 271.

Preble, Avis (Phillips), wife of Col. Jedediah, 2d, and daughter of Capt. John and Anne (Engs) Phillips, 402.

Preble, Jedediah, of Falmouth, 29; chosen councillor, 245; 264; rechosen councilllor, 272; letters to, 345, 402.

Prescott, James, chosen councillor and negatived, 272.

Prescott, Judge William, 4.

Preston, Capt., 178; Boston Massacre, 197, 198, 199; on trial, 210.

Price, Ezekiel, 49, 116, 147, 174, 194.

Price, Henry, 72, 257, 261.

Price, William, 80; death of, 216.

Prince, Capt. Christopher, 98, 145, 171.

Prince, Capt. Job, one of the proprietors of Long Wharf, 158, 186, 189, 238; 244, 266.
Pring, Capt., 64.
Proctor, Capt., 389.
Proctor, Edward, 244.
Proctor, Mr., master of one of the schools, 159, 189.
Propert, Mr., organist of Trinity, 210, 213, 235, 239.
Prout, Mr., 309.
Pryce, Capt., 341.
Puffer, Abel, 94.
Putnam's, Gen., headquarters, 44; enters Boston with some of the troops, 303, 305.
Pyncheon, Mr., lawyer, 121.

Quelch, gunner of the Beaver, 225.
Quincy, Edmund, 47, 50, 72, 112, 116, 269.
Quincy, Edmund, Jr., 72, 110, 113.
Quincy, Edmund, tertius, 122, 125, 145.
Quincy, Henry, 271.
Quincy, Josiah, 125, 224.
Quincy, Josiah, Jr., 5; one of committee of twenty-one to wait on Gov. Bernard, 166; 239; one of town committee, 270; 275, 276.
Quincy, Morton, chosen councillor, 272.
Quincy, Samuel, 37, 43, 72, 122, 125; one of committee of twenty-one to wait on Gov. Bernard, 165; 230, 254; house broken into and much damage done by the soldiers, 303.

Rand, Dr., examined before "The Body," 330.
Rayner, Capt., of the Chatham, 296.
Read, Judge William, 30, 76, 190, 358.
Reed & Pettit, Messrs., 354.
Reed, Major, 85, 138.
Reeves, Mr., 233, 298.
Regulating act, 273.
Resolutions of the city of New York, 161.
Revere, Paul, 27, 244, 245, 322.
Rhodes, Joseph, 114, 124, 337, 348.
Rice, organist at Trinity, 72.
Rich, Sir Thomas, of the Senegal, 31, 200, 202; arrives from Halifax, 207; 209, 222, 227.

Richards, Aaron, 135.
Richard's tavern, 174, 246.
Richardson, who killed the boy, 197; tried and found guilty, 201.
Richardson, James, 35, 171, 185, 207, 238.
Richardson, John and Ann, 65.
Richardson, William, 76.
Richman, 53.
Richmond, Col., 104, 110.
Richmond, Duke of, 117.
Rider, Mr. 110.
Ridgeway's plate, 106.
Robbins, James M., 39.
Robertson, Capt., and son, 29; 105, 115, 117, 178, 188.
Robertson, collector of Newport, 74.
Robins, Francis, brother-in-law to Rowe, 343, 344, 349, 352; letters to, 369, 380, 382, 404.
Robins, Mr., purser of the Lively, 270.
Robin's tavern, Walpole, 246.
Robinson, Gen., 301, 303.
Robinson, Mr. John, commissioner, 179; assaults James Otis, 192; sails for England, 199.
Robinson's tavern, Dorchester, 191.
Robson, Capt., 140, 199, 212, 214, 218.
Rockingham, Marquis of, 156.
Rogers, Daniel, 379, 398.
Rogers, Lieut., on board the Active, 268.
Rogers, Nathaniel, 145, 196.
Rogers, Mrs., 210, 214.
Rogerson, Roger, one of the proprietors of Campo Bello, 269.
Root, Capt. Joseph, Sunderland, 168.
Ropes, Nathaniel, chosen councillor, 98, 132.
Rotch, Francis, 258, 259.
Rotch, Friends Joseph and William, 340, 355, 368.
Rowe, "Jack," son of Jacob, Quebec, 235; is left at Mr. Nicholl's school, Salem, 236; 247, 249, 258, 267, 273, 287; sent home and school broken up, 271; very ill, 309; goes to Rev. Phillip Payson's school at Chelsea, 310, 317, 320, 321, 326, 327.
Rowe, Jacob, of Exeter, kinsman of John, 221, 275; death and funeral of, 276.

Rowe, Jacob, of Quebec, arrives in America, 266, 267, 273; returns to Quebec, 280; letter to, 335; 344; letters to, 347, 360, 367, 374, 378, 379, 387, 391, 394, 398, 415.

Rowe, John, birth and parentage, 2; arrival in Boston, 3; marriage, 4; becomes prominent member of Trinity Church, 16; member of Wednesday Night Club, 65; member of the Possee, 69; often on arbitrations, 67, 69, 87, etc.; on Merchants' Committee about the duty on loaf sugar, 70; one of the proprietors of Point Shirley, 75; and of Long Wharf, 128; meets committee on the excise act, 76; on committee about Mr. Hancock's donation, and gets the vote accepted by the town, 78; treasurer of charitable society, 80; is selectman for three years, 90; they meet and appoint a day of rejoicing for the repeal of Stamp Act, 95; fire ward, 91; moves into new house on Pond Lane, 112; on committee for sale of the town house, 122; meets selectmen and justices about laying out a new street in Paddy's Alley, 128; meets selectmen about paving the road by the fortfication, 132; visits charity schools with selectmen and overseers of the poor, who dine after at Faneuil Hall, 136; member of No. 5 Club with John Timmins, Major John Vassall, Robert Hallowell, Peter Johonnot, Thomas Brattle, Edward Quincy, tertius, Mr. Forrest, and George Brinley, July 4, 1767; on committee for giving instructions to the representatives, 147; on committee of nine chosen at Merchants' meeting about stopping importations, 153; which passes resolutions and recommends that a committee of correspondence be appointed, 155; meets with the Merchants, who agree to the resolutions of the city of New York, 161; on committee of twenty-one to wait upon Gov. Bernard, 165; member of Fire Club, 174, 222; receives commission from Duke of Beaufort, appointing him Grand Master of North America, 176, and is installed, 180; chosen committeeman at Merchants' meeting, 200; is offered the colonial commission by the governor, 205; gets excused from being fireward, 225; present at Merchants' meeting, where commissioners are chosen to treat with New York government, 227; on lamp committee, 239–264; present at Merchants' meeting relative to the tea, and is chosen committeeman, 256; he and Capt. Bruce sent for by the committee about the tea on board his ship, 256; on committee for filling up the town dock, 266; on committee about the granary, 268; applies for a pass to leave town, but is refused, 294; warehouse plundered by the departing soldiers, 302; chosen warden of Trinity Church, 307; on committee of nine to consult upon the best methods for immediate relief, 325; on committee of eighteen to provide corn, flour, etc., 326; member of the house, 330; town of Rowe supposed to be named for him, 330; death, and action of Grand Lodge relative to funeral, 331.

Rowe, Joseph, of Exeter, brother of John, 349, 350, 380, 384.

Rowe, Mrs. Hannah (Speakman), wife of John Rowe, 4, 64, 71, 78, 84, 85, 86, 87, 88, 88, 89, 102, 103; illness, 106–109; 112, 121, 126, 137, 139, 141, 143, 162, 164, 167, 169, 170, 173, 178, 179, 180–186, 190, 191, 196; gives a dance to please " Sucky," 197; 202, 205, 208, 209, 211, 217–223, 225, 233, 235, 237, 240, 242, 247, 248, 250; in a carriage accident, 279–281; 296, 303, 310, 315, 322, 329, 332, 336, 340, 351, 357, 361, 362, 368, 370, 378, 382, 383, 393, 397, 399, 405, 409, 416, 418, 420.

Rowe, or Roe, Lieut. Harry, 358; letter to, 370; 388, 392, 407; letter from, 418.

Rowe, Penelope (Phillips), wife of Jacob of Quebec and

daughter of Capt. John and
Anne (Engs) Phillips, 402.
Rowe, William Syntal, 400.
Rowland, Capt. George, 89, 90.
Royal, Isaac, 45; and lady, 93;
chosen councillor, 98, 132; 179;
chosen councillor, 228, 245;
resigns his seat at the board,
272.
Royal, The Misses Polly and
Bettsy, 44, 93, 179.
Ruddock, John, 15, 59, 78, 90,
118, 126, 144, 145, 162, 163; one
of committee of twenty-one to
wait on Gov. Bernard, 165;
172, 196, 199.
Ruddock, Mrs. John, funeral of,
134.
Ruggles, Gen. Timothy, of
Hardwick, 30, 31, 45, 96, 99,
127, 131, 137, 168; appointed
councillor, 282.
Ruggles, George 185.
Ruggles, Mr., the carpenter, 226.
Ruggles, Samuel, and brother,
313.
Russell, Dr., of Concord, married Miss Betty Vassall, 152;
child christened, 186, 230.
Russell, James, 69, 94; chosen
councillor, 98, 132; 216; rechosen councillor, 228, 245;
265; appointed import office,
281.
Russell, Jeremiah Condy, 348.
Russell, Joseph, 230.
Russell, Thomas, 192, 212, 227,
238, 306.
Rutledge, Mr., of South Carolina, one of three appointed
to confer with Lord Howe
and Gen. Howe, 318.

St. Barb, Capt. George, 87.
St. John, Capt., of the Garland, 109.
St. John, Feast of, Dec. 27,
dinner at Col. Ingersoll's
(Bunch of Grapes), 181; dinner at Col. Ingersoll's, present,
41 brethren, 223; dinner at
Col. Ingersoll's, present, 34
brethren, 258.
St. John's Day, June 24, dinner of the lodge at Greaton's,
167; dinner of the Free Masons at Mr. Bracket's, 217;
dinner of the lodges at
Brother Bracket's, 230; feast
at Bracket's on Boston Neck,
247; dinner of the lodges at

Capt. Marston's, 312; dinner
at Deacon Jones's, 329.
Salter, Sampson, collector of
taxes, 71.
Saltonstall, Col., of Haverhill,
41, 43, 167, 230.
Sandburn's tavern at Hampton
Falls, 313, 314, 316.
Sandford, Mr., from Bedford,
329.
Sargeant, Capt., 152.
Sargeant, Rev., of Cambridge,
death of son, 140; 160, 164, 221,
233, 283.
Sargent, Epps, of Gloucester,
30, 103, 229.
Sarjeant, Mr., theological stu-
dent from Andover, 237.
Saul, Thomas, letter to, 386; 397,
401, 417.
Saunders, Admiral, 417.
Saunders, Thomas, 76; chosen
of his Majesty's council and
negatived, 98, 133, 163, 187; re-
chosen, 228.
Savage, Abijah, 158; one of
proprietors of Long Wharf,
186.
Savage, Abram, 72, 230, 262, 263.
Savage, Arthur, death of, 75.
Savage, Arthur, appointed
comptroller of Falmouth,
Casco Bay, 84, 88.
Savage, John, 158; one of pro-
prietors of Long Wharf, 195,
238.
Savage, Thomas, 186.
Sanger, Richard, Jr., of Sher-
burne, 167.
Sayward, Jno., York, 168.
Scollay, John, 56, 74, 85, 89, 105,
115, 118; funeral of son, 152;
169, 171, 223, 302.
Scot, Capt., 145, 201, 214.
Scot, Mrs., death of, at Domin-
ico, 155.
Scot, Col., death of, 147.
Scott, Joseph, 37, 74, 75, 119, 125,
147, 156; and wife, 168; 253.
Searl, Capt., 397.
Sears, Mr., 140.
Selby, Mr., 323.
Serjeant, Mrs., 361.
Sever, William, of Kingston, 29,
31; and daughter, 161; chosen
councillor for Plymouth Col-
ony, 228; rechosen, 245; 264;
rechosen councillor, 272.
Sewall, Jonathan, Attorney-
general, 284.
Sewall, Judge Samuel, 37, 43, 78,

118, 122, 127, 132, 162, 163, 169, 230, 234.

Sewall, Rev. Dr., 21, 83, 89, 115, 165, 166, 203, 205, 225, 239, 257.

Sharp, Lieut., marine officer of the Salisbury, 217.

Shaw, Mrs., 64.

Shay, Mr., 335.

Sheaffe, Capt. Edward, of Charlestown, 41, 122, 125.

Sheaffe, William, 36, 83, 84, 88, 100, 166, 168, 173, 181, 196; death of, 222.

Sheaffe, Mrs., 83, 88, 121, 168, 173, 181.

Sheaffe, Miss Bella, death of, 200.

Sheaffe, Miss Sally, 121, 134, 173, 181.

Sheaffe, Miss Suky, 186.

Sheppard, Capt., 287.

Sheppard, Samuel, letter to, 367.

Sheppard, William, 222; death of, 228.

Sherburn, Earl, 117.

Sherburne, Mr., 348.

Sheriff, Major, 178.

Sherlock, Mr., 294.

Sherrard, Capt., 103, 345, 349, 363.

Ships of war (12) in the harbour, 175.

Shirley, Gen., funeral of, 213.

Shirley, Mr., 321.

Shouldham, Admiral, arrives, 296.

Shute, Rev., of Hingham, 21, 133, 163.

Siege of Boston, 299.

Sigourney, Charles, 202, 331.

Simpson, Jonathan, 53, 62, 67, 76, 79, 116; and wife, sponsors for Mr. Walter's son Lynde, 146; 149, 185, 191; wife and daughter, 249; chosen councillor, 282, 283.

Sinclair, Sir John, death of, 147.

Skinner, Capt. Jno., 104, 142, 163, 207, 219, 239, 321.

Skinner, Mrs. (old), funeral of, 177.

Skinner, Mrs., 181; death and funeral of, 278.

Slaver's tavern at Portsmouth, 314.

Small, Major, 178.

Small-pox breaks out in Boston, 189, 290.

Smith, Capt. Henry, 115, 120; of the Mermaid, 215.

Smith, Dr., of Newburyport, 229.

Smith, Henry, servant of John Rowe, 232.

Smith, Gen., 292.

Smith, Isaac, 127, 134, 135, 192, 195, 197, 208, 212.

Smith, James, a thief, 140.

Smith, James, 39, 104, 105, 108, 111, 113, 132, 137, 139, 155, 183; death of, 191.

Smith, Mrs. James (see Mrs. Elizabeth Inman).

Smith, Mr., from London, 125.

Smith, Richard, 68.

Snow, Mr., 117.

Snow, Mrs., 243.

Soames, Capt., 120.

Sober, Mr., and wife, 215.

Southcote, Capt., 85.

Southmead, Miss, 384.

Southmead, John Rowe, 388.

Sparhawk, Nathaniel, 42, 44, 86, 93; chosen of his Majesty's council, 98; negatived, 103; gives a ball, 104; rechosen councillor, 133; rechosen for the province of Mayne, 228.

Sparks, Mr., 293.

Speakman, Gilbert, 181.

Speakman, Hannah (see Mrs. Rowe).

Speakman, Miss Hannah, 233.

Speakman, Mrs., of Marlborough, 96, 119, 131, 137, 148, 167, 187.

Speakman, William, 84, 107, 136, 144, 157, 162, 173, 181.

Spear, Nathaniel, 125.

Spear's tavern, Pembroke, 50, 81.

Spence, John Russell, 34, 134; marriage of, to Miss Polly Hooper, 149; 156, 157, 158.

Spencer, Mr., 133, 390.

Spooner, John, 119, 157, 158.

Spooner, Walter, chosen councillor and negatived, 187; rechosen, 228, 245, 272.

Sprague, Dr., 192.

Squires, Joseph, of Plymouth, 315.

Stabo, Capt., Robert, 395, 400, 417.

Stacy, George, 114, 124.

Stamp Act, repeal of, 90, 95.

Stamp officer, hung in effigy, 88.

State Street "Massacre," 197, 198.

Stedson, Levi, 124.

Sterling, Lord, 318.

Sterns, Mr., 137.

Stetson, or Stedson, Ebenezer,

93, 99, 100, 104, 105, 107, 110, 113, 138, 140, 146.
Stevens, John, one of the proprietors of Long Wharf, 158.
Stevenson, John, 99.
Steward, collector of New London, 74.
Stewart, Mrs., 119.
Stewart, Mr., 170.
Stillman, Rev., 257, 328.
Stillwell, Mr., 337.
Stoddard, Capt., 337.
Stoddard, Col., 86.
Stone's tavern in Stoughton, 50.
Storer, Ebenezer, 212, 243, 244, 249, 274.
Storer, Mrs., funeral of, 222.
Storey, Justice, 76.
Stormount, Lord Viscount, 396.
Strand, Capt., 95.
Stratsburg, Capt., 215.
Sturgis, Samuel, 76.
Sullivan, Gen., 318; and his army retire from Rhode Island, 321.
Sumner, Mr., shop at bottom of Cole Lane, 239.
Sun, eclipse of, 106.
Swain, Mrs., 181.
Swathridge, 387, 400.
Sweetzer, John, 245.
Swift, Samuel, 35, 37, 171, 185, 190.
Sylvester, Mr., 351.
Symms, Thomas, 226, 238.
Symonds, Capt. Thomas, of the Captain, 240, 249, 268.

Talbot, Capt., of the Lively, 236, 240; arrives in the Niger, 297.
Tapley's tavern, Lynn, 50.
Tarbut, Hugh, 197.
Tasker, Mr., 399.
Taverns and Coffee Houses:
Blany's, Roxbury, 48.
Brackett's, Braintree, 27, 31, 50, 80, 106, 107, 129, 130, 160, 161.
Brackett's, on Boston Neck, 200, 217, 221, 230, 247, 254.
Brackett's, in School Street, 127, 218.
British coffee house (see Mrs. Cordis').
Bryant's, Sudbury, 50.
Bullard's, Natick, 50, 85, 101, 166, 216.
Bunch of Grapes (Col. Ingersoll's), 118, 119, 146, 153, 160, 185, 214, 226, 253, 258, 291; (Capt. Marston's) 305, 312, 326.

Taverns and Coffee Houses (continued): —
Champney's, John (The Turk's Head), Dorchester, 48, 62, 106, 127, 190.
Child's (The Peacock), Roxbury, 259, 277.
Clappam's, Mrs., 120, 225, 240.
Coolidge's, at Watertown Bridge, 48.
Cordis', Mrs. (British coffee house), 26–290.
Crampey's, 161.
Crocker's, at Sandwich, 203.
Cushing's, Deacon, at Hingham, 50, 81, 160.
Davenport's, at Newburyport, 316.
Doty's, at Stoughton, now Canton, 49, 52, 94, 101, 102, 107, 108, 109, 110, 113, 173, 413.
Ellis's, at Plymouth, 203.
Fessenden's, at Sandwich, 203.
Fisher's, on Charles River, Needham, 50.
Folsom's, at Greenland, 316.
Ford's, Elisha, at Marshfield, 50.
Furness', at Shrewsbury, 97, 131, 137.
Gardner's, Gideon, on Boston Neck, 89, 122, 123, 147.
Gay's, at Dedham, 50.
Godfrey's, widow at Norton, 109.
Goodhue's, at Salem, 50, 143, 164, 236, 247.
Greaton's, John (The Greyhound), Roxbury, 48, 100, 102, 135, 136, 167, 168, 172.
Hall's, Pembroke, 50, 106, 129, 160, 161.
Harlow's, Dr., at Duxbury, 129, 160.
How's, Marlborough, 131.
Howard's, at Easton, 107, 113.
Howland's, at Plymouth, 50, 106.
Johnson's, on Lynn Plain, 63.
Kendrick's, on Charles River, 52, 108, 132, 134, 143.
Kent's, at Dorchester, 102.
King's Arms, on Boston Neck, 48.
Kingman's, at Easton, 101.
Mackintosh's, Needham, 50, 133.
McWhorter's, or McQuarter's, Taunton, 50, 93, 104, 113.
Mann's, at Wrentham, 50, 246.

Taverns and Coffee Houses (continued): —
Marston's, Capt. Lee (see Bunch of Grapes).
Martin's, 236.
Newall's, Lynn, 135, 247, 313, 315, 316.
Newcomb's, Sandwich, 50.
Norwood's, Lynn, 50.
Noyes', Widow, at Stoughton-ham, 104, 109, 113.
Payson's, Rowley, 316.
Piemont's, at Danvers, 313, 315, 316.
Pratt's, at Needham Bridge, 50, 85.
Richard's, Roxbury, 174, 246.
Robin's, Walpole, 246.
Robinson's, Dorchester, 191.
Sanderson's, Hampton Falls, 313, 314, 316.
Släver's, Portsmouth, 314.
Spear's, Pembroke, 50, 81.
Stone's, Stoughton, 50.
Tapley's, Lynn, 50.
Treadwell's, Ipswich, 50, 229, 313, 315.
Waterman's, Roxbury, 306.
Weathersby's, at Menotomy Pond, 248.
Woodburn's, at Hardwick, 94, 96.
Woodward's (Widow Ames), Dedham, 50, 250.
Wyndship's, or Winship's, Menotomy, 51, 82, 84.
Taylor, Col. William, 42, 110, 122,
Taylor, John, 196.
Taylor, Joseph, 294.
Taylor, Mrs., funeral of, 215.
Taylor, Nathaniel, 122.
Telighman, Capt., 409.
Temple, John, Surveyor-general, 29, 88; and wife, 120; 150; and wife, 170; child christened, 178; child christened "Angela," 326.
Temple, Mrs. Robert, 29, 41, 121, 164, 170, 178.
Temple, Robert, 41, 74, 145, 163, 170, 178, 181, 184, 195, 319.
Temple, Miss Bessy, 170.
Temple, Miss Henrietta, 41.
Temple, the four Misses, 121, 170.
Thatcher, Oxna, chosen representative, 82.
Thatcher, Rev. (young), ordained, 207.
Thomas, Col., of the Provincials, 373.
Thomas, Isaac, estate of, 131.

Thomas, Nathaniel Ray, 45, 81, 161, 208; chosen councillor, 282, 283.
Thomas, of Marshfield, 74.
Thompson, Capt., of the Ripon, man-of-war, sails for England, in which Gov. Bernard goes passenger, 190.
Thompson, Capt., of the Senegal, 215.
Thompson, James, 125.
Thompson, Mr., estate of, 69.
Thompson, Mr., of Medford, 187.
Thompson, Rev., of Scituate, 128, 136, 227.
Thompson, William J., 125, 137.
Thornborough, Capt., of the Tamar, 273, 281.
Threer, Billy, 259.
Tillson, Perez, 338, 413.
Timmins, John, 28, 37, 91, 116, 123, 125, 133, 156, 168, 197, 274; sets out for two months' exile at Waltham, 315.
Toby, Elisha, 105.
Tol, the tailor, 193.
Tolcher, Mrs. Mary, letters to, 343, 349, 382, 405.
Townsend, Gregory, 120, 122, 125, 156; and wife, 162; 209; and wife, 214; 216, 230, 242, 243.
Townsend, Rev., of Medway, 144.
Tracey, Capt., 311.
Tracey, Nathaniel, of Newbury-port, 316.
Tracy, Nicholas, 229.
Treadwell's tavern, Ipswich, 50, 229, 313, 315.
Trollet, Mr., 111, 135, 140; death of, at Lancaster, 280; 333.
Troops come ashore, 175.
Trot, Thomas, Sr., 183.
Trot, Thomas, Jr., 183.
Trot, George, 183.
Troutbeck, Rev., 29; and wife, 94; 121, 128, 136; and wife, 164; 185; child christened, 210; and wife, 233; King's Chapel shut and he confined, 241.
Trowbridge, Mr., appointed judge of Superior Court, 127; 141, 262.
Truman, Capt., 13.
Trumball, of Lebanon, 125.
Trumbel, Mr., 337.
Tucker, Capt., 309.
Tudor, Mr., death of, 416.
Tudor, William, delivers an oration in Old Brick Meeting,

327; chosen representative, 328.

Turner, Lewis, death of, 227.

Turrell, Rev., of Medford, 132.

Tyler family's petition, 139.

Tyler, Joseph, 171.

Tyler, Royal, chosen of his Majesty's council, 98, 132; 162; one of the committee of twenty-one to wait on Gov. Bernard, 165; death of, and funeral, 216.

Tyng, Capt. William, of Falmouth, Casco, 72, 224, 226, 263.

Upcolis, Mr., 352.

Usher, Rev., of Bristol, 136.

Valentine, Capt., 70.

Vanhorne, David, 40; letters to, 342, 351, 390, 407, 411.

Vanhorne, Mrs. and Miss Polly, 390.

Van Ranselear, Mr., 328.

Vassall, Col. Henry, 24, 32, 43, 80, 81, 82, 111, 135, 152; death and funeral of, 184.

Vassall, Mrs., 186.

Vassall, Major Jno., 83, 88, 118, 133, 152, 179, 187, 217, 230.

Vassall, Mrs. Jno., 83, 174, 179, 217.

Vassall, William, 92; wife and daughter, 186; death of his sister, Mrs. Miller, 224; 234; chosen councillor, 282; leaves Boston with his family, 295.

Vernon, Capt., 37, 172.

Vose, Daniel, of Milton (Suffolk Resolves House), 38, 490.

Waldo, Capt. Benjamin, one of the proprietors of Long Wharf, 158, 170, 186.

Waldo, Francis, 48; and wife, 64.

Waldo, Mr., collector of Falmouth, Casco Bay, 237.

Walker, Edward, 85, 399.

Wallace, Capt., of the Rose, 286, 313.

Wallace, Thomas, 326.

Wallace, Hugh, 397.

Waller, 52, 108.

Walley, Thomas, 189; chosen representative, 328.

Walter, Rev. William, 19, 20, 23, 29, 62, 80, 81, 83, 86, 90, 92; banns published for the first time, 110; 111, 117; and wife, 121; 128, 131, 136; and wife escape drowning, 142; 143; child christened "Lynde," 146; 148,

149, 159, 172, 180, 182, 185; son christened "William," 191; 193; death of child, 201; 214, 224, 226, 233, 237, 238, 239, 242, 244, 248, 250, 252, 255, 258, 259, 260, 662, 294, 296; house broken into by the soldiers, 303.

Walton, Mr., 28.

Ward, Col. Artemus, chosen councillor and negatived, 163; rechosen, 228, 245, 271; 318.

Warden, James, 37, 69, 70, 148, 151, 178, 253.

Ware, Mr., president of the council, 316.

Warner, Mr., 316, 318, 324.

Warren, Col. James, of Plymouth, 27, 79, 263, 323, 339.

Warren, Dr. Joseph (Col.), one of committee of twenty-one to wait on Gov. Bernard, 166; 201; oration by, 225; 230, 247, 253, 257; one of town committee, 271; 276; funeral of, 307.

Washington, Gen., in Boston, 304, 305; entertained by the General Court at Capt. Marston's (Bunch of Grapes), 306; sets out to the southward with wife and family, 306; bad news from, 318.

Waterhouse, William, 222.

Waterman's tavern, Roxbury, 306.

Watson, Col. George, 81; appointed councillor, 282, 283.

Watson, Dr., of the Somersett, 324.

Watson, Miss, daughter of William, 81.

Watson, William, 81.

Watts, Capt. of the Thames, 145, 147, 181.

Watts, Col., 85, 337.

Weathersby's tavern at Menotomy Pond, 248.

Webb, Messrs., 305, 307,

Weeks, Rev., of Marblehead, 136, 275.

Weir, Daniel, or David, 344, 347, 350, 352; letters to, 359, 363; 369, 374, 378, 388, 394.

Wells, Arnold, 27; and wife, 64; 69, 98, 116; one of the committee of nine, 153; 155; one of the proprietors of Long Wharf, 158; 160, 186, 226, 238; chosen representative, 310.

Wells, Francis, 77.

Wells, Samuel, 76, 86, 121, 122, 139, 237.

Welsh, James, 62, 85, 302.
Welsh, John, 172.
Wendall, Dr. Oliver, 122, 186, 260, 308; chosen representative, 310.
Wendall, John, 171; funeral of, 224.
Wendall, Miss Katy, 168, 169, 181, 207, 225.
Wennid, John, 123.
Wentworth, Gov. Mark, 135, 313; and wife, 316; 317.
Wentworth, Joseph, 307.
Wentworth, Samuel, 29, 63, 70, 74, 88, 102, 108; funeral of, 110; 386. 394.
Wentworth, Samuel (young), 61.
West, Mr., 208.
Wethered, Miss Mollie, or Polly, 184; funeral of, 224.
Wheeler, David, tries his new engine, 84; 153.
Wheelwright, Jack, 72, 134.
Wheelwright, Nathaniel, 55, 70, 74; death of, at Guadaloupe, 99; 387.
Whipple, Col., of Portsmouth, 317.
Whipple, Miss Alice, 29, 121.
Whitaker's, Dr., meeting-house, destroyed, 58, 283.
Whitcomb, John, chosen councillor, and declines to go up, 245.
White, Capt. Gideon, 81; and wife, 106; 129, 160.
White, Miss Joanna, daughter of Capt. Gideon, 81, 106.
White, Col., of Taunton, 94, 104, 105, 110, 113, 123.
White, Cornelius, 130.
White, Dr., 241, 249.
White, Frank, 122.
White, John, 37, 111, 172.
White, Mr., of Marblehead, goes with a flag of Truce to Commodore Banks, 311.
White, Samuel, chosen of his Majesty's council 98; negatived, rechosen, 133.
Whitfield, Rev. George, 21, 22, 205, 206; sudden death of, 207.
Whitmarsh, 81.
Whitney, 65.
Whitwell, William, 195, 216; one of committee about the Granary, 268; 274.
Whitwood, Capt., of the Marquis of Rockingham, 212, 214.
Whitworth, Dr., 43, 186; son graduates, 231; and son

arrested and taken to jail, 308.
Whitworth, John, 259.
Widow Ames's, later Woodward's, Dedham, 50.
Wies, Capt., 235.
Wilcox's, Mrs., 351.
Willard, Abijah, 283.
Williams, Capt., 39th Regiment, 53, 119.
Williams, Capt. Joseph, 120, 171, 248, 249.
Williams, Col., 137.
Williams, Israel, chosen councillor, 98; of Hatfield, 168; rechosen, 282.
Williams, Jonathan, 43, 57, 121, 144, 157, 170, 229; son graduates, 230, 248, 250; one of committee on tea affair, 256.
Williams, Mr., by Pierpoint's Mills, 133, 145.
Williams, Mr. Justice, 107.
Williams, Mr., of Maryland, 218.
Williamson, Capt,, 273; Col., 390.
Willson, Capt., 121, 177, 178, 259.
Willson, Mr., of Sheffield, Yorkshire, 269, 271.
Willson, Mrs. Rachel, Quakeress, 21, 189.
Wiltshire, Richard, Barbadoes, 418.
Wimble, Capt., 337.
Winslow, Col. Job, 100, 104, 105.
Winslow, Edward, Jr., 80, 81, 86, 130, 161, 215.
Winslow, Edward, 42; and Mrs. Winslow, 81; 106, 140; and wife, 161.
Winslow, Gen. Joseph, of Marshfield, 31, 45, 77, 102, 130, 253.
Winslow, Isaac, of Roxbury, sworn in councillor, 281, 282.
Winslow, Joshua, 37, 76, 114, 116, 120, 121, 122; one of the proprietors of Long Wharf, 158; 169, 179, 186, 200, 214, 274.
Winslow, Joshua, Jr.; 38, 125; and wife, 168; death of, 193.
Winslow, Mrs., 351.
Winslow, Pelham, 81, 130, 161, 215.
Winslow, the Misses Penny and Sally, 81, 118, 161, 181, 208.
Winslow, Rev. Edward, 40, 45, 87, 128, 136, 185.
Winthrop, John, of Cambridge,

49, 232, 245: rechosen councillor and negatived, 271.
Wiswall, Peleg, funeral of, 141.
Wiswall, Rev., of Casco, 136.
Wolfe, Gen., 333, 400.
Wood, Capt., 144; cast away on Point Allerton.
Wood, Dr. Thomas, letter to 334.
Woodbridge, Timothy, elected councillor, 228; rechosen, 282.
Woodburn's tavern at Hardwick, 94, 96.
Woodmass, Joseph, letter to, 406, 409, 417.

Woodward's tavern, Dedham (see Widow Ames), 250.
Worthington, Jno., chosen councillor, 133; rechosen, 282.
Wyndship's, or Winship's, tavern, Menotomy Pond, 51, 82, 84.

York, Duke of, death, 147.
York, Sir Phillips, 396.
Young, Capt., 114.
Young, Col., 360.
Young, Dr., one of committee of twenty-one to wait on Gov. Bernard, 166, 205, 253, 259, 276.

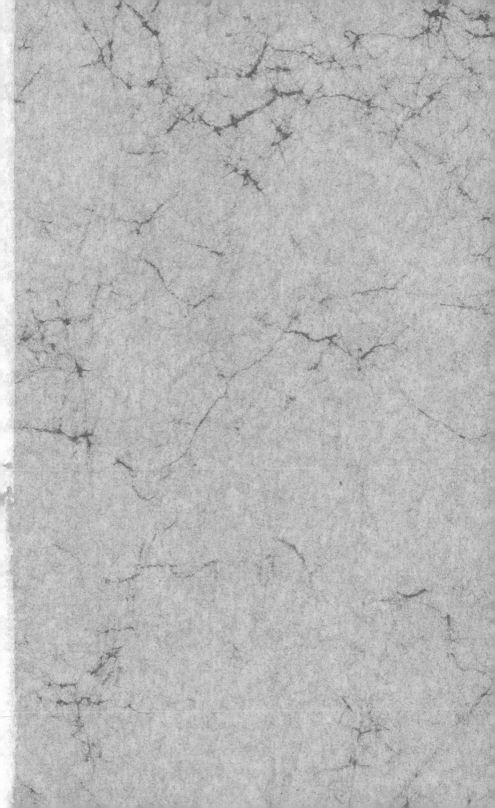